Towards
Industrial
Democracy

Towards Industrial Democracy

EUROPE, JAPAN AND THE UNITED STATES

Edited by **BENJAMIN C. ROBERTS**

An Atlantic Institute for International Affairs Research Volume

ALLANHELD, OSMUN **Publishers**
MONTCLAIR

ALLANHELD, OSMUN & CO. PUBLISHERS, INC.
Published in the United States of America in 1979
by Allanheld, Osmun & Co. Publishers, Inc.
19 Brunswick Road, Montclair, New Jersey 07042

Copyright © 1979 by The Atlantic Institute for International Affairs

LIBRARY OF CONGRESS CATALOGING IN PUBLICATION DATA

Main entry under title:

Towards industrial democracy.

(Atlantic Institute series; 2)
"Joint undertaking of the Atlantic Institute for
International Affairs and the Trilateral Commission."
   Bibliography: p.
   Includes index.
   1.   Industrial relations—Europe—Addresses, essays,
lectures. 2.   Industrial relations—United States—
Addresses, essays, lectures. 3.   Industrial relations
—Japan—Addresses, essays, lectures. 4.   Employees'
representation in management—Europe—Addresses, essays,
lectures. 5.   Employees' representation in management—
United States—Addresses, essays, lectures.
   6.   Employees' representation in management—Japan—
Addresses, essays, lectures. I.   Roberts, Benjamin
Charles. II.   Atlantic Institute for International
Affairs. III.   Trilateral Commission. IV.   Series:
Atlantic Institute for International Affairs. Atlantic
Institute series; 2.
   HD8376.5.T68   331'.09172'2   78-71100
 ISBN 0-916672-20-4

Printed in the United States of America

Contents

Tables and Figures

Foreword

This book analyzes the changing relationships of labor, industry and government in North America, Europe and Japan, a subject sometimes discussed in terms of "industrial democracy." It has very broad implications for a number of crucial elements in the enterprise and in society, such as profits, productivity, investments, working conditions, and the creation of new jobs. In its essence, the problem is one of the legitimacy of authority within the enterprise. It is frequently argued today that management authority should rest on the consent of the managed rather than on the legal right deriving from capital ownership.

There is, however, no escape from management in some form or another, since there has to be a process of decision-making and a means of ensuring that, when decisions are made, they are effectively carried out. What is at issue today throughout the world is not only the appropriateness of the traditional patterns of management, but also of the alternatives that have been proposed and in particular the role of employee participation in management.

The present study is addressed precisely to this range of questions. It is intended to throw light on problems and choices that management, labor and governments will be facing during the next few years. Through comparative analysis of several national situations, it will, hopefully, contribute to a greater understanding between countries of their different approaches and policies and will highlight any lessons or ideas which might be transferable from one political and social context to another.

The book is the result of an 18-month research project, jointly undertaken by the Atlantic Institute for International Affairs and the Trilateral Commission, under the direction of Professor Benjamin C. Roberts, head of the Industrial Relations Department of the London School of Economics and Political Science. The German Marshall Fund of the United States provided

generous support for this initiative, which brought together experts from
Europe, North America and Japan in a common research effort. The book
includes chapters on the Federal Republic of Germany, France, Italy, The
Netherlands, Sweden, the United Kingdom, Japan and the United States.
The authors of these chapters were part of a study group which, during the
life of the project, met recurrently and discussed various national experiences. The group included representatives from industry, labor, aca-
demia, and government from each country under consideration, as well as
officials from international organizations, such as the OECD. A shorter
version of the project's results by Professor Roberts, with the collaboration of
Professor Hideaki Okamoto, of Hosei University, Tokyo, and Professor
George Lodge, of the Harvard Business School, is available in the form of a
Triangle Paper, published by the Trilateral Commission.

In distributing the results of this important and so far unique project, the
Institute wishes to express its gratitude to the German Marshall Fund for
making the venture possible and to all those individuals who participated in
the effort, which proved to be a stimulating experience in international
understanding.

Martin J. Hillenbrand
Director General
the Atlantic Institute
for International Affairs

Towards Industrial Democracy

Introduction

by B. C. ROBERTS

The aim of this study was to examine the trends occurring in the patterns of industrial relations in six countries in Western Europe, North America, and Japan. The study was focused in particular upon developments in the processes of collective bargaining and other forms of employee- and union-participation against a background of ideological change and a considerable increase in the role of governments.

In examining the developments which have taken place in the recent past, country by country, the scholars responsible for writing the papers have had the assistance of business and union leaders. In the course of the study two conferences of an advisory committee, consisting of union, management, and academic representatives from each of the countries covered in Western Europe, have been held. The authors of the chapters on the United States and Japan were present. One conference in Canada, one in Japan, and two conferences in the United States of representative leaders of business and unions and academics were also held. In addition, the director of the project has also maintained contact with managers, union leaders, and academics from all of the countries concerned in this study.

It has not been the purpose of the writers to describe fully the system of industrial relations in each country, but to focus on the changes that have been taking place. These changes may be summarized as: (1) changes in the process of collective bargaining; (2) changes in the rights of individuals and the role of unions in the enterprise; and (3) changes in the role of governments in relation to the activities of employees and unions.

1

Continuity and Change: The Significancy of Ideology

Although all the systems of industrial relations examined have to some degree changed in the same direction, it is necessary to emphasize that each system of industrial relations is different in important respects. These differences arise from geographical, economic, social, and political factors that are unique to each country and which exercise a powerful influence on its pattern of industrial relations.

In spite of these differences, which are manifestly obvious, Professor Lodge has argued that the developments which are taking place in the United States are due to an ideological change, which has been even more evident in Europe and Japan for some time. The change is from an ideology of individualism to an ideology of "communitarianism." Since this change has come later in the United States than in Europe and Japan, for reasons associated with its history, geography, size of population, natural resources, and industrial structure, it is in the nature of a radical revolution, and as such it arouses doubt and opposition.

What is happening in the United States, in Professor Lodge's opinion, is the decline of the "five great ideas" that have underpinned individualistic society since they were made explicit in 17th-century England. These five fundamental concepts—property rights, contract, competition to satisfy consumer desire, limited government, and fragmentation of the social structure—are gradually being eroded by the advance of collectivist, or, as Professor Lodge prefers, "communitarian," doctrines.

With the growth of large-scale corporations and large and powerful unions and the extension of the role of government as the protector of social interests, Lodge believes the traditional pattern of industrial relations based upon the philosophic ideas of individualism to be increasingly outmoded. It is no longer realistic to perceive the modern corporation as existing simply to maximize profits for the benefit of the shareholder. To remain successfully in business, the management of a company must satisfy not only its shareholders but its employees, its customers, and the laws of the community. Since the shareholders are no longer the sole source of managerial authority, management is compelled to seek legitimacy for its decisions in the consensus of the managed, and from the law which increasingly regulates its activities. Because of this evolution in the role of management, it is necessary to develop new institutions which will enable employees and unions to participate as social partners rather than as adversaries in a war of attrition. The need to develop a cooperative relationship between management, unions, and government is already strongly recognized in Europe and Japan, and a number of different design models have been introduced.

Nevertheless collective bargaining, which has its origins in the right of individuals to protect their economic interest by forming associations, to bargain over the price of their labor and to enter into a contract, after if necessary refusing to work by going on strike, is likely to remain a dominant element in the industrial relations process in all of the countries included in this study. While it is significant that collective bargaining has grown more important at the enterprise level and at the national level in all of the European countries, there has also been a trend toward the development of consensual models of employee and union participation in the making of company policies and managerial decisions.

It may be a long time before U.S. companies adopt European models of participation, but there is evidence that the classic model of adversary-based industrial relations with its costly industrial stoppages is increasingly being called into question. Management and unions have been compelled to recognize to a growing extent that they have interests in common which can best be protected through adjustments in the bargaining process and policies of involvement, as opposed to those which inflict mutual damage.

The experimental agreement made in the steel industry in the United States in 1974, which provides for adjustments without strikes for a period of six years, is a dramatic example of this new common-interest approach. There is also in the United States a growing experimentation in new types of committee structures which is not entirely dissimilar to developments which have taken place in Europe. Some, like those associated with Scanlon-type developments, associate employee effort with increased financial benefit; others are concerned with a broader-ranged goal and affect the quality of working life.

Professor Lodge believes that, with economic, social, and political changes, the influence of government will continue to grow in America and "new forms of partnership between government, business, and labor seem likely to emerge." It is unlikely, however, that government will play as central and active a role as in Europe, since there is not in America the same readiness to welcome the intervention of the state.

Professor Lodge's thesis is a persuasive one, but he himself recognizes that there is an alternative way of interpreting contemporary developments as experimental continuity rather than radical ideological change. This view of trends in the United States has been vehemently argued by John Dunlop, who believes that the main features of the industrial relations system established in the past will continue in the future "since labor organizations and collective bargaining reflect well the character of American workers, managements, the economy and the larger society."[1] Professor Dunlop points out that there is much evidence that neither management, unions, nor political leaders would like to see any change replace the dominant method of collective bargaining, which has grown substantially in scope and complexity and been extended to new groups such as the public sector, and the secondary method of legal enactment and participation in political elections. "The American labor movement and our industrial relations system," insists Dunlop, "are distinctively American, quite different from

Europe, and while our arrangements would not work elsewhere, they have served this society and economy well."[2]

Lodge would not disagree with this conclusion of Dunlop, but he believes that the United States can no more isolate itself from changes that are of universal significance today than it could in the 17th century when it imported the ideas of John Locke. Though Lodge's focus in his chapter is primarily on the United States, he sees his analysis as one that is relevant to trends in the rest of the western world. The difference between Lodge and Dunlop is not merely one of perspective; it also incorporates deep differences in beliefs that relate to what is inevitable and what could and should be resisted. Dunlop believes his view is that of most American managers and union leaders who are firmly convinced that there is no pressing need for radical change. Such change as is necessary, argue those of this persuasion, will occur pragmatically as and when required. They also claim that this alternative interpretation of the facts of change in America as experimental continuity is to be found in other countries, as is the underlying concern with what type of industrial relations system is likely to be in the best interest of workers and managers and the wider society.

There can be no doubt that in spite of the considerable changes which have occurred in the industrial relations systems in Europe and Japan the element of continuity in each country remains strong. Although the pressure from unions often forces management to make significant concessions and persuades governments to introduce "communitarian" measures, to use Professor Lodge's word, the unions themselves are often extremely conservative organizations. In spite of demanding economic and social policies which require centralized coordination and control, unions are generally reluctant to give up their freedom to bargain or strike. Yet the exercise of these freedoms brings them into head-on collision with the policies devised by their political allies to attain the goals for which they themselves have called, the curbing of inflation and the reduction of unemployment. No matter what their long-term ideological goals might be, in terms of the short run, the behavior of the unions in all of the countries concerned in this study has been determined more by a pragmatic desire to secure immediate benefits for their members than to achieve a radical revision of society.

The attitude and behavior patterns of management are also primarily focused on the achievement of immediate goals. They would prefer to operate outside the constraints of government, but like the unions they are equally ready to seek the help of government and to accept regulation as an alternative to fighting a battle they fear they might lose. The advance of technology, economic fluctuations, and social change have made management more vulnerable to industrial pressures and at the same time compelled them to make organizational changes, which have invited a social reaction. This dialectical process contains within it both experimental continuity and radical revision, and neither unions nor management can isolate themselves from the continuing need to respond to challenges which threaten their institutional survival.

The desire of unions of all ideological persuasions to maintain their full freedom to bargain collectively in the interests of their members is strong throughout Europe, North America, and Japan. At the same time they are in favor of an increasing degree of government intervention and legal regulation to bring about full employment and more rapid rates of economic growth, to prevent inflation, and to improve the social welfare of employees. Those unions whose ideology is inspired by Marxist philosophy would like to see the role of the state extended to take over the ownership and control of the entire system of production and distribution. It is one of the paradoxes of contemporary European trade-unionism that, in spite of the evidence that trade-union autonomy is expunged in a socialist system, this is the ideological goal to which many of them give their allegiance. These unions are not prepared, however, to diminish their freedom to bargain by one jot, except under the most severe pressure, so long as the economic and political system remains capitalistic. Collective bargaining as it is perceived by the unions of the left is an integral part of the class struggle, which can only end when the capitalist system is overthrown. To agree to policies which blunt the edge of the class conflict would be, they believe, a betrayal of the ideology to which they are resolutely attached.

Unions which are less committed to a whole-hog socialist philosophy, like the unions in the United States, are also often reluctant to accept any limitation on their bargaining role, not because they seek the overthrow of the state, but because they fear that they will lose their ability to protect the interests of their members. They are ready to recognize, however, as they have done in many European countries with the possible exception of France and Italy, that the achievement of full employment and stable currencies is impossible without the concomitant policies which, although they do not entirely prevent inflation, do curb rises in pay and prices.

The role of the unions in Europe, as it has been concerned with the management of the industrial economy, has been an oscillating one. With the exception of Germany and Sweden, all the countries included in this survey have pursued pay and prices policies, which at various times have been enforced by one means or another on employers and unions. In Germany and Sweden responsibility for pay restraint since the Second World War has been accepted voluntarily by employers and unions as an economic and political necessity. There have, however, been considerable differences in the content and administrative patterns of these policies. In Germany and Sweden the employers and unions have sought to maintain an arm's-length relationship with the government, but in all the other countries, a complex structure of tripartite organizations has been developed. In no country has it been possible through either voluntary or compulsory pay and prices policies to prevent any form of inflation, or through tripartism to maintain full employment and high rates of economic growth. It is also highly questionable how far these policies have been responsible for the shift towards a more egalitarian distribution of income, which has taken place to a greater or lesser degree in every country examined.

It is quite clear that a stable equilibrium in the relation of employers, unions, and governments has not been finally established in any of the countries examined in this study. It is equally clear, however, that it is extremely unlikely that the role of government as a regulator of the economy will diminish, and that neither employers nor unions, whatever their political allegiances, will be prepared to abandon their fundamental attachment to a pluralist system of industrial relations.

The danger to pluralism, which is contingent on employers, unions, and governments observing limits to the exercise of their power, threatens from two directions. On one side are the growth of powerful unions and the reluctance of employers to recognize the need to come to terms with evolving economic and social change. In another direction the danger comes from the continued extension of the public sector and the role of governments as regulators of the economy and as employers themselves. There is a fear that a shift from a conflictual system of industrial relations to one characterized by social partnership and the desire to achieve consensus, rather than victory through conflict, will destroy pluralism, creating corporate structures in its stead. Nevertheless, there is no reason why freedoms essential to employers and unions should be undermined, if the contingencies on which they rest are understood and respected.

Since no two industrial relations systems are exactly alike, the balance in the relationship of employers, unions, and governments has been struck differently in each country. Measured by membership, the strength of trade unions ranges from a low of a little above 20 percent in the United States to a high of 80 percent in Sweden. The scale of union membership and its concentration have some bearing on the role of the unions, especially in relation to the significance of collective bargaining, and the influence they exert on the policies of governments. There is no precise way of measuring this influence so that it can be compared. Moreover, what would appear to be more important than the density of members is the role accorded to them in the state. This is determined more by the prevailing ideology than by any other factor. It is this ideology which establishes the union memberships' credibility and their ability to influence the legal framework and political context in which they exist. In this respect their relationship to political parties, especially those of the left, and the degree of political influence and power they are able to exert in this political partnership are of major significance. However, even when the partnership is organic—as in the United Kingdom where the influence of the unions is extremely great, especially when the Labour Party is in office—the processes of parliamentary democracy limit the degree of union political power. This situation could be changed, not only in Britain but also in any of the countries studied, by radical changes in ideology. It is conceivable that this could lead to the unions becoming more dominant both in the conduct of collective bargaining and participation in management and in broader government policies. It is also conceivable that should "communitarianism" continue to develop, the role of the unions will be subordinatd to the interests of the state as in the Communist countries. More probable, however, is the development of a situation in which the dominant influence in the capitalist democracies is that of the unions, as might follow if such schemes as the Meidner Plan in Sweden were enacted, since this would give the unions control over both the sources of industrial finance and the processes of production. Those who support the Meidner Plan see the development of union ownership and control of industry as a preferable alternative to centralized public ownership and governmental control. Trade union ownership of industrial capital would, it is claimed, extend the concept of collectivist pluralism, thus creating a form of social ownership less centralized and bureaucratic than the traditional forms of socialism. The passing of bills to establish an employees' investment and dividend fund, which are being urged by the trade unions in Denmark and Sweden, could provide a significant test of these points of view.

THE COLLECTIVE BARGAINING-PARTICIPATION DICHOTOMY

West Germany has developed a system of industrial relations since the Second World War, which, while giving constitutional protection to the right of unions to bargain collectively, has also extended the right of employees and union representatives to participate in the control and management of West German enterprise to a greater degree than in any other country in Western Europe. What is seen in the United States and in Europe by unions on the left and employers on the right as a contradiction, seems to have been successfully avoided in Germany, where both collective bargaining and codetermination flourish in a dualism that has come to exert a powerful influence on developments in other countries.

A significant feature of the postwar German industrial relations system was the radical reorganization of the trade unions. Instead of an ideologically divided, highly politicized trade union movement locked into a class conflict with extremely conservative employers, there arose a unified trade-union organization, strongly supportive of social democracy and a system of industrial relations in which, in exchange for a significant degree of codetermination, it has played an integrative and constructive role. The change in the philosophy and structure of the unions grew out of National Socialism and the war, but it was also deeply rooted in an earlier experience and ideology which failed in the climate prevailing at the end of the First World War. It could be argued that even more important than the change in the unions has been the change in the political environment and attitudes and the role of the employers since 1945. The dominant political parties have all accepted that the trade unions have a fundamental role to play in a modern society which demands that their right to represent their members, to bargain freely, and to participate in the supervision of the management of industrial enterprises should be guaranteed constitutionally. The employers, for their part, though reluctant to concede to the unions all that they have sought to achieve, have been pressed into accepting that the unions have a positive role to play.

The concordat achieved in 1951 and 1952 after a conflict which might have ended in disaster lasted 25 years without major revision. The new developments, discussed by Professor Hetzler and embodied in the Co-determination Law of 1976, are seen by the employers as a break with the past and an attempt by the unions to assert their dominance over the rights of property and managerial control. The unions, however, believe that the system of supervision adopted in the coal, iron, and steel industries in 1952, but which they failed to secure generally, has demonstrated their responsibility. This 1976 act is, therefore, in the opinion of the unions no more than a belated and inadequate achievement of the objective they had been wrongfully denied for 25 years.

It may be that the employers have over-exaggerated the significance of the 1976 act, which they have petitioned to ask the constitutional court to find unconstitutional, but they are afraid that unless they can obtain a ruling that will set a limit to the extension of union participation, it will be pushed to the point where the unions are the controlling power over management. It is also clear that a new radicalism is developing in Germany. This is evident in the attitudes of the younger element in the trade unions who call for more positive socialist policies. This more radical group, which has been critical of the older leadership and of the extent to which this leadership has committed the unions to policies of cooperation and against militancy, is ready to accept more open conflict with employers. The increased efforts by the unions to exercise greater influence over the works councils and to make the activities of the *Vertrauensleute*—the union representatives—more effective have reflected the rise in militancy; so too did the increase in the number of spontaneous strikes in the mid-1970s and the harder line by the unions in the collective bargaining process which threatened to result in serious industrial strife in 1976 and 1978.

The onset of recession, and with it the growth in unemployment, dampened the tempo of union-inspired activism in the plants and cooled the bargaining situation down, but it has heightened the concern of the unions over the conduct of economic policy at the levels of the Federal Republic and the *Länder*. As Hetzler and Schienstock explain, the formal breaking off of the policy of "concerted action" on wages has been a reflection of the dissatisfaction of the unions with the decision of the employers to challenge the constitutionality of the 1976 Codetermination Act, but the reluctance of the unions to embarrass the government seriously through the pursuit of aggressively militant pay policies also indicates both the general weakness of the unions in the recession and their ambivalence towards a political and economic system which has rewarded their members extremely well.

There is widespread unease in Germany that a failure to solve fundamental economic problems, especially the prevention of rising levels of persistent unemployment, and to bring about a more equal distribution of income and wealth will lead to increasing social conflict. There are proposals for radical schemes of capital-sharing, but these are far from commanding strong support. Although many German employers fear that union radicalism will grow and will not be satisfied until the unions have achieved a position of control through codetermination and an ability to intimidate the government through their bargaining strength, an equally convincing scenario is that the unions have too much at stake in the existing economic and political system to risk jeopardizing their role by creating a situation which would invite bitter conflict with the employers and the state, leading inevitably to the breakdown of democracy and a new period of authoritarianism.

The system of industrial relations in Germany and the problems which have emerged are in one sense a product of special factors unique to that country, but they are also the product of factors which have led to developments in other countries which are very similar to those that have occurred in Germany.

In one important respect there has been less change in Germany than in most other countries, namely in the pattern of collective bargaining. The determination of the basic levels of pay is still set by the tariff agreements negotiated in each *Land* by the employers' association in each industry and the unions. In most other countries in Europe collective bargaining has become much more important at the level of the enterprise, not only in regard to pay, but in relation to many other aspects of management-worker relations. In Germany the unions' bargaining role is much less evident in the enterprise, since at that level the works council, which is not a creature of the unions, is responsible for all matters of concern arising from the work activity of employees. As it has no legal authority to enforce its bargaining role by strike action, since the authority of the works council is derived not from the union, but from the law, it must rely for its effectiveness on the powers it enjoys under the Works Constitution Acts. In these circumstances the influence of the union is relatively limited in spite of the fact that 80 percent of works council members belong to the unions.

The difference in the pattern of collective bargaining and the system of co-determination through the supervisory board and the dominant role of the works council distinguish the German system of industrial relations from the other systems examined. Although there has been an increase in the militancy of works councils and a significant increase in disputes that have led to strikes, the dominant view in Germany, and this is not disputed by Dr. Hetzler, is that there is not likely to be any major change in the immediate period ahead unless the challenge by a group of employers to persuade the Constitutional Court that the 1976 Codetermination Act is unlawful is upheld. Should that happen it is likely that there will be a stimulus to militancy and an increase in union aggressiveness at the plant and company level.

In the Netherlands the social philosophy of the new FNV emphasizes the conflict of interest between management and labor, and its goal is the restructuring of the institutions of industrial relations so as to reflect the central importance of this element rather than the integrative concepts that had been of dominant importance in the aftermath of the war.

As Professor Albeda shows, the shift in trade union philosophy has been brought about by changes in fundamental economic, social, and technological factors, which had led in the 1960s to the collapse of the centralized tripartite institutions of wage determination. As in most other Western European countries in 1970, Dutch labor relations were convulsed by what has been called "the crisis of industrial relations in Europe." Starting in Rotterdam harbor there was an explosion of unofficial strikes which had an immediate and profound impact on the trade unions. "In the first place they took over the unofficial strikes, making them legal. In the second place they decided to take a more radical and more aggressive attitude in their bargaining relationship with the employers" (Albeda).

The adoption of aggressive bargaining tactics by the unions had been further encouraged by the advent of a center-right coalition government, which was unable either to curb growing inflation or to command the support of the unions. The employers inevitably sought to protect their interests by developing their own tactics of containment and concession. The replacement of the center-right with a center-left coalition which sought to re-establish a social contract, but failed to satisfy either the unions or employers, brought no immediate solution. Faced by a situation in which inflation threatened to damage the economy seriously and make worse a rapidly deteriorating unemployment situation, the unions were placed under tremendous pressure to play a more responsible role.

Following the general election of 1977 and the establishment of a new center-left coalition the government has promised to carry out an offer made to the unions by the previous government to revise the Works Council Law, bringing to an end the membership of employers, and to introduce a system of profit-sharing involving the setting up of an investment fund under the control of the unions.

It is difficult to predict the course of development in the Netherlands, since it is clear that there has been a marked shift to the left in the attitudes of union leaders and with a growth of confrontation policies. However, the demand that the unions should exercise a greater influence over the investment policies of companies and as a *quid pro quo* an acceptance of national wage policies enforced by the government through public agencies may be seen as a significant shift towards a more corporatist style of politics. There is a fear in Holland that this development, if continued, will undermine the market economy and severely constrict the bargaining role of employers and unions. This was in fact the situation from 1945 until the early 1960s. It may well be that the new trend will be no more permanent than the previous one.

The problem of relations between the unions and employers and of the government, which is responsible for preventing inflation, ensuring a rate of economic growth that will satisfy the expectations of workers and employers by keeping unemployment low and enabling a reasonable rate of profit to be earned, and at the same time meeting the challenge of those on one hand who wish to see a radical redistribution of income and wealth and those on the other who wish to see initiative and effort adequately rewarded, is not unique to Holland, it is a central issue throughout Europe. So too is the problem of the relative importance of the conflictual process of collective bargaining in the context of a market economy and the corporatist processes of tripartitism at the national level and bipartitism at the level of the enterprise.

In every country the tripartitism which was induced by inflation has been greatly strained by the efforts to constrain wage and price rises in the past decade. It has been rescued from virtually total collapse by the considerable rise in unemployment. In order to persuade governments to adopt measures of expansion trade unions have had to agree to moderate their pay demands. They have done this with considerable reluctance and not without conflicts and crisis in every country. The inflationary rates of pay increase which were a feature of the early to mid-1970s have moderated under the influence of the recession, but have not fallen, except in Switzerland, to the rates of the 1960s. There is moreover in the precarious coalitions of the center parties which govern most European countries a dangerous instability which could prove to be a fragile barrier to pressures for massive pay increases when recovery really gets under way. The economic and political climate in these respects is not very much different in Japan and the U.S.A. and Canada from what it is in the European countries. But there can be little doubt, even in North America, that there will be renewed emphasis on incomes and prices policies if inflation begins to climb again.

Although every country in Western Europe is governed by a moderate center-right or center-left coalition, there has been a significant shift in political opinion and trade union policy towards the more radical left. This takes different forms in different countries. In Italy and France the shift has radicalized the Socialists and brought the Communists into a position where, though not in the government, they exercise a powerful political influence on its policies, especially in Italy. However, the confirmed allegiance of the Communist parties to the Soviet Union and the pull that this exerts has made Eurocommunism an exciting concept for theoretical debate, but a weak ideology for revolutionary action.

The increasing support for the left parties in Italy and France has strengthened the orthodoxy of the trade unions in those countries. In neither country are the Communist and radical socialist unions prepared to support a German-type system of employee-participation. They have become more and more militant in their bargaining tactics against the larger employers. They have also raised their pressure on government to pass legislation of social benefit to their members. In both countries there has been an increase in union bargaining activity within the enterprise which has been encouraged by legislation. Professor Treu describes the change from the centralized model of collective bargaining and the factors that brought about the change in Italy. Unlike in France, plant and company agreements in the larger enterprises often anticipate agreements made at the industry level. This development has brought two important changes in trade-union structure. One has been the creation of factory committees which have had an important contributory influence on the second development, that of greater unity between the national federations. Perhaps the most significant feature of this development in the bargaining structure in Italy has been the extension of bargaining from a narrow range of issues relating to levels of pay to virtually the whole gamut of managerial decisions, including the organization of work and investment policies. The Italian unions see extension in the scope of collective bargaining as achieving, through a conflictual process, what unions in Germany have sought to achieve through the principles of co-determination.

It is evident from the analysis of recent trends in France made by Professor Reynaud that there has also been a significant change in the structure of industrial relations in France. Worker-management relations are no longer determined almost solely by the law. Nor is collective bargaining confined to the negotiation of industry-wide agreements. The role of union representatives and the activities of works councils have become of increasing importance in the larger enterprises and this trend is likely to continue. It is essentially a trend towards a greater degree of participation, which, as Professor Reynaud shows, raises for the unions, management, and government serious questions relating to their ideology and their autonomy, their traditional roles, and the future balance between policies that are based upon conflictual relations and those which necessarily involve a much greater degree of consensus.

The government of Giscard d'Estaing indicated after its victory at the elections in 1978 that it will introduce legislation to reduce inequalities of income and wealth and advance the social status of the workers. To promote a less divisive and conflictual society it will seek to give effect to some of the recommendations of the Sudreau report which recommended the development of a more participative relationship between employers and unions, but which has evoked little support from either unions or management. Whether such legislation would overcome the opposition of the French employers and the distrust of the unions with their preference for more radical social and economic developments, it is difficult to say, but in the context of the failure of the left to achieve a political victory because of the inability to bridge the gap between Communist and Socialist party organizations and the real possibility of social democracy developing from the center, some success might be achieved.

In Britain, the conflicts between those who wish to proceed toward a fully socialist society and those who wish to revert to a greater degree of individualism run deep; as does the conflict between those on the left who wish to see the full freedom of collective bargaining restored primarily as a means of carrying on class struggle against the managers, and those who are prepared to accept the implications of a social contract and a greater degree of participation in management decision-making.

What is most evident in Britain is that there is strong current in the unions in favor of a return to collective bargaining after the years of pay limitation, although there is considerable skepticism as to the extent that it will really be possible to return to completely full and unfettered bargaining. Nevertheless, this is the official policy of the unions, but they are likely to have to face continued government demands that they exercise wage restraint.

A danger in Britain is that relief to the balance of payments afforded by the substantial revenues obtained from North Sea Oil will enable unions and managers to avoid making the radical changes that are required in the structure and organization of British industry. Many of Britain's largest enterprises and most important industries, especially those in public ownership, are on all the evidence massively overmanned. So too is central and local government. There is no way in which Britain can achieve long-term prosperity and keep up with the other major industrial states unless this incubus on efficiency is removed.

The payment of high levels of compensation has made it possible for some of the most glaring cases of unrequired plant capacity to be closed down, but these are only the tip of the iceberg which the unions are determined not to permit management to liquidate. The danger which unemployment brings to the well-being of individuals is real, but in the long run the damage will be even greater if the unions prevent employers tackling the problem. The fundamental cause of the overmanning lies in the failure of management to persuade the unions to accept new equipment and to adopt new work methods. The hostility of the unions has been founded upon beliefs that the changes desired by management would not be to their benefit. The conflictual system of collective bargaining with its ingrained suspicion and deep distrust of the other side, and the apparent success of militant tactics, have made communication and cooperation extremely difficult. It will take a long and sustained period of management effort to bring about an alternative behavior pattern. Participation starting at the shop-floor level, carefully orchestrated with collective bargaining, is seen by many managers in Britain as the only way forward, since national union leadership is unable or unwilling to help managers to change the climate of industrial relations.

A number of major British companies have developed limited programs of employee participation through the establishment of autonomous work groups and consultative bodies which appear to have had a considerable degree of success. These developments are very similar to many of the experiments in workplace participation which have been undertaken in Scandinavia. They are often seen by management as an alternative to the more institutionalized systems of participation, and in non-union establishments they may in fact fulfill this purpose, but it would be unusual for them to be accepted as alternatives to the more formal systems of bargaining and participation in unionized plants and enterprises. Moreover, there is no reason why this open style of what has been called work-linked democracy should not be developed even when works councils and worker-directors exist. Participative decision-making on the shop floor is in most cases every bit as much a complement to other methods of participation as it is an alternative to them.

The political misjudgment made by the union-dominated Bullock Committee's Report, examined in Chapter VI, delayed legislation on industrial democracy, but all the main parties are committed to enacting a measure to achieve some degree of employee-participation. This will not be realized until after the next general election, but the Labor government's proposals, which would provide for one third of the members of a company policy board to be appointed as employee representatives, are likely to command a good deal of support, though the precise details may be changed as a result of the election. It is likely to be a good number of years before it will be possible to judge whether the trend towards a greater degree of worker and union participation at board and shop-floor levels in both the private and public sectors, where a number of experiments are being carried out, will fundamentally change the character of the British industrial relations system leading to a more consensual and constructive pattern. The traditional adversary model of collective bargaining is not likely to yield quickly or easily to a concept of industrial relations which seeks to resolve conflicts of interest without costly work stoppages and other manifestations of mutual distrust.

The problem of reconciling collective bargaining with participation has been taken to one logical conclusion in Sweden. The Democracy at Work Act has in effect introduced co-determination by collective bargaining. The new act gives the union power in theory to compel the employer to bargain on any issue that the union believes to be of concern. An important aim of the act has been to encourage a greater degree of union involvement in the making of managerial decision, at the level of the plant and enterprise.

Although in the last resort the management view may prevail, many managers fear the new act will lead to local union leaders opposing decisions that are essential to the efficiency of the enterprise, thus at best causing delay and at worst perhaps serious conflict. Many union leaders feel that the fears that have been expressed by managers are greatly exaggerated. In their opinion local union leaders are unlikely to respond to their new opportunities to bring pressure to bear upon managers in an irresponsible way. A good many managers share this view in spite of worries that the act creates dangers they would have preferred not to have to face.

The ultimate aim of the unions in Sweden is to bring about a system of industrial relations which is dominated by the unions. The unions recognize the need for managers and prefer to seek to protect the interests of members by the maintenance of an independent bargaining role rather than by adopting a policy of sharing power with the representatives of the shareholders on a supervisory board, though they have expressed no wish to withdraw their minority representation.

The Swedish unions in fact wish to go further by supplementing their bargaining role through the establishment of a right to acquire and manage the equity capital of privately owned enterprise.

The principal aim of their scheme, it is said by the unions, is not to give unions the power to control management in its running of enterprises, but to achieve a more equitable distribution of capital and social control of its use. Nevertheless it is difficult to believe that the independence of management would not be affected if the ownership of capital was in the hands of a fund controlled by the unions, which had the power to hire and fire the managers. Even if the unions pursued a policy of permitting them to enjoy the same degree of authority as governments give to the management of nationalized enterprises, they could not be expected to be free to pursue policies not approved by the unions any more than a nationalized enterprise is free to pursue policies disapproved of by a government.

Many other countries in Europe, as well as the United States, provide schemes which permit companies under favorable tax concessions to distribute a proportion of their profits in the form of shares or capital earnings. In France private enterprises must by law set aside up to 5 percent of net profits calculated by a complicated formula, which are credited to each individual employee as a percentage of his pay. Five years must elapse before this capital sum is distributed. It is a small but significant addition to annual salaries. There is much discussion as to how far this share in the profitability of enterprises has influenced the attitudes and behavior of French employees. Many industrialists have come to believe that, though not making for any radical change in attitudes, it has had some influence by way of encouraging a positive attitude towards the benefits of private enterprise.

The unions are extremely skeptical of any claims of this kind. They do not attack the scheme since their members are pleased to receive the annual disbursements, but they favor much more radical measures of nationalization, taxation, and social benefits as the means of achieving a far greater degree of social equity in the distribution of income and wealth and control over private industry. The CFDT and the socialists also wish to see a system of workers' control, *autogestion,* which would if ever adopted be in serious conflict, as Professor Reynaud points out, with "the strong Jacobin and centralized tradition" of the left.

The trend in the countries examined is towards a greater degree of participation in the profitability of private enterprises through a variety of schemes. Although opinion is divided, many among those who wish to see private enterprise maintained and strengthened believe that wider share-ownership would be of advantage. Few believe, however, that this development would transform industrial relations. Nevertheless, to the extent that participation in profits helps to bring about a better understanding of the functioning of enterprise, so much the better. Unfortunately it is not possible to apply these schemes to the public sector, short of returning public enterprise and service to private ownership. A radical solution would be to do this by creating cooperative organizations. In a highly stimulating lecture[3] Peter Jay has suggested that this is ultimately the only solution to the problem of the management-worker syndrome and its conflict-inspired by-product, collective bargaining, which, because it invites corporatist controls, is a threat to the maintenance of a liberal pluralist society.

The basic problem with cooperatives as a solution to industrial relations deficiencies is that to be effective and efficient they have to be relatively small unless they are run like Mondragon in Spain, or the John Lewis Partnership in Britain, by professional managers. Once professional management is employed and the organization grows to a large scale, the effect of cooperative ownership on industrial relations is diminished. It is not necessarily diminished, however, to the point where it is without any significance. Since there is little likelihood of widescale cooperative development, it will remain, therefore, necessary to improve the management-worker relationship by developing the elements that enter into motivation and behavior in cooperative organizations by other means. In this respect the pattern of management-employee relations in Japan is of some significance.

Professor Okamoto has indicated that there are strong elements of continuity and change in developments in the Japanese industrial relations system. The three pillars of the "enterprise welfarism" which dominates Japanese industrial relations—life-time security of employment, enterprise unions, and seniority pay scales based upon age and level of recruitment—remain of major significance. These three factors have had much to do with the remarkable achievements of Japanese industry. They have enabled the large enterprises to adapt their labor force without the acute difficulties faced in other countries when workmen are asked to change their skills and work practices. Since employees in Japan are not made redundant except in dire circumstances they are not dependent upon their particular skill. In exchange for the guarantees of life-time employment and continuous improvement in pay as he gets older, the Japanese worker understands and accepts the need to be retrained and to adjust his method of work to new technology and the needs of the company.

The recession in world trade in the late 1970s and the prospect of slower growth rates have imposed considerable strains on Japanese companies. The large ones which practice life-time employment have relieved their problems of fixed labor costs in a period of low demand at the expense of their temporary employees and sub-contractors. Not surprisingly there has been a considerable rise in bankruptcies and unemployment. Japan has been through these problems before, but there is now uncertainty whether there is likely to be a return to the growth levels of the 1960s and early 1970s. This prospect is leading to doubts about the possibility of maintaining the traditional pattern of employment practice. There have been some modifications in "enterprise welfarism," but Japanese employers realize that the fundamentals of their employment practices have played an important role in the establishment of the cooperative pattern of industrial relations which have meant so much to their success, and they have no wish to give them up even if the economic cost during a recession may be high.

It would be ironic if the Japanese were to abandon "enterprise welfarism" when most countries are adopting employment policies that make lay-offs extremely difficult and expensive. Although European trade unionism was traditionally organized outside the enterprise, since the Second World War it has increasingly become enterprise-oriented. The seniority pay system is rare outside of Japan, as is retirement at the early age of 55, which goes with this system of pay, but early retirement is becoming more usual in Europe and policies to achieve this goal are being advocated as a means of combatting unemployment. In all these aspects, European trends are coming closer to the Japanese model. The most significant influence on Japanese industrial relations since the Second World War has been the development of aggressive collective bargaining often supported by strike action. This development has not resulted in a breakdown of "enterprise welfarism," but it has made Japanese employers increasingly aware of the danger of an erosion of the classic pattern of employer-employee relations in Japan. Increasing prosperity, technological change, a rising tide of liberalism in family relations, and the breakdown of political authoritarianism have contributed to a weakening of the social dominance of the group and a strengthening of the principles of individualism which Professor Lodge has argued are declining in the Western capitalist democracies.

Fear of the consequences has led employers in Japan to pay attention to the developments of consultation and co-determination which have been developed in Europe. There has been some development of grievance procedure based upon the American models of collective bargaining, but neither employers nor unions have been strong supporters of a system which seems to be at the expense of the responsibility of management and the right of the employee to expect that his interests will be protected by the enterprise as a matter of normal behavior. The strength of hierarchy within an organic structure of the group, whether it be the family, enterprise, or the state, remains strong in Japan, and concessions to the interests and power of subgroups or individuals must be reconciled with this fundamental social characteristic of Japanese society.

Recent studies made in Japan indicate that the unions believed much more strongly than management that positive steps should be taken to promote participation. The survey quoted by Professor Okamoto shows that neither unions nor managers were in favor of introducing worker-directors or strongly supported an extension of collective bargaining. Both, however, apparently favor participation "as in Germany and Sweden." This result suggests that the participants were thinking mainly in terms of the role of works councils rather than German-style worker-directors or the Swedish style of extended collective bargaining.

This influence is confirmed by the strong support given in the survey quoted by Professor Okamoto, by both unions and management, to the development of consultative committees. It is interesting to note, however, that the unions in Japan are divided in their enthusiasm for worker's participation in a similar way to the European trade union federations. Domei, the moderate social democratic-oriented trade union federation, is a far more keen supporter of this idea than Sohyo, the more radical socialist-oriented federation. Sohyo's position is akin to that of the CIGL and the CGT, whereas Domei is in favor of strengthening participation at all levels, through collective bargaining, consultative committees, and the establishment of boards of auditors at the directoral level.

The board of auditors has something in common with the German supervisory board, but it does not have the same degree of executive authority. A board of auditors is in effect a consultative body, which has the right to offer an opinion on the decisions made by the board of directors, but it has no power to compel any change in the decisions the board of directors might have made. Since, however, the board of auditors is representative of a powerful constituency its comments must be taken seriously. Although the concept of a board of auditors has only been given substance in a handful of companies, it may well become, as Professor Okamoto believes is likely, a Japanese method of involving unions and employers in the decision-making processes of boards of directors without actual membership.

The concept of hierarchy and acceptance of authority is a significant cultural characteristic of Japan, but so too is the recognition of a need to foster communal participation and responsibility. The evidence of change in Japanese industrial relations points both to the maintenance and development of the conflictual pattern of industrial relations, but a pattern that is limited by the classic emphasis on group loyalty and which in the future will embrace the concept of employer and union-participation through joint committees and boards of auditors. In these respects industrial relations in Japan do not differ significantly from the trends which are occurring in Europe. In accepting the need for an organic relationship between worker and manager Japanese concepts of industrial relations move closer to those found in Europe than in the U.S.A.

Convergence or Divergence

It is abundantly evident that in spite of significant differences in the patterns of industrial relations in the countries included in this study they have all responded to the same type of technological and economic forces in a similar way. In each country employers and unions have moved towards a situation in which they have accepted a need to modify their traditional behavior towards each other. In those countries such as the United States, the United Kingdom, Italy, and Sweden in which collective bargaining has played a major role, although in different ways, there has been a common tendency for the process of bargaining to be widened and deepened with important implications for both employers and unions. In Germany and Holland the broadening and deepening has been brought about through the development of systems of employee-participation outside of the union-dominated collective bargaining activity.

Although in every country there has been an acceptance of the need to achieve a more participative system of industrial relations, in no country has this been carried as far as the unions would like to achieve, whether through collective bargaining, or direct participation on boards of supervision and management. The aims of the unions in Europe and in Japan go very much further in these respects than those of the unions in the United States. The trends of the past 30 years have brought the systems of industrial relations much closer to each other, but if the contemporary aims of the unions were to be achieved, this would bring about a divergence between Europe and Japan on the one hand and the U.S.A. on the other.

Looking not so far ahead it is probable that the convergence of the recent past will continue. Certainly within Western Europe it is likely that the convergence will be significantly on matters of substantive importance, notwithstanding the equally likely continuance of significant differences in the procedures of industrial relations.

Throughout Europe there is a strong current of support for an improvement in the quality of working life. In a wide variety of matters relating to employment security, training and education, health and safety, the advancement and protection of women's rights in employment, advances in one country influence development in another. It is widely expected that there will be a general reduction of hours of work for manual workers during the next decade which will occur more or less at the same time across the countries of Western Europe. At present there is a considerable variation in the length of vacations and number of public holidays, but these differences will probably become less.

An important factor in the transmission of ideas and influences from one country to another has been the internationalizing of trade union organization and the growth of multinational enterprises. Although the trade union movements are divided by occupational and ideological differences there has been an important measure of integration at both national and international levels. The creation of the European Trades Union Council, though weakened by political differences and mutual interests, was an important step towards greater unity in trade union policy and action in relation to the development of the European Community.

Much depends on the evolution of the EEC. If it evolves as its protagonists hope to see, it is likely to have a significant impact on trade union developments. The establishment of the directly-related European parliament might prove to be an important step in this respect, since it will offer the trade unions an opportunity to lobby for such developments as the European company statute and Directive 5, which call for the adoption in each country of systems of industrial democracy that include rights to participate on boards of directors.

At the wider international level the efforts of the unions to come to grips with multinational enterprises through the development of company councils and common action have produced little in the way of tangible results. Of more significance has been the adoption by the OECD, ILO, and EEC of codes of conduct and policy resolutions which can be used by the unions to achieve common standards of procedure and substantive conditions of employment. These are but pointers in the direction of convergence and as yet of limited importance, but they are not without significance as both unions and companies recognize.

Looking further ahead the most fundamental question open to speculation is whether it will be possible to maintain pluralist societies based upon the preponderantly private ownership of capital. If the unions make this impossible by design or their inability to adjust their behavior so as to avoid the extension of government control, the systems of industrial relations as they exist today will give way to new forms of regulation. One possibility is the development of the neo-syndicalist concepts envisaged in Scandinavia. Another possibility would be the decline of trade unionism, as it appears to be happening in the United States, together with a much wider degree of employee participation in both capital ownership and the making of managerial decisions. A major problem may be raised by the existence of multinational enterprises. They obviously provide a stumbling block to changes in capital ownership, but it is possible to conceive of arrangements in which the element of local participation is significant and in other respects they would clearly have to accept the problems of legal regulation relating to their organization and structure, as they do already. Nevertheless the problem of ultimate control would remain and could become an issue of major conflict if serious differences arose between the host country of a subsidiary and the corporate headquarters situated in another country. The development of the international codes of regulation approved by the OECD and the United Nations might provide an operational solution to the difficulties that could arise from a serious divergence in the policies pursued in the home and host countries in which multinationals have their headquarters and their subsidiaries.

Whether the extension of participation that may be foreseen is achieved in one country through collective bargaining, or in another country by other methods of representation, one of the major problems that will be generated is that there will be a tendency to encourage decisions that promote consumption at the expense of investment and to slow down the rate at which decisions are made. Workers and their unions have inevitably a shorter time-horizon than managers. It is difficult, if not impossible, for shop stewards and trade unions to feel bound to accept the consequences of decisions which may have serious effects on levels of employment, job structures, and work methods, but which in the nature of the lead time inherent in many modern technological developments had to be taken many years previously. There is moreover the problem that the satisfaction of the interests of workers may be realizable only at the expense of the other stake-holders in an enterprise, the customers, the shareholders, and the wider community. If the extension of employee-participation consistently leads to a failure to satisfy these interests, the net result, as may already be occurring, could be to reduce the rate of investment.

It may be argued that an extension of participation will bring about a greater understanding of these problems and thus improve the quality of decision-making. The extension of participation may, however, also result in a slowing down in the speed at which decisions are taken, thus offsetting other gains. Unfortunately, there is no systematic evidence available that would confirm which are the most likely results.

By making the task of management more difficult through the need to inform, consult, and negotiate more widely, the possibility cannot be ruled out that management decisions will be less well made. In some areas of management decision-making it is in fact extremely difficult and often virtually impossible for technical reasons to involve workers or union representatives in the processes that lead up to a decision. Many decisions require high levels of technical expertise and coordinated judgments that have to be taken as many sub-decisions over a lengthy time period; it is only at the end of such a chain of decisions, when for example a new process or a new plant becomes operational, that most workers will feel its effect. It is at that stage that they may wish to see changes made, but changing a major decision made in this way, so as to protect the interests of the workers, may be very costly and unjustified in the long-term interests of the enterprise and wider society. It follows that a participation system in which the representatives of workers have been drawn into the decision-making process in their early stages may turn out to have advantages, but also to lead to commitments that might be extremely uncomfortable in relation to the effect that particular decisions might have in the long term on the interests of employees. Where in a chain of decision-making, as well as by what process, participation takes place is a matter of crucial importance to the interests of employees and the efficiency of enterprises. Existing patterns of participation clearly have variable results, but there is no model that can be said to be 100 percent successful. Each gives rise to problems that can only be effectively solved in the context of the particular participation process. The way in which problems are solved is of fundamental importance both to the individuals who might be affected by a particular decision and to the enterprise and its managers who equally have much at stake in the securing of an efficient decision.

However important it might be to involve workers and their unions in the making of decisions, and of this there can be no doubt, what still remains an issue, and is likely to continue to remain an issue whatever the structural arrangements to secure this goal, is the problem of achieving the right balance between the need for technical expertise and executive authority—the managerial function—on the one hand, and, on the other, the degree of participation of all employees which will both ensure the legitimacy of the managerial role and give to employees the quality of working life that only creative involvement can bring about. There may well be a conflict of interest between long-term efficiency and short-term employee interests; it is a conflict that must be recognized and accepted as one that cannot be eliminated simply by concentrating on the virtues of participation. Managerial authority must be given its proper weight, and the role of unions, whose members' standard of life is ultimately dependent not on their bargaining power but on the efficiency of management, must be defined by that most fundamental of facts.

The countries which most successfully solve the conflicts that are inherent in the development of the new systems of industrial democracy are likely to be the ones that will be able to cope most effectively with the challenge that the evolution of modern technology and social change will bring. In searching for a solution to these problems each country will find its own balance between corporate organization and the pluralism which permits managers and unions to pursue their own interests independent of government intervention. This balance will inevitably be influenced by the powerful currents of past history and the developments taking place in other countries.

Notes

1. *Daedalus,* winter 1977, Cambridge, Massachusetts.
2. Ibid.
3. P. Jay, Wincott Lecture, Institute of Economic Affairs, London, 1977.

1

Federal Republic of Germany

by H. W. HETZLER and GERD SCHIENSTOCK

Conflict and Consensus

In comparison with other industrial countries the industrial relations system of the Federal Republic is characterized by a high degree of stability and a relatively low level of conflict. The participation of the work force in work conflicts is, for example, ten times higher in Great Britain and thirty times higher in Italy than in the Federal Republic. Within these limits, however, the statistics show considerable differences for the various years (see Table 1.1).

Generally speaking, one can say that work conflicts coincide with changes in the business cycle. The reason for this is that at the start of a recession there are excessive wage expectations, whereas in a booming economy wages are not adjusted in time with the improved situation. Although higher wages are one of the main objectives, there are other factors which influence the outcome. Political considerations, for example, were in the foreground of arguments put forward in the 1950s. In 1950-51, approximately 95 percent of the organized work force within the sphere of the Metal Workers' and the Miners' Unions voted to carry through their ideas on co-determination with the help of a strike if necessary. Further political strikes and demonstrations were directed against the passing of the Industrial Constitutional Law in 1952 and against other political decisions. At the beginning of the 1950s

Table 1.1.   Working Days Lost through Strikes and Lockouts, 1965–76

Year	Total	Per Worker Involved
1965	49,486	7.9
1966	27,284	0.1
1967	389,581	6.5
1968	25,385	1.0
1969	249,204	2.8
1970	93,203	0.5
1971	4,483,740	8.4
1972	66,045	2.9
1973	563,051	3.0
1974	1,051,290	4.2
1975	68,680	1.9
1976	533,696	3.2

Source: Presse- und Informationsamt der Bundesregierung, Gesell-
schaftliche Daten 1977, Stuttgart, 1977, p. 127.

many strikes took place for higher wages. The years 1962–63 saw another
increase in the intensity of work conflict. The most important were the
disputes in the metal industry in Baden-Wurttemberg, in which there were
many lock-outs.

After a period of relative industrial peace there were a large number of
wildcat strikes in 1969. This strike movement must be seen against the
background of economic development. After the recession of 1966–67 a
period of rapid economic growth took place in the Federal Republic. The
wages policy of the trade unions could not keep pace with this development,
and the consequence was that the collective agreements were regarded as
being too low by the rank and file. In the steel industry and in the coal mines,
spontaneous action led to a revision of the current wage agreements and to
additional extra-wage negotiations at plant level. The relevance of these
spontaneous strikes, however, went far beyond the immediate gains
achieved. They induced a discussion in the trade unions about better
representation of the workers on the shop floor and a wage policy closer to
the plant.

There were more vigorous work conflicts in 1971, particularly in the
chemical and metal industries. Wages were again the main grounds for these
disputes. The economic situation was one of marked recession. Firms reacted
to the strikes in key areas of the economy (which were supported by the trade
unions) with lock-outs. In 1973 a strike took place in the metal industry in
the Nordwürttemberg/Nordbaden region for basic improvements in
working conditions. A new skeleton wage agreement was concluded which,
in its fundamental points, stipulated the following: job security for older

workers, extension of rest periods, minimum pay guarantee for piece-workers, and a maximum work speed for assembly-line workers. In 1974 a serious strike took place in various parts of the civil service. A wage dispute in the printing industry in 1976 led the employers to resort to lock-outs, a method of conflict which had been rarely used in previous years.

In spite of these events, industrial relations in the Federal Republic have for many years presented a remarkably peaceful picture. Bearing this in mind, the Minister of Labor pointed out in a summary of social data for 1977 that between 1951 and 1976 on average the annual loss of working days per hundred wage-earners amounted to 4.1, i.e. 0.02 percent of working days per year. The largest number of working days were lost in 1971 with 22 per hundred employees, whereas a minimum of 0.1 days lost was recorded in 1964, 1966 and 1968. Several reasons can be adduced to explain the relative stability of the industrial relations system in the Federal Republic of Germany. Two main factors are most certainly the strong institutional regulations and the important role of government in industrial relations on the one side, and the overriding idea of social partnership between capital and labor on the other. Instead of concentrating on the class struggle as in other countries, the German employers' and workers' organizations both agreed during the years of reconstruction on certain basic values of a free economy—private capital, the validity of the principles of the market, and economic growth as the basis of material and private welfare.

Together with the acceptance of a pluralist political and economic system, the broad consensus on basic social values can be considered as having been one of the major conditions for constructive interaction between the parties within the tripartite system. The question is whether or not this description of past and present circumstances will also hold in the future. The answer to this is rather difficult as the German case is not characterized by spectacular events or measures, such as violent strikes, political turmoil, or excessive welfare programs as are to be found in other countries. Therefore, it is necessary to discuss a number of structural and procedural aspects to provide a sound basis for evaluating what is actually taking place. In this context it seems worthwhile to start with a brief sketch of economic developments, as these are generally regarded as being of paramount importance for the industrial relations system.

Wage and Employment Trends

The trend of economic growth in the Federal Republic has been upward over the last twenty-five years. One exception to this was the year 1967 when, due to the recession, the change in Gross National Product from the previous year was −0.1 percent at 1960 price levels. Seven years later a similarly poor result was recorded. In 1974 the increase in Gross National Product compared with 1973 was only 0.4 percent, and one year later the growth figure was negative, −2.5 percent. In contrast with earlier recessions this development was not part of the business cycle, but was caused by outside influences. While the Federal Bank still believed in 1972 that it had to prevent a boom taking place and the government had put forward a stability program in the spring of 1973 (which, above all, was supposed to lead to a cutback in investment), the oil crisis of the fall of 1973 changed the economic situation dramatically. Between this date and the fall of 1974 oil prices rose by 350 percent and prices for other raw materials were swept along with this development. According to the HWWA (*Hamburgisches Weltwirtschafts-archiv*) Index raw material prices on the world markets increased by 90 percent in this period. As the German economy depends to a large extent on exports, the oil crisis was a fundamental threat. At the same time it affected domestic prices and, as a consequence, wage levels.

Average wage costs per working hour in the manufacturing sector amounted to DM 18.30 in 1977, as compared with DM 7.90 in Great Britain, DM 10.50 in Japan, and DM 11.00 in Italy. Only Denmark with DM 18.20 and Sweden with DM 20.30 paid higher wages on average. Even the United States, a country with a traditionally high wage level was lower than the Federal Republic at DM 17.80 in 1977.[1] As Table 1.2 shows, the increase in the proportion of gross income from employment to national income (*Lohnquote*) has been accompanied by a steady decline in the share of income from self-employed work and from property.

The rise in factor costs led to a profit squeeze which in turn affected negatively readiness to invest. This is particularly true for industries with

Table 1.2.   Share of Income in National Income, 1965-76

Year	Gross Income from Employment (percent of national income)	Income from Self-Employed Work or from Property (percent of national income)
1965	65.6	34.4
1966	66.6	33.3
1967	66.4	33.6
1968	64.8	35.2
1969	66.1	33.9
1970	67.8	32.2
1971	69.1	30.9
1972	69.5	30.5
1973	70.7	29.3
1974	72.6	27.4
1975	72.8	27.2
1976	71.4	28.6

Source: Der Bundesminister für Wirtschaft, *Leistung in Zahlen 1976*, August 1977, p. 19.

declining production, such as coal mining, the textile industry, iron and steel, as well as the engineering industry. Apart from structural changes there is evidence to show that equipment in West German factories is being used for a longer period of time and is thus becoming obsolete. Although it is difficult to distinguish whether the motive to invest is primarily to enlarge capacity, to cover replacement, or to increase productivity and effectiveness, it seems to be clear that the rationalization of production has been of major importance in the last few years as a reaction to rising factor costs.[2] This is indicated not only by the fact that average investment per worker rose from DM 65,353 to DM 82,078 between 1974 and 1978 (estimates), but also by the increase in work productivity in the same period (Table 1.3).

Table 1.3. Trends in Work Productivity, 1974-78

Year	Increase in Work Productivity as Compared with Previous Years	
	(absolute)	(percent)
1974	34,738	3.3
1975	35,402	1.9
1976	37,908	7.1
1977	39,249	3.5
1978	41,118	4.8

Source: *WSI Mitteilungen*, November 1977, p. 659.

While the policy of the Federal Government and the Federal Bank before the oil crisis was mainly aimed at avoiding the negative consequences of a booming economy, afterwards it was necessary to take the opposite action, and mainly with regard to the labor market. Although it has since been possible to achieve a satisfactory rate of growth once more, the rate of unemployment has not decreased in a similar way (Table 1.4).

This comparatively high rate of unemployment by German standards has caused considerable public disquiet. This is all the more the case, as since the days of the great depression there has been a deep-rooted trauma in the German people connected with any sign of a steep rise in unemployment. At the same time it is quite a new experience that an adequate growth rate is not correlated with steady employment. On the contrary, some experts believe that the rate of unemployment could become even higher. In the present situation the return to full employment is therefore a pre-eminent political goal. There are sincere doubts, however, as to whether the instruments which worked so well in the past—such as tax relief and deficit spending— will suffice this time. The forecasts of the various economic research institutes have concentrated less on the question of how much growth is

Table 1.4.   Trends in GNP and Unemployment, 1970-76

Year	Change in the Gross National Product Compared with Previous Year (constant 1970 prices)	Unemployment Rate (percent)
1970	+5.9	0.7
1971	+3.3	0.8
1972	+3.6	1.1
1973	+4.9	1.2
1974	+0.4	2.6
1975	-2.5	4.7
1976	+5.7	4.6

Source: Der Bundesminister für Wirtschaft, *Leistung in Zahlen 1976*, August 1977, pp. 16 and 42.

necessary in order to remove unemployment, than on the question of what increases, if any, can be achieved.

It can be said without exaggeration that the employment problem is one of the main issues in contemporary industrial relations in Germany. It has been realized, in the meantime, that these difficulties have not only structural causes, but are also to a large extent the result of rapid technological change. On the one hand the government has tried to encourage technical innovation by large-scale programs which included direct and indirect incentives. It is hoped that new technologies will have a positive effect upon the employment situation. On the other hand technical change carries with it a severe threat to job security. In this connection a major part is played by "large-scale integration," a development of semi-conductor technology.[3] It is applied in two ways: either as a micro-processor where a large number of electronic elements are combined to form a minute "chip," which is able to carry out arithmetical as well as other logical operations; or, as a micro-computer where additional electronic elements make it possible to store programs and input and output data. In contrast with traditional technologies, large-scale integration allows and encourages a high degree of automation. This leads to lower manufacturing costs. While the costs of a transistor at the beginning of the semi-conductor development stage some fifteen years ago were approximately two Marks, the price has now fallen due to automation to about 0.2 Pfennings.[4] For the producers of semi-conductors the new technology means a reduction in employment in the immediate production area, at the same time as an additional need for staff in production planning. As, however, a considerable number of the mechanical parts were produced formerly by the equipment manufacturers, their replacement through electronic devices results in a corresponding reduction in job opportunities in this area. In many cases the tendency toward forward integration seems inevitable, and certain enterprises which did not adjust to this development in time, for example, several firms in the precision industry (such as watch-making and office machines), encountered great economic difficulties. Some, in fact, went bankrupt. Apart from the quantitative effects, the extension of semi-conductor technology also had major effects on the structure of job requirements. As it is a characteristic of the precision industries to employ a large proportion of skilled workers, this group was affected particularly by forward integration through the manufacture of electronic parts. It is expected that a relatively smaller number of higher-qualified jobs will be opposed to an increasing number of jobs with below-average qualifications.

The quantitative and qualitative consequences of semi-conductor technology occur not only in the area of electronic parts and equipment manufacture, but also, in particular, where these devices are used. Striking examples of these consequences can be seen in the printing industry and in the whole office and administrative sector. In newspaper printing shops, type-setting machines are gradually being displaced by light-setting equipment. Through this development skilled machine-setters are being replaced by semi-skilled typists. At the same time, the input speed is considerably increased. Further rationalization is being achieved by the introduction of new opto-electronic systems. Here journalists partly fulfil duties formerly done by machine-setters. Through the introduction of special screens it is even possible to abandon the practice of page-proofing. It is expected that light-setting alone will mean the loss of 1,000 to 2,000 machine-setting jobs annually. Technological change is regarded by the workers involved more critically as it affects a highly skilled and traditional industry.

A similar development is taking place in the office and administrative sector although, because of the different work tasks, it is less easy to observe. The "apparative intelligence" in this area is mainly used to simplify the writing, manipulation, and use of texts or other information. The use of micro-computers, for instance, makes it no longer necessary to re-write corrected manuscripts. Electronics, however, are not only being used for the rationalization of routine work, but also (as the example of computerized construction shows) for the mechanization of those areas which, until now, were regarded as not capable of being mechanized. If this development continues, office work will change its character. As there are limited possibilities for putting people who lose their jobs in offices through technical change into other jobs, the consequences for the labor economy are regarded as being even worse in comparison with manufacturing. In addition, there are unfavorable consequences for skill requirements. As the range of the job shrinks the work will become less skilled and more monotonous.

There are, of course, other technologies to be taken into consideration when one is discussing the consequences of technical change with respect for employment, job requirements, and the quality of working life. However, the development of electronic equipment deserves special attention, not only because the field of its applications is almost unlimited, but also because the social consequences are not well enough known and therefore not yet under control. Its negative impact, in particular on the labor market, makes it a central point of discussion, even though the German trade unions are more in favor of rationalization in their own estimation than are worker organizations in other countries.[5] The assumption that technical change in some industries is a source of conflict underlines this paper, and also that the development of industrial relations in the Federal Republic depends largely on returning to a state of full employment.

In the past superfluous workers in sectors with high work productivity were easily absorbed by the low-growth labor-intensive sectors. Structural changes could thus be overcome relatively smoothly. In the Federal Republic not only are the numbers of the self-employed falling—a group in which farming and small businesses are strongly represented—but the proportion of blue-collar workers is also decreasing. In contrast the numbers of white-collar workers and civil servants have risen continuously. The post-industrial society does not constitute a safeguard against unemployment. This is true for white-collar workers who have lost their jobs and also for the vast amount of young graduates—for many of whom the state is the only potential employer. The situation on the labor market will therefore depend in the short term on both the achievement of sufficient economic growth and the readiness of the Federal Government to widen the scope of its activities and services beyond those at present, even though in the eyes of some observers the range of such activities and services has already reached a critical point.

The Influence of the State on Industrial Relations

The development toward a post-industrial society, together with the economic and social problems this entails, has led to the state adopting an important position in the system of industrial relations in the Federal Republic. Quite apart from this specific situation, however, it follows German tradition that the state intervenes to a large extent, in the form of legislative measures, in the formation and regulation of industrial relations.[6] At the time of Bismarck and the Weimar Republic there was already a system of statutory safety regulations in force which were to be found in no other contemporary European country. This extremely far-reaching (for those days) social legislation was based on two fundamental assumptions. Firstly, that it would be possible for Germany, a late arrival as a nation-state,[7] to avoid those mistakes which had occurred in connection with industrialization in other European countries, and, secondly, that the state was recognized as the authoritative power by the various social groups almost without question. The strong intervention by the state singularly limited the scope for negotiation by the parties to wage agreements, but also led at the same time to a weak system of industrial relations.

The relatively strong influence of the state on industrial relations has been maintained, inasmuch as the legal tradition has continued in the industrial relations system of the Federal Republic, even though in diminished form. Social aims, as they existed among political parties of the most diverse persuasions immediately after the Second World War, were soon relinquished by them. They have not, in fact, played an important role in present-day politics.

The state's economic and social policies were very soon stamped by the ideas of the liberal concepts of the social market economy.[8] These principles are accepted as the foundation of economic and social policy by the various political parties, even though different governments emphasize different points according to their political outlook.

The social market economy has as one of its major economic concepts the synthesis between economic freedom guaranteed by the state and social security and justice. In contrast with the views of early liberalism, one proceeds from the idea that a free and at the same time socially responsible economic and social order must be deliberately shaped, and the state is expected to make constant and increasingly creative achievements as far as justice is concerned.[9] This legislative function guarantees to the state a decisive influence also on industrial relations.

In the formation of an economic and social order in the Federal Republic, the main emphasis of the state's measures lay at first in the area of social security. Legislative measures in this field included, most importantly, rectifying the outcome of the free economic process where it led to social injustices. The state's social policy was concentrated, therefore, on three areas: security at the workplace, the economic and social security of certain groups of workers, and the qualification of the work force.

Böhle and Altmann differentiate in this connection between preventive and compensatory measures.[10] Workers' protection norms and measures for influencing the qualification structure on the labor market constitute preventive measures. Workers' protection extends to security from health hazards, the determination of working hours, and protection of the work contract through regulations against summary dismissal. In the center of social security measures relating to the qualification of workers is the Work Encouragement Law, whose aim it is to enable workers to adjust to the qualification requirements of the modern production process. Among the legislative measures on social security which have a compensatory character, special attention must be drawn to national insurance (which comprises 41 percent of the social budget), health insurance, accident insurance, and unemployment insurance.[11]

In spite of the considerable extent of social security measures within the framework of a social market economy, economic growth was seen as the decisive foundation for social security. Therefore, it has always been the goal of the economic policy of the Federal Republic to secure continuous growth. Until the early 1960s, which saw high rates of growth, the state limited its role essentially to setting up the framework of conditions within which the market forces operated. Long-term state intervention for the regulation of business and the running of the economy was, however, rejected. Economic development was supposed to be accomplished by reacting to the laws of the market. The state saw its duty above all in excluding as far as possible, through legal regulations, distortions in world competition which could affect the efficiency of the market economy.

The policy of far-reaching economic restraint was rejected in the mid-1960s in favor of more overall control by the State. Decisive in this change was the fact that a long period of growth had come to an end and in 1966/67 turned into recession. In addition with the coming to government of the Social-Liberal coalition the state's economic and social policy took a new direction. This was most clearly expressed in the Law for the Encouragement of Stability and Economic Growth passed in 1967, which enlarged the range of instruments of economic policy available to the state far beyond that of the advice given by a committee of experts up to that time. Certain points are stipulated in this Law:

1) The drawing-up of a report on subsidies every two years;

2) A medium-term finance plan and a budget for investment over a number of years;

3) The setting-up of concerted action;

4) The preparation of orientation data for the development of the economy;

5) An anti-cyclical budget policy and the provision of counter-cyclical reserves;

6) In case of emergency, a change specific to the business cycle in income and property taxation.

The success of the state's economic policy in overcoming the recession of 1966–67 cannot blind one to the fact that its economic and social policy is becoming increasingly more difficult. At the same time, a falling-off in economic growth over a long period is clearly evident. In addition, there are structural crises in particular branches of the economy. However, the conditions for an active social policy by the state are no longer to hand. Not only is an improvement in the social security system being put at risk through the growing number of unemployed, but there are additional social problems which the state is expected to solve. Attempts by the state to stimulate the economy through extensive investment programs and structured measures have been unsuccessful to date. Because of this, the state's economic and social policy—which in times of stability is supported by the partners to wage agreements—has become the subject of argument between various interest groups. The employers fear that state intervention will gradually subvert the principle of economic freedom: the trade unions, on the other hand, see the insufficiently controlled production and investment freedom of the employers as a threat to the social component of the economic and social order. In this situation the state very quickly falls under suspicion of carrying out a one-sided policy. In fact, the criticism goes so far as to call into question the social market economy itself as a principle of order in the economic and social constitution of the Federal Republic. This applies even more so when economic policy is based on growth—for so long the undisputed central aspect of the social market economy and now no longer finding unreserved support in present-day society. In the argument against the social market economy, the following objections appear: there is inadequate satisfaction of collective needs, it prevents a democratization of the economy, it leads to the neglect of qualitative aspects in the world of work and favors the concentration of capital.

In view of the diverse problems with which the state is confronted in following its economic and social policy, it should make a greater attempt to establish institutions for harmonizing the interests of the various social groups. At the same time more far-reaching solutions should be striven for than those represented by concerted action.[12]

Trade Union Structure and Philosophy

Although there are the beginnings of trade union pluralism in the Federal Republic, the German Trade Union Association (DGB) has a dominant position. Among the more than 9 million organized workers—approximately 40 percent of the total workforce—around 80 percent are organized in the DGB or its member trade unions. Among the larger trade union organizations which do not belong to the DGB are the German Civil Servants' Association (DBB) of some 700,000 members and the German White-Collar Trade Union (DAG) which has organized approximately 450,000 white-collar workers. In contrast to the overriding principle of the DGB—one industry, one trade union—the DAG claims the right to represent the specific interests of white-collar workers. The arguments over organization policy between the trade unions are sharp, although their economic and social policy goals coincide to a large extent.[13]

The present structure of the DGB was largely determined by the Allied Military Government immediately after the Second World War, in that they refused to sanction a unified trade union. Therefore, all efforts were concentrated on building up a trade union for each industry. At the present time there are 16 individual trade unions represented in the DGB. To a large extent they bargain autonomously, particularly as far as wage policy is concerned. There are, of course, certain influential trade unions which decide the policy of the DGB. Among these are the Metal Industries Trade Union, the Chemical Industrial Trade Union, and the Public Services, Transport and Traffic Trade Union (ÖTV).

The number of members in the DGB increased from 5.5 million in 1950 to

7.4 million in 1974. However, the share of DGB members in relation to the working population is declining. The number of organized workers has decreased, that of civil servants has remained the same, while that of the white-collar workers has risen. In spite of an increasing degree of organization among these white-collar workers, this still lies well below that of the blue-collar workers. The degree of organization within individual trade unions varies considerably. It extends from 80 percent in the Mining and Energy Industries Trade Union to approximately 10 percent in the Commerce, Banks and Insurance Trade Union.

From the beginning of their existence the trade unions have been confronted with the following two-fold tasks: as a cooperative enterprise and organization of struggle to protect their members from the consequences of their economic and social inequality (protective function), and as a political movement to abolish the social conditions of dependence and underprivilege of the working classes (shaping function).[14]

After the Second World War the shaping of the new form of economy was in the foreground. The trade unions were among the first social groups which had developed ideas for a new form of economy. In the Basic Program of 1946 the DGB adopted the concept of economic democracy from the time of the Weimar Republic.[15] Among other things, it demanded the nationalization of basic industries, central planning, and comprehensive co-determination. However, the trade unions were forced to accept the fact that under the economic and political balance of power, a change in the prevailing economic and social structure was not possible. In its Basic Program of 1963 (which has been the foundation for the work of the trade unions up to the present time), the DGB therefore demanded the idea of providing a complete alternative to the capitalist order. It concentrated instead increasingly on its protective function and limited itself to putting forward demands and outlining goals which were closely connected with the economic and industrial interests of the workers.[16] There are signs, however, that the trade unions are again striving more forcefully to integrate general social policy and wages policy. Present trade union policy is characterized by the following features:

Strong problem orientation. That is, one attempts to see the more complex connections and no longer only single parts of the whole. In setting goals the interdependence between individual social problems—such as questions of wages and salaries, the humanizing of work, rationalization, unemployment, and education—should be more strongly reflected.

Concentration on the humanizing of work. The dominant goal of the trade unions is to make the consequences of rationalization tolerable. This includes, among other things, protection against dismissal and loss of skill.

Integration of means. There is no longer an all-embracing concept on the way to achieve the goals decided on. The trade unions no longer differentiate so sharply between structural reform policy (seen as the area for state measures) and pragmatic wage policy. Co-determination, the Industrial Constitutional Law, wage negotiations, and the exercise of influence on political decisions are regarded as instruments of equal value in the solving of concrete problems.

Widening of the planning process. The goal of the trade unions is to be informed in good time so that they can engage promptly in the solution of problems. This attitude is expressed in the demand, amongst others, for the setting-up of Economic and Structure Councils.

The trade unions are recognized—because of their cooperative orientation—as an equal party in the system of industrial relations. The trade unions emphasize their fundamental political independence. However, there is a close relationship with the Social Democratic Party and also with the present Federal Government. In any case, there appears to be a tendency in the trade unions to give greater stress to an independent position on reform and thus to risk possible conflict with the Social-Liberal Coalition Government. It is possible that this striving for independence is based on the belief that the social policy demands of the trade unions—for example, equal co-determination—cannot be accomplished by means of legislation.

A stronger trade union policy based on the interests of their members is demanded by the rank and file, particularly by younger trade unionists. This trend can be seen in a certain estrangement between the shopfloor and trade union officials, because of the fact that the trade union leadership has repeatedly deferred aggressive representation of their members' interests in favor of the interests of the community. A greater readiness for conflict on the part of the trade unions is not likely, however, to lead to a class-war posture.

Employers' Organizations: Structure and Philosophy

The organization of business enterprises rests on three pillars: the Employers' Associations, which are amalgamated in the Federation of German Employers' Associations (BDA), the Economic Associations, whose top agency is the Federated Association of German Industry (BDI), and the Chambers of Industry and Commerce, whose organizational head is the German Industry and Trade Council. The individual organizations of associated business enterprises fulfill various duties. Employers' Associations are federations of businessmen with predominantly socio-political duties. Economic Associations represent the economic interests of those enterprises amalgamated with them. The Chambers of Industry and Commerce are legally bound to represent the general political interest of all industries and branches in their respective districts. They fulfill a large number of legally enforced duties, particularly in the occupational training sector. In the Cooperative Committee of the German Trade Board (DGW) are represented the socio-political as well as the economic associations of all branches. Here, opinions on relevant themes are worked out together and agreed on.[17] A tendency toward a greater concentration in the organizations of associated business enterprises seems to have appeared when in 1977 the presidencies of the BDI and the BDA were merged. Possibly through this action it was made clear that social and economic questions increasingly overlap.

In the industrial relations system the Employers' Associations are of the greatest importance, since wages and wage agreements are among their major concerns.[18]

The present organizational structure of the Employers' Associations is extremely difficult to describe, as they include many different types. Basically, one can differentiate between industry associations at the branch level and associations at the local level. The chief interest of the Branch Associations lies in the field of wages policy; the associations formed with district interests in mind carry out rather more socio-political duties as well as looking after their members.

Membership in the Employers' Associations is basically voluntary. The proportion of business enterprises joined to the BDA through the various Associations is very high, and the number of members is rising. In the field of industry, banking, and insurance, the proportion is probably over 80 percent, while in other economic sectors it is lower because of the many nonorganized small businesses.

Within the individual Associations the valid principle is that every member, independent of size, has a vote in the BDA at the members' convention. Each member has, formally, the same opportunities for influencing the policy of the Employers' Associations. Notwithstanding this, large business enterprises and concerns appear to exercise a stronger influence on the Associations' policy, possibly because the special knowledge needed is at their disposal.[19]

The Employers' Associations in the Federal Republic no longer regard themselves primarily as an offensive or defensive association as in the early years of their establishment. They regard themselves, first and foremost, as the guarantor of the present-day economic and social order. At the same time, it should not be overlooked that they have adopted a progressive attitude in certain areas—such as the accumulation of capital in the hands of the workers and the structure of work. Economic growth, security of private property, and the ultimate right of property to make decisions are the essential goals of the Employers' Associations. They thus represent a position which finds strong support in the general scale of values of the Federal Republic. This close agreement, together with the fact that the economic situation in the Federal Republic, in contrast with other countries, can be regarded as particularly favorable (a success which is seen frequently as the responsibility, above all, of the employers), creates a strong position for the Employers' Associations in the system of industrial working relationships.

At the present time there certainly appears to be a change of orientation among employers. This must be seen against the background of a change in values in society in the Federal Republic and of a worsening economic situation, where considerations of the quality of life and democracy are increasing in importance. Both developments, in large measure, question the economic and social system of the Federal Republic in its current form. At the same time, the dominant role of business in the economic and social order is no longer accepted uncritically. A possible reaction to these trends is the greater emphasis being laid on an aggressive policy by the Employers' Associations. One sign of this may be seen in the constitutional action brought by the Federation of Employers' Associations against the new Codetermination Law.

The System of Co-determination

One of the peculiarities of the industrial constitution of business enterprises in the Federal Republic is the strong institutional security of codetermination rights for the workers. All the relevant social groups are committed to the support of the participation of workers in decisions in the plant and business enterprise. This specific German development of the industrial constitution expresses the dominant element in industrial relations in the Federal Republic, namely a social partnership based upon the balance of interests of capital and labor. Doubts about co-determination on the part of the workers stemmed from the idea that those exercising power connected with industrial technique, production, and organization should agree to the participation of those affected in the exercise and control of this power. Of course, there are different notions of the form and extent of codetermination for the workers in plants and business enterprises, which will be decided through the interests of the various groups.[20] This opposition is quite clear in the arguments about the law which came into force in 1976, giving parity co-determination to the workers.

In the Federal Republic there is a dualistic form of co-determination. At the business enterprise level, co-determination is secured institutionally through the right of the workers to send representatives of their interests to the Committees of Decision (*Entscheidungsgremien*): at plant level, however, there is a works council with an independent organization for representation of the workers.[21]

Co-determination in the business enterprise organs of supervisory board and board of directors was originally regarded by its supporters as a constituent of a far-reaching concept for the new arrangement of the economy, which should include the following:

The nationalization of key industries
An economic master-plan
The introduction of co-determination in the overall economy
Co-determination in the plant
Co-determination in the business enterprise.[22]

In 1951, co-determination of workers on the supervisory boards and boards of managers of business enterprises in the coal, iron, and steel industries was established. The law was carried through only against the wishes of the former Christian Democratic government after the threat by the trade unions of massive strikes. It stipulated an equal division of seats between the representatives of the shareholders and the workers' representatives on the supervisory board. A so-called neutral member, who is elected at the shareholders' meeting on the proposal of the remaining members of the supervisory board, is supposed to help prevent stalemate situations arising. On the board of managers there is a labor relations director, a member with equal rights, who cannot be appointed against the votes of the majority of the workers' representatives on the supervisory board.[23]

The Iron and Steel Co-determination Law applies to all business enterprises in the field of mining and the iron- and steel-producing industry with more than 1,000 workers. It has been extended in the course of time through different laws which aimed to preserve the integrity of co-determination. This additional legislation was necessitated by the fact that the number of companies affected was reduced by 50 percent between 1951 and 1969.[24]

Just two decades after the introduction of equal co-determination in the iron and steel industry, the government ordered the setting-up of a commission to examine the consequence of co-determination in industry. It was established that doubts originally expressed about the Iron and Steel Co-determination Law, as far as lowering industrial efficiency was concerned, had proved quite unfounded.

Outside the area of iron and steel, co-determination is regulated through the Industrial Constitution Law of 1952. It is laid down in this law that in all business enterprises which do not belong to the field of mining or to the iron- and steel-producing industry, the supervisory board must consist of one-third of workers' representatives.

In 1973, the question of co-determination for workers on the basis of equal numbers and equal rights for workers and shareholders was taken up again in a declaration of the Socialist-Liberal coalition government. After several years of party conflict (which also divided the coalition partners) and after wide-ranging expert hearings, a new law on the Co-determination of Workers came into force on July 1, 1976.

The jurisdiction of the 1976 Co-determination Law covers joint stock companies and is concerned with more than 2,000 workers (approximately 600 to 650 enterprises). These are required to appoint their supervisory boards on the basis of the model set out below (Figure 1.1).

Basic dissimilarities from the Iron and Steel Co-determination Law are to be found in:

1) the solution to stalemate situations on the Supervisory Board. With equality of votes, the chairman (who is always an employer's representative) receives two votes;

Figure 1.1.   Structure of the 1976 Co-determination Law

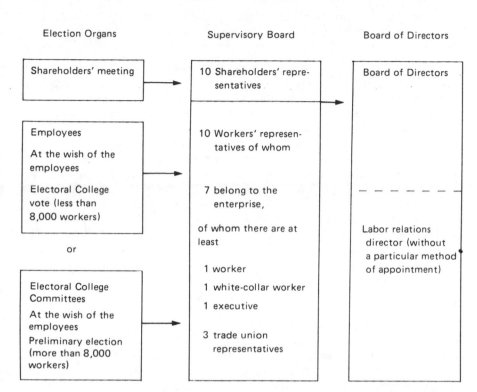

Election Organs	Supervisory Board	Board of Directors
Shareholders' meeting	10 Shareholders' representatives	Board of Directors
Employees At the wish of the employees Electoral College vote (less than 8,000 workers) or	10 Workers' representatives of whom 7 belong to the enterprise, of whom there are at least 1 worker 1 white-collar worker 1 executive 3 trade union representatives	Labor relations director (without a particular method of appointment)
Electoral College Committees At the wish of the employees Preliminary election (more than 8,000 workers)		

2) the lack of a special method of appointing the labor relations director;

3) the special status of executives; and

4) the regulation of the voting procedure.

Fundamental doubts about the law were raised by the trade unions as well as by the employers. The trade unions declared that the principle of equal co-determination was not realized, and the compromise which had been reached by the coalition government failed to satisfy their demand for parity of representation.

The employers opposed the law on constitutional and functional grounds as well as those of political order. They are of the opinion that the law

1) endangers collective wage bargaining autonomy;

2) together with the Industrial Constitutions Law causes an over-parity position;

3) results in a statutorily inadmissible restriction on the right of property owners to dispose of their property as they might choose;

4) endangers the capacity of industry to make decisions in the best interest of its shareholders;

5) concentrates power in the hands of the unions in such a way as to destroy the existence of a free and pluralistic society.[25]

Because of such fears a number of business enterprises and the Employers' Associations brought their case against the new law as a violation of constitutional rights in the middle of 1977. The trade unions have reacted sharply to this move by ceasing to cooperate in "concerted action"—an institution established by the Federal Ministry for Economics for the exchange of information between the main social groups.

In addition to the system of co-determination at the level of the supervisory board, co-determination of the workers is carried out at plant level by the works council, which is also independent of both employers and unions. In the Federal Republic, works councils were given statutory rights of co-determination in the Industrial Constitutions Law of 1952. In 1955, a similar legislative measure was enacted—the Federal Personnel Representation Law—which covered the civil service. Forerunner of the works council legislation was the Works Council Law of 1920, passed during the Weimar Republic. The important principle of economic peace, which was incorporated in the 1952 legislation, was firmly established by the Act of 1920, which laid down the obligation of the works council to cooperate confidentially with the employer.[26] This principle has never been the subject of political dispute and is also recognized by the trade unions. Their criticism vis-à-vis the Industrial Constitutions Law of 1952 is directed at the not sufficiently firmly established trade union organization in the plant and in the works council, as well as the absence of the provision of co-determination in works councils in various problem areas. A principle embodied in the Industrial Constitutions Law of great importance is their independence of the trade unions. Although they have no legal power to call a strike, the works council is free to enter into commitments with employers who interpret agreements made by the unions at other levels. The cooperation between trade unions and works council is largely secured by the high degree to which their members belong to unions—in 1973 it was 80 percent.

On the employers' side, there was no resistance to the Industrial Constitutions Law, as the binding of the works council to the well-being of the plant and its formal separation from the trade unions corresponded with their aims.

The Industrial Constitutions Law of 1972 differentiated co-determination rights and participation rights. There is only a qualified co-determination for the workers' representatives in social matters. In this case the new law has certainly widened the rights of the works council at some points. Of importance, above all, is the works council's right of participation in matters which can affect the technically organized design of the job, work flow, and the working environment; the right to co-determine short-time working and overtime; and the possibility of establishing a co-determined social plan for the enterprise. Decisions which concern the structure of an enterprise and questions of production in its development and planning are subject alone to the arrangements of the business enterprise. The importance of the law for the workers can be seen, above all, in the fact that it contains a list of socially protective measures and provisions against abuse by employers of their authority.[27]

Table 1.5 sets out in condensed form the different co-determination regulations valid in the Federal Republic. The widening of co-determination will also in the future be one of the most controversial problems in industrial relations for the Federal Republic. A consequence of the law passed in 1976 could be that the trade unions will accord greater weight to an autonomous collective wage bargaining policy than to legislative measures, through disappointment with the compromise made by the Socialist-Liberal coalition government.[28]

Table 1.5. Federal Republic. Forms of Codetermination in Operation Coverage

Form of Codetermination	Number Workers (in millions)	Sectors
Codetermination (according to the most recent law)	4.5	Large corporations
Iron and Steel Codetermination	0.6	Iron and steel industry
Third party	0.6	Small corporations
Codetermination at plant level (Law of Staff Representation)	3.6	Civil service
Codetermination at plant level (Industrial Constitutional Law)	9.3	Remaining industry
No codetermination	3.4	Small firms (fewer than 5 employees)

Source: *Handelsblatt.*

The question of total industrial co-determination is also increasing in importance. Ideas on this, which partly tie in with the concept of "concerted action," have been developed by the Social Democratic Party as well as by the trade unions.[29] The aim is the establishment of Economic and Social Councils representative of the various social groups, which should be effective as information, advisory, and co-ordination committees directed for total economic development.

There seem to be signs of a widening of co-determination at the level of the workplace.[30] The beginnings of this development can be seen in various business enterprises in the Federal Republic. The Federal government's Program for the Humanizing of Work is probably giving further impetus in this connection. However, the concept of greater autonomy at the workplace is in dispute and is repudiated by certain trade unions, in particular by the Metal Industries Trade Union.

Among the innovations introduced into the field of industrial relations can be included the numerous attempts to humanize work in industry and in administration. This development can be seen as being partly due to a change in values. After a long period in which growth was regarded as the supreme goal of economic policy and work efficiency and as a valid maxim for the structure of work organization, the demand at the end of the 1960s for a better quality of life brought a change of direction, which has not failed to have an effect on politics, science, and a section of the public. In the declarations of the Federal government, there has been quite as much emphasis on the quality of life as on the quality of work, a perspective which was set out in a concrete form in an Action Program.[31] The following aims are contained in this Action Program:

Development of a job technology more fitting to man's needs;
Use of suggestions and models for the organization of work and structure of workplaces;
Propagation and use of scientific findings and industrial experience that would be of benefit to workers.

The largest number of projects begun under this program fall within the sphere of ergonomic and technological themes. The field of work and industrial organization contains, however, a number of projects which are particularly complex and which, therefore, have a central position in the overall program.

The problem under research is seen from two standpoints: "one, the consequences of technical change in the world of work are to be analyzed in detail, and, two, to prepare the scientific foundations for the removal and prevention of negative effects in future."[32] It must be emphasized in this connection that the Federal government is, to a greater extent than ever before, including the social sciences in developing its program, and social scientists are being drawn in increasing numbers into research dealing with the testing of new forms of work organization.[33]

As can be seen from their participation in research projects promoted with money from the Federal government, the employers have adopted a positive stance towards redesigning jobs to fit them better to the workers' needs.[34] For example, Work Report No. 36 produced by the Federal Alliance of German Employers' Associations contains a series of proposals for the creation of more self-contained workplaces, the limiting of monotonous work, and better understanding for colleagues' work, as well as for job organization which would allow a greater development of individual talents at the workplace.

While the employers have engaged more and more in the discussion about new job structures, after an initial period of reservation, the trade unions have adopted a more skeptical attitude, at least when this is restricted to direct changes in work organization. The reason for this is that, for the trade unions, treating the problem of humanizing work in isolation leaves the present structures of interest and power untouched.[35]

With regard to the charge of having adopted a party political approach, it must be conceded that the Federal government also sees its efforts to improve the quality of working life as part of an overriding strategy. The legal results of the program are an amendment to the Industrial Constitutions Law, the Work Security Law, the New Workplace regulations, the regulations covering dangerous places of work, the law governing protection of youth at work, and the Co-determination Law.

The above list shows the improvement in legal norms which is characteristic of the German system of industrial relations. Among specific statutory regulations the new Industrial Constitutions Law deserves particular attention.[36] The rights of co-determination and participation of the workers in force up to that date were extended to include the design of the workplace, flow of work, and work environment. One important innovation is that the established trend towards job bargaining is strengthened by legal methods.

The second aspect which should be raised at this point concerns the intention expressed by the law that when techno-organizational changes take place "reliable work study findings with regard to redesigning work to fit the workers' needs" must be taken into consideration (clause 90, Industrial Constitutions Law). The works council also has the right to intervene in cases of changes in work organization "which obviously contradict reliable work study findings on redesigning work to fit the workers' needs" (clause 91). These definitions have led to a lively discussion. On one side is the problem of specific scientific competence. The difficulty here lies in the fact that individual sciences consider certain aspects only of a larger problem. The practical application of the results gained thus remains imperfect, if it is not possible to take into account at the same time an integrated research assessment[37] of the extremely complex circumstances of the problem. On the other hand, it must also be stated that work-study perceptions only partially fulfill the criterion of general validity. Thus, work norms dependent on experience and expenditure vary from those which are regarded as being technically possible and which conform to the value concepts of society. The work-study man can therefore no longer put forward the claim (as representatives of scientific management have postulated) that there is *one best way* of finding out, against which there is no protest possible because an alternative is lacking. This point of view has shown itself to be untenable, not only because of its one-sided nature, but also because it overlooks the fact that ideas of work organization are dependent on various interest groups and must, accordingly, be subject to negotiations. The inclusion of experts, therefore, not only is necessary, as is suggested at the conclusion of the Survey for Economic and Social Change,[38] in order to strengthen the relationship between theory and practice, but also because they fulfill a structural need. What differentiates the various efforts at humanizing work in the Federal Republic from parallel endeavors in other countries, apart from the initiatives which the state and the legislators have taken in this field, is in the novel role (still requiring clarification) of work studies in the context of industrial relations at shopfloor level.

Workers' Property Formation

The possibility of giving the workers a share in productive property is one of the central points in the conflict of interests between capital and labor. The need for the accumulation of property in the hands of the workers is based, on the one hand, on the unequal distribution of income and the impossibility of achieving a redistribution by means of a conventional wage policy, and, on the other hand, on the argument that property which has originated through social production must also be made accessible to the parties concerned in this production. A third argument is that the diminution in profits caused by retrograde economic developments has reduced margins for wage and salary increases and, therefore, workers are entitled to seek an alternative source of higher income in a property policy. This aspect is of greater relevance in that the present economic position is characterized not only by stagnation, but also by inflation. Advocates of property plans by the employers do not fail to point out that too high an increase in wages will immediately affect demand, leading to price increases, which will again cause the growth in income to come to nothing. This view is based on the Leber Plan (named after the former Federal Minister of Defense and past chairman of the Industrial Union of Bricklayers). The question will be left open as to how far this perception can be maintained in the present economic situation, as too high a rate of consumption can give rise to as much economic concern as an equally high propensity to save.

Although there has been no lack of examples in the past of workers sharing in productive property, industrial property-sharing "did not succeed in emerging from the sphere of the 'social romantic' and of being accepted as a future concept of business enterprise policy until the 1970's."[39] This statement is supported by an empirical investigation of the Institute of the German Economy (which is closely connected with the employers) and the Society for Inter-Industrial Cooperation, which has led to the following conclusions:

1. In the Federal Republic of Germany 770 industrial enterprises provide for employee equity participation, that is, approximately 1 percent of all enterprises concerned. According to the evidence 134 joint stock companies

have distributed staff bonds to their workers—that is, 6 percent of all joint stock companies. The ten largest industrial enterprises in the Federal Republic are, without exception, profit-sharing enterprises.

2. Nearly 800,000 workers—6.2 percent of all workers in profit-sharing enterprises—are included in these schemes for employee equity participation. Of this number almost 700,000 are owners of staff bonds.

3. Profit-sharing workers hold a capital of DM 2.3 billion, of which DM 2.1 billion is risk capital.

With regard to these consequences, it must be emphasized that (1) they are essentially the successful outcome of the profit-sharing policy of business enterprises in the 1970's; (2) that the introduction of profit-sharing schemes was carried out on a completely voluntary basis; and (3) business enterprises in favor of profit-sharing have even today to overcome fiscal and legal barriers.

This positive balance should not lead one to ignore the fact that there are basic differences between management and labor on the question of the accumulation of property for the workers. These are connected with the disparate attitudes on the function of property accumulation, as well as the level and form of its realization. Opinions differ with regard to the goal—whether the accumulation of property should be regarded primarily as an instrument of economic redistribution, or as a means of social policy. Different forms of property accumulation have been proposed from time to time in pursuit of this goal, which were variously criticized by management, labor, and the government, the evaluation of the goal they were intended to meet has fluctuated. The underlying lack of certainty in the whole affair is evident when consideration is given to the fact that the motion carried by the Federal government at the beginning of 1974 for the "Outlines of a Property-Sharing Law" has been officially withdrawn on the grounds that a balanced and rational solution raises difficulties nationally that are insoluble at the moment because of legal and technical considerations.

The discussion of a suitable form of property accumulation concentrates (apart from the basis of evaluation), in particular on whether participation should be at an industrial or higher level. As far as the basis of evaluation is concerned, the different viewpoints can be divided between those in favor of a collective bargaining agreement and those who prefer the legally anchored linking of wages to profit-sharing. The first position takes the view that the wage contains the component affecting property formation independent of the economic circumstances of the business enterprise, while under the conditions of profit-sharing for capital-formation the worker receives a share only when a profit is made. As far as the accumulation of capital is concerned, in contrast to the traditional wages system a part of current income is not made available to the worker for private consumption in the medium term; instead it is invested to achieve the objective of capital accumulation.

The current argument also relates to the method of bringing about capital accumulation. While the employers have unequivocally taken up a position in favor of business enterprise-based capital accumulation, the trade unions would prefer supra-industrial capital accumulation which they believe would be an alternative means of collectivizing capital to that of state ownership. The formation of a central fund would be in conformity with the aims of the Social Democratic Party of Germany for the participation of workers in the growth of productive capital. Business enterprises would pay a fixed percentage of their profits into this fund. All workers up to a fixed income limit would receive certificates free of charge from the fund which would be subject to a seven-year sale embargo, together with accrued income. The employees would administer the fund, which would also take the public interest into account.

However, opinion is divided within the trade unions on the suitability of this means of capital accumulation in the hands of the workers. The Metal Industries Trade Union has rejected the idea because the dependence of the worker is not altered by this arrangement and its socio-political effects are limited. It advocates instead, on basic trade union and political considerations, a collective wage-bargaining policy which will secure for the workers a higher proportion of the national product. Before considering capital accumulation, it believes priority should be given to the building of collective security and co-determination as the means of limiting economic power.

In general, the trade unions and also the Expert Commission of the Social Democratic Party of Germany object to company-based capital accumulation, in that a capital-sharing scheme in the company in which the worker is employed not only burdens him with a risk to income, but also a capital risk. It is further pointed out that because of the different positions of various industries and enterprises, the chances for capital accumulation are unequally distributed.

Those trade unions which, with reservations, have spoken out for a capital accumulation policy prefer the solution of an investment wage secured by collective bargaining. An investment wage is an addition to the ordinary wage which is paid by the employer free of tax and must be placed in an investment fund or savings account of an approved type and only withdrawn after a specified time period. Under the 1961 Act to Promote Workers' Participation in Capital Formation, as amended in 1965, a union may secure by negotiation with an employer an agreement that he should pay up to 624 Marks a year—which may be supplemented by a workers' contribution of a similar amount, which is then invested under favorable tax provisions. A collective bargaining wage-agreement on these lines was concluded for the first time in 1965 by the Bricklayers' Industrial Trade Union. The advantages of this settlement were, above all, to be seen in the fact that all business enterprises coming under this trade union were similarly affected. Marginal industries and labor-intensive industries are stimulated to greater rationalization efforts as a consequence.

Retirement Pensions and Occupational Saving

A legislative measure has followed in the field of industrial old-age pensions. In order to help their workers increase their income on retirement and also as recognition of long service to a firm, many business enterprises have agreed to pay industrial pensions in addition to the legal old-age pensions. Certain disadvantages have arisen in this connection in that where a worker changed his employment his rights in an industrial pension were not transferable. One disadvantage, too, of the recognition of the seniority principle was that the mobility of the individual worker was circumscribed. A further criticism related to the fact that the accumulated rights to a pension were not always adequately safeguarded against firms going bankrupt. Furthermore, the question of the age of retirement must be settled once again, as workers now have the possibility (after the introduction of a flexible retiring age) of retiring before their 65th birthday for men, and before their 62nd birthday for women. It is basically a question of regulating afresh these points which were covered in the law of 1973 on the improvement of industrial old-age pensions.

Questions of occupational training and in-service training were for a long time among the less disputed areas in the Federal Republic's system of industrial relations. In the last few years, however, primary occupational training at least has become the subject of heated argument. A decisive factor in this change of attitude was that in 1974 the downward swing of the economy coincided with a big decline in the number of apprenticeships available, thereby producing considerable unemployment among young people. Between 1969 and 1973 the number of reported apprenticeships declined approximately 50 percent, from 650,000 to 370,000. The unemployment rate among young people in 1974 was 3.3 percent, appreciably higher than the average unemployment rate for that year of 2.4 percent.

It was not until 1969 that the Occupational Training Law was passed, covering occupational primary training in the whole of the Federal Republic. This law was supposed to influence the quality and continuity of apprentice training. Among other things, requirements were formulated on the teaching capabilities of instructors, later supplemented by a regulation laying down the qualifications of instructors (*Ausbildereignungverordnung*), as well as prohibiting the carrying out of duties other than those of an instructor. Beyond that, new training regulations were demanded covering all jobs, to be enforced at the beginning of an apprenticeship, to give a better orientation within the wider field of employment and thus increase job flexibility and mobility. To meet the growing theoretical demands with a comparable occupational training, a basic educational year of occupational training (*Berufsgrundschuljahr*) was introduced by some Federal *Länder* in 1972, to be counted as part of the period of apprenticeship.

In 1973, the government coalition put forward the main features of an

Amendment to the Occupational Training Law (*Berufsbildungsgesetz*). The most controversial points in this bill are the dual training system and the financial regulation of training. The trade unions are striving, first of all, for a totally new adjustment of the primary training set-up in order to get rid of dual training. According to the trade unions, increasing demands for theoretical knowledge and greater specialization have made systematic and practical training in the plant almost impossible. Therefore, workshop training and occupational instruction must be abandoned in favor of scholastic training. The integration of occupational training and general education is also demanded by the unions, and as a consequence of this, the setting-up of integrated comprehensive schools. The trade unions argue further that a public occupational training system will not only achieve more functional training, but ensure that sufficient apprenticeships are made available.

Trade organizations are in favor of a continuance of the dual system. Their chief argument is that a school can never provide basic occupational instruction, and, therefore, that no such deterioration in occupational training should be tolerated. It was proposed instead to improve the present training system in order to achieve, in particular, more harmony between school curricula and the occupational training regulations. In addition, to reduce unemployment among young people, the trade organizations in 1975 offered 40,000 extra apprentice vacancies, so long as the dual training system remained untouched.

Another controversial point in connection with primary training is its financing. After long discussions—including also those between the governing coalition parties—the Training Encouragement Law came into force in 1976. It provides that if the supply of apprenticeships is no more than 12.5 percent above demand, then the business enterprise must pay the equivalent of 0.25 percent of the wage and salary bill when this rises above DM 400,000 annually.

In 1977, the Ministry of Education presented a report in which it came to the conclusion that this occupational training levy had to be paid as the supply of, and demand for, apprenticeships did not coincide with the method prescribed under the law. The levy was not, however, collected at this time, because the basic principles for calculating costs between industry and government agencies (*Staatliche Stellen*) could not be agreed upon.

New legal regulations have been created also in the area of in-service training and retraining, because of the high rate of unemployment. At the beginning of 1977, the scope of the Occupational Training Encouragement Law was extended. The main conditions are that the applicant be unemployed (or threatened with unemployment) and that his participation in these measures is necessary for him to obtain an adequate job.

In the area of in-service training the introduction of day-release training in the various *Länder* represents the first step towards an institutional provision of life-long education; this should abolish the division between the phase of education and occupational training on the one hand and

practical application on the other. Day-release training should, furthermore, motivate those groups of workers to participate who, up until now,
have been excluded from in-service training measures.

The *Länder* laws for regulating day-release training differ quite
considerably from one another. The Joint Education Plan envisages the
step-by-step introduction of day-release training at Federal level by 1985. Its
aims are, of course, still controversial. The employers demand educational
goals which are occupation-related; the trade unions, however, consider that
quite apart from occupational training, political education is urgently
required.

For various reasons questions of occupational training and in-service
training will increase in importance in industrial relations. Technical
change and modifications to the economic structure require a greater job
flexibility from labor. On the one hand, primary training must adapt to this
requirement and, on the other hand, the possibilities for occupational in-
service training must be improved. From the point of view of equality of
opportunity the question of how to remove educational deprivation will be
increasingly discussed. On the question of the organization of primary
training, the trade unions will be concentrating on their demand for
codetermination in the occupational training service. Finally, the financial
regulation of occupational training and in-service training will be a major
point of controversy, the solution of which depends, not least, on an
expansion of occupational and in-service training.

Summary

After a long period of economic growth and full employment, the Federal
Republic is confronted with increasing economic difficulties. These are of a
structural nature and are therefore more serious and of more far-reaching
importance than economic crises in the past. As far as the participants in the
industrial relations system are concerned, the state no longer confines its
activities to laying down the legal conditions of economic and social life, but
exercises more direct influence by means of structural measures and in the
field of collective bargaining. Consequently, the principle of a free market
economy, which served as the ideological basis for the socio-political system
up to the present time, is losing its former credibility to the same degree as it
is failing to provide the means of solving existing and emerging social
problems. Whereas management continues to use the concept of free
enterprise as a basic principle, the trade unions regard the problem of social
security as the most important issue. Apart from collective bargaining this
conflict in values is demonstrated by several issues, such as codetermination,
work organization, property policy, and education. There are several signs
that in the period ahead the industrial relations system of the Federal
Republic will increasingly develop elements of conflict instead of
integration, by which it was characterized for so long in the post-war period
of reconstruction.

Notes

1. *Die Zeit*, October 21, 1977, p. 35.
2. W. Gerstenberger, "Zuviel Rationalisierungsinvestitionen?" IFO–Schnelldienst, May 1977, pg. 7.
3. *Rationalisierungskuratorium der Deutschen Wirtschaft, Mikroprozessoren und Mikrocomputer, Zwei Studien*, Frankfurt am Main, 1977, 11.
4. F. Baur, "Technologische Entwicklungen und ihre Auswirkungen auf die Situation der Arbeiter," in *Industriegewerkschaft Metall* (ed.), *Strukturelle Arbeitslosigkeit durch technischen Wandel*, Frankfurt am Main, 1977.
5. G. Friedrichs, "Das RKW und die Gewerkschaften," in *Rationalisierungskuratorium der Deutschen Wirtschaft* (ed.), *Produktivität und Rationalisierung*, Frankfurt am Main, 1971, p. 33.
6. L. Unterseber, *Kollektivies Arbeitsrecht und Tarifsystem*, Dissertation, Frankfurt am Main, 1975.
7. H. Plessner, *Die verspätete Nation. Über die politische Vergügbarkeit bürgerlichen Geistes*, Stuttgart, 1959.
8. W. Eucken, *Grundsätze der Wirtschaftspolitik*, 4th edition. Tübingen, 1968; A. Müller-Armak, "Die Wirtschaftsordnung, sozial gesehen," in *Ordo*, Vol. 1, 1948.
9. H. Lampert, *Die Wirtschafts—und Sozialordnung der Bundesrepublik Deutschland* 5th edition. Munich, Vienna, 1976.
10. F. Böhle and N. Altmann, *Industrielle Arbeit und soziale Sicherheit: Eine Studie über Risiken im Arbeitsprozess und auf dem Arbeitsmarkt*. Frankfurt am Main, 1972.
11. H. Braun, *Soziale Sicherung—System und Funktion*, 2nd edition. Stuttgart, 1973.
12. *Bericht der Kommission für wirtschaftlichen und sozialen Wandel* (ed.), *Gutachten der Kommission*, Göttingen, 1977.
13. D. Schuster, *Die Deutsche Gewerkschaftsbewegung, DGB, DGB Bundesvorstand*. Düsseldorf, 1969.
14. G. Leminsky and B. Otto, *Politik und Programmatik des Deutschen Gewerkschaftsbundes*. Cologne, 1974, p. 66.
15. F. Naphtali, *Wirtschaftsdemokratie, Ihr Wesen, Weg und Ziel*. Frankfurt am Main, 1966.
16. G. Leminsky, "Die Zukunft der Gewerkschaften in der Wohlstandsgesellschaft" in G. Friedrichs (ed.), *Zukunft der Gewerkschaften*. Frankfurt am Main and Cologne, 1972, pp. 11-44.
17. G. Zepter, *Da haben wir die Verbände*. Cologne, 1975.
18. W. Büchi, "Arbeitgeberverbände" in E. Gaugler (ed.), *Handwörterbuch des Personalwesens*. Stuttgart, 1975.
19. Zepter, op cit.
20. G. Apel, *Mitbestimmung—Grundlagen, Wege, Ziele*. Munich, 1969.
21. G. V. Schenk, "Wirtschaftsdemokratie," in *Gewerkschaftliche Monatshefte*, No. 26. 1975.
22. B. Muszynski, *Wirtschaftliche Mitbestimmung zwischen Konflikt und Harmoniekonzeptionen, theoretische Voraussetzungen geschichtliche Grundlagen und Hauptprobleme der Mitbestimmungsdiskussion der Bundesrepublik Deutschland*, Meisenheim am Glan, 1975.
23. R. Kirchenmeister, "Mitbestimmung im Vorstand," in *Das Mitbestimmungsgespräch* No. 15, 1973; S. Viesel, *Der Arbeitsdirektor—Aufgaben und Pflichten*, Cologne, 1973.
24. Muszynski, op. cit.
25. *Gutachten der Kommission für wirtschaftlichen und sozialen Wandel*. Göttingen, 1977.
26. H. G. Schweppenhäuser, *Der Kampf um die Mitbestimmung. Ein Schlagwort und seine sozialen Konsequenzen*. Frieburg im Breisgau, 1967.
27. G. Schaub, *Der Betriebsrat* (Munich, 1973).
28. H. Günter and G. Leminsky, "Labour in the Twentieth Century. The Federal Republic of Germany," Fourth World Congress of the International Industrial Relations Association in Genf, 1976.
29. Kommission für wirtschaftlichen und sozialen Wandel, DGB, SPD Paper.

30. F. Fürstenberg, "Mitbestimmung am Arbeitsplatz," in *Gewerkschaftliche Monatshefte*, No. 24. 1973; F. Vilmar, *Mitbestimmung am Arbeitsplatz, Basis demokratischer betriebspolitik.* Neuwied und Berlin, 1971.

31. *Der Bundesminister für Arbeit und Sozialordnung, der Bundesminister für Forschung und Technologie, Forschung zur Harmonisierung des Arbeitslebens, Aktionsprogramm,* Bonn, 1974.

32. *Forschungsberich IV der Bundesregierung.* Bonn, 1972, p. 55.

33. W. D. Winterhager (ed.) *Humanisierung der Arbeitswelt,* Berlin, 1975.

34. *Bundesvereinigung der Deutschen Arbeitgeberverbände, Erklärung zu gesellsohaftspolitischen Grundsatzfragen Entwurf.* Cologne, 1974.

35. *Gutachten der Kommission für wirtschaftlichen und sozialen Wandel.* (Göttingen, 1977, p. 445; W. Vitt and H. O. Vetter "Humanisierung der Arbeit durch Mitbestimmung" in *Humanisierung Aufgabe.* Frankfurt am Main, 1974.

36. B. Natzel, "Zur Mitbestimmung bei der menschengerechten Gestaltung der Arbeit" in *Recht der Arbeit.* 1974, p. 280; H. Pornschlegel and R. Birkwald, "Ebenen und Kategorien gesicherter arbeitswissenschaftlichen Erkenntnisse im Sinne, 90 und 91" in *Afa Informationen 1973* (6), p. 79.

37. F. Fürstenberg, "Konzeption einer interdisziplinär organisierten Arbeitswissenschaft." *Schriften der Kommission für wirtschaftlichen und sozialen Wandel,* Vol. 64, Göttingen, 1975.

38. *Gutachten der Kommission für wirtschaftlichen und sozialen Wandel.* Göttingen, 1977, p. 423.

39. *Wirtschaftswoche,* No. 32, July 7, 1977.

2

France

by J. D. REYNAUD

What have been the principal tendencies in the evolution of industrial relations in France in the last ten years? Even if there is agreement over the facts, putting them into perspective requires examination. What are the future tendencies? Here, intuition, with all its vulnerability to the preferences and self-interests of the author, plays the leading role. Finally, presenting these tendencies in a very restricted space prohibits the accumulation of data and reinforces the impression of arbitrary interpretation. The following exposé should therefore be read as an essay, with the corresponding uncertainties. It goes without saying that other perspectives are possible.

The Sources of Change

THE GENERAL FRAMEWORK

The principal causes which have brought about the change in the substance, procedures, and results of collective bargaining are shared by the majority of the countries involved. Everywhere, economic growth has changed the distribution of the active population between sectors and has increased the proportion of wage-earners in this active population and the proportion of highly-skilled and skilled workers among the wage-earners. It has raised standards of living often in a spectacular way, thus causing not only the disappearance or diminution of some problems but also, and above all, the awakening and development of new requirements. Everywhere, it has remodelled economic structures and rendered efficiency and market constraints more perceptible. Everywhere, it has encouraged financial concentration.

Moreover, in all the countries concerned, development of education (and most particularly the explosion of university education) has created a strong ferment of social unrest. By putting on the market young people who are more educated and more demanding and who are confronted with the devaluation of diplomas, difficult problems of employment have been created (and most particularly of the level of employment) and of careers. The focus of education at all its stages has tended to be academic, and many employers believe that it has given those entering industry relatively little understanding of basic economic and industrial problems.

Finally, in all countries, the crisis of 1973, rather than revealing new problems, accentuated and intensified problems which had been with us for years: foremost, inflation, but, just as important although less visible, also the changes imposed on the machinery of production by what is termed, by contrast, the new international economic order.

What, in this general framework, is more particular to France? The thrust of the new demands were expressed in France in a brutal and explosive fashion. The impact of these new demands was particularly great on the highly-skilled categories, in both the private and public sectors. The ties between industrial relations and political life are close in France, and the great stability of the political majority for the previous twenty years increased the importance of possible political and social changes.

A MILITANT UPSURGE

Seen from afar, the French situation may appear to have been one of a major crisis in 1968, and, contrary to many European countries, a relatively calm period thereafter, at least if one judges by the number of strike days per year. However, this overall view conceals the importance of the appearance of the new "active minorities," i.e., new militants, which throughout the period had a significant influence on public opinion. The most important factor therefore is not the combination of events which led to the great explosion of 1968. It is the constant pressure for social change which prevailed during this entire period.

This pressure has three characteristics:

1. In the first place, it comes from the grass roots. Although the trade union organizations have rarely been put into difficulty, the initiation of demands like those relating to working conditions or to employment certainly does not come from the national institutions, but from within firms and workshops. This is where, very often, the genesis of conflict has been centered. Many important strikes have been started and often even conducted at the workplace (the national organizations stepping in mainly

to end them). The trade unions have recognized this openly, by trying to give the voice of the wage-earners more influence, or, stated another way, to extend internal democracy.

2. New categories of workers which, up till now, had not been in the middle of conflicts and negotiations have been mobilized; women and immigrants, unskilled or semi-skilled workers, bank and insurance company employees, and a variety of technicians (including air traffic control assistants and computer programmers). The new pressures have brought on the scene actors who were previously only marginal, and made it possible for them to voice specific claims and demands, and this is particularly evident for the less-privileged categories.

3. The pressure for social change has not been limited to professional problems and issues, nor restricted to those within the framework of the trade unions. On the contrary, it has found expression in a great number of movements and associations, sometimes short-lived, sometimes disclosing, in spite of organizational difficulties, deep sources of discontent. Housing and transportation problems, the problems of women workers, health problems, and many others have given rise to action groups, movements, and demonstrations, often local, sometimes coordinated. Behind the tumult and sometimes the scandal, it is necessary to recognize that the result has given a new depth to the discussion of social issues and produced a diverse variety of social conflicts.

THE ADMINISTRATIVE FRAMEWORK AND ITS PERPLEXITIES

The fact that it was necessary in France to invent the notion of *cadres* (superior employees), which does not exist in other countries, demonstrates no doubt that, for a long time, those in this stratum of foremen, engineers, and administrative officers had been aware of their own peculiar problems, which recent developments have considerably increased.

In the first place, this was because there has been created, as elsewhere, an important category of specialists having no leadership responsibilities and no contact with the client or the market, especially in the cases of researchers or laboratory assistants. As in some other countries, this category of intellectuals in the economic field was more sympathetic to the ideas of the new left than were traditional business executives. In France, a good portion of the militants and the extreme left-wing voters was to be found in this category, which as a group possibly voiced its opinions more freely than elsewhere.

Secondly, growth and centralization reinforced the administrative framework and multiplied bureaucratic and management posts, and thus probably accentuated the break between the head office and the branches, and between the management and the men in the field (sales and production). More elaborate methods of management and supervision popularized the idea of delegating authority, of reaching pre-agreed objectives, and of the autonomy of local managers. Paradoxically, this has often reinforced the isolation of those in the provinces and the executants of decisions taken centrally. The principal cause of the *malaise des cadres*, to which the Patronat (employers' federation) has given more attention, probably lies here.

Because of the militant upsurge which we have just mentioned, and the lack of conviction and aims in the administrative framework, all the elements were assembled to raise the question of the legitimacy of authority (and, of course, the problems of structure on which it depends) in a deep, if not acute, fashion. However, in spite of some conflicts this challenge has not led to a paralysis or freeze within companies, but there is a general feeling that the problem has been placed on the agenda and that much imagination will be needed to find a solution.

THE POLITICAL CONTEXT

As in Italy, two of the principal French confederations of labor (and the two principal ones in private industry) are profoundly attached to a program to achieve a fundamental transformation of society. This ambition is not simply a device to glorify or magnify the daily task of defending the interests of the workers; it inspires the union militants and enables them to recruit; it draws them together in a common endeavor; it determines very concrete choices of protest policy. It leads finally to ties with the political parties: for the CGT a close relation with the Communist Party, with whose framework it intersects; more difficult for the CFDT and Socialist Party whose relationships are still unsettled and changing. *Force Ouvrière*, represented particularly in the public sector but a significant influence on negotiations in many areas of employment, insists on its political independence, despite its common roots with the Socialist Party. This neutrality as far as the political parties are concerned no doubt reinforces its diverse membership, but it does not stimulate the recruitment of militant members.

Moreover, and we shall return to this later, the trade unions, to a greater extent than the political parties, have probably given rein to the expression of needs and new tendencies. The CFDT has probably been the most welcoming to the new radical tendencies and therefore has been the most involved in recent upsurges.

On the other hand, and this constitutes the main difference with Italy, a firm majority has governed France since 1958. Although the trade unions consider it to be right-wing and although it is often accused of expressing the points of view of the Patronat, the majority has not been incapable of either economic or social initiatives. In fact, despite an opposition to intervention on principle, the government has played an important role, and in certain aspects, a major role, in industrial relations, and the continuation of negotiations with the employers and the unions and evolution of the legal settlements contrasts with the explosions and sensational turns of the political scene. The objectives and the coherence of the government's social policy may merit criticism, but what is certain is that the government is not a missing or an immobile actor.

Moreover, the union of the left-wing parties around a government program, enabling them to enjoy the hope of attaining power, has reinforced their representative role. At the beginning of the 1960s, in the confusion of the parties who have passed from power, the trade unions were, with some secondary movements, the main spokesmen for the opposition. This is no longer the case today, and the decisions of the political parties are starting to weigh very heavily on industrial relations.

The stability of the majority in power increased the importance of the 1978 elections (for the first time, the opinion polls regularly showed the union of the left to be in the lead). The two parties benefitted from magnifying the stakes, one by planting fear and the other hope. However, even if one is of the opinion that a change in government would have had less dramatic consequences than the election battle would have had us believe, it is true that such a change would have posed very important problems for the trade unions, particularly in view of the economic situation. Even if a left-wing government had tried to reduce costs by stimulating production, the field of action would have remained extremely restricted. It is difficult to see how, by wanting an important revision of salary scales, the trade unions could have avoided stating the boundaries of their independence faced with those they had wished to see come to power.

Employers and Their Policy

Employers are one of the groups which has altered the most in French society, if only because they are directly connected, actively and passively, with the economic changes which have affected it. Growth and the development of new management and forecasting methods and the increase in welfare responsibilities (and undoubtedly in social costs) have all contributed to altering the characteristics of the "boss," who is often a salaried manager. Relations between firms and the state have also altered, as a result of the changing policies of employers' organizations which have become less concerned with protectionism and more with expansion and export. The aim of the *Conseil National du Patronat Français*, when it equipped itself with new statutes in 1969 and elected a new president soon afterwards, was certainly to take the initiative in the field of social policy.

TAKING THE INITIATIVE

The social policy of the CNPF was not born in 1968. The succession of agreements that at the end of the 1950s and the beginning of the 1960s laid the basis for the establishment of pension schemes, and their coordination between different sectors of industry, and the unemployment benefit scheme from the first agreement of 1958 to that of 1969 and the amendments of 1974 that grant up to 90 percent of gross salary in the case of dismissal for economic reasons, show a continuity of intention and a coherent philosophy. Supplementing the social security schemes with their inefficient bureaucracy (and, above all, the weight of the administration) by schemes administered through equal representation, they escape the fluctuations of the political situation as well as the bureaucarcy of the public services. Even if their motivation was very different, the trade unions could not refuse to be a party to these agreements, nor refuse a round-table approach, even if their divisions weaken their bargaining position opposite a single partner representing all the employers.

One of the first major agreements stemming from this compact was an agreement on further training (July 1970), which has since been amended and improved several times. At the same time as creating a right to further training which the wage-earner may claim, it established consultation and study procedures (equality committees) and, since the agreement of 1976, procedures for examination as part of the company's training program. The agreement of 1970 was an important step forward in the training of adults at work. Although the unions are not satisfied with their role in the administration of the training scheme and emphasize that management basically makes the decisions, it would not be correct to describe the program as unilateral.

A broadly similar policy has been followed in the field of employment. In 1969 an agreement was made which was innovative in giving companies objectives as far as maintenance of employment was concerned and in establishing procedures through which these objectives would be adhered to. The 1973 economic crisis led to the development of these procedures in the agreement of 1974, by ensuring that the works council examine redundancy plans and by supporting the joint examination of disputes in the regional and national employment commissions. Moreover, numerous disputes over employment have led the most enterprising part of the Patronat to take initiatives to save companies from bankruptcy, where the folding-up of a company would present major local and regional employment problems, with, it must be said, a varying degree of success—failure at Lip and at Romans, where the employers' federation of shoemakers had become involved, and relative success at Rive de Giers.

An effort has been made to follow the same policy in connection with negotiations on work conditions. The CNPF was the first, just ahead of the CGT, to take a public stand on these problems, but the serious deterioration of the economic situation between the beginning of these negotiations (1973) and the end (1975), and maybe also the difficulty of dealing, jointly, with problems which consisted entirely of economic and technical constraints within the sector or within the company, have made the agreement something of a failure.

PROCEDURES AND ORGANIZATION

As we have already shown, this policy of initiatives by the CNPF has manifested itself in new bargaining procedures.

The employer-union agreement is not really entirely new because this system was employed in 1947 to create a management pension fund. At least it has acquired increasing importance, and the 1971 law provided it with all the characteristics of a collective wage agreement. This plan was indispensable for social security agreements and was taken up again in 1971 to provide women workers with full pay during maternity leave. It could, in these cases, permit, or perhaps even invoke, sectoral agreements to adapt or improve it, as in the case of complementary pension funds. But in the case of employment, staff training, work conditions, or even the system of monthly payments, its role was less of fixing an appropriate framework than of setting the principles, application of which would be achieved by the sectoral agreements, supplemented where necessary by agreements at the company level. This mechanism has functioned quite efficiently in some cases, and less so in others. For example, the diffusion of agreements up to company level, officially regarded as desirable by the CNPF President, has only partially been achieved.

Should it be concluded that the company agreement (officially recognized as a collective wage agreement by the law of 1971) has not developed to a very great extent? Although company agreements are important, especially for the large firms, it does not appear that they have become very widespread. In fact, even in the large companies, a major proportion of the bargaining system takes place on an informal basis within the company or on the occasion at a works council meeting, or, even in the instance where negotiations result in a signed agreement, deals with questions as they are raised, rather than trying to establish a fixed pattern which traditionally constitutes collective bargaining in France. In small and medium-sized companies, the absence of formal agreements is the rule; this does not exclude discussions and claims, sometimes supported by a stoppage and sometimes resulting in an explicit compromise.

Although industry-wide agreements remain of predominant importance in France, the thrust of negotiation has increasingly come from the top of the CNPF and the union agreement and from the base of the company, mainly in the case of the large companies. This is perhaps partly because the large companies, who have discreetly managed to maintain their autonomy as far as unions are concerned, seem to be more influential at the level of the CNPF than at the level of the industry.

It should be emphasized that this development of the bargaining system has resulted, in the large companies, in important steps forward in those departments specializing in social problems. Under various headings (human relations, social relations, and, more traditionally, management of staff), these have gained in resources and in authority. A considerable effort seems to have been made to strengthen the social responsibilities of company chiefs and, more generally, of executives, and to equip them to deal with the internal conflicts which frequently arise.

This change reflects a change in the structure of the organization. The reform of 1969 gave the CNPF more opportunity for initiative as compared with the industry federations. It also facilitated direct contact with the larger companies, and the CNPF used these opportunities to hold regular meetings on burning issues, from work conditions to further training, exports, and growth.

In effect, the CNPF has taken on the responsibility of defending the company *vis-à-vis* public opinion, and this has obliged it to intervene much more actively in the main public debates.

THE LIMITS OF MOBILIZATION

Despite the success of these developments there has been only a limited extension to medium and small-sized companies.

First of all, it would appear that the joint arrangements at the regional level (with very different names and structures) have scarcely functioned. If the CNPF has taken the initiative on a national scale, the industry associations maintain control of the regional situation. Common efforts have been only slightly successful, if the example of the Rhone-Alps region is anything to go by. Of little importance for the large companies, whose headquarters is nearly always in Paris, and who have no difficulty in communicating with their provincial establishments, this failure is very serious for the small and medium-sized companies. For these, the economic crisis, principally felt from the end of 1974, aggravated the position. The general confederation of small and medium-sized companies hardened its view and stood by the rights and the position of the "real employers" *vis-à-vis* the "technocrats" of the CNPF and of the large companies. The agreement on staff training was not easily accepted by all. The agreement on work conditions created much bad feeling. A series of incidents, notably on problems of security, increased the grievances of the small employers.

Although bargaining itself is not in question, it is essentially industry bargaining which seems legitimate to the employers in small and medium-sized companies. But, on the other hand, they are not prepared to accept that the union should be the only mouthpiece in the company. The law of 1968 obliges them to recognize the existence of union delegates and to give them the practical means to fulfill this role—free time, putting up of notices, and opportunity to meet off the premises and not during working hours—but the employers do not wish to make a privileged spokesman of the union. The law helps employers by defining the role of staff representatives and works councils. It is clear that, in the last ten years, they have been more and more accepted by the employers, since their number has increased quite considerably.

The revolutionary ambitions of the CGT and the CFDT, expressed in the position that the two organizations have occupied in political debates and notably in the elections, have strengthened the reserve and sometimes the hostility of the employers.

Of course, it is difficult to generalize about a group as diverse and disorganized as that of the small and medium-sized companies, and it is doubtless improper to try and describe them as a whole. But the popularity of the campaign against "union monopoly" (the right reserved to local union organizations to nominate candidates for the first round of union elections) was so strong that the CNPF had to pretend that it was their initiative. The present state of union power has made possible the generalization of bargaining at company level. The CNPF has not allowed the unions to be the recognized spokesmen in the companies, but at least they can have their representative elected to the works councils. Full recognition of the unions is more than a purely legal problem.

THE RESERVED DOMAIN

The scope for bargaining has expanded because today this covers employment, staff training, and work conditions. On the other hand, as far as purely economic decisions are concerned, the unions' right to take part has scarcely been extended; rather to the contrary. Sometimes, this is because they refuse to take any responsibility of an economic nature. But this is far from being the only reason.

The most striking example of this limitation of unions' bargaining activity is that of wages. Bargaining in France fixes base or minimum rates. Even if it is necessary to leave a flexible margin for the companies to meet economic fluctuations, or to enable the company to take on more staff, this margin should not be excessive, otherwise minimum rate bargaining would lose all its relevance. In those industries where there is bargaining over base-rate wages which have a direct repercussion on the wages being paid, company bargaining is very much a minority practice. Expansion and inflation have, of course, both helped to emphasize the problem of wage bargaining. On many occasions, employers' organizations, like the one in the metal industry, have recognized the problem and attempted to correct it. Success has so far been very mediocre. The Barre Plan, which limited salary increases to the equivalent rise in the cost of living in 1977, aggravated the problem by practically halting all bargaining for that year. It did not create it. The level of wages in practice remains essentially the employers' prerogative, moderated by waves of bad feeling from the employees in the company.

Decisions on industrial policy have become increasingly void of union influence. At the beginning of the 1960s, the Plan offered the unions a means of participating in the work of the commissions who prepared and set it up. Although no decisions were taken at these meetings, they did permit the unions to exert quite an influence over the economic orientation of the company. The CFDT had even sketched out, on this subject and based on this experiment, what democratic planning would entail (the CGT, as well as FO, were much more reserved). Today, the importance of the commissions of the Plan has diminished—and even more so in the eyes of the unions—as the example of major changes in the steel industry demonstrates. The reorganization of the steel industry in 1946-47 was designed by a commission presided over by a CGT member. In 1966 a major policy question was considered between the government and the industry, but linked to the discussion of a wages agreement finally signed by all the unions. In 1977 an evaluation of the problems of the industry was undertaken by the government alone, but an agreement was signed later by the employers and by the "moderate" unions, but not the CGT nor the CFDT. This is not a unique example. As for sharing in the economic decisions of the company, notably in the form of participation, with the right to speak and vote on the board, this is a subject on which the employers (with the exception of an association of Christian employers) and the unions (except for executives and the small Catholic confederation) are remarkably united in expressing their disgust. The very moderate propositions of the Sudreau Committee, for optional organization of co-determination in the very large companies, aroused little interest. The unions would like to have more information on economic matters at the works council, but they do not wish to participate in management, for different reasons according to different unions.

Employers do not have to refuse what is not asked of them. And it is evident that the emphasis placed by the large unions on wage claims, due first of all to the militant explosion of 1968 but reinforced by the economic crisis and the recession, has scarcely led them (except in relation to certain employment problems, to which we will have to return later) to demand economic responsibility. But this situation does explain perhaps why the CGT and the CFDT tend only to touch on economic problems in the context of their pay demands. Maybe this is a wise division of the work. It is certain, in any case, that since the crisis union members and wage-earners endure it with increasing impatience.

The Unions and Their Objectives

ORGANIZATION

The French unions have been less affected than others by the change in the distribution of the economically active population. They have never been exclusively made up of industrial manual workers. A long while ago, municipal employees and civil servants were organized in unions, and civil servants have enjoyed a very important position since the 1930s. Technicians and executives are also unionized. Staff employees are one of the bases of Christian trade unionism. An important proportion of the *cadres* (without doubt, the majority of those allied to a union) belong to the independent Confédération générale des Cadres; and for the most part, teachers also belong to an autonomous federation.

Perhaps the organization of these new unions has been made easier by the fact that union structures are fundamentally based upon industry. Although it could be wrong to underestimate the strength of the tradition of worker solidarity, particularly evident in the cases of the printers or the dockers but nevertheless present elsewhere, control of entry into an occupation, of work practices, and of techniques is rare and very limited in France. The door is not, therefore, closed to professional employees who wish to have their own independent organizations.

Limited financial resources, a small number of permanent staff, little internal discipline, and a low level of regular dues-paying members means that gradually, but not consciously, the basis of union organization is moving away from the member to the sympathizer who votes indifferently and irregularly. This relatively loose attachment of the member to the union has weakened the organizations of labor in France if we compare them to their British or German counterparts. But nevertheless, and this is the compensation for the weakness, because their power rests on the mobilization of a base which is never finally conquered, French unions have to be sensitive to new claims and demands and are capable of rapidly and adroitly interpreting them. The spontaneous thrust towards militancy since 1968 took the unions by surprise and threw them off balance; but this thrust has also fed and reinforced their role in France.

EXPRESSION OF NEW NEEDS

The strength of French unionism is to be found in its militants. Their enthusiasm does not replace necessary administration, but the unions have developed in the last ten to fifteen years measures which assure a more stable income and more effective basis for industrial action, like the strike fund of the CFDT and its policy of insisting that all sections of organizations contribute financially. But, on the whole, what assures the survival of a union in competition with other unions of a different ideology and in disputes with employers is the presence and action of those who inspire the confidence of the membership and whose leadership is accepted.

Not only is sensitivity to what is happening, understanding of new needs, and capacity to formulate the claims in which these are expressed necessary to preserve the basis of the organization. It is necessary also for the organization itself to have support, especially from among the unpaid activists who, working full-time in the shop, provide the militant base which is indispensable for political and industrial action. Unions in France have not lacked this grass-roots leadership.

It is, therefore, not surprising that the French unions have, on the whole, been able, if somewhat hesitantly, to respond to new currents and new pressures. When the subject of improving working conditions was introduced by small left-wing groups, who were extreme in their demands, it took several months for the unions to examine the problem, to formulate propositions, and incorporate the new theme into their programs and preoccupations. They responded in a similar way in developing their policy over employment. The CFDT, during the 1960s, was probably the most militant supporter of "maximum employment"; it sought to make forced mobility acceptable to workers by insisting on compensation for redundancy, payment of redeployment expenses, and the facilitating of further training. The CFDT was also perhaps the first to understand that, in difficult regional conditions, maintenance of employment in the region was more important than financial compensation. The Lip troubles showed this in no uncertain terms as early as 1973. The social costs of forced mobility can be very high, but those who refuse to see their company closed down are not necessarily right in economic terms. However, the closure of a company with a large loss of jobs and no alternative employment does reveal a deficiency in protective measures. This reaction, which is deep-rooted and reinforced rather than diminished by the industrial expansion of the last 25 years, cannot be ignored by the unions. It is one of the tasks of the unions to suggest measures that have a reasonable chance of success and to press them on governments.

The two examples of unemployment and mobility which we have taken affect working life. But, in fact, the unions, essentially to remain in contact with their militants, have often linked up with movements from outside working life. This has sometimes not been without serious problems, as the CFDT found with committees of soldiers, which were an embryo union. The best example is probably that of the problems of women. After much effort to make this issue just one among others, so as not to make a special case of women's *vis-à-vis* the problems of wage-earners in general, the CFDT and then the CGT have had to take full account of them. But should women who are not employed wage-earners be admitted into the trade union movement? Nobody has yet decided, or established a formula. Between the sections of the union who deal with female problems, and the "women's groups" who seek to impose a feminist view on all problems, relations are sometimes strained. One can well understand, given this example, why it is in the interest of the union movement to maintain their annoying and awkward contact. It is often persons who belong to both sides who debate the issues, and the union movement benefits from this exchange, even if it sometimes results in serious difficulties.

The differences are very noticeable, in this connection, between the organizations (it is clear that the CGT is more suspicious than the CFDT as far as anything that resembles the "new left" is concerned). More important than these differences is the common preoccupation with belonging to this newly-woven association which makes up local life. The interaction of peasants', regional, and feminist movements with union organizations, traditionally urban, political and masculine, may give the impression of a heterogeneous coalition to all those opposing it—and it may be that this is precisely what it is. However, if movements are not defined in the abstract by their public aims and doctrines, but in terms of practical problems, these can be effectively dealt with by unions and managers.

ACCESS TO RESPONSIBILITY BY MOBILIZATION

In the case of the CFDT, the change since the beginning of the 1960s has been spectacular. Before it was a confederation which believed in the opportunity to influence decisions within the *commissions du plan*, to reconcile social demands and economic reasons; today, it is preoccupied with bringing out what those at the base think and want, to permit them to establish their plans and demands, to fight their own battles. In this way, it may be asked, have they not abandoned all social responsibility? By giving priority to the expression of interests as opposed to coordination and hierarchical organization (articulation as opposed to aggregation) are they not confining themselves to blind opposition, since the role of the union is also to enlighten and to lead along practicable paths?

The conflictual process has often been followed, particularly at the CFDT, but also, with slightly different arguments, by the CGT. It requires examination on at least three levels.

First of all, it would be absurd to reduce union action simply to open conflict and militant strike action. Because they disturb and cause problems, conflicts and breakdowns attract our attention. But daily life in companies also involves adjustments and problems to be resolved. Bargaining certainly practically broke down in 1977, due to being unable to affect wage levels. But, even then, it did not entirely collapse. There is virtually no significant area in which agreements of substantial importance have not been reached in the last three years. An organization like FO, for this reason, plays a role which is often decisive by ensuring, sometimes under very disagreeable conditions, the continuity of negotiations and bargaining institutions. The CGT and the CFDT sometimes accuse FO of going too far and of playing the employer's game. But if, sometimes, opposition is real and profound, it can happen that the sharing of tasks between the federations allocates to one the safeguarding of what has already been acquired, and to the other the demanding of more for the future. And, even as far as the CGT and the CFDT are concerned, it is true that when expression and coordination are in conflict, the unions usually favor the former. But they are not always in conflict and, more generally, the union organizations are required not only to recognize and support disputes locally initiated, but also to lead them to a conclusion.

Secondly, it would be quite unrealistic to be against responsible unions who know how to decide on their priorities and in favor of irresponsible ones who limit themselves to following their rank and file. If there could be—and in fact there are—discussions and disagreements on the conduct of the contractual agreement, it remains true that a responsible union is the one which makes agreements which it can honor. In a system where, for reasons which are often given, organization is weak and discipline nonexistent, the only agreements which can be made are those on which there is a sufficiently strong mobilization of wage-earners. To give priority to mobilization can mean, at least in certain cases, to gain access to responsibility.

Disputes over employment, which we have already mentioned, attest to this fact. It is less interesting to bring out the means used (occupation of the premises, unsupervized production, and sales) than the opportunity which they have given, in practically each case, to analyze the economic situation and its constraints and to take responsibility for the plans to sort out the company in difficulty. Supported by the mobilization of those concerned, the CGT in the case of the Rateau conflict and the CFDT in the case of Lip discussed and negotiated investment plans, if not in detail at least the major characteristics.

Thirdly, the priority given to expression (and to the means to publicize it) is perhaps more justified in a political and economic system where decisions are very centralized. It was the scandal which Lip provoked that caused a very reasonable law to be passed ensuring compensation of wage-earners in the event of bankruptcy. It was the strikes of skilled workers in 1971 which led all professional organizations to take a position on improving work conditions and the government to prepare a bill. It was the experience of disputes over employment which permitted the agreement of 1974 and the law of January 1975 to be passed on procedures to be adopted in the event of redundancy.

Perhaps we should add that many union members are suspicious (this is a very old tradition) of distant objectives and multiple projects. What is demanded now, and under present circumstances, the aims which can be attained in the immediate future, are obvious. The place and role which all these would have in a large-scale plan are much less evident. Those who wish to change society want to do so starting with the part they know and which they master little by little: pragmatism and skepticism join forces when faced with distant objectives.

The unions are perhaps better prepared than they might seem to tackle a situation where their powers are increased, where the public authorities would more often be their allies, and where their responsibilities would be greater. They are very well aware of the distance separating an idea, however good, from its adoption by those concerned. The experience of numerous conflicts in the recent past has made them realize how much effort and time is needed before those concerned take responsibility and know how to lead a militant action. This knowledge of the problems and cost of winning support and the possibility of carrying the policy out is not of course all there is to democracy, but it is nevertheless an indispensable element.

THE UNION IN THE ENTERPRISE

By and large, employers offer limited scope to the trade unions in the company, but it should be added that they are perhaps aided in this respect by the union members themselves who seem uncertain of the responsibilities they wish to take on.

Besides the trade union delegates, which each union elects according to its own system, the company employees have other representatives whom they elect by direct vote; spokesmen for the staff (for grievances and claims) and representatives on the works council. Works councils have gradually been accepted, having been treated very coldly by the employers at the outset. The law, but also collective bargaining, has multiplied their responsibilities and their tasks. Not only are they informed of and consulted on economic problems, but they examine the staff training program; any possibility of a mass redundancy is considered with them directly or through the setting up of a special commission; they examine working conditions and possibilities for improvement. Most frequently, it is they who sign the so-called sharing agreements (in effect, profit-sharing). A social account will increasingly be submitted to them as the Act of 1977 becomes effective. A detailed list of the rights of the council would be very long. Although one can justifiably criticize the lack of consistency of a body which has been the result of its pattern of development, it is necessary to recognize its importance. The number of works councils has more than doubled in the last ten years—many companies who managed very well without this institution having no doubt changed their minds due to union pressure.

In the face of the development of works councils, union attitudes differ. They sense the danger which an institution, over which they have no direct control, could represent for them and which has, increasingly clearly and despite its legal standing, developed a negotiating role. *Force Ouvrière* without doubt stresses the danger of this development most clearly and has demonstrated the importance, in its view, of union organization within the company. Although all the federations emphasize the significance of the role of the union in the enterprise, most of the time they settle quite happily for a situation which is not entirely without its advantages. First of all because, in large firms, the representatives on the works councils are those whom the unions put forward (it is only really any different in firms with less than 100 employees), and in this way the union can keep a certain grip on the situation. It is also because discussion at council level allows all points of view to be submitted to the employer and the elections ascertain the weight that each should carry—and it is this which many employers appreciate. Finally, and most importantly, there are many delicate problems, for which trade unions do not wish to assume responsibility but which they do not wish to leave entirely to management, which may be dealt with through the works councils. Unions do not care much for profit-sharing agreements, but it was difficult to refuse the advantages, however limited, which they would bring. It was, in the end, the works council which signed them in spite of complaints by FO about this breach in the union monopoly of the bargaining system. Redundancy plans have to be discussed step-by-step, but when these cannot be dropped, the unions prefer not to take any responsibility for the dismissals which occur. The works council, which has only a consultant capacity, may challenge redundancy decisions and do their utmost to limit the damage. In the same way, it is not altogether unfortunate that responsibility for the staff training programs lies with the works council, but the unions would like an agreement whereby, in case of dispute, the plans would have to be negotiated with them.

In a strictly legal sense, the council is a consultative body and the union maintains a monopoly of bargaining rights except for agreements on profit-sharing, but for all practical purposes the council has become the arena for preliminary discussion, or what might be called pre-negotiation. There is no institutional operation to ensure that, in a disagreement between management and employee representatives on the works councils, the problem becomes a matter for negotiation—a procedure which the unions would like to see implemented. In the more important cases, and in the larger firms, the union's opportunity to initiate a dispute entirely fulfills this desire. Both the proceedings and the length of the consultations where, for example, employment is concerned result in a strengthening of this opportunity for the union. Open dispute is the channel through which, in the event of failure, relations with management pass from the informal disagreement and pre-negotiation to true bargaining.

This process is both costly and inconvenient, but it does have the advantage of making clear the issues and the extent to which the union can mobilize support. In those cases where installations are few and far between and the management uncooperative, a major problem may arise since the council may then have the last word and the question may be asked of whether it is replacing the union.

It is therefore not surprising that the attitude of the unions and the manner in which their discussions are held vary considerably with the size of the company in question. In large firms, the variety of employee representative bodies complicates matters, but is not usually threatening. In small firms, apart from the fact that the impartiality of management in works council elections is sometimes questionable, the unions are often effectively split. This uncertainty over the allocation of responsibility between the various representative bodies also creates difficulties when new problems arise.

Work conditions can serve as an example. In the sense in which this term has been used in the debates since 1971, it concerns the organization of work and the distribution and nature of tasks, as well as the material conditions under which an employee works. This last point is the traditional subject of claims by the unions and they feel quite assured about it, but what is to be done *vis-à-vis* the organization of work? Leave it the employer? It is obviously management's responsibility, even if his mistakes and weaknesses come in for criticism. That was the first reaction of the CGT, but it quickly took stock of the problems of this attitude. If the employers consult the white-collar workers, should the unions remain in the background as far as these consultations are concerned? Leave the details to the employer and preoccupy themselves only with the most important aspects, wages and employment? This of course would mean losing a lot of ground. The CFDT, on the other hand, solved these problems by distinguishing between the role of the workers who, organized into groups on the basis of similarity of their tasks, were to take responsibility for their own work conditions and the role of the unions, its local leaders, and members of the union's information and coordination staff who were not directly involved. In practice, these work divisions carry the risk of reducing themselves to mere work teams, thereby eliminating the role of the union in the enterprise. Today, the different union federations have come closer in their respective outlooks. The FO places more importance on the index of the quality of life at work, but the CGT joined it in July 1977 by signing a company agreement on this subject. Unfortunately, the most important problem has not been resolved: can all responsibility be left to the employer for the organization of work, despite the fact that the subject is of direct personal interest to the workers? On the other hand, can the unions take on these responsibilities without jeopardizing their bargaining position?

In another guise, the same dilemma arises when employment within a company is seriously at risk. Emergency situations, the declaration of bankruptcy, and the difficult rescue operation permit the problem to be straddled, but what is to be done when management puts forward a carefully calculated proposal? To what extent can a union get involved without accepting responsibility? On the other hand, can it wash its hands of the whole affair?

The problem put this way is, of course, what is known in other countries as the problem of participation. It is clear that the French experience is not in the direction of co-management, of joint decision-making on a board of directors or a works council, but of negotiation and therefore of conflicting participatory schemes. This is closer to the American and British experiences than the German one. But what shape can the *participation conflictuelle* take in these new areas where either the bargaining in the traditional sense of the word is too inefficient and awkward a method, as in determining working conditions, or when the responsibilities an agreement would involve are virtually unacceptable to the two parties, as in the case of lay-offs? Under the legal fiction of frequent consultations, there are perhaps new structures, or, at least, a new framework, coming into existence in France.

UNIONS IN POLITICS

There is little doubt that industrial relations play a part in the political system. In various ways, they mold industrial laws by explicit or implicit representation to the authorities (and not without their intervention). In a stable, or at least sufficiently unchanging, situation the place allotted to industrial relations in political life does not pose many problems, and one can appreciate the statement that relations in a place of work have nothing to do with politics, but at least one of the actors aims to transform society. The problem arises once more—how can laws and national decisions, social representatives and political parties and those in authority be compatible? In France it is impossible to avoid the dilemma inherent in this situation.

It should be noted that the answer, for the unions, is not clear and they are not at all unanimous on this point. FO probably has the most stable and best-defined position because it is, above all, attached to the principle of autonomy of negotiation, and in this respect its commitment to the aims of social transformation is limited. Therefore, to keep one's distance as far as political problems are concerned is a tenable attitude, although it is, in fact, accompanied by the exertion of intense pressures on, and lobbying of, the authorities. The reply in principle of the CGT is evident: it considers itself to be a mass organization with some links with the *avant garde* of the working classes, which is the Communist party. (It is necessary to recall that this was Lenin's plan?) Today, however, the CGT is increasing its independence, and taking its role of mass organization very seriously. The CFDT has dreamed for a long time of creating its own labor party, but has grown closer, although its outlook is not identical, to the new Socialist party, having previously flirted with a small extreme left-wing party, the *Partie Socialiste Unifié*. The CFDT is not prepared, however, to sacrifice its independence which it fiercely asserts; the coming into power of the Left, which CFDT hopes for and supports, would not change its attitude.

The fundamental question is not a theoretical one and is not put merely for academic reasons. The economic crisis, and especially the combination of inflation and unemployment, makes this a very real problem. Even if the diagnoses of the left-wing economists had been accurate and their remedies efficient, even if the new economic policy would have been entirely successful, there would still be a necessity to impose strict limits on wage increases, especially if differentials were to be noticeably altered and the rate of unemployment reduced. In short, quite simply, a program that will be coherent and effective requires the unions and those in authority to resolve issues on which they are often fundamentally sharply divided.

The problem is aggravated by two factors:

1. The unions overall have been more sensitive and more open than the political parties to new leanings and needs. They have retained the impression that they are more far-sighted and less attached to traditional doctrines. Their open-mindedness is their strength. And they have often taken account of the conservatism, or at least the caution, of politicians. Perhaps they would resist all the more the imposition of the left-wing parties if they were ever to come to power.

2. Much uncertainty remains as to the aims of the unions. Even if, in the spirit of mutual reconciliation, the unions today avoid verbal battles on

autogestion (worker self-management) and bureaucracy, it is clear that not only two doctrines, but two schools of thought, two entirely different currents exist reluctantly side-by-side: one current is based on Communist attitudes, in which social change would be achieved by the defeat of the capitalist state and the establishment in its place of a state-controlled socialist economy; the other is the liberal current for which change would principally be in the taking over of responsibility by the organizations and groups in the community.

Failure of the Left in the elections of 1978 of course saved the unions from a crisis that might have arisen, but it has left them without any clear-cut solution to the problems which they face. It is unlikely, however, that they will attempt to become a coherent political opposition to the new government. The election result will probably reinforce the tendency towards political pragmatism without leading to any change in fundamental ideological connections.

The Authorities and Their Intervention

It is only by enormous simplification that one can describe the action of the authorities in industrial relations as coherent. Despite all the efforts of coordination and consistency by governments and administrations, there exists no established harmony between the state legislator, represented, for example, by the Minister for Labor and the Labor Inspector, the state responsible for economic policies and financial equilibrium, and the state as employer, or at least protector of public companies. The economic crisis since 1973 has exacerbated the differences of viewpoints that exist within the organization of the activities of the state.

THE BROADENING OF THE AUTONOMY OF SOCIAL SPOKESMEN

France has a reputation for settling by law many problems which are dealt with elsewhere by collective bargaining. The facts now show that for twenty years this has not been so. It has already been pointed out that it is through bargaining that redundancy payments and pensions have been both generalized and improved. The major problems of the last ten years have been dealt with as much by bargaining as by law. On the whole, not only has the scope for bargaining grown but the autonomy of the social negotiators has increased.

This is true in both the legal and in the bargaining sense. The law of 1971 which introduced limited but significant modications on collective bargaining was, in fact, drawn up through consultation in an *ad hoc* group with such efficiency that it was afterwards unanimously accepted by Parliament. In this instance, the social partners largely established, by a compromise which did not entirely satisfy them all, the basis for their meetings.

It occurs frequently that the law generalizes, by making available to all, a practice developed by voluntary agreement, but it also happens that it often rids the agreement of any interest. The 1971 law on further training of staff has generalized, and in some cases improved, the previously jointly-adopted policy but has left all the ways of applying it to be reached by negotiation and agreement. In this case, so great is respect for the parties' autonomy that some employers fear that this unusually liberal attitude conceals a trap. The January 1975 law relating to mass dismissals follows the same principles. It stipulates the procedure to be followed for mass redundancy and the rights of the works council in this respect, essentially drawing on the agreement made in the autumn of 1974. By so doing, the center of gravity of the process is altered. Although the Labor Inspector retains the right to refuse his authority for planned redundancies, he is not, as in the preceding cases, the only recourse. This is now fundamentally to be found in the examination by the works council and possible reference to the joint commissions concerned with employment.

So, in some cases, the agreement requests and obtains a modification of the law or decree. In this way, the negotiations on monthly wage payment, a subject proposed by the President of the Republic, have required that two laws be altered, one on the weekly payment of wages and one on the system of maternity leave. Going much further, the agreement of 1970 on further training sketches out a complete reform of the education system, and it is probable that, in the near future, this could be followed up.

This growing autonomy does not represent a separation. In the most important negotiations, not only is the exchange of information constant between the private negotiators and the authorities, but the former will request confirmation or promises from the latter; for example, at the time of the discussions on complementary redundancy pay, the undertaking by the government to improve and generalize the public assistance system was one condition of success.

Should we conclude that the authorities have simply become more discreet? The change goes much deeper. It concerns the very nature of their intervention.

A NEW STYLE OF INTERVENTION

That the state is not solely a partner in industrial relations on an equal footing with the others is too obvious to require any evidence. The law stipulates the procedures and the rights of the actors; the government defines and executes an economic policy; the authorities, at their discretion, intervene where the public interest could be harmed by individual agreements, or, more simply, where their efficiency has decreased to too great an extent. Can the state *also* be a partner? Is it possible to distinguish between its various functions and to maintain, in some cases, the role of authority? This has been illustrated, since 1968, by the policy of the state as an employer, which in France is known as the *politique contractuelle*.

In the legal disguise of protecting the large national enterprises, and directly for the civil servants, the government, the ministries involved (Secretary of State for Public Affairs or Ministry for Industry), the Ministry of Finance, even the Prime Minister or the President in difficult cases, maintained a general control over wages and work conditions in the entire public sector. This was not without growing difficulties and frustrations. The unions would not tolerate the fact that the negotiators with whom they dealt were never in a position to make a decision, and that those who were remained inaccessible. Thus those who were required to adhere to the undertakings were not those who made them. After much hesitation, the most concrete outcome of which was to make the problems clearer and more apparent, under the *politique contractuelle* responsibility was handed back to the management of national companies and to the Office for Public Affairs for negotiating and signing. The first agreements attempted to incorporate into their text national economic constraints which pressed on the main state monopolies. In this way, the first agreement of Electricité de France in 1969 connected salaries to the growth in GNP and to the balance sheet of the company. Under pressure from the unions, and in particular from the CGT, the rules have been simplified and returned to a percentage-based increase, almost completely indexed to the cost of living. This policy has not attained all its aims: it has not succeeded in developing the "contractual undertaking"; it has not created rules of the game which are unanimously respected; and it has scarcely served as a model for the private sector. It has renewed social relations in the national enterprises, not only by the agreements themselves, but by stimulating an already important mechanism for the application and definition of these agreements. Finally, this policy is not limited to fixing wage levels, but has systematically served to extend their scope; it has dealt with problems of modernization, of the length of the working day and working conditions. It has indeed developed a very broad area for negotiation.

A study of the figures shows that the renewal of negotiations has not been obtained by excessive concessions on the part of management. The economic responsibility which was left to them under this policy of devolution seems to have been taken very seriously.

The *contrats de progrès* (this term was repudiated by the CGT and then by the CFDT) were supposed to be "program contracts," that is, agreements between government and company management to define their obligations and aims, leaving themselves a considerable amount of freedom for carrying them out. For this reason, social change relied on economic change, on the autonomy of the companies, and in the realm of negotiation on the autonomy of their management.

Although the same method cannot of course be applied to civil servants, in their case also bases for negotiation have developed along similar lines and with similar aims, notably the increase of the lowest wages. The opinion of the different unions varies greatly: FO and the *Fédération de l'Éducation Nationale* support a policy, of which they are the principal partners, against the criticisms of the CGT and the CFDT, and the differences became more acute with the economic crisis. However, one cannot question the change, not only of the attitude, but also of the role of the authorities.

More generally, the government chose to play a role in industrial relations, of encouraging more than deciding, and through negotiation more than arbitration. The government did not avoid indicating its aims. The agreement on employment in 1969 was the result of negotiations which were primarily intended to reply to suggestions in a letter from the Prime Minister. The monthly wage system was an initiative of the President of the Republic taken shortly after his election (1970). An office has been created in the Department of the Secretary of State to coordinate action on the condition of manual workers; the agreement is rather broad in its aims, if not on the means to attain them. Finally, the entire *politique contractuelle* in the public sector served as an example to the private sector and it has, in fact, opened the way, for instance in the scarcely-concealed indexation of salaries to the cost of living.

This encouragement has left an important area to be covered by negotiation and assumes an implicit consensus of the parties. The social partners have not been told on what they should agree. They have been left free to occupy the area they were offered, and they have left their mark.

In an area such as that of working conditions, this effort to encourage and to support is particularly evident. The 1973 law created few new obligations. It provided a place for discussion within companies, a committee of works council to deal exclusively with work conditions. A public agency has been created to study the problems, to gather and disseminate information, and to support experiments and attempts at improvement. A special fund will cover part of the expenses incurred by the most worthwhile projects. Along similar lines, a policy research and training of specialists is being adopted by the General Delegation to Scientific and Technical Research. Decisions and the carrying out of them remain in the hands of the social partners. Interventions by the authorities favor dialogue, providing financial and intellectual support and undertaking to publicize the results.

We could compare these interventions with those which were less successful in both their methods and their results. The large concept of the Participation Bill of 1967 has been diminished to a deferred participation, on the whole rather limited, in profits—the amount of which is probably not negligible as far as the economic status of the wage-earners is concerned (it is an experiment in saving) but which has little impact on the relations between management and workers. Actions taken to revalue manual work have stimulated a combination of irritation and interest; irritation in view of a publicity campaign, the usefulness of which is not apparent, and interest in the concrete measures such as compensating overtime by additional days of leave, early retirement for those in difficult jobs, or the limiting of night-shift or Sunday work.

MAINTENANCE OF AUTHORITATIVE CONTROL

Is this new style of intervention now dominant? Experience has shown that it was not strictly connected with the policy of one man and one Prime Minister; its social roots were already well established. There are, however, two major obstacles which reduce its effectiveness or prevent its working altogether: the traditional centralization of the administration and the constraints of the economic crisis. The latter are more apparent. The former are undoubtedly just as important.

Nobody is opposed to the *politique contractuelle,* but if it is a fact that "progress contracts" are only in effect "program contracts" then this could exert a decisive influence on the future of this policy. It is clear that despite the affirmation in principle that national enterprises should maintain a broad management autonomy, discussion over the "program contracts" has progressively restricted this policy. It has been necessary to readjust the contracts because the rate of inflation was increasing more rapidly than forecast. In order to come to terms with the energy crisis, Electricité de France's investment program has been turned upside down. Each reshuffle has provided the occasion for a battle for management control, a battle where traditional concepts of finance gained a lot of ground.

The danger is all the greater because politicians set much store by the *politique contractuelle* for their social reputation and because, on many occasions, the skepticism of traditional administration on new procedures appeared like the defense of responsible economic conduct *vis-à-vis* the extravagance of the politicians. To point out the traditional controls and their logic can only strengthen the position of the former.

The crisis, for its part, has led to authoritarian decisions. After the price freeze of the autumn of 1976, the government decided to limit wage rises to the increase in the cost of living for the year 1977. Very precise details were sent to the unions; this increase could neither be exceeded nor anticipated. Effective sanctions through price control enabled this decision to be carried out. Its immediate effect was virtually to eliminate the revision of wage levels in the private sector. It also led to real difficulties in the public sector; Electricité de France management, for example, was obliged to abolish a clause in its wage agreements which by mutual agreement had provided for a percentage increase. Although the Prime Minister has confirmed his support of the *politique contractuelle,* it has been virtually dispensed with for the period of wage restraint. Agreements were, in fact, signed in 1977, but the results were hardly convincing.

The method adopted by the government was noteworthy. It would have been unreasonable to reproach the government for not having attempted the negotiation route, since the attitudes of the unions would have meant certain failure of the social contact, but the government could at least have backed up its decision by law, after parliamentary debate. Whatever the reasons might be for its not wishing to do so, the method selected had the effect of stressing its authoritarian approach and of putting all the pressure and responsibility on the employers, leaving the unions only the option of indignant protest at the austerity policies imposed on wage-earners.

Would these two reasons to maintain (or reestablish) the authorities' controls have been weakened by a change of the party in power in 1978? It is extremely unlikely. Despite the adoption of the system of *autogestion* by the Socialist party, the Left has a strong jacobin and centralized tradition, and the Communist party would not appear to be attracted by the charms of *autogestion*. As for the economic crisis, other solutions may be found, but it is not certain that these solutions would have given a more autonomous role to the social partners.

Examination of the problem of a revision of wage structure which has been much discussed quickly shows the difficulties. The numerous discussions which the problem has engendered have raised questions relating to what is the acceptable scope. Is it desirable? How should the differential be calculated? Gross? After tax? But the most important problem to emerge has been what proportion of the task should be allocated (1) to collective bargaining and (2) to the law. In which domains should the partners be left a certain amount of freedom? Should negotiations be limited? A settlement between the different trade unions, however divided they might be, seems to be within reach on the point of giving priority to collective wage agreements. Public sector precedents show that it is possible. It is not the least paradox of the situation that the CFDT and CGT, who have taken a front-line position on problems of differentials, must, to demonstrate the realism of their point of view, rely on the policy adopted by FO and the FEN.

More generally, what capacity for reform and fundamental change would collective bargaining have, what role would be allotted to the authorities? On this point, opinions and proposals differ. Past experience has scarcely made it possible to reply.

Future Prospects

THE CONSEQUENCES OF THE 1978 ELECTIONS

For the industrial relations scene, the unexpected outcome of the March 1978 elections—the government winning a clear victory after a tight contest—had a sobering effect. The heat of the political debate tended to exaggerate its stakes. The failure of the newly divided Left brought back many union activists to the slower but safer channel of industrial action.

The first consequence, which should not be underestimated, will be the weakening of the two unions which took a resolute stand in the electoral contest, and the corresponding strengthening of the "apolitical" ones. The disillusion of the activists and the loss of influence due to too narrow party identification will be particularly felt for the CGT, as recent works-committee elections show.

To the new context created by the government victory, the CGT and CFDT tried to respond immediately by falling back on bargaining channels and industrial issues. This opening was accepted by the new government and by the employers' top organization. Important negotiations will take place during the summer and fall of 1978.

What deserves to detain us here is not the tactical situation. We will not try to guess the outcome, in itself very uncertain. But the interest of these events is that they throw light on basic long-term trends in industrial relations.

SOME BASIC TRENDS

The influence of central union organizations is, in many cases, stable or declining. Whatever the effects of political events, centralized control has been weakening in the last ten years. The pressure and militancy of a part of the rank and file, though somewhat mitigated by the adverse employment situation, did not find adequate expression, whether in the organizations or in bargaining. A large degree of informal relations does not eventually result in a new system of agreements or, more generally, of well-defined relations.

Several large firms have elaborated a policy of decentralization for social problems, giving more authority to the local managers and to the whole of management *encadrement*. But this policy is at best applied very gradually by those who advocate it and has had little echo among the great bulk of medium-sized companies. The trend toward plant or shop bargaining and toward some degree of direct expression of work groups found no institutional expression, and it was severely constrained by the economic crisis. The narrow margins for bargaining in the summer of 1978 were not incidental. Without discussing whether the adjustments of wages of lower-paid and of manual workers may provide enough substance for an agreement, it is clear that, more generally, the extent of possible concessions by the employers is strictly limited and, what is still more important, that the government will maintain strict supervision and control of these limits.

This means too that local problems of wages, hours of work, and job content and context will be intermingled with general economic policy problems. Will the hours of work be reduced to allow for some work-sharing, with or without adjustment in rates of pay? Will the retirement age be set earlier with the same purpose? These are not local decisions, and no government will stay a passive spectator to negotiations about these topics.

But it implies, as we already said several times, that unions will take more, and not less, interest in national economic policies; and this interest implies, in its turn, some forms of political participations by the unions, whether it be through political parties or directly (or both).

The prospect for industrial relations taking on more importance, more weight, and more autonomy in the next five years seems rather good. But this development will not go back to the traditional lines of industry bargaining. It will, on the contrary, include local, plant, and shop forms of discussion and negotiation. It is likely, on the other side, to include the consideration of broader policy, and hence political issues. This trend, which is fundamentally changing the practice and pattern of industrial negotiation, is not specific to France. Comparison of the institutional solutions that emerge in different countries may be an interesting and fruitful exercise.

3

Italy

by T. TREU

Historical Background

Italian industrial relations have undergone profound changes during the postwar period, yet present problems cannot be understood without taking into account the trends in recent history and the contradictions not resolved in the past. The system built immediately after the Second World War, which lasted until the end of the fifties, was strongly influenced by Italian tradition in all its basic features. Collective bargaining and labor union organizations were highly centralized, the most important issues being decided at the industry confederation level, and by means of interconfederation agreements covering a whole sector of the economy (e.g., industry, agriculture, services). Labor unions were organized along the two traditional lines of organization, vertically (i.e., on an industrywide or category basis) and horizontally (cutting across different categories and embracing all workers in various geographical locations), but with a clear dominance of the latter—the confederation at the center, and the chambers of labor at the provincial level being the strong points of the organization.

Until the late 1960s, labor unions were on the whole very weak and almost completely non-existent at the company level. The only representative body within the enterprise was the "works committee" (*commissione interna*), elected by all workers, irrespective of their union affiliation, which, only being precariously linked with the unions, lacked any formal authority or substantial bargaining power. After a short revival in 1945–47, collective bargaining remained almost static, wage gains being very moderate, much less than productivity increases, and normative innovations almost non-existent. These features, rooted in Italian history, were linked to the economic and political situation of the country. Centralization and horizontal unionism, traditionally dominant in the strong Marxist wing of Italian unionism, were held necessary to control a labor force which was highly fragmented in small industrial firms and in agriculture, and basically weak in the labor market due to the high rate of structural unemployment. After 1948, these features of union organization were also considered necessary because of the contemporary political climate (ousting of the Communists from the government, the cold war, etc.). They were strengthened by the need to face a powerful and united employers' front (united because of the wide export opportunities and weak competition). The centralized model of organization also reflected the strong political orientation of the Italian working class and, more precisely, the Italian labor unions' dependence on the major political parties. In fact, for different reasons, the model was favored by both the Socialist-Communist and Christian Democratic components of the labor movement.[1] For the former it was the most suitable instrument through which to direct all efforts towards the class struggle or more simply, according to the ambivalent aims of the left-wing parties, against the government. For the latter it was a convenient way to control industrial conflict at the plant level, where it was most dangerous, and to keep labor's behavior compatible with the country's reconstruction program and with monetary and economic stability. The dependence on political parties was a product of the weakness of the labor unions, and in turn contributed to reduce further their bargaining capabilities. Last, but not least, this pattern of industrial relations was influenced by an established tradition of centralism and bureaucracy affecting, by and large, all Italian public life and institutions even before Fascism. A centralized model of collective bargaining, possibly subject to state control, was also assumed as a basic norm in the Italian constitution (Article 39).

Until the end of the 1950s the rigid structure of Italian industrial relations did not impair its stability. This was because of the inherent weakness of the working class in the labor market, which favored, particularly in the early period, the central control of the federations by their respective parties. An element of control was fostered by the state, which responded to the political use of conflict by the Socialist-Communist union, CGIL, through the courts or by administrative or police intervention. The authorities used these informal methods of countering union political action since legislation had proved impossible due to the stubborn resistance of all the trade union federations.

This rigid, centralized model of industrial relations began to be challenged in the early 1960s, due to basic changes which occurred in both the economic and political situation and the labor movement. The end of the reconstruction period combined with growing economic prosperity: a reduction, although temporary, of unemployment; the lessening of political tensions at both the international and national level, which led to the first coalition governments open to the Socialists; a parallel rapprochement between the three confederations, which increasingly led them to experiment with "unity of action"; a more liberal attitude towards industrial relations on the side of the state, which adopted a policy of collective *laissez faire* and even encouraged new, more decentralized, patterns of collective bargaining through the diffuse network of state-owned enterprises.

Economic growth and technological development contributed to the strengthening of industrial unions and their peripheral structures, particularly in the northern areas of the country. The centralized structure of bargaining proved inadequate in coping with the different capacities for pay and working conditions in various sectors and enterprises (wage-drift having reached a very high level). A more dynamic structure was instituted in most industrial sectors, whereby industry-wide bargaining, while controlled at the central bargaining level, could be modified by plant- or company-wide bargaining on a limited range of matters, defined at the same national level. These innovations—although favored by the benevolent attitude of the state—were not covered by any legislation, or state regulation of bargaining procedures, scope and contents. The rejection of positive state intervention in industrial relations, and resistance to the system of union registration provided for in article 39 of the Constitution, while originally motivated mainly by tactical and political considerations (the fear of a hostile government and dissidence between the various unions), became consciously applied principles of the Italian unions, accepted to a large extent by management and by the public authorities. Freedom from legal regulation came to be recognized as the most suitable environment for promoting effective bargaining and improving relations between social partners—a drastic transformation for a country in which the prevailing ideologies and traditions favored union action within a well-defined institutional framework. In general terms the prevailing attitude in the 1960s, a time of great technological optimism, showed an unprecedented faith in the capability of the social partners to regulate by common consent all the major problems of social and economic development. A central tripartite bargaining system was proposed (but never implemented), as the best way to establish comprehensive national planning. Management of conflict, like that of bargaining, was to be by the self-restraint of the parties, and by bargaining itself; for the first time no-strike clauses were included in most national collective agreements. Whereas in other countries run by a clearly pro-labor government, unions were able to grow with direct political help from the state, this was not true for Italy in the sixties. Here the growth of the unions, particularly at the end of the decade, had to start from the plant level and be sustained mainly by direct conflictual action.[2]

These attempts to institutionalize agreement by mutual consent in industrial relations were already proving to be illusory by the mid-sixties and were officially buried with the wave of strikes of 1968–69; an unprecedented and unforeseen explosion of conflict, which Italy was not alone to suffer. The crisis of 1968–69 and the subsequent instability of Italian industrial relations were caused by factors which had been emerging during the sixties. Some of these factors were related to the quality and quantity of manpower: the decline of traditional professions; the growing number of unskilled workers, mostly young, provided with increasing levels of education (compulsory education up to 14 years was introduced in 1962) and with social expectations higher than in the past; and the growth in the number of workers in the labor market, particularly in the northern industrial and urban centers. Other factors were related to working conditions: the growing exploitation of manpower, especially in mass production systems exposed to international competition; the excessive wage and social inequalities between manual and non-manual workers, between workers with differing job qualifications, and in different economic sectors. The potential for conflict could not be reduced in Italy, as in other countries, by resorting for the hardest and lowest-paid jobs to immigrant workers, who were not culturally and politically integrated in the host society, and therefore less prone to protest against adverse working conditions.

The pattern of bargaining and of labor management relations was not suitable for dealing with these problems. The bargaining structure, too rigidly limited to plant-wide bargaining, was still too centralized to be able to impinge on working conditions at the workshop level. At this level unions were still non-existent or not recognized by management, which was stubbornly resistant to accepting them fully as bargaining agents, in spite of official declarations to the contrary. The continued centralization of the unions made them less responsive to the rank-and-file and unable to control it, particularly when their ability to come up with monetary returns was reduced by economic difficulties (the depression of 1964–66) and by the still limited strength of union organization. Indeed the "rational" and controlled model of the sixties presupposed a labor movement which was well organized and fully recognized. Yet this was not the case. Not until after 1969 did unions obtain full legitimacy, from the employers, the state or the workers. From the sixties onwards, the dichotomy between the centralized system of industrial relations and that at the plant level proved to be the major malaise of the system both in Italy and other countries. In Italy, the potential for instability was increased by two factors: the scant success of Italian capitalism in ensuring stable development and rewards for the workers, as opposed, for instance, to Germany; and the obvious incapacity of the weak center-left governments to put into effect some basic social reforms in public health, education, housing and transportation and to cope with the serious social and economic imbalances between different areas of

Italy and between various groups of the population—employed, unemployed, retired people, industrial and agricultural workers. From this point of view many aspects of the 1968 crisis and the objectives pursued by the labor movement can be seen as directed at redressing historic gaps and lags in the development of the Italian social and economic system. The seriousness of the gaps partly accounts for the violence of the conflict, the difficulty in controlling it, and for the radical demands for change advanced by the unions which at that time were supported to a large extent by the left-wing parties.

The Turning Point of 1968-69

The changes introduced in Italian industrial relations since 1968-69 affect all the basic features of the system: forms and objectives of conflict, structure and content of bargaining, forms of union organization, particularly at the plant level, and relations between the unions, the political parties and the state. Industrial conflict, which reached a peak in 1969 (302,597,000 hours lost in strikes), and was also exceptionally high in the following years is now showing an increasing independence from the economic cycle in spite of growing economic difficulties. Since the end of the sixties considerable use has been made of new and radical forms of struggle, although these have mainly been declared illegal by the courts. They are aimed at drastically reducing industrial production with a minimum wage loss by the workers, and are particularly effective in systems of mass production, characterized by a highly interdependent and integrated work organization and technology. They include slowdowns, working-to-rule, rotating strikes, occupation of the plants, and work-ins, all these often accompanied by tough picketing. (It must be borne in mind that strike funds are unknown in Italian tradition.)

Conflict has been centered in the plant, producing a growth of union power and collective bargaining at this level without precedent in Italian history. The articulated bargaining structure of the past has been replaced by a much more dynamic pattern, whereby plant and enterprise arrangements are by and large independent of the bargaining taking place at the two broader levels, industry-wide and between the national federations. This means that any matter can be bargained at any level at any time. Coordination between the different levels of bargaining and industrial peace for the duration of the agreements are not guaranteed by any bilateral obligation, but depend upon opportunistic judgments made by the bargaining agents themselves and on the capacity of the central organizations to control decentralized initiatives.

Collective bargaining is considered by Italian unions to be a continuous process in the sense that any matter can be negotiated at any level at any time. Time is rejected as an essential element of the agreement. Lacking an explicit peace obligation clause, the agreement is considered to settle only the existing conflict and not to contain any promise to avoid future conflicts both on the interpretation of the agreement and on "new" issues.

Since 1969, enterprise agreements can be counted in their thousands every year, and they are accompanied by a tight network of informal bargaining extending down to the single shop or department. Plant- or company-wide bargaining no longer merely extends national agreements locally, but often anticipates the results of the latter. This has been the case with many of the recent major innovations in bargaining matters. National agreements continue to maintain their important role—providing a uniform platform of treatment for all employees in various sectors most relevant to the large number of small and very small firms, which account for a substantial part of the Italian industrial structure—where plant bargaining is less widespread and less effective. Attempts to rebuild some form of tangible coordination among the three levels of bargaining, through strike clauses or similar obligatory clauses, have so far been unsuccessful, due to strong union opposition.

This intense union activity at the enterprise level has been made possible by the profound change in the form of union organization and has been sustained by the closer unity of action by the three major confederations, aimed at eventual unity of the organizations. These facts have allowed the unions rapidly to assume control over the diffused and partly spontaneous pressures coming from the rank-and-file; unofficial strikes have always remained very rare. The Italian labor movement has been able, more than other labor movements, to use these pressures and demands for change coming from the workshop to strengthen its general position as a bargaining agent. In this it has been favored by its long tradition of political radicalism, by the competition between its different ideological and political components, and also paradoxically by its relative weakness, whereby it could not use the strength of organization to resist the demand for spontaneous action.

This has expressed itself in a profound change in union organization, particularly at the plant level. The old works committees, worn out by bureaucratization and by a long history of isolation and ambiguity, have been replaced, in almost all industrial sections, by the "delegates" elected in each department, shop, or office of the enterprise by all workers, unionized or not, in assembly meetings, regardless of union affiliation and without pre-selected lists. The shop delegates make up the "factory committees" (*Consigli di fabbrica*), which have been recognized not only by the unions, but also by management, as bargaining agents at the enterprise level. It is the first time in Italian history that this recognition has been granted to a structure representing workers within the company. The delegates and the factory committees have acquired the double aspect of being direct representatives of the workers and of the first level of union organization, and filling a double function as instruments of union democracy and as institutional structures for industrial relations. The number of committees

Table 3.1. Trend of Strikes in Italy, 1960–76

Year	Number of Strikers (thousands)	Working Hours Lost and Number of Strikes								Average Hours Lost per Striker
		Company-wide		Industry-wide		Intercategorial		Total		
		Hours (thousands)	Strikes	Hours (thousands)	Strikes	Hours (thousands)	Strikes	Hours (thousands)	Strikes	
1960	2,338							46,289		19.48
1962	2,910							181,732		67.27
1965	2,310							55,943		24.13
1966	1,887							115,788		61.22
1967	2,243							68,548		30.34
1968	9,862	21,704	2,860	25,477	489	26,737	28	73,918	3,377	15.12
1969	7,507	21,908	3,219	230,620	548	50,569	21	302,597	3,788	40.3
1970	3,722	30,214	3,537	115,842	614	156	11	146,212	4,162	39.3
1971	3,891	35,284	4,831	64,476	725	830	42	103,590	5,598	26.6
1972	4,405	23,164	4,099	108,434	639	4,882	27	136,480	4,765	31.0
1973	6,133	15,483	3,225	138,429	523	10,023	21	163,935	3,769	26.7
1974	13,287	32,918	4,731	42,043	818	60,657	20	135,618	5,569	10.2
1975	20,867							181,381	3,568	8.9
1976	11,898							177,643	2,706	15.0

Source: Institute of Statistics.

Note: Official data for 1977 are not yet available, but the number of hours lost for strikes seems to have declined sharply.

and rotation of their members have contributed to creating a large number of union militants and officials and to extending the unions' presence in the vast area of small enterprises, traditionally not unionized. The unions control informally nearly all the delegates elected, and the unitary structure has provided an organizational basis for proceeding towards unity between the confederations.

The intense union activity and the removal of organization since 1968 contributed to an unprecedented growth of membership, made more stable by the introduction of check-off in most collective agreements. Meanwhile, the change in bargaining structure has been accompanied by a similar innovation in bargaining practices and results. Since 1969 wage increases have been considerable, on the principle of equal amounts for all employees, regardless of their job and basic wage rates, and in a few years have brought Italian average industrial wages near to European levels (not beyond—as it

Table 3.2. The Degree of Unionization in Italy, 1949-76

Year	CGIL	CISL	Metalworkers (CGIL, FIOM)	Metalworkers (CISL, FIM)	Agricultural Workers (CGIL, Federbraccianti)
1949	4,988,271	--	637,290	--	1,046,059
1950	4,634,200	1,200,000	589,178	--	949,639
1951	4,490,756	1,360,000	549,997	80,927	1,016,022
1956	3,118,936	1,340,000	265,836	120,410	778,032
1960	2,584,215	1,340,000	191,162	90,498	586,138
1962	2,694,615	1,420,000	222,262	115,524	504,059
1963	2,616,307	1,470,000	292,201	150,436	460,786
1966	2,453,444	1,430,000	240,210	139,840	392,597
1969	2,625,442	1,620,000	327,020	189,642	366,979
1970	2,943,314	1,790,000	452,872	258,762	362,248
1971	3,136,345	1,950,000	463,862	255,792	379,691
1974	3,827,175	2,460,000	514,203	300,546	517,257
1975	4,081,480	2,593,540	548,556	311,119	560,670
1976	4,300,969	2,823,735	565,827	323,192	591,002

Sources: CGIL, *Qualerni di Rassegua sindicale,* num. 50, 1975, and official data for 1975-76.
CISL, *Conquiste del lavoro,* num. 26-28, 27 Nov. 1975, and official data for 1975-76.
FIM, official data published up to 1971 in Cella Manghi Pasini, *Un sindicato italiano negli anni '60,* Bari, De Donato, 1972, pp. 318–319. These official data are reliable for the first time. Similar data for UIL are not available. According to the last official data available (1976), UIL members are 1,104,000; UILM 140,038.

Note: About 55 percent of regular Italian workers belong to the three major trade unions. The degree of unionization is still higher in the public services than in agriculture and in industry. White-collar workers, with the exception of the public services, are much less organized than blue-collar workers.

Table 3.3. Total Hourly Wages of Blue-collar Workers in Industry, 1965–75

Sector	Year (lire)				Percent Increase 1965 to 1969	Percent Increase 1969 to 1974	Percent Increase 1974 to 1975
	1965	1969	1974	1975			
Mining	646	812	1,904	2,359	25.7	134.5	23.7
Manufacturing industry	527	653	1,684	2,171	23.9	157.9	28.8
Construction	571	678	1,491	1,893	18.7	119.9	26.9
Electricity, water, gas	1,085	1,336	2,586	3,066	23.1	93.6	18.5
Total industry	547	675	1,687	2,167	23.4	149.9	28.4

Source: Ministry of Labor.

Note: The hourly wage is calculated by dividing the monthly total wage by the number of hours actually worked during the month. The data for 1975 are an overestimate because the number of hours worked was reduced due to the economic crisis, whereas the monthly wage has decreased less than proportionally (due to social security benefits).

is sometimes claimed—particularly if the lira devaluation is taken into account). This egalitarian policy of the Italian unions has caused a relative reduction in wage differentials between jobs—differentials which were traditionally rather high in Italy. According to the most accurate, although admittedly partial, estimates, the variation in total hourly wages of blue-collar workers in industry decreased, between 1969 and 1974, from 17.8 to 13.9 percent.

The scope of bargaining, mainly under the influence of plant bargaining, has been extended from merely economic matters to all aspects of labor relations: organization of work, job content, work-loads, subcontracting, controls on overtime, and, most recently, information and control of management investment policies. This intensive use of bargaining has provoked strong reactions among Italian employers. They were not accustomed to industrial conflict and were preoccupied with keeping labor costs within well defined limits; they now feel hampered in their management by the rigid control of labor mobility exercized by the factory committees. Finally, the use of industrial conflict has been extended from industrial disputes to broad social objectives: better housing, public transportation, health, social security and schools. The unions have thus assumed a direct political role, acting as the counterpart of the public authorities, in addition to or instead of political parties, whose initiative has been hampered by, among other reasons, the persistent tensions between the Christian Democrats, and the conservative interests represented in this party and the Communist opposition. The growth of unions' power makes them now more protective of their autonomy *vis-à-vis* the political parties, although no less politically committed in their own name.

The changes described above caused, and in turn were sustained by, the changed attitude of the public authorities. The state shifted from a role predominantly of non-intervention during the sixties to a clearly supportive attitude towards labor, or more specifically towards the three major confederations. The failure, during the sixties, to achieve voluntary regulation of industrial relations, the persistent weakness of the unions, and therefore the scanty development of collective bargaining as a means of promoting social peace, made clear that the state could no longer stay aloof. The most evident example of this new attitude was the 'Statute of Workers' Rights' (1970). This gave strong incentives to union action within the enterprise, granting the workers' and unions' representatives some basic rights: time off for union activities; the right to call meetings during working hours within the plant and paid by the company; check-off; protection from "unfair" labor practices; the right to control the working environment; protection against dismissals, transfers, and changes of jobs.

According to the Statute of Workers' Rights, employees can be transferred from one productive unit to another only for proved and objective reasons. Their jobs can be changed only if the new job is professionally equivalent or corresponds to a higher classification than the old one. They can be dismissed only for just cause or justified reason, such as serious violation of workers' obligations, reasons concerning the organization of work, and/or the productive activity of the enterprise. Both concepts are narrowly interpreted by the courts, which are empowered to order the reinstatement of the worker unjustly dismissed. Moreover, job security is indirectly protected by a special social fund which guarantees almost complete income for long periods of time (sometimes indefinitely) to workers laid off or working short-time, due to various economic difficulties in the enterprise, thus helping the entrepreneur to avoid or postpone collective dismissals. These legal guarantees, coupled with tight union control on labor mobility, have greatly reduced the discretionary powers of the employer in the use of manpower.

Backed by a liberal interpretation by the courts, this law has significantly contributed to consolidating the unions' position as bargaining agents within the plants and indirectly as political agents in the social sphere. Since 1968, mediation by the Ministry of Labor, its peripheral offices and other public authorities has been of growing and sometimes decisive importance in the solution of major industrial disputes and has been directed at the same goal as the Statute; i.e., to promote unions as bargaining agents at all levels. At the same time workers have been granted nearly full wages in case of layoff, or reduction of working hours, due to economic difficulties. This was made possible by a series of contractual and legislative provisions which increased the unions' bargaining powers in time of crisis and contributed, as mentioned above, to the greater independence of industrial conflict from the economic cycle. Finally, union pressure for social reforms has been supported by the Constitutional Court, which recognized the lawfulness of strikes for political and social objectives.

This type of state intervention in industrial relations has certainly been directed at strengthening the unions against revolt by the rank-and-file and the Italian employers' resistance to a bilateral and more equitable regulation of industrial relations. Yet, while it has succeeded in these purposes, it has not managed to institutionalize industrial conflict. This failure is bitterly denounced by employers. Although they partly recognize the advantage of promoting union bargaining power, they stress the partiality and incompleteness of the law and the need for more "positive" state intervention. The latter would stabilize industrial conflict and ensure the attainment of profitability and efficiency—two basic conditions for the viability of the enterprise.

Against this background it is understandable that there has been no room in Italy for any form of institutional participation by workers in decisions within the enterprise, nor even for cooperative bargaining. Until the late 1960s the question could not even be proposed to employers, who had been enjoying great freedom in handling unilaterally the most crucial aspects of industrial relations. Italian employers were too conservative to accept even marginal experiments in co-determination or too conscious, with good reason, that in the highly conflictive environment of Italian industry these experiments could hardly be used to stabilize industrial relations. They were afraid that co-determination would result in a substantial loss of their power, while contributing to the strength of unions within the firm.

On the other hand, the degree of consensus on basic issues of social and economic development was too low and the imbalances in the distribution of income, education, and social services too great to make institutional participation possible, or even conceivable, on the side of the labor movement. The weakness of the unions kept them away from crucial issues concerning the enterprise and work organization for a long time. On the political front the existence of strong parties of the Left, particularly the Communists, who were consistently in the opposition and had great influence on the major confederation, CGIL, was an obstacle to any form of rapprochement within the enterprise. Other forms of "involvement" of the workers in industrial economics (such as profit-sharing or shareholding by workers) had, for similar reasons, little chance of success either in theory or in practice. That is why highly conflictive bargaining has been, up to recently, the principal means by which workers and management have sought to influence each other's behavior. A major exception to this rule was the public service where there were various forms of joint committees and workers' representatives on the administrative boards of public institutions. However, these forms of workers' participation are closely linked to the peculiar nature of the employer and to the labor tradition in the public sector, and therefore not necessarily readily adaptable to the private sector.

Collective bargaining has been used very effectively by the unions, particularly in the period between 1969 and 1974, and has produced important results for them, but the advances achieved have been set back by subsequent economic difficulties. The major results were an unprecedented rate of wage increase, a reduction of weekly working hours to 40, rigid union control of overtime and of labor mobility, reduction of wage differentials, and equality of treatment between blue- and white-collar workers with the introduction of a common job-classification system.[3] Most recently there has also resulted a better defense of workers' wages against inflation, by means of a sliding-scale mechanism which ensures automatic wage adjustments in relation to cost-of-living increases, nearly equivalent to full adjustment up to a certain sum for the majority of blue-collar industrial workers, and unions have also won the right to be informed of and to "examine jointly" with management its policy on investment and employment. This right, first sanctioned in some company-wide agreements in 1974 (FIAT and others)[4] was recognized in the major national agreements of 1976.[5] The results are less satisfactory in terms of the unions' political objectives; most of the social reforms demanded are by and large still unaccomplished. This failure has more than one reason. It is questionable how far even the most "modern" among Italian entrepreneurs are prepared to support the rationalizing of the economy and society and in isolating those groups which are only concerned with profiting from their advantageous economic situation. It is also doubtful whether they are willing to give up the substantial government assistance and protection from which they have so far benefitted. Finally, their willingness to accept a new economic model, preferring social to individual consumption, is not at all clear, although an important acknowledgment of the need to move in this direction has recently come from the dynamic new leadership of *Confindustria*. Union action itself has proved weak in many respects—too often merely ideological, inclined to overestimate the positive effects of general social agitation, incapable of identifying concrete and relevant targets as well as their real counterparts in the highly fragmented scenario of private and public authorities.

The Impact of Political and Economic Instability on Industrial Relations

Italy's economic difficulties since 1973 have put increasing pressure on social partners to revise their attitudes on industrial relations. The dynamics of collective bargaining have highlighted dramatically the problem of the competitiveness of the Italian economy. The elements of crisis, some of which are common to other western societies, are increased by difficulties specific to the Italian situation: the structural weakness of the industrial system, the endemic agricultural crisis, the inefficiency of public administration, in particular of the public institutions directly operating on the labor market, and the serious gap between the products of the educational system and the demands of the labor market. Political instability, a traditional feature of Italian society, has so far prevented the public authorities shaping a planned development policy and satisfying the demands for social reform coming from the people. The ensuing social tensions have been transmitted to the sphere of labor-management relations within the firm and have become an additional reason for industrial conflict. The growing polarization of votes around the two major parties (Christian Democrats and the Communists) at the expense of the smaller ones, with the lack of clear and stable agreement, has so far had only a limited stabilizing effect on Italian social and political life.

On the other hand, the lasting political tensions between the major parties and the persistent difficulties in building a more efficient formula for government had major consequences for labor unions, in terms of their relationships with both the political system and with their rank-and-file. These tensions undermined the drive for unity among the three major confederations and provoked lasting disagreement among the different political components within the CGIL, CISL and UIL. The process towards unity, clearly postulating a similar rapprochement on the political scene, is now postponed *sine die*, if not forever. The appeals to political loyalty, especially within the CGIL and CISL by Communists and Christian Democrats respectively, are, on the other hand, reducing the autonomy of unions in both their bargaining and political activities. There is now a growing feeling, even among the parties of the left, that union action has exceeded its "natural" limits and must be checked in order to give back to the parties their traditional role in the political system, that of the definition of economic policy.

Since the June 1976 elections, these parties have, for different reasons, made serious efforts to regain control of the unions, particularly those of the most militant industrial categories, and to have them control their workers so that excessive social conflict does not "disturb" the parties' plans for a big coalition and a more stable government. Pressure on the unions was particularly great during the events which led to the agreement for a new government, in February 1978, between the Christian Democrats and the Communist Party. This was a precarious agreement indeed, in spite of the large majority in Parliament officially endorsing it.

The slowing down of the unification process and the increased proportion of political matters in union activities, coupled with a new centralization of decision-making in crucial bargaining issues, have often reduced the initiative of the factory committees, as well as their effectiveness as basic channels of communication between the workers and the union. Signs are in fact visible of a growing difficulty on the side of the federations in controlling the rank-and-file and having them accept a policy of self restraint and austerity, by way of persuasion and collective bargaining. How to maintain internal democracy and operating contractual autonomy in a period of growing union involvement in the economic government of the country and of greater political influence by left-wing parties, has become, more than ever, the crucial question for Italian unions.

The use made of bargaining power by the unions has been judged severely, and not only by employers, as having contributed to increasing, instead of reducing, the dualism of the Italian economy, i.e. the inequality between the well-protected unionized industrial workers and the weaker part of the labor market. The latter includes the workers of the smallest productive units, peripheral workers, homeworkers in particular, and the growing number of unemployed, concentrated mostly in the underdeveloped south and among the young and women. It is quite likely that the growing tendency by employers to decentralize systematically production from large enterprises, where union control on wages and labor organization is strong, to smaller units or to home work, reflects a reaction to the new drive of collective bargaining.

A further serious phenomenon, connected with this situation, has been the slowing down of capital investment and the process of industrial restructuring aimed at increasing productivity and labor mobility at the inevitable expense of employment. The excessive rigidity of manpower, even more than the growth of labor costs, is considered, not only by employers, the major obstacle to both national and foreign investments and to the firms' capacity to adapt to market demands. The guarantees of salary in case of lay-offs, coupled with the tight judicial control on dismissals, is believed to reduce beyond reasonable limits the right of the enterprise to get rid of redundant workers. The apparently paradoxical result would be that an excessive protection of already employed workers has blocked new opportunities of employment and reduced the protection of marginal workers.

These political and economic difficulties have already reduced the dynamic and innovative impulse of collective bargaining. Unions are bound to try to defend the results so far achieved and to protect the workers' purchasing power and employment. They are faced with the difficult alternative of maintaining a tight relationship with the stronger, traditionally unionized, part of the labor market which is showing growing dissatisfaction with the demands for austerity, even though they come from the Italian Communist Party; and on the other hand representing the weaker but growing part of the population, which has traditionally been non-unionized. Furthermore, inflation and the economic crisis are fostering discontent and hostility among medium-to-upper-level white-collar workers and public employees, who feel hindered by the egalitarian policy of the unions and want to maintain their position of relative privilege, which they consider to be in danger. These reactions run counter to the declared intentions of the confederations and of the left wing parties to make allies among these crucial middle-class strata for their objectives of social and economic rationalization.

If the factors mentioned so far do not support the recurrent forecast of a decline of union power in advanced capitalistic societies, certainly they alter the nature of the industrial relations system which was in force between 1968 and 1973. First of all the implicit assumption that collective bargaining could expand potentially without limits in a fast and regularly developing economy, and with a relatively high degree of autonomy from the political system, is clearly not valid any more. The traditional methods of collective bargaining have reached a peak, which can hardly be exceeded, yet they appear insufficient to meet the new problems associated with the present crisis of the economic system. The institutionalized and continuing intervention of the state to support entire sectors of the economy, ignoring the distinction between private and public enterprises, has reduced, probably irreversibly, the autonomy of Italian industrial relations, so that these are more and more determined by and related to "political" events. In this context the factors causing political instability mentioned above have become direct determinants of the instability in the system of industrial relations.

Perspectives of Change in Industrial Relations

While the signs of crisis in the old system are clear, the directions for possible change are not, and probably will not soon become so. Any analysis of future trends in Italy must take into account the general uncertainty about the future. So much more because the Italian economy, given its strong dependence on foreign trade, is more closely linked than others to international economic conditions, which are themselves largely undetermined and unstable. Management, so far largely inactive in shaping industrial relations policies, is preoccupied by the decreasing legitimacy of its power within the enterprise and also within the socio-political system, following the drastic political changes and the growing power of the left. On the other hand, the management of large companies in particular realizes that sheer resistance to the encroachment of trade unions is not enough. Positive solutions need to be offered to the demands for more participation in decision-making, better working conditions, more equitable distribution of income and of employment opportunities, coming from the labor struggles of these past years. The new leadership of *Confindustria* seems to realize that both public inactivity in the field of social reforms and the costs of financial assistance are becoming an unbearable burden for vital parts of industry and for society as a whole; to the point that the growing influence of the Communists in the government is seen with cautious favor or with resignation as the only (or most effective) way to break the present political and economic impasse. The leadership of *Confindustria* appears also to agree that the objective of more stable industrial relations cannot be attained by simply going back to the rigid bargaining structure of the sixties or by reducing the scope for industrial conflict through legal regulations. It seems aware of the need to form a consensus on unresolved issues through bargaining, with labor unions fully recognized as bargaining and social agents, and to improve information and consultation procedures, in order to foster more rational industrial relations. This does not mean, however, that all the different components of Italian industry, particularly those small firms traditionally living on expedients and characterized by paternalistic, authoritarian industrial relations, agree in practice on these attitudes or can be induced to implement a new, more rational industrial relations policy. Employers' associations are themselves facing problems of political mediation and bargaining with their rank-and-file. Not only the dualism of the labor market, but also the dualism of the Italian industrial structure is a major problem to be solved in order to achieve more stable and consensual industrial relations.

On the other hand, even the most militant unions admit that changes must be introduced in the system of industrial relations. The need is increasingly and widely felt for more consensus and for a more pragmatic approach to the crucial problems of the moment—recovery of the economy, full employment, and improvement in the quality of life. Some changes are already visible. We have already mentioned the reduced use of traditional patterns of collective bargaining, particularly on economic matters; the main concern in the future is likely to be the maintaining of existing standards of living. The emphasis of bargaining seems to be shifting already towards "qualitative" objectives: conditions of work, work organization, and, at a broader level, control of investment, manpower policy and employment. It is generally felt by the unions that simply maintaining employment, company by company, cannot be defended "at all costs." The point is not to reduce protection of job security, which is a worldwide trend, but to shift from rigid and static types of guarantees (job-by-job protection) to dynamic bargaining and control of overall employment stability. It is understood that some sort of labor mobility, both within the single plant and among different firms or sectors of the economy, must be allowed and even promoted, provided that it is controlled through bargaining and connected with similarly controlled policies of industrial restructuring, professional retraining of manpower, etc. A major possible point of consensus between unions and management is the need for a better use of manpower resources, both quantitatively through the more intensive use of industrial capacities and qualitatively through the selection and improvement of professional skills and of labor mobility. Some basic principles have already been expressed in the agreement made between the national federations on January 26, 1977. This introduced the opportunity to negotiate the introduction of work shifts, which up till then had been strongly resisted by the unions, in order to increase productivity, to implement labor mobility at plant level and a tighter control on absenteeism, and to admit exceptions to the existing maxima for hours of overtime. The commitment to favor labor mobility, to give absolute priority to employment security, and to restrain wage demands—in exchange for a new economic policy by the government—has recently been renewed and specified in a comprehensive document solemnly approved (February 1978) by the three major federations, after extensive consultation with the rank and file throughout the country. This document is the greatest effort so far made by Italian unions to adapt their bargaining policy to the seriousness of the economic situation. It challenges the new Communist-supported government to confront the economic and political crisis by making constructive and responsible proposals. Furthermore, greater attention is being given to new organizational techniques directed at improving the quality of work, particularly in the most repetitive jobs. Some commitment in this direction was introduced by the national agreements of 1973 (mainly job rotation combined with on-the-job training under union control), but remained largely unfulfilled. Now the initiative is taken mostly by employers, preoccupied by the very high rate of absenteeism and by the urgent need to increase productivity. Experiments in job enrichment, teamwork with considerable autonomy of decision by the workers and reduction of supervisory activity, mechanization of the most repetitive jobs, etc., have been introduced, apparently with good results, in major companies such as Fiat and Olivetti. Unions have accepted these experiments, although with some diffidence; they seem to feel an urgency to regain the initiative, if not in order to find a totally new organization of work as some dreamed in 1968, then at least not just to accept passively the employers' plans.

A major point of weakness in reaching greater labor mobility and professional improvement is the traditional inefficiency of the public bodies in charge of manpower policy and professional education. While the latter has recently been decentralized to the regional level and is undergoing a process of reform, the former are still centrally organized, bureaucratic and unable to provide the necessary help and guidelines for better organization of the labor market. This means that the strict legal rules which govern manpower recruiting, prohibition of direct hiring and obligation to recruit employees from the public manpower agency not specifically by name but by qualification and number, are not adequate to control the labor market and produce equilibrium between labor supply and demand. These rules either are circumvented or reduce labor mobility and employment opportunities. Almost completely lacking is any initiative by the public powers to improve the quality of life and the working environment, either in the factory or in the region.

Another major point of debate and of possible innovation in future bargaining concerns the present structure of wages. In Italy indirect labor costs, social security contributions, automatic wage increases due to seniority, seniority allowances, Christmas and annual vacation bonuses, are exceptionally high compared with other countries. There is a feeling that these elements must somehow be reduced, to lessen labor costs and keep their increase in line with the European average, without reducing the salary actually paid to the employees, and without blocking completely the possibility of wage bargaining particularly at the plant level. Some agreement to reform the structure of wages would seem the best, although not the easiest, compromise between the urgent need to control the evolution of labor costs agreed by the government and by the major political parties and the need—recognized also by employers—not to limit the capacity for bargaining and the unions' power too much if for no other reason than not to increase the difficulty of the confederations in controlling the rank and file.[6] This is even more necessary because the possibility of strong control of wages by the authorities is remote in the present political and social situation; it would be opposed not only by the unions, but also by the parties of the left, and it could not be balanced by any reliable promise by the government to control prices in a similar way.

A rationalization of the wage structure would indeed involve much broader problems; first of all a reduction in wage differentials among the various sectors of the economy, particularly in public employment and services. It is in these sectors that inequalities reach a maximum, causing serious discontent, waste of resources, and hampering labor mobility. To intervene in this area is not easy, either for the unions or for the employers, since such action would arouse strong reaction from the privileged groups of the labor force. That is why the confederations are moving very cautiously and are not in a hurry to implement the agreement of January 1977. They do not feel very safe, particularly in public employment and services, where central control has always been very weak. The reduction of social contributions paid by enterprises, on the other hand, requires a drastic reform of the inefficient and costly public institutions in charge of social security, and a change of fiscal policy to bring fiscal revenues closer to European levels. Naturally these matters are external to the system of industrial relations, and involve a reform of public policy and public administration.

Despite the political difficulties already mentioned, the urgency of controlling labor cost increases has forced the government to intervene, with the decided abstention of the Communists, and with the forced consensus of the unions, to restrict collective bargaining through anti-inflation measures partly similar to those enacted in other countries. An initial and temporary measure (of November 1976) aimed at reducing the effectiveness of the sliding scale mechanism, which some consider to be a primary cause of inflationary pressure. Wage increases due to the sliding scale clause for workers with a yearly income of above 8 million lire (net of social security benefits) are paid by the employers not to the workers but to a special public fund, which will be used to finance investments in small to medium-size enterprises. The workers receive in exchange public certificates of credit, not convertible for five years. The same wage increases for workers with a yearly income of between 6 million and 8 million lire are paid 50 percent to the workers and 50 percent to the special fund. This system of forced saving has been applied to a growing proportion of the labor force, due to the rapid rate of inflation, but its duration is limited in time (expiration was on April 30, 1978).

This measure having been held insufficient to curb inflation, and following very difficult negotiations with the unions, the government has adopted a more direct system of intervention to reduce labor costs to employers. It includes a change in the evaluation of some basic goods from which the consumer price index is calculated, so as to make the sliding scale less sensitive to cost-of-living increases, and a partial reduction of social security contributions owed by the firms, which are instead paid out of the general state budget. In exchange for these legislative restrictions on collective bargaining, whose efficiency in curbing inflation is still to be seen, the government has repeatedly promised the unions vigorous action to support investment and employment. This promise cannot be merely ritualistic, since a violation or postponement of its implementation could seriously increase the tensions which have developed among the rank and file of the labor movement as a result of the acceptance of the government's measures by the three confederations; the difficult discussion on the document approved by the confederations in February 1978 (quoted above) confirms this diagnosis.

Another new trend is emerging towards the centralization of bargaining, not so much through formal clauses, as through *de facto* concentration of the major powers of decision at the federal level. Inter-federation bargaining is regaining a crucial role, parallel to the growing importance of macro-economic considerations. The need is felt to control decentralized bargaining and also to bring it into line with the egalitarian goals proclaimed by the unions in recent years. The unions seem to realize that centralization of major decisions and of wage differential negotiations is of major importance in an era of high inflation. We have already mentioned the agreement of January 26, 1977, and the agreements on guaranteed wages in case of lay-off. Particularly important is the agreement of 1975 on the functioning of the sliding scale mechanism, to which the unions have assigned the basic task of defending the workers' purchasing power at a time of inflation. This mechanism has in itself a centralized controlling effect on wages and indirectly reduces the possibility of enterprise bargaining on wages. Of course this control, being indirect, is also elastic, and leaves room not only for adaptation to the different circumstances but also for evasion by the union plant structures with the tacit consent, or claim of non-responsibility, of the superior levels of the unions. But it is probably the maximum which can be obtained in the near future, without prejudicing too much the relationship between the plant level and the general policy of the confederations. Another significant trend in this direction instigated by the unions, but not resisted by management, is to reduce the amount, traditionally high, of industry-wide bargaining, through a process of rapprochement between or unification of the agreements concerning various sectors of the same branch of industry (for example, the textile, chemical industry). The goal—not universally shared, but likely to emerge—is to produce agreements of wider scope, aiming at a single agreement for the whole industrial sector, in order to reduce excessive wage and normative differentials among categories of workers, which are considered a major reason for tension and recurrent wage push. The trend is parallel to, and favored by, a relative reduction of the importance of industry-wide bargaining, due to the nature of the results which it has reached in the past.

Finally, territorial bargaining might well assume a new importance, particularly at regional level, because of the new competence of the regions, particularly in problems of territorial planning, industrial location and investment, and also as a means of coordinating the company-wide bargaining which is bound to increase on these issues.

The Issue of Workers' Participation

Finally the problem of workers' and unions' participation has begun to be discussed openly among employers, within the political parties and also by the unions. The problem has regained importance in Italy for reasons largely common to all industrial systems. An important impulse has come from the labor movement itself, but others have come from within the political system. The widening of the scope of collective bargaining to include such matters, traditionally regarded as managerial prerogatives, as manpower planning, work organization, job security, investment and industrial restructuring, has posed new problems for the trade unions concerning the strategies of private enterprises and their future. This already goes beyond the traditional frontiers of bargaining and calls for more "involvement" of the unions in enterprise decisions, whatever the form thereof. Meanwhile the unions have become involved more and more frequently in the country's major economic decisions, either by way of formal or informal consultation by the public authorities, or through the co-opting of union representatives in a growing number of institutions, not only those administering social services, the most traditional area of union participation, but also those governing the labor market, industrial restructuring, territorial planning and other major aspects of public policy. The state and the major parties, in search of a more stable political and economic organization of society, need the help of organized labor. This need is to become clearer and clearer with a formula of government, based somehow on the Communists' consensus.

Foreign experience of co-determination and the EEC proposals for the reform of company law, suggesting employee representation on the supervisory board, and for a European statute are being taken into consideration. The trend towards an increasing participation by union representatives within public institutions is likely to develop further, even if with some difficulties and ambiguity. The debate on the proposals to adopt some sort of institutional workers' participation within the enterprise, on the contrary encounters more difficulties. A tentative and very cautious draft from the Ministry of Labor has so far been either ignored or criticized by the unions and viewed with indifference by the industrial employers' association. No experiment, even in formal workers' participation, has so far been proposed by management in Italian enterprises. A few cases exist of self-management by the workers under a cooperative form, in generally small firms facing economic difficulties. But the idea of self-management is being considered with interest by some sectors of the unions (particularly CISL and UIL) and by the Socialist Party as an important guideline, although utopian and necessarily projected in the long run towards a new set-up of society.

The reasons for the unions' diffidence towards co-determination are the same as ever: mainly the fear of being involved in responsibilities which limit their autonomy more than they give them real powers, not only in labor matters but also in the main strategic decisions of the employers. Union diffidence is increased by the serious difficulties of the Italian economic and political situation, which justify requests, on the side of the employers, that the unions become more responsible and moderate, but cannot guarantee a new and more balanced economic growth capable of adequately compensating the moderation and sacrifices asked of the workers. In spite of this, the very seriousness of the economic crisis and the growing power of the unions spur them from merely negative attitudes in bargaining, to making proposals concerning industrial policy, work organization, investment policies, and the reduction of absenteeism or labor's excessive rigidity. The necessity for a more positive attitude on economic issues is widely recognized by the unions, as we have already underlined. The occasions to test this goodwill are also there. In particular the unions stress the urgency that the government finally adopt a policy of "sectoral planning," in order to guide industrial development towards more rational and socially adequate objectives which the unions would contribute to shape. The institutional frame for this industrial policy was fixed by an Act of August 1977, which provided for an extensive program of financial help to all industrial enterprises submitting plans for reorganization and for new investment on conditions stated by the law and controlled by administrative authorities. But the evidence of a real capacity to shape such a new industrial policy through the exercise of government is yet to be seen.

Italian union federations prefer to talk of *union control* rather than *union participation* to underline the fact that the growing influence of organized labor on economic decision-making must not be to the detriment of union autonomy nor lead to a subtle confusion of roles between unions and management. Beyond this point there is no united position within the trade union movement itself on the possibility of institutionalizing this union control in some way. The most realistic solution, and also the most cautious, could be for the unions to broaden and reinforce, if necessary by means of legislation, their right to disclosure of information and to negotiate with respect to investment, job security, manpower planning, etc., as already recognized in some national agreements. Moreover Italian unions and the major political parties to which they are related firmly believe that no form of union participation or control at the enterprise level can be significant and successful if it is not connected with increased influence by the workers on the major decisions and on the economic planning which determine the enterprise's policies. The means for the achievement of such democratic planning, however, are not at present available.

Employers are also very cautious and have no standard position on these issues. Declarations in favor of some sort of institutional co-determination within the undertaking coming from some employers (young employers particularly) have received a rather cold reception from the leadership of *Confindustria*, which is apparently skeptical on the applicability of co-determination formulas, given the present Italian social and political situation. Moving along this road would imply, for the employers, giving a more definite guarantee of social and industrial peace, to counter the unions, than they are willing and able to give. It would also lead to a parallel stabilization of the political situation, mainly through a strengthening of the Communist involvement in the government, which is not necessarily in the employers' interests. For the time being, management stresses the value of new procedures of information exchange as a means of reaching agreement and of building a more solid enterprise. However, the right to information is considered only a first step by the unions on the way to real participation in power. *Confindustria* has repeatedly proposed to extend the information and tripartite bargaining procedures from the enterprise level to broad economic issues. But "tripartism" is hardly acceptable to the union federations as a substitute for, or as a form of, democratic planning and anyhow presupposes a consensus on basic issues of the economic and political future of the country which is still far from being achieved.

Reasons for Instability

Most of the elements so far mentioned seem to be directed towards a growing institutionalization and central control of Italian industrial relations. But other facts contradict this tendency. Some of them have already been discussed: first of all the serious and probably non-transitory political uncertainties. No significant progress towards a more consensual and stable industrial relations system can be made in the present climate of political tension. Labor, more clearly than ever, is being asked by the state to give its consent to a particular type of social order, and its consent is essential to the success of any national economic policy.

The powerful and militant Italian unions have shown themselves—as has already been seen—inclined to moderation and even to austerity; but on the condition of a new government economic policy, in which labor is to acquire greater influence, able to direct public and private investments with an eye not only to capital growth, but to the crucial issues of employment and a more balanced development and distribution of wealth. The rapprochement of the Communist party with the government—recently accelerated—can have a stabilizing effect. But it is hardly sufficient. A political agreement, although important, cannot alone control social and industrial conflict. Someone on the left wing of the unions stressed that this rapprochement would be illusory or even dangerous in the present situation, if obtained at the price of an excessive reduction of trade union autonomy and absence of social change. The crucial problem of the relationship between trade unions, political parties, and the political system generally is more controversial and unresolved than ever with the growth of union power and of the left-wing parties. The political role of the unions is largely undetermined and raises strong opposition, even from the left. The major unions, for differing reasons, hesitate to draw all the political consequences from their growing social power and to make open and clear choices of the major problems to be solved. Beyond the traditional scope of industrial relations the following problems have also to be handled adequately: the objectives and form of democratic planning; public control of the economy for more balanced growth; political and administrative decentralization to make public administration more efficient and capable of meeting social demands; and generally finding a means of revitalizing the forms of representative democracy and of integrating it with social democracy. The point anyhow is whether any future government—or the whole political system generally—will be able to give sufficient reward or reliable promises to the unions, in terms of employment, quality of life, and social reforms, to enable them to accept a "social contract" and to control industrial conflict in the name of the democratic national interest. So far this has not been aimed at. There is a growing consensus that the old order must be changed, but not enough consensus for a choice of clear alternatives to be made and put into practice.

In particular the employment situation is serious and not adequately faced. The number of unemployed in 1977 reached 1.6 million (7.7 percent). The level of the economically active population in Italy is one of the lowest in the industrialized world (about 39 percent) but there is a large number of irregular and peripheral workers (homeworkers are estimated at about 2 million). The public authorities have so far intervened to stimulate economic growth mostly through massive financial assistance for enterprises in difficulty, or by planning the reorganization of production to create jobs for laid-off employees. While this intervention has reduced the impact of the economic recession on the workers already employed, it has not prevented a constant decline of total employment, due to non-replacement of staff, and early retirement. In fact, the authorities lack adequate controls to ensure that public assistance is used to benefit enterprises so as to create new jobs, or to maintain the present levels of employment. On the other hand, the cost of this assistance is dangerously adding to the already heavy deficit on the state budget.

A new source of social conflict of unforeseeable violence is the growing number of young workers, with relatively high levels of education and expectations, who are unemployed and without any realistic possibility of employment matching their professional status. The number of unemployed below 29 years of age is estimated at 1.2 million, 36 percent of these having a high school or university degree, while there is also a large number who only work part-time or with irregular jobs. A law has recently been passed (July 1977) providing financial incentives for private enterprise to hire young workers on a temporary basis both on regular labor contracts and on so-called "formation" contracts and directing the public administration to employ young workers in public works of social utility. However, these incentives have proved insufficient to stimulate new employment in the private sector so far.

Employment in the public service also cannot be expanded beyond narrow limits, due to budgetary difficulties. The inefficiency of public institutions in charge of manpower policy, training and retraining, makes them completely inadequate for handling this massive phenomenon of young unemployed and for helping to bridge the traditional gap between school and work, which is at least in part responsible for the difficulty of young people in finding employment.

These new "marginal proletarians" do not feel represented and do not appear to be easily controllable either by the traditional parties of the left or by the unions. Some sectors of the left, within the unions in particular, proclaim vigorously the danger that a too "moderate" and cooperative union policy would completely undermine the relationship with this crucial group of the population. The revolt of young students is only the most serious symptom—they claim—of the general situation, which proves that the labor movement cannot wait inactively for a miraculous change of the economic and social conditions via uncertain or insufficient agreements, without losing the confidence acquired over the years among the majority of the Italian working class. The changes in the age, employment opportunities, and education of the working class, coupled with the growth of non-institutional and decentralized work, represent a modification of this class even deeper than that of the sixties, and that is not transitory in Italy as it is in other advanced capitalistic societies. A further problem is that there is no possibility of continuous high economic development to absorb the tensions deriving from the structural dualism of the labor market (between internal and external or marginal workers) as there was in the 1960s. The unions must become representative of these young proletarians and peripheral workers if they want to keep their role of political and social mediators and enable a solution of these new tensions to be negotiated. This is also essential for the state, which needs unions that are as representative as possible in order to create social consensus. The difficulty is that labor unions are traditionally built to represent the workers already employed, even in Italy where they have been very sensitive to the general problems of the working class. The attempts to find an organizational or political link with this "new working class" have so far failed. The planned extension of the factory committees outside the firm by electing area committees including all workers is encountering serious obstacles, and it is even more difficult to open these committees to unemployed or marginal workers. On the other hand the state is not doing enough—deliberately or not—to help the unions to become representative of workers external or peripheral to the organized labor market.

The seriousness of labor market dualism also influences the union attitude to the handling of labor relations in the strong areas of the market, making them more and more reluctant to limit their commitment to the defense of the regular organized workers and to accept the proposals of "cooperative" co-determination or participation.

This impasse is weakening the image of the union federations with the rank and file and giving rise to limited but unprecedented tensions between plant level representatives and the central levels of the organization. The control of plant bargaining for wages is by no means successful, even in the areas traditionally most "disciplined." Decentralizing pressures are particularly difficult to control in the public sector, where the federations have always been weaker and which is now in turmoil, because it feels itself left behind by a wage policy too favorable to the industrial sector. Collective bargaining, recognized formally in the public service only a few years ago, may be an instrument of modernization of labor relations in this area and indirectly of social control of the public administration, traditionally separated from society and highly bureaucratic. However, it is also putting new pressure on the already serious Italian budget deficit. The dichotomy between labor relations in public and private employment, due, among other things, to the fiscal crisis of the state, may in the future be a major source of social conflict.

Italian industrial relations, as in neighboring countries, stand clearly at a crossroads where contradictory pressures for consensus or conflict, for political centralization or for cooperative segregation meet. The causes of instability are still deeply rooted in the structure of Italian society and economy and are not likely to be removed in the short term. Even on the hypothesis that the present weak signs of political stabilization, of a more consistent government economic policy, and of union self-control, continue, it is not reasonable to foresee a rapid increase in the institutionalization of an industrial relations system following the German and Scandinavian patterns. Instead a slow evolution, not ratified formally, toward a more consensual government of industrial relations and a greater *de facto* control of conflict and collective bargaining, widened in scope as mentioned, will probably continue to be the main trend in industrial relations, and—possibly encouraged by the public authorities—this will deal with matters that are elsewhere handled by institutionalized systems of co-determination.

Notes

1. CGIL, the major confederation, has always been of Socialist and Communist allegiance; CISL, originally composed of Catholics and linked to the Christian Democrats, is now partly linked to this party, partly politically non-committed, and has groups connected with the non-Communist left (Socialists, New Left); UIL is composed of Socialists (now in slight majority), Social Democrats, and Republicans. In 1976 CGIL declared 4,300,969 members, CISL 2,823,735, UIL 1,086,630. Of minor importance is CISNAL (the neo-fascist confederation), while a few strong independent unions exist in the public service.

2. A Pizzorno *"Fra azione di classe e sistemi corporativi"*, in *Problemi del Movimento Sindacale Italiano, 1943–73*, Feltrinelli, 1976.

3. In the mechanical engineering industry, for example, the traditional classification of personnel in thirteen categories (or more in case of firms adopting job evaluation systems) has been replaced by a classification in seven categories (often six, the first being transitional) whereby white-collar jobs are distributed from the second to the seventh level and blue-collar from the second to the fifth. The criteria of classification have also been changed by giving weight, in addition to the characteristics of the job done, to the self-defined qualifications of the manpower (e.g. studies completed) and to seniority as grounds for automatic advancement (especially from the lowest categories). Wage differentials between the lowest- and the highest-paid blue-collar workers, according to the sample adopted by a recent Parliamentary Commission (1977), are 100-143; between the lowest- and highest-paid white-collar workers they are 100-294.

4. In the FIAT agreement, the enterprise was committed not to reduce personnel during the whole of 1975, to replace the turnover (only) in southern Italy, to bargain with the unions on timing and extent of lay-offs and on making additions to salaries from the special fund mentioned above, and finally to examine jointly with the unions the amount of production, of overtime and the implementation of investment commitments. In exchange, the unions agree to bargain on labor mobility within the single plant and among different plants, to accept lay-offs and short-time in case of excess production, jointly ascertained. The real value of these agreements, particularly after 1975, has not been on negotiating new investments, but in maintaining existing employment.

5. The actual content of the national agreements is less significant than intended and often proclaimed by the unions. They fall short of giving the unions a real right to bargain on investments; and the right of the unions to be informed is shaped in such a way that it is likely to be effective only in large firms.

6. A commitment to revise the present structure of wages is included in the inter-federation agreement of January 26, 1977 mentioned above; but there is no sign that the revision will be rapidly agreed upon.

4

The Netherlands

by W. ALBEDA

A Slow Start

The organizations of employers and workers, their mutual relations, their behavior, and the role that the government plays in the field of the making of rules for work and the conditions under which work takes place, in short the system of labor relations, can only in theory be separated from the rest of society. It is, therefore, impossible to describe and to explain the system and also to explain and predict changes in it without leaving the system.

The Netherlands is a small country, situated on a favorable strategic corner of Western Europe. It has always been highly exposed to strong influences from abroad. Situated at the crossroads between the main cultures of Western Europe, Anglo-Saxon, German and French, and with a tradition of openness towards influences from abroad, economic and cultural, the country always underwent strong pressures from abroad and was therefore much less self-sufficient and perhaps less self-centered than the bigger nations of Europe. Periods in which French influences were more fashionable were followed by periods when German cultural modes were more important; the British, and of course, later on, American influences were always strong.

The country was late to develop a modern manufacturing industry. Traditionally, commerce and transport, as determined by geographical position and strengthened by the large colonial empire, shared the economic scene with an important, productive, and not very traditional agriculture.

This is, of course, not the kind of surrounding in which industrial relations would have a rapid start. Although there were early beginnings (in printing, in diamond-cutting, and other skilled trades), modern labor relations developed after strong trade union movements had evolved in Germany and Great Britain.

When, around 1900, the now existing trade union federations were formed, they had foreign models which could be copied or even adapted. The Dutch trade unions were organized following the example of the Germans, taking over not only the organizational forms (and sometimes even copying the names), but also the pattern of having socialist and Christian unions side-by-side (although these were divided on confessional lines). However, within the German structures which had been borrowed, the British philosophy had a strong influence in trade union federations. It was not uncommon to find Christian socialist writings of the nineteenth century being studied alongside German corporatist authors.

The development of Christian trade unions can be explained only in the broader context of the nineteenth century. Holland always had both important Protestant churches and a strong Catholic population (mainly in the south). However, the country was governed until the end of the nineteenth century by a rather liberal elite. That century brought the emancipation of the Catholics (who, since the struggle for freedom of the sixteenth and seventeenth centuries, had been treated as second-class citizens) and a "Calvinist revival." These two, not totally unrelated, developments led to the political struggle for confessional schools, to the development of confessional political parties, and—after some abortive attempts to form general trade unions—also to the development of Christian trade unions. A similar pattern can be formed in the world of the employers. Although the employers were rather late in organizing themselves, when they finally formed their central organizations (for industry and trade, for small scale enterprises, and for agriculture in three different groups), they followed the pattern of a "neutral" organization alongside one with a religious base.

Around 1900, the radical wing of the trade union movement was strongly influenced by anarcho-syndicalism. But the General Strike of 1903 convinced the majority of trade union leaders and workers of the wisdom of opting for reformist tactics. After 1903, the radical trade unions withered away, although, of course, an undercurrent of radical thinking both inside and outside the official trade union movement has remained up to the present day. Some of its influence can be identified in the docks of Amsterdam and Rotterdam and in the poorer regions of the north. The mainstream in the Dutch trade union movement was, especially after the railway strike of 1903, represented by the three trade union federations: NVV (socialist), the NKV (Catholic), and the CNV (Protestant). The Catholics and Protestants together covered somewhat more than half of the organized workers. Since the Second World War, the three trade union federations have worked more closely. More recently, the pattern of cooperation has been influenced by two distinct trends. The first is the growth of white-collar trade unions. The second is the growing distance that separates the Protestant federation (the CNV) from the other two central federations. This has led to the development of a new structure for the Dutch trade union movement which has replaced the structure of three closely cooperating trade union federations of the last thirty years.

The three trade union centers have always claimed to represent workers from all levels. In 1945 they accepted the principle of "industrial unionism"—the adherence of all workers in the same industry or group of industries to the same union. The three federations accepted the same borderlines between these unions. Although the Catholic federation accepted the industrial-union principle only half-heartedly and maintained a group of white-collar unions, the principle was adhered to until recently. However, it was never accepted by all white-collar workers. In the public sector, almost one-half of the unionized workers joined independent unions. In the private sector, smaller groups of white-collar unions carried on. Since the late 1960s and the beginning of the 1970s, however, the white-collar unions received an impetus from the federations' policy of demanding a general levelling of wages received by different groups of workers. This issue came to the forefront in 1973 when the trade unions in all industries asked for a levelling of wages by raising the level of the lower paid in maximizing the compensation for price increases in wages. This helped to stimulate the formation, in 1974, of a new federation of white-collar trade unions with about 120,000 members. A major contributing factor was the break-away of two white-collar unions from the NKV during 1973.

A second important development was the growth of cooperation between the NKV and the NVV. Since 1971 discussions had taken place which aimed at the formation of a confederation of the three trade union centers. In the course of 1974, it became evident that there was a difference of opinion on the implications of such a confederation. The CNV wanted to retain its own

Table 4.1. Members of Trade Unions, 1971–77 (in thousands)

Date	NVV	CNV	NKV	Others	Total
1.1.71	613.0	237.8	404.5	322.7 (20.7%)	1,578
1.1.72	623.8	239.1	399.7	354.1	1,616.7
31.3.73	656.6	234.9	396.3	366.4	1,654.2
31.3.74	670.7	231.4	397.9	394.4	1,694.4
31.3.75	683.8	228.1	360.4	437.6 (25.6%)	1,709.9
31.3.76	702.6	230.0	352.8	440.0	1,725.9
31.3.77	720.3	258.8	347.2	443.1	1,769.4

identity, in particular the possibility of retaining its independent decision-making process (before entering into discussion with the other two) and the possibility of voicing minority opinions. The other two aimed at the creation of a new unit which was virtually tantamount to amalgamation.

The attitude of the NKV has to be seen in the context of developments in the Catholic world in the Netherlands. The Catholic church had always (much more than the Protestant churches) strongly advocated the existence of Catholic organizations in social, cultural, and political fields. Now that the church no longer takes this view, the Catholic organizations amalgamated either with their Protestant counterparts (e.g. in politics, where Catholic and Protestant partners now form the Christian Democratic Party [CDA] and in the employers' organizations) or with the non-denominational groups (e.g. the farmers' organization, the organizations of small employers, etc.).

On January 1st, 1976, the new FNV (Federation of Dutch Trade Unions) came into existnce. In different industries NKV and NVV unions have already formed federations, and now plan amalgamations. The FNV decided to limit its collaboration with the CNV to "incidental contacts," meaning that where the FNV and CNV have the same objectives they can work together, but that in general no real attempt would be made to reach agreement with the CNV.

The existence of the FNV, of course, has its own consequences for the development of industrial relations. Intensive cooperation within the FNV leads to a definite convergence of opinions, although here and there differences survive. (In general, NVV members are socialists, while in the NKV many members and secretaries are Christian Democrats.) The CNV, left to itself, has arrived at a difficult situation in those industries where its membership is weak (manufacturing, urban industries), although here and there in works councils, CNV groups have developed a form of collaboration with the white-collar unions. Perhaps this could become a pattern in the future. Its own relative dependence on white-collar membership has increased. Moreover, some Catholic unions (civil servants, police, and unions in the field of education) are joining CNV. The Christian federation is rapidly approaching 300,000 members, but its weakness in the blue-collar field is becoming more pronounced. An important element in the future could be that intensive dialogue no longer takes place between the CNV and the FNV unions. The "ideological gap," which had been reduced to a considerable extent in the post-war years, is now opening again.

Early Centralization

Several factors can explain the early and persistent tendency towards centralization in the Dutch industrial relations scene.

Since the beginning of this century, Christian Democracy has played an important role in Dutch politics. The Christian Democratic parties, although often conservative in their outlook, were never without a strong trade union wing. Governments, therefore, have always played an active, rather paternalistic, role with regard to the development of collective bargaining. In its socio-economic policy, the government furthered the growth of centralized organizations by its introduction of early legislation on collective agreements and its acceptance, since the First World War, of a consultative role on the part of both employers and trade unions.

These centralized organizations were rather weak and divided, owing to religious splits and the slow growth of modern enterprise. For both internal and external reasons, it was necessary to form trade unions encompassing more than one trade. The pattern of the German *"Industrie Gewerkschaft"* was repeated in Holland after the First World War, and was rationalized and further developed after the Second World War. As social legislation became more significant, it was of growing importance to develop central organizations with a minimum of staff.

During the formative years of the system (especially the period between the two world wars), the labor market was constantly in a depressed state, although unemployment was high in that period, approaching, or—as in the 1930s—surpassing 10 percent. Trade unions have found that in a depressed labor market a larger bargaining unit is preferable to a smaller one. Under such conditions, competition in product markets and on the labor market pushes wages downwards. The immediate aim of the trade unions from the beginning was to form national collective agreements for whole industries (printing, building, the metal industry, etc.). This was brought about initially by accepting long wage scales with important differences between urban and rural areas. Then, particularly after the Second World War, these differences were suppressed (at least in the collective agreements; in the real world it turned out to be more difficult). It is interesting to note that, although the full employment situation of the first 25 years after the Second World War could have led the unions to seek smaller bargaining units, the habit of centralizing labor relations, the continuing strong role of the government, and—especially during the first 15 years—the fear of inflation and unemployment, led to a continuation of large bargaining units in most industries.

Integrative Labor Relations

Labor relations in the Netherlands, as elsewhere in Europe, have an "integrative" character. The same factors which lead to the relative centralization of the unions, and the centralization of the system itself, played a role in the development of this character. It was further strengthened by the development of institutionalized and permanent bargaining. The government introduced legislation to establish the framework for institutional contracts between employers and trade unions, partly to help weak trade unions and, more importantly, to further the development of peaceful labor relations. The law on industrial councils (*Bedrijfsradenwet* 1937) and the law on industrial organization (*Wet Bedrijfsorganisatie* 1951) aimed at the establishment of semi-official bodies with the authority to make regulations in the social field for the industry in which they were set up. Such bodies developed particularly in industries dominated by small-scale enterprise, such as retailing, agriculture, handicrafts, and building. In other industries, private bargaining bodies were set up. These bodies, like the ROM (*Raad van Overleg in de Metaalindustrie*) in the metal industry, or the *Vakraad voor de Textielindustrie* in the textile industry, are witness to the need of the organizations concerned to have more than just incidental contacts. They feel that it is not enough to conclude a collective agreement each year, but that these organizations should react to daily and weekly developments. It is clear that in so far as such bodies really work, they help the bargaining process run smoothly. People meet each other regularly, get to know each other, are involved in a common process of problem-solving. Personal relationships may develop, which do not totally eliminate conflicts, but which make them scarcer and more easily soluble.

The move towards integrative labor relations was also furthered by developments on the ideological front. Socialist trade unions gradually turned themselves away from class-war ideology, first for pragmatic reasons, and later also as a consequence of more sophisticated views of the developing welfare state. From the beginning, the Christian trade unions had based their strategy on a rejection (sometimes too easy) of class-contradictions. The close collaboration between the different trade union groups, especially after the Second World War, led to a convergence of ideologies.

A factor that played an important role in the years preceding and following the Second World War was the fairly intensive contact between confessional organizations on both sides. Many questions were discussed between functionally different groups accepting the same ideology, which made the differences between them more relative and sometimes enabled the groups to find common ground.

The symbol of Dutch integrative labor relations remains, of course, the Foundation of Labor, a private organization set up by the central organizations of the trade unions and the employers' organizations. The Foundation is at the same time the institution where top-level discussions take place between trade unions and employers, where guidelines for wages for the whole country are discussed, and solutions are found for threatened conflicts within industries, and the body that discusses matters of socio-economic importance (especially the yearly wage discussions) with the government. It has all the advantages of a permanent bargaining body at the industry level. In some ways, it is amazing that the Foundation still exists after 32 years, yet one could even say that since 1972 its importance has grown again. Perhaps as a child of emergency, the Foundation feels more at home in emergency situations like the present economic crisis. For the role of consultation, the government created in 1951 the Social Economic Council (*Sociaal Economische Raad,* SER for short). When it was established, the SER was seen as the summit of the *Bedrijfsorganisatie,* mentioned before. From time to time, it was thought that after the creation of the SER the Foundation could disappear, but this never happened.

Because the organization of industry intended by the 1951 law never really occurred, the role of the SER as the summit of that organization never became important. Instead, its role of advisor to the government became much more substantial. Its very composition made it well equipped for this function, and less fit to take over the role of the Foundation. The SER is composed of 45 members (each with his deputy-member). These members are appointed by the Crown; 15 of them are proposed by the central organizations of employers, and 15 proposed by the trade unions. The remaining 15 members are appointed by the Crown on the basis of their ability to keep in mind the general interest. In the last group (the "Crown members") we find the President of the Central Bank, the Director of the Central Planning Bureau, and a group of social or economic experts. The government is obliged to consult the SER on all new legislation. The SER is also authorized to give advice on its own initiative. Moreover, the SER has some policy functions, and it plays a role in the execution of some laws (e.g. the law on works-councils).

In the course of the last 25 years, the SER has played an important role, both in preparing new legislation and in preparing and executing socio-economic policy. The most important example of the last function has, of course, been the management of the wage policy in its more rigid form between 1951 and 1963 and in many different forms since then. With regard to wage policy, in the course of time a convenient division of labor evolved between the Central Planning Bureau, preparing the numerical basis and economic analysis, the SER, evaluating the CPB material and advising on policy, and the Foundation, bargaining on the basis of the material developed by the SER. Of course, such a division will never be complete. The trade union leaders, in discussing the economic report that will serve as a basis for bargaining later on, already have an eye to this bargaining, but the presence of the third group sometimes functions as a bridge and sometimes as a neutralizing agent in discussions that could come too close to bargaining too early on.

The social organizations are in these ways intimately involved in the process of legislation and policy-making. It is difficult for them to give the impression that they live in an alien, capitalist world, where only the voice of the owners of capital is heard. On the other hand, what happens in the Social Economic Council is often very removed from what happens in the real world, and this they see as a problem. It is not always easy to explain to the members what happens in the sphere of econometrics and legislation, where expert opinion is more important than the political or ideological insight of trade union leaders.

A Top-Heavy Set-up

The position of the trade union federations within the SER highlights a basic problem of the Dutch system of labor relations and, perhaps, to a certain extent of labor relations in general, in countries where trade unions are involved in national policy-making. This is the spatial and intellectual distance between the most important trade union activities and the members of the trade unions.

The intellectual distance is not just a distance marked by the use of macro-economic analysis or complicated mechanisms for managing the social security system of the country; in a sense, it is more basic. There is a real difference between the way a problem poses itself on the national and on the local level. On the national level, the wage rate is an element in a system of national accounting. In that system it is not too difficult to show how the financial health of the nation and the wage level are mutually dependent. Let the financial system get out of hand, and you will see that the resulting pressure on wages will be unbearable. On the other hand, let the wage bargaining get out of hand, and the whole financial management of the country is undermined. On the local level, workers are confronted with an economy that shows a different face from enterprise to enterprise, from industry to industry, and from economic sector to economic sector. It is very difficult to convince building workers on a big site in Amsterdam that is hampered by lack of sufficiently skilled workers that their wages should be kept down, in order to prevent a general increase in the wage level which will trigger off a new wave of inflation.

How can a union be deeply involved in national policy-making and at the same time represent its members? How can it function as a reliable partner of government and employers, and at the same time react to the fears and wishes of its members?

This basic problem lies at the heart of the strange history of Dutch wage policy, and of the hesitant involvement of Dutch trade unions in policy-making. Hesitant, because on the one hand they know that they should be involved in order to influence policy, and on the other, it is only by keeping their hands free that they will be able to react to the day-to-day needs of their members.

The attitude of both the government and the social partners in Holland cannot be understood without taking into account the traditional centralization of the system, and the traditional involvement of the government in labor relations. Therefore, it is necessary to say something, albeit rather brief, on the Dutch wage policy of the first 18 years after the war.

The post-war situation was rather unique in more than one sense. In the first place, at the end of the German occupation, there was the possibility of the "new start." Everybody could see that the economy was depressed and that only a common effort and common sacrifices could help us out of the difficulties. Moreover, the confrontation with an alien and evil system contributed to a certain lessening of tensions that had previously existed between groups that were functionally or ideologically separated. It was this phenomenon that made the establishment of the Foundation of Labor possible and provided the basic common understanding necessary for a concentrated action to turn a devastated country, bereft of its overseas colonies, into a modern industrial nation.

Wage policy was an important element in this effort. Between 1945 and 1963, the government acquired the authority to give prescriptions for the process of collective bargaining concerning wages, job classification, wage systems, etc. This authority was utilized in close cooperation between the Ministry of Social Affairs, the Foundation of Labor, and the Social Economic Council. Initially the wage level was geared to the cost-of-living index, but later different criteria were introduced, for example the increase in productivity of the country as a whole, and later the increase in productivity of the different industries. For a time, an attempt was made to keep the wage element in the national income at an acceptable level.

When this policy failed after 1963, the most important factor was, of course, the disappearance of the unique constellation that had made it possible. Reconstruction was over. The fear of unemployment had disappeared. Old controversies made themselves felt again. In short, the national economy went back to normal and, unsurprisingly, labor relations went the same way.

But at the same time, more and more fundamental changes took place:

1. The wave of economic development in the 1950s led to new patterns of economic activity: employment among agricultural workers dropped rapidly to about 6 percent; the structure of manufacturing industry changed; new industries came into being (e.g. chemicals). Consequently, old ideas of "industry as a community" disappeared.

2. In 1958 the Netherlands entered the Common Market. This meant that the example of other countries, with a free system of collective bargaining, was brought home more clearly to trade union members, and also that the influence of higher wages and higher prices in neighboring countries made itself felt.

3. It could be said that the re-establishment of the pre-war trade unions and employers' organizations was an example of restoration, rather than of renewal, in more than one sense. The structure of the industrial relations system, as set up during the 1940s and 1950s, was highly dependent on a certain docility on the part of the leaders of the social organizations. The Netherlands has for a long time been a rather traditional country, where what one could call "pre-industrial values" (e.g. respect for authority, the acceptance of leadership) play an important role. "Pillarization"—the system of rather top-heavy organizations split in terms of socio-political principles (based on religious differences) but working closely together at the top level—was based upon this attitude.

In this sense, it could be said that a modern policy of linking wages to the macro-economic possibilities of the nation was made possible by the rather traditional behavior of most workers. The self-same economic development that resulted from this policy therefore undermined the possibility of its continuation. This economic development may be seen as an example of modernization. One instance is the rapid reduction in the number of agricultural workers from 15 percent in 1945 to 7 percent in 1960. But, of course, there is one very important element that cannot be found in the statistics—namely the growth of modern, large-scale manufacturing industries which have replaced small family enterprises. Also the mass media (especially television) have a strong influence in eroding traditional attitudes and dividing lines.

4. The relatively peaceful, and seemingly problem-free, development between 1945 and 1963 was not unique to Holland. Perhaps one might say that the temporary "end of ideology" made itself felt strongly in the Netherlands because it fitted the mood of the population so well in the post-war period.

The so-called wage explosion of 1964 may therefore be seen as an early reaction against the atmosphere of harmonious cooperation of the 1950s, an atmosphere that, on looking back, appears almost unreal. In the wage explosion we find all the elements that were mentioned before, but the most fundamental aspect was the fact that the constituency, both of the employers' organizations and of the trade union federations, simply refused to follow their leaders and thereby reduced the value of central bargaining almost to nothing.

Since the story has been told several times,[1] I can be brief. The three main parties in formulating wage policy were not slow in their reaction. They were willing to change their attitude almost overnight. The same Minister of Social Affairs who just before had refused to accept a wage increase of more than 3 percent, suddenly accepted a proposal from the metal unions to increase wages by no less than 8 percent, and at the end of the same year the central organizations accepted a general increase of no less than 10 percent. The objective of the three parties was not to put an end to the wage policy. What they really wanted was to renew their grip on what was happening in local labor markets. It was hoped that increased wages could ease the tension and thereby open the possibility of continued guidance on wage development from the central organizations.

However, this operation failed in practice. An important element in this failure was the unexpected reaction of the economy to the shock of the sudden wage increase. In 1964 average productivity in the Dutch economy suddenly went up by no less than 9 percent. This figure put the cautious views of economists of government, employers and trade unions in a new and not too favorable light. Their authority was undermined. Their reasoning, that increased wages will only after a certain period lead to important changes in the level and structure of production, did not impress the constituent parties very much. These "kept to the facts" and concluded that, rather than leading to unemployment, higher wages would promote increased productivity and real welfare.

The wage explosion was not, of course, totally unexpected. Since the second half of the 1950s there had been symptoms of a reaction from trade union members and local trade union functionaries against the centralizing influence of the centrally guided wage policy on the trade union movement. Sociological studies carried out during the 1950s[2] and early 1960s had confirmed the existence of two important problems: (1) There was virtually no impact by the trade union on the firm, especially at shopfloor level, and (2) given the predominantly national activities of the trade union movement, influence from below (within the trade unions) on trade union policies was almost impossible.

The wage explosion and the discussions which followed confirmed the warnings of social scientists and experienced trade union leaders alike: the over-centralization of policy had led to an over-centralization of trade union organization. Since then, the trade unions have embarked upon an extensive program of internal reform and revision of their policies.

Trade Union Organization and Trade Union Presence Within the Firm

In 1964 the ANMB (Metal Workers Union, now part of the *Industriebond NVV*) published *Trade Union and the Firm*. In this pamphlet, the first conclusions are drawn from the sociological studies mentioned above. It links the two basic problems: the absence of the trade unions on the shop-floor level, and internal trade union democracy.

According to the ANMB, the firm's policies are determined in the first place by its attempt to achieve certain standards of technology and efficiency, so there is a danger that the worker suffers as a vulnerable human being. Therefore, the enterprise needs an active opposition, which should function not only externally when a collective agreement is concluded and its functioning is watched by the trade union, but also from the inside.

Therefore, within the enterprise, the members of the trade union have to organize themselves in a trade union group which functions as a permanent opposition within the firm. It was not the idea of the ANMB that this trade union group should approach shop-stewards and engage in collective bargaining itself. It should be interested in the conditions under which work is carried out, and the organization of the work itself. It should pass on complaints to the trade unions. Within the two confessional metal unions, similar ideas were voiced. There was, however, a difference in that the two Christian organizations gave less emphasis to the element of opposition. Also, they tried to make a link between the trade union group and the works-council.

The activites of the trade unions on the plant level have developed in two ways since 1964. Firstly, a number of collective agreements extended facilities for trade union group work in the firm (e.g. in the metal, building, and printing industries). These facilities include the appointment of group chairmen who may spend a certain amount of time on trade union activities; the use of localities within the plant for union meetings; and of the firm's information board to tell trade union members of trade union activities. Secondly, the trade union groups within the firm were used as an element in the restructuring of trade union organization. Before the 1960s, most unions were based upon geographical, rather than functional, organization. Every trade union member was a member of his local trade union group. The groups elected district councils, and the district councils elected a national council that was the main governing body of the trade union. General meetings were constitutionally more important, but were rather big and costly. Therefore they took place only once in every three or five years, and so could not play a very important role in the day-to-day policy of the organizations.

Now the *Industriebond NVV* has decided to have the district council of the union elected by the two basic units of the organization: the local group and the union group within the plant. It is felt that the internal trade union groups are more "action-oriented" and have a better day-to-day contact with the ordinary members.

The Trade Unions and the Development of Industrial Democracy

INDUSTRY LEVEL

One aspect of the over-centralization of Dutch industrial relations was the tendency, before 1960, to prefer forms of "industrial democracy" that operate on the national and industry level to forms that operate on the enterprise level. The law on industrial organization (mentioned above) provided for the establishment of industrial councils with the authority to make regulations in the social and economic field. The idea behind this legislation was that it should be possible to extend the sphere of collective bargaining by including economic items in the process, and to broaden collective bargaining into a form of bipartite government for each industry. A basic problem for such a form of industrial democracy would be that in a modern and growing economy the definition of what is an industry or a sector changes continually. Moreover, extending the field of bargaining into the sphere of economics could easily eliminate competition and thereby impair the economic viability of Dutch industry in general. The scheme, therefore, met with determined resistance from employers and, apart from the industries mentioned before, was never realized. Of course, there was one notable exception, the establishment of the SER, that played such an important role in the preparation and execution of socio-economic policy on the national level.

One could say that the idea of industrial organization has possibilities only in a depressed economy, where saving the existence of small firms is deemed more important than promoting the expansion of profitable ones. In the years of rapid economic growth between 1950 and 1972, nobody was interested enough in the existence of marginal firms (outside marginal industries) to press very hard for the application of this legislation. It is interesting to note, however, that now that we are again witnessing economic depression, the ideas behind the law on industrial organization have come back. Trade unions want to bring investment decisions into the sphere of bargaining. A discussion is going on about the possibility of introducing a form of indicative planning in which new industrial councils could play a role in both the preparation and the execution of the plans. In its last White Paper on economic growth[3] the former government proposed consultative groups composed of employers and trade union representatives, which would play an important role in the restructuring of the economy. In practice, such consultative groups already play an important role in restructuring industrial sectors. Especially in cases where mass lay-offs are inevitable, no important steps are taken without the assistance of such bipartite groups.

FIRM LEVEL, WORKS COUNCILS

In the 1950s, there was a certain tendency to look upon schemes of industrial democracy at the firm level as a part of a hierarchy of forms of industrial democracy set up on the national (SER) level, the industrial level, the firm level, and ultimately on the shop-floor level. The role that the SER and specialized bodies at the industry level (*Bedrijfscommissie*) play with regard to the works councils bears witness to the original conception.

The original idea of dealing with industrial councils and works councils under one law was abandoned. As a consequence, the first law on works councils was accepted in 1950. This law was succeeded by the law in 1971. It is expected that a new law on works councils will be introduced in 1978.

The three laws are built on different conceptions of workers' influence. The 1950 law wanted to create an advisory body within the enterprise. It stipulated that the independent function of the employer should not be impaired by the authority of the works councils. The works council, the law said, should contribute to the optimal functioning of the firm. The works coucil, one might conclude, had as its main function two-way communication, but it held no real power to influence the decisions of management.

The 1971 law differs in two respects from the previous one. In the first place, the law implicitly envisages a works council that is not only concerned with the position of the firm, but that, at the same time, is a forum for discussion on the interests of the workers. In the second place, the works council's position is strengthened.

The present works council is elected in a secret ballot by all workers (whether organized or not). It has between 3 and 25 members (including the chairman, who is a member *ex officio*). Trade unions have the right to introduce lists, but a group of workers of sufficient size (30) can also do this. The works council now has the following rights:

1. *Information.* The works council has the right to be informed about (a) financial figures and (b) facts on lay-offs, education and wages.

2. *Consultation.* The works council has the right to be consulted on (a) *economic matters* (in general, the employer is obliged to ask the opinion of the council before a decision is taken on important resolutions such as selling the firm, closure or partial closure, important expansions, reorganization, removal, permanent alliance with another firm) and (b) *social affairs* (wage systems, education, merit-rating, criteria for lay-offs and careers, social work).

3. *Co-determination.* The council has the right to veto decisions with regard to work regulations, pension funds, profit-sharing plans, saving systems, working hours, holidays, and safety and hygiene, in so far as this has not been dealt with by the collective agreement.

The works council has the right to meet during worktime, and the chosen members have the right to hold closed meetings without the chairman to prepare their position. They are obliged to maintain secrecy. They are protected by special rules for dismissal. Bigger companies with affiliates in more localities can install a central works council, elected by the works councils of these plants. In the case of a conflict the council, or its chairman, may appeal to a bipartite industrial committee; one for each industry.

The proposed new law will be built upon two main principles. One is the attempt to create greater independence for the elected members, the other is the proposal to enlarge the power of the works council.

Their powers are to be enlarged in two ways. A works council will have the right to advise on important decisions (e.g., new investment plans). This will be enforced through the right to appeal to a court if the advice is rejected without good reason. The works council will have the right to advise on nominations of members to the managing board.

The new law is based upon a compromise between the views brought forward by the FNV (Federation of Dutch Trade Unions) and the Labor party, on the one hand, and on the other hand, the views of the Christian Federation of Trade Unions (CNV) and the Christian Democratic Party. (The two sets of views are not homogenous, but can be brought under two headings.)

In the view of the FNV, the works council should be converted into a "workers' council." The manager should not be a member of the council, and the council should evolve into the top of the on-site trade union organization. Works council members should be protected from the danger of manipulation by the employer. Their most important function would be to protect the rights of the workers.

In the view of the CNV, development as seen in the laws of 1950 and 1971 should be extrapolated, the works council remaining as it is, but with greatly increased responsibilities.

In short, the FNV wants a more independent, more worker-oriented workers' council in a position of permanent opposition to management, while the CNV wants a works council based upon the idea of collaboration, rather than opposition. The two lines of thought are fundamentally opposed. However, the Socialist-Christian Democratic government had to make a compromise. This compromise gave the works council the independence asked for by the FNV (the chairman is elected by the members; the manager is not a member), but the council has to make its decisions "in the presence of the manager." The powers of the works council will be enlarged, especially in the economic field.

It is clear, however, that much depends on the attitudes of the members of works councils. It may well be that members who have a rather antagonistic attitude will not change their attitude when the works council changes. The same, of course, is valid for members with a more collaborative attitude.

In practice, some works councils already operate as a permanent opposition. Where the *Industriebond NVV* is strong, especially, the members tend not to take any decisions without first asking the decision of the trade union group within the firm. Difficult situations arise when CNV, white-collar unions, and unorganized workers oppose the policy of the FNV members. This is happening more and more, although it certainly does not occur in the majority of cases.

The future development of the works council is not yet very clear. On the one hand, the FNV, especially in the manufacturing industries, has an overwhelming strength. On the other hand, certainly over half of the FNV members of works councils do not follow the hard line prescribed by their unions (and not all unions prescribe this hard line). Moreover, the influence of the white-collar unions is growing fast, so that the FNV members often do not have majorities in works councils.

An important influence in the development of the works council has been, and will be in the future, the relationship between the works council and the Supervisory Board.

THE SUPERVISORY BOARD

The Dutch corporation is organized in a two-tier system: the managing board leads the day-to-day operations, while the board of directors (or supervisory board) has the responsibility for fundamental and long-range developments.

Since 1973 the works councils have been given rights regarding the nomination of members of supervisory boards. It is interesting for several reasons to look at the development that led to these new rights.

In the 1960s, quite a debate took place with regard to the composition of supervisory boards, a debate that found a (temporary) conclusion in the new legislation of 1973. There were at least three different views on the desirability of introducing a system of co-determination along the lines of the German model. In the first place, the employers' view was that the composition of the board of directors or supervisory board should be broadened by the introduction of people with a certain expertise in the social field (social legislation, personnel policy, labor market, labor relations, etc.). However, employers objected to the proposal that directors should be elected by the works council and the shareholders' meeting. They feared the introduction of contradictory opinions and interest groups into the boardroom.

The NVV at that time hesitated to propose the election of worker directors because they feared that this could involve a certain commitment by the trade unions. Trade unions could perhaps lose the freedom to criticize and oppose the employers' policy by accepting worker directors. The CNV, on the other hand, wholeheartedly accepted the idea of co-determination on a bipartite basis, as in the German *Mitbestimmung* model.

As far as the situation in the Netherlands is concerned, the government had already by 1960 set up a State Commission of experts to study the issue. The Verdam Report, proposing minority worker-representation on the boards, was published in 1964.

Then the government asked the SER to give its opinion. Given the three points of view, mentioned above, it was not easy to find common ground. Then Mr. J. de Pous, the president of the SER, found a beautiful compromise: the board of directors would have the right of co-optation; however, both the works council and the shareholders' meeting would have the right to propose names for nomination, and to veto nominations.

The three groups could reconcile their positions in the proposal in the following ways: (1) There would be no direct representation, and no commitment of the trade unions. (2) There would be a new group of people, with new expert knowledge on the boards. A compromise should be made on each candidate; extremists from both sides could be excluded. (3) In the long run, the system could even lead to bipartite boards.

This compromise was accepted by the government. According to a law in 1973, all firms having a capital of at least 10 million guilder, who are legally obliged to have a works council, and have at least 100 workers in the Netherlands, should have a Board of Directors. This Board has most of the functions previously belonging to the shareholders' meeting. The Board appoints the members of the Board of Management, determines the contents of the annual report, and makes proposals for the distribution of profits.

The law has been functioning now for four years. It is too early therefore to draw conclusions from the experience, but perhaps two remarks could be made.

Owing to the lack of involvement on the part of the trade unions, the influence of managing boards and existing boards of directors on the selection of newcomers was important. The necessity of compromising on each candidate narrowed the chance of finding new members who were middle-of-the-road people, with a trade union or political background, and who were not too far on the left.

It is of itself interesting that the law necessitates the development of a dialogue between works councils and boards of directors. In the beginning, this dialogue was limited to the appointment of new directors, but there is an evolution in the direction of greater and closer contact between the board and the council.

In the meantime, there are new developments. Although (or perhaps I should say, partly because) management is happy with the experience gained from the new legislation, the trade unions do not share this enthusiasm. They have been working hard to find a common understanding in this matter. As a result, the FNV is now demanding the introduction of a system of tripartite co-determination, whereby workers and shareholders have equal representation, and a third and small group represents the general interest. Instead of the present system they now want directors to be nominated directly by the workers, as a first step towards some form of workers' control. Like anywhere else in Western Europe, there has been a development in trade union thinking about industrial democracy. Two years ago a pamphlet from the *Industriebond NVV* stirred up strong reaction from employers, and also from center groups in the political field. It was entitled (in many eyes rather fittingly) *Fijn is anders* ("Nice is different."). It had two main elements. In the first place, it had a fairly consistent acceptance of the so-called confrontation model. In the second place, the pamphlet proposed the introduction of a system of workers' control within the context of a planned economy. It is clear that the two elements are connected. Because the union rejects the present economic system, it is not prepared to accept a form of collaboration within the context of that system. It is curious to note that the union does not always follow its own prescriptions. Many members still play a positive role within works councils. Moreover, in later publications the *Industriebond* showed its willingness to play a rather pragmatic role, compromising with the employers on many practical issues.

In a recent report, the Federation of Trade Unions within the food and agricultural industries (*Voedingsbonden FNV*) proposed the same model for the future as the *Industriebond.* However, although the report contains rather radical aims (workers' control, the abolition of all income differentials not based on job characteristics, etc.), the confrontation model is not used in the very consistent way of the 1975 pamphlet. My impression is that, perhaps as a result of the economic recession, the trade unions are accepting more pragmatic policies without abandoning their final aims. In this sense, it could be possible that the trade unions are in the course of recovering from the shock that the end of the 1970s will mean for them.

The Christian Democrats and the Liberals, who form the new cabinet, have agreed to evaluate the results of existing legislation and to ask the advice of the Social Economic Council on the desirability of proposing direct election of members of the supervisory board by workers and shareholders, the system of tripartite co-determination which—as written above—the FNV wanted. On the other hand the Labor Party chose the system of co-determination on a tripartite basis which the CNV prefers. Consequently, the new cabinet will probably propose new legislation to replace the existing scheme. In one sense, it is deplorable that the experience of an interesting compromise situation may thus be a short one. From the European point of view, however, the Dutch system comes close to other European examples (Germany, Scandinavia). Both elements will play a role in the process of decision-making by the government.

SHOPFLOOR DEMOCRACY

The 1971 law on works councils includes an article that states that the works council "organizes shopfloor democracy" (in Dutch, *werkoverleg*).

Forms of shopfloor democracy have been introduced in the Netherlands mostly on the initiative of employers and social scientists. Philips introduced its system of work structuring at the beginning of the 1960s. The policy was inspired particularly by absenteeism and by the tight labor market. The initiative was firmly in the hands of management. Some assembly lines were abolished, there were experiments with semi-autonomous groups, hierarchical lines were shortened, etc. However, the trade unions were not really involved in these experiments. The Philips works council criticized the company's approach. It did not like the one-sided initiative and the uninvolved attitude of management, that did not commit itself to carrying on experiments which had disappointing results, or which had led to negative economic developments.

An example of the initiative taken by academics can be seen in the line taken by the Department of Industrial Sociology of the Free University of Amsterdam. Under the leadership of Professor Van Zuthem particularly, this group tried to carry out experiments inspired by socio-ethical convictions regarding responsibility and work, and power relationships in work. The group carried out a number of experiments, firstly under the sponsorship of the Federation of Christian Employers, then later working in firms where management was willing to collaborate in experiments. The results of the experiments were not very encouraging. At first, the trade unions were not sufficiently interested to give strong support to the experiments. In later experiments, the attempt of the research group to change the power relationships within the firm met with strong opposition from the management of the firms.[4] The tendency for the research group's attitude to radicalize after the disappointing results did not help it to win the confidence of managment, although its standing with the trade unions gained considerably.

In addition, socio-technic systems, as developed by the Tavistock Institute, were introduced in a few cases. My own institute is carrying out some experiments based upon the power reduction theory, inspired by Professor Mulder.[5] In these experiments the collaboration of the trade unions is seen as a necessary condition for success. On the whole, it seems that the experiments carried out in different forms and by different institutes remain much too isolated from each other, and from the main developments in the system of industrial relations. One gets the impression that traditional issues like wages, other conditions of work, and formal structures of industrial democracy absorb too much of the energy of the different parties involved to leave enough room for experiments of this kind.

Developments in the Field of Collective Bargaining

The wage explosion of 1964 marked the end of the centrally guided wage policy. It is perhaps no exaggeration to state that the collapse of the wage policy was a traumatic experience for many trade union leaders. Suddenly they had to change their policy. They had committed themselves very strongly to uphold the wage policy. Among the elements in their attempts to find a new basic policy and regain the confidence of their members were efforts to change the organizatonal structure of the trade unions, the new stress on developments within the firm, and initiatives to organize the trade union presence at the shopfloor level.

Not surprisingly, however, the main interest was taken up by the developments in the sphere of collective bargaining. The employers' organizations saw the failure of the wage policy in quite a different way from the trade unions. For the trade unions, a fundamental reappraisal of trade union strategy and tactics was necessary. For the employers, collaboration with the government and the trade unions in the post-war period did not necessitate a very different approach to collective bargaining. The new arrangements did not fundamentally change their basic role. Perhaps the only change for them had been that the government and the central trade union organizations helped them to fulfill their main target: control of the wage level. The failure of the wage policy brought the employers back to their traditional role, with their traditional opponents. It is not surprising that from 1964 onwards their main aim seems to have been to re-establish some form of wage policy.

In this aim they found a constant ally in the government. The ministers of Social Affairs could not easily reconcile themselves to the roles of neutral bystanders that the trade unions would have liked to see after 1963. Consequently, between 1963 and 1972 the field of collective bargaining was characterized by attempts by the government to regain a grip on the development of the wage level. In this they were helped by the employers and resisted by the trade unions. Attempts to hand over the responsibility for wage policy to the Foundation of Labor failed. The central trade union federations were not prepared to turn down proposals for wage increases that were accepted by employers in the different industries.

The government attempted to regain some control of the cost of labor by using the power they had possessed since the Second World War to regulate wages, and by introducing new legislation. This led to their complete alienation from the trade unions. The fact that since 1959, with a brief interlude from 1964 to 1966, the government has been based upon the collaboration of Christian Democrats and Liberals (Conservatives) made understanding between government and trade union movement anyhow difficult.

As in most other Western European countries in 1970, the Dutch labor relations system was struck by what has been called the crisis of industrial relations in Europe. A wave of unofficial strikes took place in September 1970, starting in Rotterdam harbor, then spreading everywhere else. The direct motive for the strike (the differential in wages between temporary and permanent workers in shipbuilding) was not that important. The significance of the "revolt from below" was, like the wage explosion of 1963, an indication of widespread feelings of frustration: this was caused by the pressure of inflation in a tight labor market and set against the background of the new revolutionary mood that persisted in the aftermath of the May 1968 revolution in France.

The wave of unofficial strikes prompted an immediate reaction from the trade unions. Firstly, they took over the unofficial strikes, making them legal. Secondly, they decided to take a more radical and more aggressive attitude in their bargaining relationship with the new employers. In 1971 this led to a strike in the building industry, and in 1972 there was a bitter strike in the metal industry, where the socialist metalworkers' union (later part of the *Industriebond NVV*) went on strike against an agreement made with the employers by their confessional and white-collar counterparts. The strikes that took place in the spring of 1973 were another example of this more radical attitude.

However, the 1973 strike movement also marked a change in the attitude of the employers. Up to 1973 they had always been able to count on the open or silent sympathy of the government. In 1973 this was no longer the case. The issue on which the strike took place—the demand for a levelling of wages and salaries—met with a certain amount of sympathy from the Minister of Social Affairs, who was at that time very involved in the preparation of a new coalition government, this time with the socialist party. The employers felt that they had to rely on their own strength and decided on their action accordingly. They organized a fund for mutual assistance and were able to hold their ground. The demand for the levelling of wages was brought down to a harmless proposal for a common study of the issue.

It is interesting to note that this whole development took place at the same time as important changes at the central level. The acceleration of inflation and the first symptoms of the worldwide recession of the 1970s had, in 1972, brought the central organizations and the government around the table once more. For the trade unions this was a very difficult step. They had opposed every deal with the existing center-right government. On the other hand, the emergency gave the trade union leaders the feeling that something should be done. Moreover, the attitude of the Minister of Social Affairs, Mr. Boersma (a former CNV official who had only reluctantly accepted a seat in a center/right government) gave them some confidence.

The trade unions, then, expressed their willingness to make a "social contract" with the employers and the government. This contract would include the trade unions' intention to reduce their wage claims, and the government's promise to show their goodwill by introducing new legislation. To the surprise of nearly everybody (including the trade unions), this proposal was accepted by the government.

An important debate took place inside and outside parliament on the implications of this social contract. A government that makes a deal of this kind with the trade unions (while the employers took a rather passive attitude, watching the bargaining between government and trade union with interest but without commitment) maneuvers parliament into a difficult position. If parliament rejects the deal, the result is a government crisis, with new elections, and there is the added danger of social chaos at the same time. The social contract was criticized by left- and right-wing politicians alike. The contract was seen as a form of corporatism and, in my opinion at least, not without reason. However, it is difficult to see how the government could have acted in any other way.

It was somewhat tragic that the first (and, up to now, only) social contract did not bring industrial peace, but instead the major labor unrest of 1973. The two basic trends—one towards a new centralization and the other in the direction of a harder confrontation between trade unions and employers— interfered with each other.

One (but certainly not the most essential) of the reasons for the change in the government coalition that came about in 1973 was the realization by the responsible political leaders of the Christian Democratic center that a coalition with the socialists was essential for an understanding with the trade unions. The government, headed by the socialist Den Uyl, saw as one of its most important tasks the re-establishment of collaboration between the government, the central federations of trade, unions, and the employers' organizations on the central level. In this the government had limited success. It turned out that improved collaboration with the trade unions was possible, but at the same time it became clear the better understanding with the trade unions was leading to alienation between the government and private enterprise. This alienation showed itself on different occasions.

In the first place, the attempt to make a new social contract in November 1973 failed as a result of a revolt within the employers' organization, where the rank and file refused to accept the agreement. The government then took action and introduced the so-called "Authorization Law" (*Machtigings-wet*) whereby they were given the authority to interfere with all incomes in the country. This rather unprecedented step was taken under the influence of the oil crisis (the Netherlands was threatened by an Arab boycott). In the second place, ten leaders of important companies sent a letter to the Prime Minister at the end of 1975, reproaching the government for its lack of understanding of the problems confronting private enterprise. In the third place, there are examples like the letter from the Board of AKZO to the Prime Minister in 1976, when he had made a statement about the difficulties between AKZO and the ICF (International Chemical Federation).

The pattern of the 1960s, when government and employers sought to find a way to re-introduce a central wage policy, was thus followed by a period where the government came closer to the point of view of the trade unions than to that of the employers. It was, however, difficult to find a solution to the wage problem. The coexistence of these two trends, towards a new centralization and towards confrontation, made the trade unions a rather difficult partner to deal with.

In 1974 an attempt to make a new social contract failed again, although the following round of negotiations did not create any important problems. Undoubtedly, rising unemployment was important here. In 1975 attempts to reach an understanding failed again. The government then decided to make use of the wage law of 1970. The trade unions were very upset at this unfriendly action from a hitherto friendly government. However, the government promised two consolations: a law on profit-sharing (VAD) and a new law on works councils.

The VAD is not a simple profit-sharing plan. The main idea is that workers should have a share in that part of the profits that remains after all other reasonable claims to them have been fulfilled (dividends, management rights, etc.). Realization of this idea is not simple. The former government did not get its project accepted by parliament. The present parliament is now considering a new project. According to this, different schemes will replace the old proposal. One is an obligatory "surplus profit-sharing plan" for all firms. The other amounts to the establishment of a collective fund, governed by trade unions and government representatives and collected through a small increase of company tax.

The new government is reconsidering the relative shares of individual and collective funds and the structure of the collective fund.

It is interesting to note that the Dutch VAD will be the only plan of its kind to be realized so far. We must wait and see how far it will go towards setting a precedent.

Employers point to two main dangers: The VAD (1) could damage the industrial relations climate in the Netherlands in relation to other countries, and (2) will increase trade union power in the firm.

Trade union leaders point out that other countries will follow the Dutch example, and the burden of the VAD will be very light, given the present profit situation of most enterprises. Moreover, shareholders have virtually no power in companies in the Netherlands. In what way, then, could workers holding shares be so important?

In 1977 the frustration of the trade unions over the 1976 wage freeze and the frustration of employers over what they saw as an unfriendly government led to a severe conflict. The immediate reason was the decision of the employers to cease to accept an automatic price index clause in the collective agreements, and their readiness to confront the trade unions on this issue. A solution at the central level proved to be impossible. Bargaining within all industries led to the same stalemate. The government did not intervene, although it offered to help find a solution. Then the trade unions (FNV, CNV and the independent unions alike) decided on a strategy of strikes in selected firms. The employers gave in after four days, and a compromise was reached. For 1977 the automatic clause would be operative. Before the end of the year, a study of the clause would be undertaken. In addition, a common study was announced on a number of so-called unmaterial claims of the trade unions: particularly on the relationship between higher profits and more work.

The trade unions decided to embark upon their own program to keep as many jobs in the economy as possible by introducing schemes for early retirement, five-shift schemes, shortening of working hours. During the bargaining in the early months of 1978, the demand for "job agreements" (arbeidsplaatsenovereenkomsten) became one of the most important issues. Job agreements may include the right of the trade unions to be involved in decisions concerning recruitment and lay-offs, but also could go as far as granting the trade unions the right to have their share in decisions concerning investment. A very interesting proposal was that made by the Industriebond NVV to accept a 1.5 percent decrease in wages of all workers within an enterprise as a means of paying for schemes of work-sharing (as in the case of Hoogovens). They asked the government to pay their, far more important, share in such schemes. In an attempt to remain on speaking terms with the trade unions, the government expressed its limited willingness to finance some elements in such job agreements, as long as they did not become too expensive, or decrease labor mobility.

The elections of 1977 resulted in an important gain for the socialists. This gain was not made at the cost of their main rivals (the Christian Democrats and the Liberals), but was achieved largely because, as a result of the breakdown of the smaller left-wing parties, a continuation of the Christian Democratic-Socialist coalition seemed logical.

The attempted formation of the new center-left coalition cabinet was interesting in so far as the claims of the trade unions (mainly the FNV) played an important role in the bargaining between the two parties. The Prime Minister wanted to develop a socio-economic policy that would make it possible for him to convince the trade unions of the desirability of accepting a wage freeze for the first two years of the new government, in order to reduce unemployment. In this sense, the social organizations played an important role in the political process preceding the installation of the new cabinet. The strong connections between politics and the social economy in the Netherlands were illustrated clearly on this occasion.

When the attempt to make a new center-left coalition failed, a coalition of Christian-Democrats and Liberals was formed. The trade unions (and especially the FNV) voiced their discontent with the new government. Complaints were heard about the "limited social support" of the government.

The trade unions, however, did not change their policy, based upon the acceptance of no increase in real wages in 1978.

The Involvement of the Social Partners in Economic Policy

In more than one respect, the economic scene in the Netherlands presents a rather gloomy picture. The country is highly dependent upon exports—it has to export more than 50 percent of its total output—and is therefore vulnerable to high production costs, including high direct and indirect wage costs, in competitive export markets. Government expenditure and expenditure on social security have expanded vastly during the 1960s. The wage level has developed into one of the highest in Europe. As a consequence of the export of natural gas, the exchange rate of the guilder is high, making export difficult. This state of affairs leads to hesitancy on the part of employers to invest in the Netherlands, thereby adding to the general trend to expand private enterprise in the U.S.A. rather than in Western Europe. In short, the immediate economic prospects are rather depressing.

Under these circumstances, and with the growth of the Labor Party, trade union opinion has gained in relative importance. It is difficult for both the government and the social partners to adapt to this new reality. It means, of course, that the trade unions can no longer dream of beautiful schemes that could be realized if only they had the power. They have to realize that some of their schemes can be put into operation only if they are willing to compromise with the still powerful political center. It is not by accident that a new realism has made itself felt since 1973 within the trade union movement. Symptoms of this new realism are: the willingness to accept wage control in 1974 and 1976; the attempt to make a deal with the government, even before its formation was concluded in 1977; and the readiness to play a role in both the preparation and the execution of the new industrial policy.

The employers have greater difficulty in following this development. They are used to a position of more power, and more influence in the political field. Suddenly they find themselves in a minority position. This does not mean that their influence has suddenly dwindled to nothing— everybody, including the trade unions, knows that the nation needs their collaboration. It is clear, however, that the new formula for tripartite collaboration has not yet been found. The proposal of Mr. De Pous, President of the SER, during a meeting at the Amsterdam Palace in April 1977, to introduce a system of medium-term indicative planning with full involvement of trade unions and employers' organizations, may be seen as a first attempt to find a new form of collaboration. Mr. De Pous is a shrewd observer of existing trends and it is just possible that the social partners may try to embark upon this kind of adventure. However, the wounds of the 1977 conflict are still fresh and painful. It is not impossible that the employers will need a little more time to get used to the new balance of power.

The creation of the new government has of course reduced the alienation between the employers and government. However, because of its limited support in parliament, the cabinet cannot afford to go too strongly against the wishes of the trade unions. Their position remains, therefore, important, although their relationship with the new government is far more uneasy than under the former government.

Notes

1. John P. Windmuller, *Labor Relations in the Netherlands*, Cornell University Press, 1969.
2. M. Van de Vall, *De Vakbeweging in de Welvaartsstaat*, Amsterdam, 1964.
3. *Nota selectieve groei*, 1976.
4. A. Walraven, *Veldexperimenten met industriele democratie*, Assen, 1977.
5. M. Mulder, *The Daily Power Game*, 1977.

5

Sweden

by N. ELVANDER

The aim of this paper is to analyze post-war changes in industrial relations in Sweden with a focus on the roles of trade unions, management and government in the fields of collective bargaining and employee participation. We shall try to determine which pressures for or against change in the systems of collective bargaining and participation have come from the three groups of actors. Recent developments from the beginning of the 1970s to summer 1977 will be emphasized. An attempt will also be made to assess some probable future trends.

Collective Bargaining 1945–77

A GENERAL SURVEY

Since the end of the 1930s the system of industrial relations in Sweden has been regarded as a model for other industrial countries. The famous "Saltsjöbaden Agreement" of 1938—the Basic Agreement between the Swedish Trade Union Confederation (*Landsorganisationen*, LO) and the Swedish Employers' Association (*Svenska Arbetsgivareföreningen*, SAF) on procedures for bargaining and conflict resolution—became a symbol for a system of labor market relations which was characterized by friendly cooperation between strong national organizations, a peaceful climate, reasonable compromises, and freedom from state intervention in the bargaining process. In the 1970s, however, important changes have occurred on the Swedish labor market which are often regarded as the beginning of the end of the "Swedish model." The so-called "Spirit of Saltsjöbaden" is said to be dead, or at least withering away. Is this really true? To what extent have the basic elements in the Swedish model changed? What groups have initiated or opposed changes? In order to answer these questions, the basic elements will have to be identified in a short historical survey of the post-war development. The following characteristics of the Swedish system will be discussed: the structure and the powers of the labor market organizations; the collective bargaining system; the rate of offensive industrial action, including illegal strikes; and the role of the state, including tendencies towards an incomes policy.

With the possible exception of Israel, Sweden seems to have the strongest and most centralized system of interest organizations in the world. This is particularly true of the labor market, which is dominated by a few large top organizations. Most of the employers in the private sector are organized in SAF; nearly 40 percent of Sweden's working population are employed in the 30,000 companies affiliated to the SAF associations. Because SAF was at its founding in 1902 built up as a defense organization, directed against the trade union movement, it had a strong and highly centralized structure from the beginning. Thus the central bodies of SAF have the exclusive power to enter a final decision on a central agreement with the employee organizations. The employers in the public sector also have bargaining organizations with practically the same amount of centralized power as SAF: the National Collective Bargaining Office (*Statens Avtalsverk*, SAV) for civil servants and other state employees, the Collective Bargaining Board for State-owned Enterprises, and the federations of communes and country councils.

When LO was founded in 1898 it was a weak central organization; the formal power to negotiate collective agreements and to decide on offensive industrial action was vested in the national unions. The Basic Agreement in 1938 and a constitutional reform in 1941 indicate the beginning of a process of centralization of formal and real powers which has continued in the postwar period. Centralized bargaining with SAF, starting in the middle of the 1950s, and the creation of large central economic and administrative resources are the main results of this process. A parallel development was a process of integration which reduced the number of national unions from 46 in 1945 to 25 in 1976. At the same time the number of local units was reduced from a maximum of 8,950 in 1948 to less than 1,800. Most of these integration processes occurred in the 1960s, and they were mainly caused by the necessity to adapt the union structure to processes of concentration within business and to the strong centralization on the employers' side. Many small, old fashioned craft unions have been replaced by large industrial unions. An important motive for the merger of small local units into large regional branches was a desire to strengthen the bargaining resources of the branches through regularly employed union officials. Collective bargaining has

become a more and more complicated affair, and the trade union movement
has set up a wide range of societal goals, covering almost the whole political
agenda. Therefore, a process of professionalization has been unavoidable,
particularly on the central LO level.

Needless to say, all these changes towards centralization of decision-
making powers, integration of unions and branches, and professionalization of union staff have created problems of internal democracy. The old
direct democracy in the many small local units has been substituted by
representative bodies in the new large branches, and the system of
consultative referendum on collective agreements was in reality abolished
in the middle of the 1950s as a consequence of the transfer to central
negotiations.[1] Although the political views of the elected officials at different
levels seem to be fairly representative of the views of the rank-and-file,
problems of membership apathy and alienation can easily be found within
the trade union movement, partly as a result of bureaucratization and the
growing distance between the members and their representatives.[2] It should
be pointed out that according to an election study in 1976, as much as 27
percent of the LO members voted for non-socialist parties. This is
astonishing, considering the fact that LO and the Social Democratic Party
have maintained an intimate cooperation from the start, reflected in
collective affiliation of local unions to the party, joint commissions and
campaigns, parliamentary representation of unions through the party, etc.

The same developments can to a large extent be observed within the
whitecollar organizations. It should be pointed out, however, that in these
organizations problems of centralization, integration and internal democracy have not at all been subjected to such a penetrating political science
analysis as in the LO.[3] The biggest white-collar federation is the Central
Organization of Salaried Employees (*Tjänstemännens Centralorganisation*,
TCO). TCO was founded in 1944 as a top organization of white-collar
unions in both private and public service. From the start, TCO has adhered
to a policy of neutrality in relation to the political parties. The membership
of TCO has expanded rapidly, reaching 1,007,000 by December 1976, which
was more than half as large as LO's membership of 1,961,000. TCO is a much
more loose and decentralized organization than LO, which is demonstrated
by the fact that TCO has taken part in central wage negotiations only on one
occasion, in 1956. Special bargaining organizations have been created by the
unions of state civil servants (TCO-S) and local and county council officials
(TCO-K). In 1973 a Private Salaried Staffs' Cartel (*Privattjänstomannakar-
tellen*, PTK) was founded by the three biggest TCO unions in the private
sector and a number of small SACO unions. The membership of TCO
belongs to the middle and lower income brackets, and most TCO unions are
vertically organized according to the industrial union principle, which is
also dominant within LO.

The other large white-collar federation is called the Central Organization
of Swedish Professional Workers (*Sveriges Akademikers Centralorganisa-*

tion, SACO) and was founded in 1947. SACO was based on the horizontal principle, implying in this case that the union members usually have a university degree and belong to some profession. Membership numbers in SACO have been growing rapidly, like in TCO, and particularly so in 1975 when a merger occurred with a minor federation of civil servants (*Statstjänstemännens Riksförbund*, SR). SACO-SR, which is the name of the amalgamated federation, now has 178,000 members. Unlike TCO, SACO-SR has the right and the power to bargain and make central agreements for its member unions in the public sector, whereas members in the private sector usually have their wage negotiations carried out through the PTK.

The large membership of LO, TCO, SACO-SR implies that the so-called organization percentage is very high in the Swedish labor market. With about 90 percent of the blue-collar workers belonging to the LO unions, LO takes a top position in any international comparison. Even more unique is the fact that as much as 75 percent of white-collar workers are organized.[4] Given the fact that no "closed shop" or "union shop" clauses exist on the Swedish labor market, the high percentage of employees who belong to unions must be regarded as exceptional. Of course, this is a tremendous source of strength for the Swedish trade union and white-collar union movements. The three big national federations can speak with considerable authority for almost all wage-earners.

Before 1956, collective bargaining in the private sector was usually carried on at the national union level. On some occasions in the 1940s centralized stabilization agreements, aiming at a wage and price freeze, were concluded at the request of the Social Democratic government. Although inflationary pressures and balance of payment crises sometimes presented as strong arguments for stabilization agreements in the following decades as they had in the 1940s, there was never any question of re-introducing an incomes policy. Another instrument for the necessary wage restraint was created, which was better suited to the traditional Swedish doctrine of "the freedom of the labor market." The new instrument was the system of centralized negotiations between SAF and LO, which was first applied in 1952 and then again in 1956—this time including even the TCO groups. SAF was the driving force behind the introduction of centralized bargaining. Its arguments about economic balance and the necessity to preserve the competitive position of Swedish exports were reluctantly accepted by the LO. Economic considerations of this kind and a loyalty towards the government's economic policy were the decisive motives for LO's acceptance of central agreements in 1956 and afterwards. A secondary motive, which became dominant at the end of the 1960s, was LO's commitment to a so-called solidaristic wage policy. Only by means of a central agreement, through which special supplements for lower wage-earning groups were made possible, could continuing wage differentiation between "strong" and "weak" industrial branches be avoided—such was the argument within the LO.[5]

The central agreements usually cover a two-year period; there has been a variation, however, between one and three years. During the contract period a peace obligation prevails; offensive actions are possible legally only after the cancellation of the contract. On the LO side the draft agreements have the character of recommendations to the national unions, which are usually accepted. If a union tries to withdraw from the central co-ordination—which has sometimes happened—it will be exposed to heavy pressures not only from the LO but also from the SAF, which may forbid its member associations to sign agreements with the unions until negotiations are completed at the central level. It should be pointed out that the national unions and the corresponding employer associations carry on negotiations of their own during the whole period of central bargaining, and particularly after this period. When the national-level agreements are concluded, a period of local bargaining begins where they are applied to local conditions. In this way the whole bargaining process on all levels may take a full year. Given the fact that preparations in the form of statistical analysis, membership polls, discussions in representative bodies, etc., sometimes cover another full year before negotiations start, there is no doubt that modern collective bargaining is a continuous and extremely complicated process; in fact, it has no end and no beginning.

On the whole, the picture of the LO-SAF bargaining system holds true for the private and public white-collar sectors as well. The contract periods are usually the same, and the LO-SAF agreements—which normally precede the other agreements—provide norms for wage-setting in other contract areas as well. In the private sector the two big TCO unions of clerical and technical employees in industry (*Svenska Industritjänstemannaförbundet*, SIF) and supervisors and foremen (*Svenska Arbetsledareförbundet*, SALF) have signed central agreements with SAF since 1957. Now PTK plays about the same role as LO at the central negotiations. As will be demonstrated later, all attempts at coordination of bargaining between LO and the PTK groups had been unsuccessful until the wage round in 1976–77. The main obstacle to co-operation has been different views on wage drift. Whereas wage drift for large groups of LO workers in industry accounts for wage increases which may parallel or even exceed those specified in collective agreements, white-collar employees can hardly take advantage of any wage drift. Therefore, PTK demands full compensation for wage drift. Until 1977, LO dismissed these demands because wage drift was regarded as an expression of a justifiable differentiation of wages, based on hard rationalization of production and on the relative difficulty, danger of accidents, working environment, etc., of various jobs.

In the public sector centralized collective bargaining was a practical reality a decade before civil servants and local government employees were given the full right to negotiate, including the right to strike, in 1966. Before 1966, when SAV took on the function as the government's agency for collective bargaining, a government department negotiated directly with

TCO-S, SACO and the unions of state employees within LO (now united in a single federation called *Statsanställdas Förbund,* SF).[6] Co-ordination between the three civil servants' organizations was almost non-existent in the 1960s but has increased since the beginning of the 1970s, particularly as regards TCO-S and SF. The civil servants, and the local government employees as well, have one great interest in common, namely to get a nominal wage increase which gives compensation for inflation and wage drift in the private sector. Sweden never had any automatic index regulation of wages—unlike the other Nordic countries—and public employees have no wage drift at all. Therefore, nominal wage increases in the public sector are sometimes much larger than those in the private sector. This situation creates mutual irritation, particularly between the SACO and the LO groups. Two big crises on the post-war Swedish labor market were in fact caused by tensions of this kind: open conflicts occurred in the public sector in 1966 and 1971. A brief analysis of these conflicts will give a proper background to the discussion of present problems in the collective bargaining system.

In 1966 the new bargaining system in the public sector had a bad start. Three-year agreements on moderate wage increases were concluded in the private sector after very hard bargaining and the threat of a major LO-SAF conflict. The example was followed by the civil servants, with the exception of the teachers' unions in SACO. Because the teachers' salaries had been left unchanged for some years, negotiations on their high compensation demands were postponed. In the autumn a SACO strike broke out, followed by a big SAV lockout. After a few weeks the conflict was brought to an end when SACO and SAV agreed on a contract which gave the teachers more than twice as much as the LO groups. This was in fact a Pyrrhic victory for SACO; the strike and its outcome caused tremendous harm, particularly within LO. Since that time LO has insisted on coordination of all agreements for the entire economy. The LO groups no longer wanted to lead the bargaining process and let salaried employees put in delayed claims for compensation which make all levelling of wages between blue-collar and white-collar employees impossible.

The crisis in 1966 provoked an intense debate on equality, wage policy, and bargaining structures. The debate led to an agreement between SAF, LO, and TCO through which a common investigation group was established with the task of analyzing the economic role of wages. The group was composed of the research leaders of the three organizations and it was called the EFO group.[7] In 1970 the EFO group published its famous report "Wage Formation and the Economy." Inspired by a Norwegian government committee, the Aukrust Committee, the report constructed an econometric model of the Swedish economy. In this model the economy was divided into two different sectors, one exposed to foreign competition and one protected from it. The "competitive" sector is mainly made up of manufacturing export industries, whereas private services, agriculture, and trade belong to the "sheltered" sector. Within the competitive sector prices are decided by the price level of the world market, and productivity is higher than in the sheltered sector. According to the EFO model, the competitive sector should be the "wage leader," which means that general wage development over the long term is decided by the productivity and price level within that sector. Due to, *inter alia*, union claims for a solidaristic wage policy, a wage increase in the competitive sector proportionate to its productivity growth will extend into the less productive sheltered sector and cause a rise in prices and taxes; this is the price one has to pay for wage solidarity.

The EFO group found that a total cost increase, including wage drift, of about 9 percent a year in both sectors would not damage the capacity of Swedish industry to compete in the world market. It would also be compatible with domestic economic balance, provided that productivity could be increased and the rise in prices reduced in the sheltered sector through greater efficiency. However, this recommendation was based on the international price increases of the 1950s and 1960s, which were in the range of 0.5 to 1.5 percent annually. Of course, the dramatic increase in international inflation in the 1970s has changed the conditions for the application of the model, although the model as such is still a useful instrument for a responsible wage policy that is consistent with economic balance.

The EFO report has played an important role in the Swedish debate on wage policy. It furnished arguments for the wage-earners' organizations when they maintained that there was more room for wage increases than SAF had been willing to admit from the traditional standpoint that wages should depend on average productivity increases in the whole economy. Although the report never was officially adopted by SAF or by LO and TCO, it is a remarkable sign of consensus in perceptions among the parties on the labor market that the EFO model was worked out by the central offices of the three organizations. The report was particularly useful for the TCO unions when they formulated wage policy programs which gave up the traditional comparison with industrial workers' wages, previously so much critized by the LO.

One of the TCO unions that clearly based its wage policy on the EFO report was SIF, which is the biggest and most independent of the TCO unions. SIF broke away from the coordination demanded by the LO and signed a separate one-year agreement with SAF for 1969 before LO reached its own agreement. Coordination was instead pressed upon the civil servants who got a two-year contract with only minor increments; they had to pay the price for the "equality policy," at this time strongly urged by the LO and the Social Democratic government. In the autumn of 1969 SIF, together with SALF, followed up its separate line and negotiated a five-year agreement with SAF, based on the EFO model. This was something quite new. The salaried employees in the private industrial sector spoiled LO's coordination efforts and took the lead in the wage settlements. Although the experiment with such a long contract period as five years was a failure because of rising inflation (consumer prices increased about 12 percent in 1974 compared to 4 percent in 1969), the idea that the white-collar groups in the private sector should play a more independent and leading role in the bargaining process has important implications for the future. These ambitions are borne out by the creation of the PTK in 1973. The fact that already now as much as 40 percent of the total payroll of the SAF-affiliated companies goes to white-collar groups, and the future prospect of salaried employees being a bigger group than manual workers, indicate that PTK will become an even more prominent actor in the Swedish labor market than it is now.

At the beginning of the 1970–71 wage round very strong tensions had developed in the labor market. Wage drift was exceptionally high in 1970 because of a boom in the economy and a wave of wildcat strikes, partly inspired by the large and protracted illegal strike at the Lapland iron-ore fields in the winter of 1969–70. Total wage increases in the contract period 1969–70 amounted to more than 20 percent within the LO-SAF area. For the civil servants it was only 10 percent, and far less for the highly-paid SACO members. Nevertheless, the employers in the public sector demanded a continuation of wage-levelling. When the bargaining started at the turn of 1971, TCO-S and SF got a prompt and positive answer from SAV to their wage demands, particularly as regards the low-paid civil servants. For SACO and SR, however, bargaining as well as mediation were without results, and strikes broke out in February 1971, followed by a major lockout. In the end the conflict embraced nearly 50,000 higher officials in state and municipal services; railway traffic was paralyzed and military officers were notified of an impending lockout. The conflict was regarded by the government and the opposition parties as so damaging to the country's vital interests that it had to be stopped after 40 days through state intervention. Parliament enacted an emergency law that prolonged existing contracts for six weeks.

In June 1971, three-year agreements were concluded in the public sector which provided for a total increase of 22 percent, most of it to the lowest paid groups. The negotiations between LO and SAF did not result in an agreement until after most of the bargaining was concluded in the public sector. LO issued strike warnings and the SAF leaders gave in, probably because they knew that the government was prepared, in case of a large conflict, to legislate on the basis of the mediation proposal. A three-year contract was concluded with a total increase of 28 percent (including social fringe benefits).[8]

The 1970–71 negotiations are exceptional in many ways. The initiative passed from SAF and LO to the parties in the public sector. The coordination desired by LO did not work; obviously, it could be realized only through better co-operation on the employers' side. SAF was put under severe constraint, and its endeavor to attach the agreement with LO to the SIF-SALF five-year contract (with an annual wage increase of 7 percent) failed. The conflict in the public sector, which was in fact the largest conflict on the Swedish labor market since 1945, caused the first compulsory intervention by the state in the history of Swedish industrial relations. The negotiations were politicized even in the sense that the state as employer pursued an independent wage policy and acted as a "wage leader," contrary to the EFO model. The events in 1970–71 indicate a tendency towards state interference in the wage negotiations, although the parties in the public sector acted more carefully in the following years in order to avoid a recurrence of direct state intervention.

Another factor indicating a tendency for state interference is the development in the field of tax policy. The burden of direct taxes in Sweden is probably the heaviest in the world. In the beginning of the 1970s, marginal tax rates became so high even in "normal" income brackets that wage-earners could attain improvements of their real incomes after taxes only through very high nominal wage increases. Thus, taxes tended to become a driving force in a dangerous cost-inflation process, at the same time as mounting inflation caused an automatic tax increase for most wage-earners. In the 1960s SACO alone tried, in vain, to draw public attention to the effect of taxes on real income and inflation. However, in 1973 the problem was observed even within LO. Two economists in the Metal Workers' Union suggested that direct state tax should be reduced in exchange for wage restraint by the unions, and that the state should be compensated through an increase of the so-called employers' charge ("payroll tax"). This idea was carried through in a modified form; after negotiations with LO, TCO and SACO, government and parliament decided in the autumn of 1973 that a basic pension charge should be transferred from taxpayers to employers. In the springs of 1974, 1975, and 1976 agreements of this kind, implying further tax reductions and increases of the payroll tax and some social security charges on employers, were concluded between the government and the organizations. In the so-called Haga negotiations (after the name of the house where the meetings were held) in 1974 and 1975, even the opposition parties participated. The agreements were supported by the Liberals and in 1975 by the Center Party as well. It was the parliamentary deadlock created by the election of 1973 that made it necessary for the government to seek the support of the opposition.[9]

The "Haga policy" of tax revision was intended to make it easier for the unions to accept a policy of wage restraint. This intention was fulfilled in the wage round of 1974 when one-year contracts with a very moderate wage increase were concluded after an unusually short period of negotiations. In 1975, however, wage restraint was hardly visible: two-year contracts were concluded which led to a total increase in wage costs for 1975–76 around 40 percent (including wage drift of 13 percent and a rise in employers' charges of 7 percent). Once again, as in 1971, the contracts covering the public sector were signed before LO and SAF reached their agreements. Attempts at co-ordination between LO and TCO unions failed, mainly because PTK demanded full compensation for the industrial workers' wage drift. Against opposition from the PTK member union SALF (which was in favor of co-operation with LO) the PTK leader Ingvar Seregard enforced a very favorable solution of the compensation issue; this was done with threats of strike after the conclusion of all the other agreements. The growing power of PTK was clearly demonstrated.

The extremely high rise in wage costs in the 1975–76 agreements became a strong argument for the employers when the next wage round started late in 1976. SAF, led by a newly elected and militant chairman, former chief manager of ASEA Curt Nicolin, argued that there was no room for wage increases because wages and employers' charges had exceeded the space according to the EFO model with 18 percent in the 1970s which had resulted in a serious reduction of export industry's market shares, particularly in the last two years. In order to improve the competitive position of exporters, SAF demanded productivity guarantees and some reduction of sickness benefit to counteract an alarming increase in the rate of absenteeism. The last-mentioned demand was dismissed not only by LO, PTK and the mediation commission but also by the new non-socialist government. On the other hand, the government had the same gloomy view of Sweden's economic situation as SAF; in fact, this view was confirmed by an unprecedented series of industrial crises in the winter of 1976 and the spring of 1977. The economic crisis, the change of government, and SAF's unusually tough lead at the beginning of the wage round created a harder climate than ever before on the post-war labor market.

Another notable thing happened in February 1977: LO and PTK succeeded in co-ordinating their wage demands, which meant that LO accepted PTK's principle of full compensation for wage drift. Probably, this astonishing change of position can be explained as an element in a far-reaching strategy, aiming at the consolidation of a "wage-earners' front" against SAF's hard stance, concerning not only the on-going wage round but also coming negotiations on the implementation of the new Co-determination Act. The collaboration between LO and TCO with respect to the participation issue, which is an important part of the background to the sudden emergence of the LO-PTK coalition in 1977, will be discussed later. However, the new wage-earners' coalition was exposed to severe strains in the protracted wage negotiations. In the middle of May the mediation commission presented a final proposal with a modest wage increase, which gave PTK a compensation for wage drift that amounted to 80 percent only. The proposal was accepted by LO and SAF, but rejected by PTK. After two weeks of strikes among 3,000 PTK members and some other offensive actions and after a new mediation round, the parties were prepared to sign a one-year agreement with almost the same content as the mediation proposal. PTK had to give up its claim for total compensation. In fact, it was abandoned for ever; PTK promised—in a declaration together with LO on conditions for further cooperation between the two organizations—not to raise the compensation issue again. Obviously, LO's moderation was more successful than PTK's militancy. The most important outcome of the 1976–77 negotiations in the private sector is, however, that the newly created LO-PTK coalition remains intact.

Negotiations in the public sector did not come to an end until August. In spite of some very high wage demands from neglected groups, such as the nurses, agreements were reached on a total increase in wage costs for 1977 around 10 percent. This is about the same as the average wage increase in the private sector, but the rate of inflation for 1977 was higher. As a result of Sweden's depressed economic situation, large groups of wage-earners have experienced a decline in real incomes for the first time in many years.

The image of Sweden as the land of labor peace *par excellence* has been revised to some extent during the past ten years. As Table 5.1 shows, the rate of legal labor disputes was very low between 1946 and 1966, and particularly since the beginning of central negotiations in 1956. In 1945, 120,000 metal workers were striking for four and a half months, inspired by Communist agitation against the policy of wage restraint during the war years. Foreshadowed by the teachers' conflict in 1966, a period of labor unrest started at the end of 1969 with the large wildcat strike among the mine workers at the state-owned LKAB iron mines in Lapland. A series of minor wildcat strikes occurred in 1970 and another in 1974–75.

In 1975 a large illegal strike took place in the forestry industry, partly owing to Communist agitation against employers and the national union as well. The mounting rate of labor disputes indicates that disagreements between labor and management have increased since the end of the 1960s. Another sign of this development is the fact that the government has been compelled to appoint special mediation commissions for all wage-rounds since 1964—which was not the rule earlier—and that the country has been on the brink of a major labor conflict on many occasions from 1966 to 1977.

What are the main reasons for the tensions that are revealed in the increasing rate of labor conflicts? The answer to this question has to be preliminary because thoroughgoing scientific analyses are still missing. The two conflicts in the public sector in 1966 and 1971 can be said to indicate that the equality policy, carried out jointly by the Social Democratic government and the LO through, *inter alia*, a levelling of high wages and salaries, has resulted in rising disagreement and an increase in the risk of conflicts. This is true not only for the public service sector but also as regards some highly-paid groups of manual and white-collar workers in industry. The solidaristic wage policy has been successful, particularly since the end of the 1960s. The range of wages in the LO-SAF sector today is less than half what it was in 1959. The very success of the wage solidarity policy, especially during periods of economic prosperity, seems to have contributed to labor market tensions. In the years preceding the LKAB strike of 1969–70, for instance, the relative wage position of the miners compared to other workers had declined sharply. Another aspect of the miners' strike was, however, a distrust among the members of the union leaders. Such distrust was also revealed in the

Table 5.1.   Number of Working Days Lost due to Industrial Action, 1946–76
(in thousands)

Year	Total Numbers	Days Lost through Illegal Conflicts
1946	27	
1947	125	
1948	151	
1949	21	
1950	41	
1951	531	
1952	79	
1953	582	
1954	24	
1955	159	
1956	4	
1957	53	
1958	15	
1959	24	
1960	18	
1961	2	
1962	5	
1963	25	
1964	34	
1965	4	0.2
1966	352	0.7
1967	0.4	0.1
1968	0.8	0.5
1969	112	64
1970	157	157
1971	839	27
1972	11	8
1973	12	12
1974	58	23
1975	398	343
1976	26	19

Source: Statistics from SAF.

Note: No statistics on illegal conflicts were available until 1965.

forest workers' strike in 1975. In both cases these sentiments were skillfully exploited by the Communists. Dissatisfaction over the centralization of the collective bargaining process and a feeling that the union leadership is bureaucratic, distant, and difficult to influence is sometimes a contributing factor to wildcat strikes. On some occasions in the beginning of the 1970s, such sentiments were instigated or exploited by extremist Communist groups, sometimes inspired by the student revolt of the late 1960s.[10]

Sociological studies have indicated that an important cause of wildcat strikes before 1969 was a growing dissatisfaction with the working environment. The wave of intense rationalization that swept through Swedish industry after the Second World War led to more monotonous work processes and a more hectic working pace. The piece rate system became more and more unpopular; piece rate setting was a common source of wildcat strikes. There is today a widespread endeavor within the trade union movement to abolish piece-work, and even management is looking for other forms of incentive. One possible remedy against wildcat strikes seems to be doing away with piece work and making other improvements in the working environment within an effective system of employee participation. However, according to a recent LO report most illegal strikes are now caused by purely economic motives. The strikers want to press for higher payments in the local bargaining than the central agreements allow. The picture is complicated, indeed, and there is no simple remedy against wildcat strikes.[11]

SUMMARY AND CONCLUSIONS

This survey of post-war trends in collective bargaining shows that the initiative for the most important change, the introduction of central agreements, came from SAF. In other respects SAF played a relatively passive role, with the exception of the initiatives in connection with the wage round of 1976–77. Although SAF's proposals for productivity guarantees and reduction of some social benefits were rejected, the parties agreed on further investigation of these problems. SAF's initiatives may result in future changes in the object of negotiations, aiming at productivity increases.

The bargaining system has remained basically unchanged since the central negotiations started in the middle of the 1950s. Those changes that have occurred were initiated from the union side: co-ordination between LO and PTK, the tax revision agreements with the government, the introduction in some branches of monthly salary instead of the piece-work system, etc. It is in the nature of things that the unions should be the active party in changes of this kind. However, the resistance from SAF has not been particularly strong. There is still a basic consensus between labor and management on the rules of the bargaining game which helps SAF to accept minor changes that are demanded by the unions. The joint initiative to the EFO report—the most important theoretical innovation in post-war wage policy—is a remarkable expression of this consensus.

Until 1971 the role of the state in the bargaining process was just as passive as it should be according to the "Swedish model." The direct intervention in 1971 was exceptional and it will probably not be repeated. The fact remains, however, that the central government—and the local and county council authorities as well—have come to play more and more important roles as employers. It is now generally accepted that the public sector should not act as a wage-leader, as it did in the 1970–71 wage round. With almost 1,300,000 employees the public sector has, however, a strategic position in employment and wage policies, and the public employers can to a large extent decide the general profile of wage distribution, for instance in a levelling direction. Therefore, some degree of co-ordination of wage policies and bargaining between the public and the private sectors is necessary. Much remains to be done in the way of better coordination of this kind.

The most notable innovation by the state in connection with wage negotiations in the 1970s is the "Haga policy" of tax revision. The first agreements were regarded by many critics as a threat to the right of free bargaining and as a beginning of some kind of incomes policy, weaving together taxes and wages. The Haga policy could also be criticized as an encroachment on the right of politicians to decide on tax policy. Before 1973, tax policy was regarded as the exclusive domain of the political parties, and the labor market organizations were not invited by the government to influence it in such a direct way as was done in the Haga negotiations.[12] However, apprehension founded on principle had to give way to the political necessity to reduce inflationary pressures through wage restraint and attain broad political agreement in an unstable parliamentary situation.

LO and TCO repeatedly declared that the tax policy agreements should not be regarded as a permanent element in wage policy or as a beginning of an incomes policy. It was also stated by the organizations, and the non-socialist parties as well, that improvisations of this kind should come to an end when a more permanent solution of the tax issue is created. The new non-socialist government has promised to carry through such a solution, and it has already proposed a partial reform in 1979, implying an index regulation of income-tax scales. In this way, the automatic increase in marginal tax rates due to inflation can be avoided. The proposal is rejected by the Social Democratic opposition and the LO because it gives more tax "reductions" to highly-paid groups than to low-wage workers. The principle of protection against inflationary tax increase has been accepted, however, by TCO, although this position is somewhat modified in recent statements. The "wage-earners' front" is still incomplete as regards tax policy because the members of LO and the highly-paid TCO groups have different interests in this case. Probably, LO will claim compensation for its lowly paid members for the tax benefits in higher income brackets that are produced by an index regulation. The connection between tax policy and wage negotiations cannot be totally removed by the new tax system. Somehow, the state will always interfere in wage policies on the labor market through its tax policy, although its interference may be less direct and less frequent in the future than it was during the "Haga period."

To what extent have the basic elements in the Swedish system of labor market relations changed in recent years? Can the Swedish model survive? Let us sum up by returning to these questions.

As far as the system of collective bargaining is concerned, no basic changes have occurred and no immediate threat to the Swedish model can be observed. The structure and the powers of the organizations remain intact. The high percentage of union membership and the authority of the leadership are strong guarantees against disruptive tendencies and a decay of the bargaining system, followed by direct state intervention. Problems of internal democracy within the wage-earners' organizations are admitted by the leaders and will probably be met by, *inter alia*, a stronger emphasis on local bargaining rights. Together with improvements of the wage systems and the working environment, a certain degree of decentralization of the bargaining system within the frame of central negotiations will probably be one of the most important remedies against wildcat strikes. There is nothing inevitable in the recent trend of labor conflicts; the picture may be changed through reforms which give the employees more influence on their wages and working conditions. The top leaders of the labor market organizations are well aware of the tremendous damage that a major conflict would do to Sweden's depressed economy, to the system of free bargaining, and to the welfare of the membership. This is clearly demonstrated by LO's cautious behavior and PTK's retreat in the wage negotiations of 1977.

Given this pattern of continuing basic stability in the Swedish system, the risk of large-scale state intervention may seem insignificant. In case of a major conflict, government and parliament would probably interfere after a while through legislation on the basis of the final mediation proposal. On the other hand, this prospect is one of the strongest guarantees against the outbreak of a large conflict. The parties want to preserve the "freedom of the labor market," and they know that once a major state intervention has occurred a tendency to irresponsibility and reliance on future interference may develop. The resistance to all forms of state intervention in the bargaining system is specific to Sweden, even in a Nordic perspective. The relatively limited formal power of the mediation procedure, compared to the other Nordic countries, the absence of compulsory arbitration of the Norwegian type, and the strong distaste for the Danish model of conflict resolution through legislation *in casu*, all underline the strength of the Swedish tradition of freedom from state intervention.[13]

Concerning future tendencies towards an incomes policy, the development in the field of tax policy since 1973 indicates a trend in this direction. Although the tendency will probably be modified through the recent initiatives of the non-socialist government, it cannot be disregarded when future prospects are evaluated. More important is, however, the risk that a continuation of the present economic crisis in Sweden—characterized by a very negative balance of payments, a weakening of the competitive position of exporters, and a series of structural crises in the main export industries— will call for a more far-reaching incomes policy. The last OECD report on Sweden's economic situation (July 1977) gives a clear warning in this direction. It depends on the strength and realism of the labor market parties if such a development is to be avoided.

The relatively bright prospects of the bargaining system may, however, be disturbed by political conflicts concerning some aspects of employee participation or co-determination, particularly as regards capital formation. A major political controversy on the current issue of wage-earners' funds may "spill over" into the arena of collective bargaining and cause a deterioration in industrial relations which may become a threat to the "Swedish model." If the concept of the Swedish model is taken to include even a basic consensus on a mixed economy with a large private sector, a system of exclusive trade-union ownership of all big companies in the present private sector may be regarded as incompatible with the concept according to both definitions. On the other hand, a system of far-reaching participation, including wage-earners' influence on capital formation, can be seen as a condition for labor peace and thus for a preservation of the present bargaining system. It is a paradox, indeed, that participation may entail the destruction as well as the survival of the Swedish model as regards collective bargaining.

Employee Participation 1945–77

THE ISSUES OF INDUSTRIAL AND ECONOMIC DEMOCRACY

Employee participation in decision-making at the company level, which is usually called industrial democracy, was not an important issue in the period 1945–70, either in Swedish politics or in negotiations in the labor market. In the 1970s, on the other hand, industrial democracy came in the forefront in both arenas. What are the reasons for this change? To what extent were participation reforms initiated or opposed by trade unions, management, and the political parties? What are the effects of participation and what are the future prospects?

At the end of the Second World War there was a short period of active interest in participation reforms. The main result of the debate was an agreement between SAF and LO on the creation of works councils, which was signed in 1946. Later on, similar agreements were concluded between TCO and SACO on the one hand and SAF and the public employers on the other. The joint councils had narrowly defined consultative functions only, and their primary task was "to maintain continuous collaboration between employer and employees in order to achieve the best possible production." The wording of the LO–SAF agreement is characteristic of the attitudes of management and labor at this time; productivity was regarded as the underlying motive for participation reforms. For a long time the unions were content with a limited influence on management and gave priority to wage increase through high productivity and rapid economic growth. In 1966, LO, TCO, and SAF signed new agreements on works councils. The areas of information and consultation were expanded to, for instance, personnel policy, a limited right of delegation of decision-making from management to the councils was created, and the formal position of the unions in relation to the councils was strengthened. The practical outcome of these changes was, however, insignificant. The extent of the councils' influence was still largely dependent upon the employers' benevolence. Sociological studies indicated that the works councils had a limited importance in the decision-making processes of the companies.[14]

At the end of the 1960s growing discontent with the working environment, structural transformation, etc., among industrial workers and a general radicalization of the political climate led to intensified claims for participation reforms among union leaders. Several LO unions expressed dissatisfaction with the new agreement on works councils, and radical demands for co-determination were raised in a committee on industrial democracy which was appointed by LO in 1969. Managerial prerogatives came under attack.

The elements of these prerogatives were concentrated in the famous Article 32 of the SAF statutes, according to which collective agreements signed by SAF member companies must contain a clause conceding to the employer the right to hire and dismiss workers freely, to direct and allot work, and to use workers regardless of whether or where they are organized. There were similar reservations in the laws concerning the bargaining rights of central and local government employees. In fact, the principles of Article 32 covered the entire labor market. The principle of managerial prerogatives had also been stated by the Labor Court on several occasions since 1933. Although the employers supreme right to engage and dismiss workers had been somewhat reduced through central agreements, beginning with the Saltsjöbaden Agreement in 1938 and followed by another contract in 1964, the unions had so far failed to bring about any real change in the power relationship between labor and management. Around 1970, a total abolition of Article 32 became a primary union objective.

The TCO congress of 1970 and the LO congress of 1971 mark the beginning of the new era. There was an almost total meeting of minds between the two confederations in their approach to industrial democracy. TCO approved the principle that industrial democracy must be given equal status with wage and employment conditions in the work of trade union organizations. According to LO, industrial democracy must be regarded as an essential part of the democratization of society as a whole. LO stated that equality between labor and management could only be achieved through legislation which removed Article 32 and the legal practices created on the basis of this article. The two organizations demanded that the right to bargain should be extended to include personnel management, work organization, etc., and that the employer's traditional right of precedence in interpreting agreements should be limited or abolished. Security of employment should be improved through legislation restricting the employer's right to dismiss and lay off employees. Finally, the LO and TCO congresses put aside all hesitation on the issue of employee representation on the boards of companies. The problem of double loyalties, which was earlier regarded as a decisive argument against union representation on the boards, was no longer seen as essential because all the other participation reforms would strengthen the position of employees. In the context of a general democratization, a minority representation could be regarded as a matter of justice and as a valuable channel of information.

The new demands from TCO and LO are remarkable in many ways. Suddenly, a far-reaching radicalization is demonstrated. Previous hesitation in relation to union responsibility for the management of companies is swept aside. Legislation is demanded on matters which were previously regarded as proper objectives for collective bargaining agreements. Claims for co-determination supersede the earlier consultation model. How was this drastic change in attitudes possible? Probably the most important motive power was the spontaneous dissatisfaction among industrial workers, and salaried employees as well, with a trying working environment and increasing insecurity of employment in a period of intensified structural transformation, implying production cutbacks and closing down of whole companies. The union leaders were forced to act by membership opinion. The LKAB conflict and other wildcat strikes in 1970 may have underlined the strength of this opinion. It should also be kept in mind that labor unrest and demonstrations with radical claims for a general democratization of society were an international phenomenon at this time. The obvious radicalization of the political debate on participation in Sweden should be seen in this international perspective. The union leaders were probably influenced by this debate, particularly when demands for industrial democracy were raised in several political party statements around 1970.[15]

The demands for new legislation from LO and TCO were promptly met by the Social Democratic government. A number of investigation commissions were appointed. Most important was the Commission on Labor Law, popularly known as the "Article 32 Commission," which was appointed in the fall of 1971. The outcome of commission deliberations and the final reforms decided by parliament were to a large extent identical with union demands. The decisive influence of LO and TCO on participation reforms in the 1970s is obvious. The objections of SAF and its insistence on a continuation of collective bargaining agreements instead of legislation were disregarded. The reform proposals were largely supported by the opposition parties.

The most important new laws are the following:[16]

1. *Laws on representation of employees on the boards of private companies and public agencies (1972, 1974).* On an experimental basis, employees in larger private companies and economic associations were allowed to elect two representatives on the board. Elections are carried out through the local unions. The employee representatives have the same rights and obligations as other board members except that they may not participate in deliberations on issues concerning industrial action and collective agreements. In 1974,

similar representation was introduced for central government employees. Since 1972 a number of municipalities and county councils have pilot projects giving employees the right to attend the meetings of politically appointed boards and committees; the representatives are not allowed, however, to take part in any decisions. As regards representatives on the boards of central government agencies, they may not participate in decisions concerning the aims and direction of the agency's activities. The idea is that public employees should not interfere in the functions of political democracy, which means that they are not allowed to influence issues that fall within the domain of elected political officials.

In 1978 the right of employee representation on the boards of all companies employing more than 25 persons was made permanent.

2. *Security of Employment Act and Promotion of Employment Act (1974).* Through these laws the employer's right to dismiss workers was finally broken. An employee can only be dismissed on "reasonable" grounds such as shortage of work. Priority rules in cases of grounded dismissals, for instance the seniority principle, are specified, and older employees are entitled to a longer period of notice. According to the Promotion of Employment Act, the employer is obliged to give notice to trade unions before dismissals or layoffs and to negotiate with labor market authorities and unions in order to find solutions for older and disabled employees in particular.

3. *The Workers' Protection Act (1974).* In order to meet union demands for an improvement in the working environment, new rules on workers' protection were enacted in 1974. The new law emphasizes the importance of collaboration between labor and management on industrial safety. The local unions and the safety stewards have gained a stronger position and a greater direct responsibility for worker protection. Through their representatives on safety committees, employees now have much greater influence over working environment issues than previously. This development will continue through a new Working Environment Act which came into effect in 1978. Working environment is here defined much more broadly than industrial safety is defined today, including such things as work organization, work hours, and adaptation of work to psychological human needs.

4. *The Codetermination Act* (Medbestämmandelagen, MBL, 1977). The main attack on management's prerogatives came through the Codetermination Act, which was decided by parliament in 1976 on the basis of a joint minority report from the LO and TCO representatives on the "Article 32 Commission" and came into effect in January 1977. The new law replaces earlier labor laws on mediation, collective bargaining, and right of association. It also supersedes most of the collaboration agreements between the parties on the labor market, including the Saltsjöbaden Agreement. The

provisions of earlier laws have been modernized and worked into the new law. The position of the employees is considerably strengthened, however, through a new legal framework for collective agreements between the employers and the local trade union branches on participation in decision-making. Such matters as the direction and allotment of work, personnel management, supervision of work, and working environment are now negotiable, and contracts can be concluded in this area. By means of the so-called residual right to industrial action, the parties may resort to industrial action if matters concerning co-determination are not regulated in a collective agreement. Provided that union demands for a participation agreement are presented at tne same time as wage negotiations, there will be no peace obligation on participation issues until an agreement is concluded, even if a wage contract is already signed. Obviously, the residual right to industrial action may become a powerful weapon in the hands of the unions.

The power of the local union branches is strengthened in many other ways. The so-called priority of interpretation in case of disagreement on the interpretation of a collective agreement is transferred from the employer to the union. The primary obligation to negotiate on matters where the employers have the right to decide requires that the employer initiates negotiations with trade unions before making any changes in management or supervision of work. If the parties are unable to reach a local agreement, the negotiations may be moved up to the central level. The employer is required to provide employees with information on the company's production plans, economic situation, personnel policy, etc., without the trade union having to request it.

Finally, it should be added that the principles of the Codetermination Act have been applied to the public sector through a special act and a basic agreement. The same kind of guarantees against union encroachment on the area of political decision-making are constructed as in the laws on employee representation on the boards of central and local government agencies. However, the problem of drawing a demarcation line between political democracy and public employees' demands for democracy on the job is by no means finally solved. It can be questioned, for instance, whether such negotiations between the civil servants' unions and government departments on budget issues which have been going on since 1977 under the provision of the primary obligation to negotiate are compatible with the basic constitutional principle of sovereignty of political democracy. There is also an obvious risk that the efficiency of public administration is severely hampered by unwieldy forms of co-determination. In many agencies the local unions are now negotiating with representatives of the agency board on a vast area of management issues.

The Codetermination Act was decided by parliament before the elections of 1976 and the change of government. The basic elements of the government bill were supported by the non-socialist parties, particularly the Liberals, but the Center Party and the Conservatives had some reservations in line with SAF's critical remarks. On some details, the opposition parties were able to amend the bill with the help of the lot (the method that it was necessary to adopt to break the parliamentary deadlock after the 1973 election); thus, damages against employees taking part in wildcat strikes were sharpened. The Social Democratic government immediately appointed a new labor law commission with the task of examining some remaining problems, following up the implementation of the new law, and proposing an abolition of the amendments. Certainly, the political debate on co-determination will continue for a long time. Finally, it should be pointed out that central negotiations between SAF, LO and PTK concerning a national agreement on co-determination have been going on since autumn 1976. No result can be expected within the near future. According to a provisional contract of December 1976, the old collaboration agreements are still used.

As regards the practical effects of the participation reforms on, for instance, management efficiency, the role of the unions, and the attitudes and behavior of employees, it is probably too early to say anything precise. According to preliminary reports from sociological studies of the implementation of the Codetermination Act, no important changes have occurred so far.[17] However, some effects of the Security and Promotion of Employment Acts are already visible. During the present recession, beginning in 1975, unemployment in Sweden has been very low on an international comparison. This is partly due to the fact that it was possible through these laws to find work assignments, retraining opportunities, etc., for people who would otherwise have been unemployed. On the other hand, the admission of young people to apprentice jobs may in some cases be blocked by job security for older workers, particularly in small, un-unionized firms.

The picture of participation reforms would be incomplete, however, if nothing were said about "shop-floor participation," i.e. socio-technical experiments and reforms which were introduced even before the enactment of the new laws. In this field SAF played the most active part. In the 1960s, management began to accept the idea that work satisfaction should be included as an explicit goal of enterprises and always taken into account in the organization and designing of jobs and in personnel management. Jobs should be so designed that they give the worker a meaningful and stimulating activity, thus building into the job a natural incentive for productivity. Job enlargement and parity self-steering groups were seen as promising solutions. Experiments of this kind were carried out, for instance, in Volvo and Saab, and often with good results. According to the SAF view, a condition for success is that organization plans are generated within the management-controlled "line system" and that workers' participation is fully integrated in the ordinary work organization. Socio-technical ideas and reforms have been supported by the trade union movement. Part of the research and experimental work has been carried out through the joint SAF-

LO-TCO Development Council. The basic attitude of the trade unions is, however, to regard socio-technical reforms as part of the industrial democracy and as tied to changes in the power structure. The employers prefer "practical co-operation" and "everyday democracy" on the shopfloor to "heavy" formal procedures and structural re-organization, whereas the unions insist upon far-reaching changes of power relations, with the Co-determination Act as the main instrument.[18]

All the participation reforms which have so far been discussed here express the idea that the employees' influence should be based on their work. This is the micro dimension, industrial democracy. However, another dimension of participation came to the forefront of political debate in the middle of the 1970s. It was the societal macro dimension of "economic democracy," according to which employee participation should also be based on a collective ownership of capital and a wage-earners' share in the growth of private corporation capital. The idea of economic democracy, which might properly be called *Socialism*, was initiated by the LO at the same time as the radicalized ideas of industrial democracy. Thus, demands for a change in the power relation between the parties on the labor market were combined with the demand for a change in the existing structure of ownership and capital formation in the whole economy. Why did socialism come into focus in this way? To what extent were participation reforms or reform proposals, based on employee ownership of capital, initiated or opposed by trade unions, management, and the political parties? What are the future prospects for economic democracy?[19]

Proposals for employees profit-sharing on an individual basis were initiated by the Liberal Party on many occasions since the end of the 1940s. However, the Liberal idea of creating more harmonious industrial relations and an increase in productivity through profit-sharing was rejected by the parties on the labor market and the other political parties as well. LO and SAF did not want any state interference in labor market relations through legislation of this kind. In LO's opinion, individual profit-sharing was particularly distasteful because it was regarded as a threat to the solidaristic wage policy. Such a system would be unduly favorable to employees in profitable companies; trade union efforts at wage-levelling between high-profit and low-profit industrial branches would be impeded, and the necessary mobility on the labor market would be made more difficult. On the other hand, problems inherent in the solidaristic wage policy became a decisive motive when LO finally took an initiative of its own concerning employee influence on capital formation.

Along with equality goals, the desire to achieve high productivity and rapid economic growth was a main driving force behind the wage policy of solidarity. In the 1950s and 1960s LO had a positive attitude toward industrial rationalization and mobility of the labor force. Large profits should remain in the sector of the economy with the greatest competitive power, thereby helping this sector to consolidate and expand more rapidly.

The disadvantage from the LO's point of view was, however, that the employees who have helped generate the earnings of the most profitable companies did not receive a "reasonable" share of these profits. The highly-paid LO members have seen their relative position compared to other LO groups become worse at the same time as the companies they work for have earned high profits. The desire to solve the inherent conflict between the solidaristic wage policy on the one hand and the wish to achieve a more equitable structure of ownership on the other finally became a strong motive for the trade union movement to create a system of wage-earner investment funds on a national branch level.

Proposals for industry-wide funds were discussed at the LO congresses in 1951, 1961, and 1966. On the first occasion, the idea was that the funds should be used directly for wage-equalization purposes. In the 1960s, this idea was discarded in favor of proposals for branch rationalization funds which were to be established as instruments for an industrial policy through collective agreements between unions and employer associations. However, all these proposals were disregarded by the majority of the LO congresses. Not until 1971 did the LO congress decide to authorize a study of the issue of employee influence on capital formation. The task of preparing a report for the next congress in 1976 was delegated to a study group within LO's research department, led by the economist Dr. Rudolf Meidner. The following goals were indicated in the directives to the study group: to solve the problem of "excess profits" in profitable branches; to counteract the concentration of property that followed from autonomous capital formation within the companies; and to increase the influence of wage-earners on economic processes.

The congress decision and the preparation of the report did not attract much interest until 1974. In that year, the issue of wage-earners' funds suddenly came into focus. This was partly due to the rising interest in industrial democracy within the trade union movement and in political debate as well. A more direct impulse to an intensified debate on employee influence on capital formation was created by the fact that many large companies earned so-called excess profits during the boom of 1974. When the Meidner report, which was published in August 1975, was discussed among a selection of LO members in the autumn of 1975, it was clearly shown that the problem of excess profits was regarded as one of the main motives for a reform in line with the proposal. Another current aspect was the extremely uneven distribution of shares on the Swedish stock market. According to the Meidner report, the holding of shares is increasingly concentrated in the hands of a few private persons and institutions (investment companies, family foundations, insurance companies, etc.). This aspect of the problem of capital formation was strongly emphasized in the campaign for wage-earners' funds, which was launched jointly by LO and the Social Democratic Party in the autumn of 1977.

Equality aspects of this kind were dominant in the trade union debate.

The idea that some kind of wage-earners' funds could be a valuable, and even necessary, contribution to the formation of future investment capital was not paid much attention to until 1978. However, this idea was in reality an important motive for Meidner and the LO leaders. In particular, it was stressed in public statements by Olof Palme and other leading Social Democrats. No doubt, an understanding of the necessity of creating a broader base for capital formation in relation to future investment requirements will be of decisive importance when a solution of the fund issue is finally reached.

The Meidner proposal rejects the idea of using wage-earners' funds for wage-equalization purposes. The problems of excess profits and the solidaristic wage policy are reduced to secondary motives for a reform. If earnings from the most profitable companies were transferred to less profitable companies in order to give them a greater capacity to pay wages, this would help maintain production in those parts of the economy where Sweden's competitive ability in international terms is limited. Instead of subsidizing unprofitable enterprises, the fund system should promote the formation of capital in industrial sectors that are successful on international markets. The profits should remain in the companies where they originated, but they should not stay in the hands of either the existing private capital owners or individual employees. The solution of the capital formation issue has to be collective ownership of shares.

According to the Meidner report, large private companies should contribute to wage-earner investment funds in the form of so-called compulsory directed stock issues. The profits are not removed from the company but issued in the form of new shares of corresponding value. How rapidly ownership of a company will shift in favor of employees will depend on the size of profits and how large a percentage of profits is set aside for the fund. The report suggests that 20 percent of profits are transferred each year to the funds. After a few decades the majority of shares in big companies may be owned by the funds. The number of funds is not settled, but a system of numerous branch funds or regional funds is suggested. The alternative of having a central fund is rejected as leading to an undesirable concentration of power, whereas a system of company funds is regarded as incompatible with the trade union philosophy according to which solidarity should not be limited to one's own company. The dividends earned on employee-owned capital are to be paid into a so-called central equalization fund. This money can partly be used for the benefit of all wage-earners in the form of training for employee representatives on the boards of companies, research in the field of the working environment, and so on. In this way, employees in the sectors of the economy which are excluded from the fund system—i.e., small private companies, consumers' cooperative organizations, and all public agencies and companies—will derive some advantage from the system. The influence of the employees on the companies within the fund system is channelled through representatives on the board, jointly elected by the local unions and the branch funds. The boards of all funds are elected jointly by all national unions, but the branch funds may also have political representatives elected by public authorities.

After some revision, the Meidner report was accepted by the LO congress in June 1976, although with further modifications. For instance, the size limit of companies included in the fund system, which was tentatively set at 50-100 employees in the original report, was left undecided. This time, the idea of wage-earners' funds received strong support at the LO congress. The radicalization of active trade union opinion was revealed by the fact that many congress delegates wanted to include even small business in the system. Therefore, the issue of a size limit was not settled in the congress decision. To a large extent, the LO proposal had the character of a vague outline.

Even more sketchy than the LO report, however, was a report on wage-earner influence on capital formation which was discussed at the TCO congress in 1976. Several alternatives were considered, including a system of individual shares, but some precedence was given to collective ownership. A collective system was regarded as a more effective instrument for wage-earners' influence on the economic decisions of private companies than individual profit-sharing. However, TCO has demonstrated less interest than LO in the societal macro dimension. The issue of wage-earners' funds is seen from the point of view of industrial democracy rather than economic democracy.

The LO proposal became one of the most hotly debated issues in the election campaign of 1976. It was heavily criticized not only by SAF and some independent economic experts but particularly by the non-socialist parties. According to the critics, such a system of "trade union socialism" would result in a dangerous concentration of enormous economic and political power in the hands of a few central trade union leaders. LO's desire to achieve decentralization rather than centralization of power was disregarded. The government and the Social Democratic Party were put into an awkward position. They were unable to give a clear answer to the opposition parties' demand for a declaration of the Social Democratic Party's position to the LO proposal. It is astonishing that the party did not discuss the issue in 1975–76, because the party congress in September 1975 adopted a new program which emphasized "the third stage of democratic development" as an immediate task. Political and "social" democracy (i.e. the welfare state) are already accomplished; now the time has come to carry out economic democracy, which implies not only public planning and a reinforcement of the co-operative sector but also a wage-earners' share in the growth of private corporation capital. Despite this programmatic declaration of principle, Olof Palme and other leaders were compelled to give evasive answers to opposition attacks on the LO proposal.

The obvious lack of co-ordination between LO and the Social Democratic Party was partly due to the fact that the issue of wage-earners' funds at the same time was under deliberation in a public commission. The commission was appointed in 1975 by the government in accordance with a promise to the Liberal Party in the first Haga agreement in 1974. In the election campaign of 1976, the Social Democrats tried in vain to avoid the socialization debate by referring to this commission, which was supposed to be investigating the fund problem for many years to come. Olof Palme repeatedly declared that the fund issue could not be solved until the beginning of the 1980s and should be thoroughly discussed in such a way that broad parliamentary support for a good solution could be obtained. However, tactical considerations of this kind were not the only reason for the Social Democratic reluctance to go along with LO's offensive line. Objections founded on principle were also raised in the internal debate, mainly concerning guarantees for a broad public influence on capital formation; in fact, the LO report left this important problem unresolved.

Indeed, LO was far ahead of the party. Never before did the two branches of the labor movement appear so divided in an election campaign, as they did in 1976. After the election, the LO president Gunnar Nilsson publicly deplored the failure of LO and the Social Democratic Party to co-ordinate their ideological positions on the issue of economic democracy. He suggested that the party's defeat and loss of governmental office partly was caused by its defensive and unclear position.[20] Opinion polls and election studies, indicating very limited public knowledge of and interest in the LO proposal and an increasingly negative attitude during the election campaign towards collectivism and trade union power, do not contradict this statement.[21]

The LO proposal for wage-earners' funds can be criticized from many different points of view. This is not the place for a detailed account of all the arguments that have been directed against the plan. However, some of the principal lines in the great debate and some alternative solutions, which were presented by non-socialist as well as Social Democratic debaters, will be briefly outlined. My own opinion on the weak points of the LO plan, and of some objections against it as well, will not be concealed.[22]

The non-socialist points of attack can be divided into economic and political arguments. The main economic argument is that a realization of the LO plan would lead to a drastic fall in stock market prices because the present shareholders would try to sell out shares in those companies that are supposed to be included in the fund system. A collapse of the stock market may result in a much swifter transfer to full-fledged trade union socialism than Meidner envisaged, followed by economic and political chaos. The administrative guarantees against such a development which are mentioned in the LO report are either insufficient or have to be so drastic that the present economic system, and the political system as well, cannot survive. In any case, a confiscation of property, particularly through a slump in the stock prices, would cause an increase in capital costs and a serious reduction of capital resources for all the enterprises concerned. The "confiscation" argument seems to be convincing; in fact, the final LO report admits the risk of capital destruction due to counteractions by present shareholders. Another strong economic argument says that small firms will try to hold back or conceal their development in order to avoid being swallowed up by the fund system. In this way, too, Sweden's economic prosperity may be seriously damaged. It should also be pointed out that relations between LO funds and the multinational corporations is a difficult problem which has not been solved by Meidner and his associates. In sum, the fund system is probably incompatible with a market economy.

The political argument from the non-socialist side boils down to the conclusion that the above-mentioned economic problems of the transition period, and the final outcome of the fund-building process as well, will result in a situation where political democracy is destroyed or at least seriously weakened. The process is irreversible; all opposition against the tremendous concentration of power in the hands of the trade union leaders will be silenced; most of the press will be included in the fund system; legal security is imperilled. In short, if dominant, a system of wage-earners' funds is incompatible with democratic pluralism. However, most of this criticism seems to be somewhat exaggerated. The fund system can be modified or even abolished through a political decision, at least in the beginning; there are elements of decentralization of trade union power in the scheme; newspapers will certainly not be included; legal guarantees against the abuse of power can be created, and so on. The most difficult problems from the point of view of political democracy will probably appear in connection with the hard administrative actions which may be necessary to combat economic chaos during a rapid transition.

A more fundamental objection to the democratic pretensions of the propounders of the scheme is, however, an argument which has been put by some Social Democratic critics. According to this argument, the fund system implies a form of economic democracy which is incomplete because public influence on capital formation and on the use of fund capital is insufficient. A minority representation of the public interest on the boards of the branch funds is not enough; the political representatives should have a stronger position in the fund system. The LO proposal gives no guarantees against conflicts of interest between the unions and the government's economic planning and industrial policies. The supremacy of political democracy may be endangered by trade union power; the public interest may be forced aside by particularistic interests. The wage-earners' funds must be transformed into citizens' funds, and they must be subordinated to government and parliament. This is an important democratic aspect which was totally disregarded in the LO report.

Social Democratic critics have also observed the problem of double loyalties which may be embarrassing for the unions when they assume management responsibility through the funds. The unions may lose their position as independent representatives of the workers' interests. On the other hand, risk-taking and necessary structural rationalization may be obstructed by the employees' short-term interests. This is one of the reasons why the economic arguments against the fund system cannot be totally disregarded. On the whole, the Social Democratic critics admit that the economic consequences of the LO plan have not been sufficiently analyzed in the report.

No detailed counterproposals to the LO scheme have been presented. However, a brief outline of a voluntary wage-fund system with some state subsidies was propounded in a joint report from SAF and the Swedish Federation of Industries, which was published in May 1976. The report gives a detailed account of the international debate on participation in capital formation. Experiences of profit-sharing systems (which are almost non-existent in Sweden) lead to the conclusion that a saving system based on wages is a better solution of the conflict between the need for an increase in company profitability and the demand for a more equal distribution of property. In this way, necessary investment capital and a more dispersed share-holding can be obtained without undesirable concentration of power.

The idea of a branch fund system based on wages and not on profits has been proposed even by Social Democratic debaters, particularly by the economist Villy Bergström as early as 1973. Unlike the SAF-inspired outline, this early proposal aimed at a combination of increased capital formation and wage-earner power. The wage funds will finally be the owners of all large companies, and no individual shares will be allowed. In this respect, the proposal is similar to the LO report. However, the negative economic and political consequences of "capital confiscation" in the LO plan can be avoided, and capital formation will probably be much larger than in a system based only on profits. If such a wage-fund system can be combined with effective guarantees for democratic pluralism and the supremacy of political democracy, it may very well become a key to a future solution of the issue of collective capital formation. Another advantage of a system based on wages is that employees in the public and co-operative sectors can be included.

A wage-fund system was in fact presented in February 1978 by a study group appointed in the autumn of 1976 by LO and the Social Democratic Party (the LO-SAP group). The basic motive for the new proposal is the need for an increase in investment capital, which is demonstrated in the report by figures on the drastic decline in industrial investment since 1975. In order to regain the former strength of Swedish industry, a large collective capital formation is said to be necessary. This is to be done through a sort of payroll tax on all wages, which are collected in a fund system. Two nationwide "development funds" will be created, one with a majority of political representatives and the other with a majority elected by the unions. The big national funds are supplemented by a system of small regional funds, the boards of which will be elected by the county councils. The wage-fund system implies enormous capital formation since the charge on wages will be as high as 3 percent at the end of the first five-year period. Every fifth year the size of the charge and the structure of the fund system will be decided by Parliament.

However, the wage-fund system is to be combined with a collective profit-sharing system which is based on the same principles as the LO proposal of 1978. According to the LO-SAP group, wage-earners must be compensated in this way for their giving up of a large part of future wage increases to the wage funds. The new proposal differs from the LO plan in the following ways:

1. The compulsory part of the profit-sharing system will be restricted to the biggest private companies with more than 500 employees. However, smaller firms, as well as public and co-operative companies, are given the chance to join the system after negotiations with the unions.

2. The role of the central equalization fund in the LO proposal will be taken over by a co-determination fund, based on a one percent charge on the wage sum of companies which remain outside the compulsory system.

3. The idea of branch funds is given up, with the exception of a vague proposal for consultative branch councils. Instead, a system of regional representations of all wage-earners in each county is combined with a representation of the employees in the big, collectively-owned companies in such a way that the local trade union influence is maximized to 20 percent of the votes at the shareholders' meetings.

4. Although most of the stock market will be eliminated in the future, when the majority of shares in the big companies on the stock-exchange list are owned by the wage-earners' funds, the interests of the present individual shareholders are taken care of in a better way than in the LO proposal.

The new fund system is a very complicated construction because it is a compromise between LO's demand for trade-union power, based on ownership, and SAP's insistence upon a broadly-based system of capital formation and guarantees for the supremacy of political democracy. However, the democratic guarantees seem to be insufficient; the decisive power over the funds and over the economy as a whole will remain in the hands of the unions. All the objections which could be raised against the LO plan are still valid. There will be no citizens' funds and thus—according to a proper definition of democracy implying the principle of one man, one vote—no economic democracy. Instead of democracy, there will be a tremendous concentration of economic and political power in a complicated corporatist system, far away from ordinary citizens.

A few days before the LO-SAP report, another proposal for wage-earners' funds was presented by a TCO committee. It is based on the same principles as the LO-SAP plan. The main difference is that the guarantees for a decisive public influence on the fund system are even weaker in the TCO scheme than in the LO-SAP report. The new proposal will be discussed by the TCO unions, but it is likely that a final decision will be taken at the TCO Congress in June 1979. The Social Democratic Party discussed the fund issue at the Party Congress in September 1978, but it was unable to agree on more than support for the general principle of wage-earner's funds. The voters will decide the issue after the Royal Commission has reported in the early 1980s.

Finally, it should be pointed out that so far, no other political parties have presented any sort of concrete plans for fund systems, profit-sharing, or wage saving. The non-socialist parties and the present government are waiting after the Congress decisions of the Social Democrats in 1978, for the TCO Congress in 1979 and the Public Commission report. After the change in government the Commission was supplemented with some more non-socialist members, and a new Commission was appointed with the task of working out an individual saving system.

The Conservatives tend to prefer the stimulation of voluntary individual saving and wide-spread ownership of shares through state subsidies or exemption from taxes. The Center Party has the same general outlook but is less precise than the other non-socialist parties. The Liberals maintained their traditional preference for individual profit-sharing on company level until the middle of the 1970s. Then they accepted the idea of wage-earners' funds, although with some form of individual connection. In a proposal to the Liberal Party Congress in summer 1978, individual and collective profitsharing are combined together with a fund system which is based on wages in approximately the same way as in the TCO and LO-SAP reports. The Communists, finally, seem to prefer traditional state socialism to trade union ownership and wage saving. They may accept a fund system which is based on profits and large property incomes, but they firmly reject the idea of funds based on wages.

SUMMARY AND CONCLUSIONS

The distribution of initiative concerning employee participation forms a simple pattern: with the exception of socio-technical reforms or experiments at plant level, SAF had a totally defensive role, and all reforms or reform plans in the 1970s were initiated by LO and TCO. Resistance from the SAF and pressure from the unions have been much stronger than in the field of collective bargaining. Obviously, membership opinion in the unions was a much more active driving force for change in employee participation than in collective bargaining. The reasons for union activism have already been discussed and will not be repeated. However, some reflections concerning relations between LO and TCO and the relative distribution of initiative and influence between the two federations still remain to be made. SACO-SR can be disregarded in this context; no important initiatives have come from this organization, and its role in the debate on participation reforms has been fairly passive.

One of the most important changes on the societal and political scene in Sweden in the 1970s is the emergence of an intimate cooperation between the manual workers' trade union movement and the white-collar unions. Future developments in the labor market, concerning collective bargaining and employee participation, and in the electoral and parliamentary arenas as well, will to a large extent be decided by the future course of this collaboration. In my opinion, the interests of manual workers and whitecollar groups are becoming more and more identical, and therefore a continuing and intensified co-operation between LO and TCO on all levels is the most probable development. This prediction is based on an analysis of the societal reasons for the emergence of the so-called wage-earners' front, which will be briefly outlined. It should be pointed out that the term "wage-earners' front" is applied not only to cooperation between LO and TCO unions in collective bargaining but also to the recently developed community of interests as regards employee participation; defined in such a broad sense, the term is almost part of common political parlance in Sweden today.

When attempts to organize salaried employees in private and public service into large national federations started in the 1930s, many white-collar workers still tended to feel a stronger loyalty to the employers than to the manual workers' unions. Since the Second World War, however, the pattern of identification has totally changed. Today, salaried employees realize that they are confronted with basically the same problems of employment insecurity, working environment, etc., and have the same need for participation as the manual workers. In addition, social and economic distinctions between the two categories are levelled out by technical changes in production processes, such as the routinization of clerical jobs and the substitution of manual work with supervision of complicated machines. Social changes of this kind are the basic reason for the community of interests between LO and TCO groups which was manifested in the 1970s in the form of intensified co-operation on collective bargaining and employee participation. The development towards a united "wage-earners' front" is probably more advanced in Sweden than in any other European country. The process seems to be almost irreversible. Tax policy, and to some extent wage policies, are still the cause of conflicting interests, but these differences are likely to disappear in the future when wage systems become more similar.

Being a relatively young organization, TCO tends to display greater militancy than LO. This difference is reflected not only in a higher rate of legal strikes, or threats of strikes, among the TCO unions but to some extent also in different attitudes towards employee participation. With the exception of the issue of wage-earners' funds, participation reforms were initiated at an earlier time by TCO (1970) than by LO (1971), and they were sometimes handled in a more aggressive way by TCO unions—particularly in the public sector—than by the more cautious LO unions. Differences of this kind may to a limited extent impede collaboration between the two federations, although they are likely to disappear when participation reforms are further developed.

A more fundamental obstacle to future co-operation may, however, be created by the contrast between the political commitment of LO and TCO's neutrality in relation to political parties. Up to now, this difference has been no problem for "the wage-earners' front." As regards collective bargaining and industrial democracy, different political commitments are no obstacle to further collaboration. However, if the issue of wage-earners' funds were to be solved in accordance with the principal lines of the LO-SAP proposal and if non-socialist opinion among the TCO members gets the upper hand, TCO may split in the same way as it did during the great political controversy on the Supplementary Pension reform at the end of the 1950s. In order to avoid such a situation, TCO will probably try to exert a decisive influence on the final solution of the fund issue. If LO wants to preserve successful cooperation with TCO, it is bound to pay great attention to TCO's position and give up some of the most controversial demands. An agreement between LO and TCO, accepted by the Social Democrats, and to some extent also by the Liberals, is the most likely outcome of the controversy on the fund issue. Obviously, TCO holds the key to a broad solution, through which the "wage-earners' front" will be consolidated.

Another condition for a consolidation of the wage-earners' front seems to be relaxing the ties between LO and the Social Democratic Party, particularly as regards collective affiliation. Apart from the political aspects of this problem, which will not be discussed here, the system of collective affiliation of local LO branches to the Social Democratic Party creates a psychological distance between the LO groups and the salaried employees which is likely to be more accentuated in the future. A less primitive and more voluntary form of political commitment on the LO side may in the future facilitate an even more intimate collaboration with the TCO unions. On the other hand, TCO will never abandon its political neutrality. This policy is firmly based on the fact that salaried employees tend to distribute their political sympathies among all the parties in roughly the same proportions as the electorate as a whole. According to election studies in the 1970s, between 30 and 40 percent of the TCO members voted for the socialist parties; the Liberals and the Center Party came next with about 20 percent of the TCO votes for each party. Obviously, the emergence of the wage-earners' front does not automatically give the Social Democrats an absolute majority in the electorate. They tried, however, to make the most of it in recent election campaigns.

The Social Democrats played the most active part in political decisions on participation reforms, followed by the Liberals. However, the former government, and the non-socialist parties as well, did not initiate the reform process. The role of the government was mainly limited to an accomplishment of reform proposals that had been worked out by LO and TCO. The opposition parties supported the basic elements of the government bills on industrial democracy. The only exception to this pattern is, of course, the fund issue; in this case, the political parties did not act merely as executors of union demands.

Corporatist trends are very strong in the Swedish political system of the

1970s. Everywhere local and central unions are negotiating with representatives of the private companies, the state, or the local and regional communities. Decision-making processes become more and more complicated and ineffective. Public opinion is almost totally dominated by a favorable attitude toward union demands, created by the unions with the help of the mass media and most of the political parties. Who has the courage to be critical of the wage-earners, the vast majority of the Swedish people? However, a popular reaction may come in the near future against the rapidly growing power of the new class of national union officials. Interesting omens of such a reaction are revealed in a political science study of the 1976 election. A majority of the electorate, even among the Social Democratic voters, is almost as critical of the centralized power of the LO as of the power of big business. The negative attitude towards top union officials will be strengthened if the demands from the LO-SAP majority of the new Labor Law Commission are carried through. According to the majority report, the salaries of 4,000 so-called regional union functionaries should be paid by tax-payers at the beginning of the new system and then by public and private employers. The proposal deserves no comment.[23]

Sweden stands at the crossroads between a pluralist economic and political system and corporatist socialism. Whether Sweden's prosperity and the Swedish model of peaceful and orderly labor relations will be preserved depends largely on the ability of the decision-makers in political parties and trade unions to find a solution to the issue of "economic democracy" which may broaden the base of capital formation without sacrificing political democracy.

Notes

1. Axel Hadenius, *Facklig organisationsutveckling. En studie av Landsorganisationen i Sverige. Skrifter utgivna av Statsvetenskapliga föreningen i Uppsala*, no. 75, 1975, Stockholm: Rabén & Sjögren, 1976, pp. 193-201.

2. Leif Lewin, *Vem styr facket? Om demokratin inom fackföreningsrörelsen. Skrifter utgivna av Statsvetenskapliga föreningen i Uppsala*, no. 73, Stockholm, Rabén & Sjögren, 1977, *passim*.

3. Short reviews of the white-collar unions are given in English by: Nils Elvander, "Interest Groups in Sweden", *The Annals of the American Academy of Political and Social Science*, Vol. 413, 1974, pp. 27-43; Nils Elvander, "In Search of New Relationships: Parties, Unions and Salaried Employees' Associations in Sweden,". *Industrial and Labour Relations Review*, Vol. 28, 1974, pp. 60-74; Lennart Forsebäck, *Industrial Relations and Employment in Sweden*, Stockholm, The Swedish Institute, 1976, pp. 20-41; Christopher Wheeler, *White-Collar Power. Changing Patterns of Interest Group Behavior in Sweden*, University of Illinois Press, 1974, pp. 8-65.

4. Forsebäck, *op. cit.*, p. 30.

5. Hadenius, *op. cit.*, p. 68-122. *Cf.* Nils Elvander, "Collective Bargaining and Incomes Policy in the Nordic Countries: a Comparative Analysis", *British Journal of Industrial Relations*, Vol. 12, 1974, p. 426; Rudolf Meidner, *Coordination and Solidarity: An Approach to Wage Policy*, Stockholm, Prisma, 1974; and Derek Robinson, *Solidaristic Wage Policy in Sweden*, Paris, OECD, 1974.

6. Nils Elvander, "Collective Bargaining by Civil Servants in the Nordic Countries", in

Charles M. Rehmus (ed.), *Public Employment Labor Relations: An Overview of Eleven Nations*, Ann Arbor, Institute of Labor and Industrial Relations, 1975, pp. 147-170.

7. The EFO group got its name from the initials of the participants' surnames: Gösta Edgren in TCO, Karl-Olof Faxén in SAF and Clas-Erik Odhner in LO.

8. A detailed description of the 1970-71 wage round is given by Svante Nycander, *Kurs på kollision. Inblick i lönerörelsen 1970-71*, Stockholm, Askild & Kärnekull, 1972.

9. The recent development of tax policy and the wage rounds of 1974-77 have not yet been subjected to scientific analysis. They are mentioned briefly in Hadenius, *op. cit.*, pp. 112-116, and Forsebäck, *op. cit.*, pp. 131-135. The presentation in this paper is also based on reports from the organizations and newspaper articles.

10. Forsebäck, *op. cit.*, pp. 67-70, 80; Elvander, *op. cit.*, *Industrial and Labor Relations Review*, Vol. 28, 1974, p. 65.

11. Edmund Dahlström, "Efficiency, Satisfaction and Democracy in Work: Conceptions of Industrial Relations in Post-War Sweden", *Acta Sociologica*, Vol. 20, 1977, pp. 33-37; Bo Ohlström, *Vilda strejker inom LO—omradet 1974 och 1975*, Stockholm, LO, 1977.

12. Tax policy before the 1970s is analyzed in Nils Elvander, *Svensk skattepolitik 1945-1970. En studie i partiers och organisationers funktioner*, Stockholm, Rabén & Sjögren, 1972. A summary of the book is given in Elvander, "The Politics of Taxation in Sweden 1945-1970: A Study of the Functions of Parties and Organizations", *Scandinavian Political Studies*, Vol. 7, 1972, pp. 63-82.

13. Elvander, *op. cit.*, *British Journal of Industrial Relations*, Vol. 12, 1974, p. 426. *Cf.* Elvander, "The Role of the State in the Settlement of Labor Disputes in the Nordic Countries: A Comparative Analysis", *European Journal of Political Research*, Vol. 2, 1974, pp. 363-383.

14. Forsebäck, *op. cit.*, pp. 51-52; Dahlström, *op. cit.*, pp. 37-38, 41.

15. Bernt Schiller, "LO, paragraf 32 och företagsdemokratin", in *Tvärsnitt. Sju forskningsrapporter utgivna till LO:s 75-årsjubileum 1973*, Stockholm, Prisma, 1973, pp. 283-398. *Cf.* Dahlström, *op. cit.*, *pp. 41-42.*

16. For a more detailed presentation of the laws, see Forsebäck, *op. cit.*, pp. 54-55, 117-126.

17. Reports from *PA-rådet*, July 1977.

18. *Job reform in 500 Swedish firms*, Stockholm, SAF, 1975. *Cf.* Dahlström, *op. cit.*, pp. 32-37, 44-46.

19. The following account is mainly based on the LO reports *Löntagarfonder*, Stockholm, LO/Tiden, 1975, and *Kollektiv kapitalbildning genom löntagarfonder*, Stockholm: LO/Prisma, 1976; the LO-SAP report *Löntagarfonder och kapitalbildning*, Stockholm, LO/Tiden, 1978; the TCO reports *Löntagarkapital*, Stockholm, TCO, 1976, and *Löntagarfonder ur TCO-perspektiv*, Stockholm, TCO, 1978; pamphlets from *Moderata samlingspartiet* (the Conservatives) and *Folkpartiet* (the Liberals), published in 1978; and Erik Åsard, *LO och löntagarfondsfrågan. En studie i facklig ideologi och strategi*, unpublished dissertation manuscript, Department of Political Science, Uppsala, 1977.

20. Berit Rollén (ed.), *Vi kommer tillbakai*, Stockholm, Pogo, 1977, pp. 109-110 (interview with Gunnar Nilsson).

21. Hakan Gergils, *Svenska folket och Meidnerfonderna. Utdrag ur och kommentarer kring fem Sifo-undersökningar*, Katrincholm, Aktiespararnas skriftserie, No. 3, 1976; Hans L. Zetterberg. *"Opinionen och makten över företagen,"* in Carl-Johan Westholm (ed.), *Vi kan ännu välja. Fakta om Meidnerplanên*, Bôräs: Askild & Kärnekull, 1976, pp. 23-40; Olof Petersson, *Väljarna och valet 1976*, Stockholm: Statistiska centralbyrån, 1977, pp. 88-97, 230-231.

22. The following account is based on Westholm, *op. cit.*; Åke Wredén, *Kapital till de anställda? En studie av vinstdelning och löntagarfonder*, Stockholm; Studieförbundet Näringsliv och Samhälle, 1976; *Löntagaraktier eller fackföreningsfonder? Alternativ i debatten om löntagarfonder. En sammanfattning av Waldenströmrapporten*, Stockholm, Svenska Arbetsgivareföreningen, Sveriges Industriförbund, 1976; Villy Bergström, *Kapitalbildning och industriell demokrati*, Uppsala, Tiden, 1973; articles in the Social Democratic journal *Tiden*, 1976-77.

23. Petersson, *op. cit.*, pp. 110-111; *Fackliga förtroendemän, möten på betald arbetstid och arbetslivs forskning, Delbetänkande av Nya arbetsrätts kommitten*, Stockholm: Statens offentliga utredmingar, 1977.

6
United Kingdom

by B. C. ROBERTS

The British system of industrial relations was, until the last few years, less legally regulated than any other system of industrial relations in the world. The central feature of the system was that wages, and increasingly salaries, and the main terms of employment for the great majority of employees were settled by agreements made voluntarily by negotiations between employers and trade unions. It was true to say that although the state had come to play a much larger role in protecting the economic and social interests of the worker, it had virtually no influence on the procedures and little more effect on the substantive terms and conditions of employment agreed by employers and unions through the collective bargaining process.

The pattern of industrial relations in the United Kingdom was often described as voluntaristic and the role of the state as non-interventionist.[1] Although neither descriptions were ever totally true, they described a system in which, up to the 1970s, the unions received little positive help from the state to secure recognition and to bargain, but were protected from legal actions by employers by immunity from actions in tort and by the exclusion of collective agreements from the Courts. Employers were free to refuse to enter into negotiations with unions, as in fact they still are, and bargaining depended essentially on the strength of the unions to force them into negotiations, but agreements when made had no force other than the willingness of both parties to ensure that they were observed.

Voluntarism also extends to the trade unions and they have flourished under it. At the present time, there are some 462 unions in existence with a total membership of 12.3 million, which is about 50 percent of the employed labor force. There is, however, a high degree of concentration with some two-thirds of the membership to be found in eleven large unions with more than 250,000 members. Two hundred and fifty of the unions have an average membership of less than 1,000 and account for only 0.6 percent of all union members.

During the past 25 years the growth in trade union membership has mainly come about by the organization of white-collar workers and especially those employed in the public sector. The growth in the readiness of white-collar workers to join unions has been encouraged by the great increase in their relative number, and by the decline in the advantage they used to enjoy in pay levels and terms of employment over those of manual workers. Increasingly, white-collar workers have turned to unionization as the means of safeguarding their economic position. A similar development is now taking place among higher-level technical, professional, and managerial employees. These groups of employees have traditionally belonged to professional associations which are now often becoming trade unions. A feature of this development is the bitter competition between these organizations and the mainstream of trade unions, affiliated to the Trades Union Congress. Attempts have been made to organize a trade union center of independent professional unions, but so far with little success.

Year by year the number of unions fall as the smaller ones amalgamate with the larger organizations. This process of amalgamation unfortunately has not altered one of the most significant features of the structure of British trade unions, which is its heterogeneity. The unions in Britain were originally based upon the occupational activity of their members, and many of them retain this characteristic although there are very few pure craft unions left. Many unions now organize workpeople in a wide range of occupations, some organize, at least in theory, any variety of employee from the manual laborer to the managing director, others confine their membership to a single industry, but there are relatively few of these. Others still confine their membership to clerical, technical, or administrative grades in the public sector and some to both public and private sectors. The result is a pattern of organization which leads to multiple unionism in almost every plant and enterprise and unit of public employment.

Unlike the United States, the concept of exclusive jurisdiction has never been embraced. The most the unions have been willing to accept is that they should not commence to organize workpeople in a bargaining unit where another union is already recognized. It is the responsibility of the Trades Union Congress to enforce this rule, but it is one that is not infrequently breached. The problem is particularly acute in the rapidly expanding areas of technical, professional, and administrative employment especially in the private sector which the unions are now vigorously competing to unionize.

The Changing Pattern of Collective Bargaining

The structure of the trade unions has been of particular importance in the evolution of the collective bargaining system. The classic system of collective bargaining in Britain, which developed in the nineteenth century and predominated until the end of the Second World War, was based upon negotiations between federations of employers and federations of unions in each industry. These industrywide agreements established the basic rates of pay and main conditions of employment in each enterprise that was affiliated to the employers' federation. This system of collective bargaining broke down under the inflationary demand for labor and the growth in the size of enterprises which occurred after the Second World War. Under these conditions, the shop stewards' committees, which had existed for more than half a century, but except in the First World War had not played a significant role, developed a power and influence which changed the character of the collective bargaining process.

Gradually realizing that they were in a position to negotiate improvements in pay and terms of employment superior to those settled at the level of industry, the stewards began to bring pressure upon employers who were at first reluctant to negotiate with them, by calling strikes unofficially, that is, without the approval of the unions. As employers began to make concessions these strikes were encouraged; they became the predominant form of industrial dispute and seemed beyond the control of either the trade unions or employers' organizations.

Unofficial strikes mainly occurred over demands for improvements in pay, but they also often happened when employers sought to introduce new machines or new methods of production. They were thus closely related to the persistent tendency for earnings to rise at an inflationary pace and to the failure of industry to invest in new equipment to the same extent as European and Japanese enterprises that were not confronted by similar militant opposition.

It was this apparent breakdown in the traditional pattern of industrial relations that led the Labour Government, which had taken office after thirteen years of Conservative rule, to announce in 1965 the appointment of a Royal Commission on Trade Unions and Employers' Associations with very wide terms of reference.

Royal Commission on Trade Unions and Employers' Associations

The diagnosis of the Royal Commission which was accepted by all its members was that the British system of industrial relations had become dysfunctional because of a failure to adapt to the fact of the development of plant bargaining. In the opinion of the Commission, Britain was suffering from the fact that there were in existence two systems of collective bargaining, one at the level of industry which was orderly and smooth-working but of limited relevance, and another at the level of the plant, where bargaining was meaningful but often disorderly and lacking well-developed procedures. The two systems were, as a result, in conflict with each other.

Since the diagnosis of the Commission pointed to the need to reform plant bargaining by making it more systematic, it was necessary to find a means of achieving this objective. The majority of the Commission, strongly influenced by the voluntaristic tradition, and sympathetic to the predica-ent of the unions, sought to find a remedy which would strengthen their role and without major changes in the legal framework. They found the solution in the compulsory registration of collective agreements made by all companies employing more than 5,000 employees. It would be the duty of a new Commission for Industrial Relations to monitor the register and to offer its services on a voluntary basis to help management and unions, where they were faced by intractable industrial relations problems, to develop new procedures.

These proposals did not satisfy a minority of Commission members who were of the opinion that what was really required was a reform of the law which would make the unions legally liable for breaches of contract brought about by wildcat strikes and secondary boycotts. Nor did the proposals of the Commission satisfy the Labor Government, which did not believe that they went far enough. The government gave notice of its own proposals, which included giving the Secretary for Employment power to declare strikes damaging to the national interest, to impose a cooling-off period, backed by fines on those who refused to accept it, and to hold a ballot of those on strike. These proposals were bitterly opposed by the trade unions who threatened to withdraw their support from the Labor Government. Faced by this intransigent opposition, the government withdrew its White Paper. It was defeated at the polls soon afterwards.

Labor Law Reform

The incoming Conservatives, who had campaigned on the importance of the reform of industrial relations, introduced a series of sweeping changes in the law in their Industrial Relations Act of 1971. The aim of the Act was to make collective bargaining more orderly by giving the unions certain advantages if they registered under the Act, but also making them liable for actions for damages if they went on strike in breach of agreements which, unless they specifically affirmed otherwise, were to become legally-binding contracts. After three years of uncompromising opposition from the T.U.C., the 1971 Industrial Relations Act was repealed by the incoming Labor Government in 1974. The Act had failed, but some of its most important elements were to be incorporated in new legislation passed in the next three years.

The Trade Union and Labor Relations Act of 1974 repealed the 1971 Act and restored the limitations on the legal liability of trade unions which had existed before 1971; it re-enacted sections of the 1971 Act relating to unfair dismissal from employment, which included giving workers protection against dismissal for belonging to a union or taking part in its activities. In 1975, the Employment Protection Act extended the role of Industrial Tribunals, established an Employment Appeals Tribunal in place of the Industrial Relations Court, which had been established by the 1971 Act, and introduced new machinery to assist the unions to gain recognition, to extend collective bargaining, and to improve industrial relations through the settlement of industrial conflicts.

The Advisory Conciliation and Arbitration Service was established in place of the Commission for Industrial Relations. The A.C.A.S. also took over the long established conciliation and arbitration functions previously discharged by the Department of Employment.

In conformity with the return to voluntarism which the new legislation sought in some respects to foster, the A.C.A.S. was to have no legal authority to impose a settlement on the parties to a dispute. An important responsibility that it took over from the C.I.R. was that of assisting unions to gain recognition where this was refused by employers. On receipt of a complaint from unions, the A.C.A.S. is called upon to investigate. If, after a preliminary enquiry, it is satisfied that the union has sufficient support to give reasonable grounds for thinking that it would be accepted by the employees concerned as their bargaining agent, it first seeks to persuade the employer that he should recognize the union. If the employer refuses to grant the union recognition, the A.C.A.S must then seek the employer's co-operation to carry out an inquiry. The procedure A.C.A.S. has developed is to conduct a ballot of all the employees the union seeks to represent to discover not only how many members the union has secured, but whether there would be support for the union if it were recognized by the employer.

The A.C.A.S. does not have any legal power to compel an employer to give it facilities to conduct its inquiry and it may, therefore, have to rely on the union for the names and addresses of members and of non-member employees. The A.C.A.S. does not have a legal right to make a recommendation to recognize, if this is based solely upon a survey of union members and not of all those employed in the bargaining unit to be established. The A.C.A.S. is also free to ask the union to withdraw the reference if the preliminary inquiry indicates that it is unlikely to have sufficient support to warrant a recommendation in favor of recognition.

The law lays down no specific procedure that the A.C.A.S. must follow to discover whether there is sufficient support for it to recommend recognition. Whether it conducts a ballot, and the form of the ballot, are matters that lie within the discretion of the A.C.A.S. Thus the procedure is not the simple question of discovering whether the union has a majority of the employees in membership, as in the N.L.R.B. system in the U.S.A.; it is a discretional procedure based upon the judgment of the A.C.A.S. officers and its Council. The crucial evidence on which the Council has relied has not been the percentage of union members, but the percentage of those who say they would like to have their pay and conditions of employment determined by collective bargaining, and who would be prepared to join a union if one were recognized. Thus, if the union has far less than a majority of employees as members, but a reasonable proportion indicate a desire for collective bargaining and a willingness to join after recognition, A.C.A.S may recommend that the employer recognize the union.

This method of procedure has been bitterly attacked by employers who see it as a device to put pressure on employees to say that they would join the union in the hypothetical circumstances of recognition, but who have not been prepared to join of their own volition as a means of assisting the union to gain recognition. Since the composition of the Council of A.C.A.S. has a clear majority of members who are known supporters of the unions, there is a low level of employer confidence in its role in recognition cases. The A.C.A.S. rejects criticism that it is biased, by reference to the Employment Protection Act which calls upon it to assist the unions to gain recognition, if it is satisfied that this will promote good industrial relations.

The effect of this new procedure has not been quite so dramatic as some trade union leaders hoped. It has undoubtedly led to the unionization of a number of small firms and has led to an extension of recognition in insurance and other financial institutions, but it has not brought about recognition in a number of other well-known non-union firms which were prime targets.

In the I.B.M. ballot, the percentage of members which voted in favor of accepting a trade union was only 4.4. In other cases, the determined opposition of the companies and the clearly small number of employees unionized has led to unions withdrawing their complaint against the employer, since if the A.C.A.S. carries out an inquiry which produces evidence of very little support for the union, a further claim for recognition cannot be lodged with the A.C.A.S. for another two years.

Where a recommendation in favor of recognition has been made by A.C.A.S. and the employer has refused to make it effective, the union may then submit unilaterally a substantive claim for an improvement in pay and conditions of work before the Central Arbitration Committee, which has been established in place of the Industrial Court, set up under the 1971 Industrial Relations Act. So far only a few cases have been brought before the C.A.C. The general attitude of the unions seems to be that if they cannot fairly quickly persuade the employer to grant recognition, after a favorable recommendation by A.C.A.S., there is not much point in relying on a rather weak legal remedy.

The discretionary latitude allowed A.C.A.S. and the ambiguities and uncertainties to which this gives rise, may be seriously criticized as fundamentally in conflict with the rule of law. Rights and duties are obscured, issues in conflict are determined by an administrative process, and when an employer acts within his legal right not to recognize a union which may have only a small percentage of members, he is, in effect, deprived of this right by the exercise of what employers consider to be arm-twisting by a public body. On the other hand, if the employer stands firm, there is little that the union can do but turn to exercising traditional pressures which may be soured by frustrated expectations.

One of the most important developments in the encouragement of the unions has been the introduction of a legal right to gain access to information without which the union would be materially impeded in carrying on with collective bargaining. There is no obligation on the employer to disclose information that would be unlawful under some other legislation, or which would cause substantial injury to the undertaking, or which relates to any individual without his consent, or which would involve the employer in an amount of work compiling the information which would be out of all reasonable proportion to its value in collective bargaining.

It is too soon to judge how far this right of access to information will be used and the extent to which it will have any material influence on collective bargaining.

Another new right that may be of substantial benefit to shop stewards and other union offices is one that enables them to have reasonable time off to carry out their trade union duties. Employees are also entitled to have time off for any public duties they may undertake, for retraining, and to search for new jobs if they are threatened with loss of employment.

The Growth of Workplace Organization

There can be little doubt that the new legislation has strengthened the role of the union representatives at the place of work, and helped to consolidate the activities of the shop stewards' committees.

One of the most significant trends in this respect has been the growth in the number of shop stewards, which has probably increased by well over 50,000 in the last decade, to a total of some 300,000 throughout British industry. A factor of particular interest in this connection has been the increase in the number of full-time shop stewards. Recent studies have shown that there were probably about 5,000 full-time shop stewards in 1977 compared with perhaps 1,000 at the time of the Royal Commission inquiry in 1967. In the private sector of industry, the shop stewards' committee has become the main instrument of the development of an increasingly autonomous system of plant bargaining. With this development the desire of the Royal Commission to see a more orderly and systematic pattern of bargaining at the plant level has, to an important extent, been achieved in the larger companies.

This development suggests that in the private sector of industry the shop steward is becoming a more experienced and professional representative who is capable of carrying out his role with little outside assistance from the union. However, in the public sector, where bargaining remains more centralized than in the private sector, there is more reliance upon the permanent officials of the union than is the case in the private sector.

There are nevertheless considerable weaknesses in the shop steward committee system. These committees rarely represent all the employees, since it is common for white-collar stewards to have a separate committee. Moreover there are often conflicts of interest between the stewards representing the skilled grades and those representing process workers and the less skilled. The fragmentation which arises from the multiplicity of unions in British industry continues to give rise to serious problems and is an obstacle to the development of a more cooperative system of plant industrial relations.

The establishment of plant bargaining has also had significant effects on the role of the trade union and employers' federations. Industry-wide agreements continue to be negotiated, but they relate virtually entirely to the establishment of minimum rates of pay and conditions of employment. These agreements no longer set a pattern which is followed by most firms. Their role has become one of following the trends established by plant agreements by raising the minimum from time to time. The industry-wide employers' associations are now mainly concerned with representing the interests of their members with reference to new legislation and in providing information in this field. Many companies are now questioning the role of the employer's organizations. The trade union federations are in an even more serious state of decline, having no function now that they have no significant bargaining role.

The development of plant bargaining has led to problems, which are becoming more important, in multi-plant firms. Although shop stewards' committees at plant level have become the normal pattern, what are much less well-developed are shop steward committees at the enterprise level that are capable of developing negotiations with the enterprise as a whole. Employers have resisted the growth of company-wide bargaining, since this would entail limitation of the autonomy of plant management.

The development of company-wide bargaining also gives rise to problems for the unions, since the balance of inter-union power might be different from what it would be on a plant-by-plant basis. Therefore, even where employers have a preference for company-wide bargaining, as with the case of British Leyland, they might find it difficult to achieve.

In many cases, of course, the activities carried on in the various plants of a company may be so different as to make a company-wide agreement virtually impossible. Whereas in the case of the automobile manufacturing companies, the plants are producing the same product, or parts used in a common product, the case for a uniform company agreement is often very strong. If there are different rates of pay and conditions of employment in each plant, this may well give rise to demands for parity. Problems also arise, especially in periods of pay-restraint policies, when one plant is making its settlements at a different date from another.

An outstanding example of these problems has been produced by the British Leyland Company. This company has been seeking to reduce the 58 separate agreements made at different times of the year in 34 plants to a single master company-wide agreement. This policy was accepted by all but the largest union, which was not prepared to go beyond reducing the agreements to one for each plant. After long and bitter negotiations a majority of the employees voted to adopt the company scheme of one bargaining unit, but this was achieved only by making considerable improvements in pay and fringe benefits conditional upon a reform of the bargaining structure. The first step towards a single agreement will be to conclude the existing agreements on a common date, thus bringing to an end the leap-frogging and re-opening of negotiations which has been a feature of British Leyland's industrial relations in the past. It still remains an open question whether a single master agreement will ever be effectively concluded.

In spite of the difficulties of British Leyland, there are other companies which have had considerable success with the development of company-wide bargaining structures. The Ford Motor Company is a conspicuous example in this respect. It is likely that the advantages of company-wide bargaining will be increasingly stressed since they have significant implications for the evolution of pay bargaining as well as for the role of the unions in the enterprise.

Collective Bargaining and Inflation

Some form of national incomes and prices policy has been in force in all but five of the last seventeen years. In most of these years the trade unions have reluctantly accepted the limitations on their right to bargain which the pay policies have implied. Their support has, however, in each policy period, gradually eroded, and the policy has been ended with the vain hope that a return to free collective bargaining would prove to be durable. Both Conservative and Labor Governments have declared their opposition to national incomes and prices policies and both have found it necessary to resort to them again.

Less than a year after taking office in 1964, the Labor Government established a National Board for Prices and Incomes and embarked upon a policy which it had denounced before taking office. The story was virtually repeated in 1971, when a Conservative Government, which had been returned to office pledged to get rid of statutory pay and price controls, was obliged after a period of vain exhortation to the employers and unions in the private sector to hold pay down, to introduce a statutory pay freeze. This was followed by a second stage in which employers were allowed to raise pay by

£1 a week, plus 4 percent—a policy which was designed to give the lowest paid a much larger percentage increase. The succeeding stage three repeated this formula, but at the more generous level of £2.25 or 7 percent, whichever was greater. These pay restrictions led to massive strikes in 1972 and 1974, which in the end brought the government down.

The Labor Party came back to power pledged to end the Conservatives' pay restrictions and to enter into a social contract with the trade unions. The terms of the social contract worked out between the T.U.C. and the Labor Party before the election of 1974 were that in exchange for a government pledge to bring in a new era of labor law, a considerable advance in social security benefits, and a policy to lower prices, which in the aftermath of the oil crisis were rising rapidly, the unions would exercise restraint in their pay demands. There was no employer participation in the making of this policy; it was simply between the T.U.C. and the Labor Party. After a year of massive rises in pay and prices the government was compelled to extend the social contract to include a quasi-voluntary limitation on pay increases. The fundamental feature of this policy was that it involved direct bargaining between the T.U.C. and the government. The outcome of the negotations was not only an agreement that involved the union in a "voluntary" acceptance of limits to pay increases, but also an undertaking by the government that it would adjust the level of taxation and influence the level of prices so as to ensure that the membership of the union would enjoy a minimum rate of increase in real wages.

The problem with this policy was that the government was compelled to give a hostage to fortune by lowering taxes and holding prices down before the unions had delivered their side of the bargain. In practice, however, the government has more control over tax levels than it does over prices. Prices did not fall to the levels forecast by the government, mainly because earnings had risen well over the levels agreed with the unions, and there was a severe devaluation of the pound, thus forcing up the price of imports which had to be passed on to consumers. Had this price rise not been allowed, there would have been a staggering rise in bankruptcies and lay-offs leading to a massive increase in unemployment, which would, in turn, have brought the social contract to an end. Faced by a collapsing pound, the government persuaded the trade unions to accept pay increases limited to £6 per week on the assurance that price increases would have fallen by the end of the year to 10 percent, and the danger of a massive increase in the already high levels of unemployment would be averted. These aims were not achieved, and a stage two was agreed upon, again with the purpose of achieving single-figure price inflation, and again the target was missed. Nevertheless, the government stuck to its belief that price increases would come down to single figures if the unions accepted pay increases of less than 10 percent, and unemployment would also gradually fall.

In the event, the unions only agreed to observe the rule that they should observe a minimum period of twelve months after the last pay increase before demanding another—the twelve-month rule. The government insisted, however, that no pay deal should lead to an increase in earnings of more than 10 percent unless this could be justified by proven increases in productivity, which must be achieved before pay was increased. By early 1978, aided by a fall in the rate of increase in the price of imports, single-figure inflation was achieved, but unemployment showed no sign of falling significantly.

At no time since the social contract was agreed had the pay restraint policy been based upon a law that was enforceable on the trade unions. It has, on the other hand, been enforced upon the employers. Under the legally enforceable price code the government threatened employers with the penalty of disallowing price increases if they failed to adhere to the pay guidelines laid down by the government. In the first two phases of the policy, these were agreed with the T.U.C.; in the third phase they had only the tacit support of the General Council. Nonetheless, the government has taken action against a number of companies by depriving them of the right to use such arrangements as the Export Credit Guarantee scheme. They have also threatened to bar firms from access to government subsidies and contracts if they violate the pay restrictions.

This so-called voluntaristic pay policy has given rise to much misgiving. It is thought by many to be an abuse of the rule of law, since it involves the government enforcing its will on the basis of a general parliamentary approval of its policy, but without specific legal powers being obtained to ensure that in detail its policy is carried out according to law. The Acts which the government has used to bring pressure to bear upon employers for not accepting the voluntary pay policy were not passed for this purpose, and it is possible that sooner or later some employer will take the government before the Courts to test the legality of its use of its powers under this legislation. To make the matter even more sinister, the government refused to make public the names of the companies who were on its blacklist, until forced by a public outcry to do so.

The significance of the government's policy is not in its desire to keep pay increases down to rates that will bring price increases down to European inflation rates, but the manner in which this has been done. The "non-statutory" approach to pay policy has been consistent with the demand from the unions that they should enjoy the benefits of voluntarism, including the freedom to make demands and negotiate settlements well above the maximum levels established by the government. Securing compliance by putting doubtful legal pressure upon the employers to ensure their rejection of union demands avoids direct legal control of pay determination, but it is clearly not consistent with a return to free collective bargaining.

The debate on the fundamental question as to whether it is possible to maintain full employment, high rates of economic growth, and collective bargaining without running into the problem of inflation remains unsettled. There are those who believe that the inflationary consequences of collective bargaining can be prevented by the tight control of monetary and budgetary policies, without necessarily incurring high levels of unemployment. An equally significant group believes that there must be a permanent incomes policy, administered by an appropriate machinery, since in its opinion collective bargaining is incompatible with the attainment of goals of full employment and high growth rates without high levels of inflation. It appears unlikely that a Labor Government seeking high levels of growth and employment will be able to dispense completely with some form of pay policy no matter how much the unions might protest. It remains to be seen whether a Conservative Government, should one come into office, would be able to steer the economy by monetary, fiscal, and expenditure policies without running into the same difficulties as the Labor Government and being forced, as in 1972, to resort once again to some form of pay restraint policy.

The Reform of Pay Bargaining

The persistent tendency for wages to rise at rates causing considerable price inflation, and the effects which inflation and the efforts to control it have had on pay structures, have given rise to demands for reforms in the pay bargaining system. There has been a long-term trend which has led to a dramatic narrowing of pay differentials and a much more equal distribution of income. During the past five years, the pay levels of the higher-wage and salaried groups have been relatively firmly held down by the pay policies of both the Conservative and Labor Governments, while those below the average level have gone up rapidly. The squeeze on the higher-income groups, brought about by pay policies, has been aggravated at the same time by swinging increases in income tax, which have been made all the more savage by the effects of inflation.

The squeeze on differentials has been a potent factor in stimulating the unionization of the salaried grades of employees. It has led to a growing revolt of skilled workers and technical, professional, and managerial employees against the continuance of pay policies, and in certain cases to the establishment of militant breakaway groups. That the narrowing of differentials has gone too far and is having serious social consequences has been generally recognized, but finding an acceptable way of reforming the patterns of pay determination without generating further inflationary pay demands is not easily accomplished.

One of the most coherent and cogent sets of proposals has been put forward by the Confederation of British Industry. In a discussion document, *The Future of Pay Determination*,[2] the C.B.I. rejects both the idea of permanent controls and the almost total reliance on market forces within a system of strict monetary and fiscal controls, in favor of a policy of free bargaining within monetary disciplines, but with some central influence on the level of pay claims and settlements.

The C.B.I. sees change as being necessary on four related points:

1) action by government as financial controller and as pay bargainer in its own right;

2) creating wider understanding of and agreement on the nation's economic circumstances and implications for pay;

3) restricting bargaining arrangements to reduce competitive bargaining between groups and encouraging greater recognition of real interests;

4) restoring greater balance in bargaining power over the long term between employers and employees.

The government must play its part by creating a favorable economic climate in which monetary, taxation, and expenditure policies are properly coordinated. As the largest employer in the land the role of the government in collective bargaining has become crucial. It must impose effective cash limits on the public sector so as to ensure that unbudgeted costs are met by savings made elsewhere.

The role of the government as legislator must be to ensure that the law will protect society from the abuse of power by sectional interests. It should not create an unstable balance of bargaining power by protecting the unions at the expense of the employers.

There is, the C.B.I. insists, an urgent need to reduce competitive bargaining between groups to restore stability within individual plants and companies; to synchronize dates of settlements to prevent leapfrogging; and to ensure that the structures of bargaining are revised and controlled so as to prevent rapid erosion. To achieve these ends, it is necessary for employers to be prepared to sink their differences and seek to develop greater solidarity and strength, and perhaps to re-establish a strong role for employers' federations.

For their part, the trade unions must seek to reduce the adverse effects of multi-unionism; to be willing to cooperate in larger and fewer bargaining units. Unions must reassert their control over their members. This they could achieve by becoming more representative. If there were rank-and-file participation in the bargaining process, there might be a better understanding of what is at issue. Unions should be ready to agree to a more formal framework for collective bargaining which would involve a clearer definition of when a strike might take place. The situation which exists in a number of other countries where a strike or a lock-out is not permitted during the term of a collective agreement, if adopted in Britain, would lead to greater stability especially if it was linked to a well-developed procedural arrangement.

The C.B.I. is strongly of the view that while it would not be appropriate that British companies should adopt a formal system of mandatory works councils on the German model, it does recommend that a body similar to the worker's economic committee, which is set up in German enterprises and meets regularly with management to discuss the financial situation of the company, could well be borrowed and adapted to British needs.

The first step in this new process of pay bargaining would be to reach some consensus with the T.U.C. and the government on the national economic situation and policy options. This would be followed by the budget and then the bargaining round which would take place within a limited period. Alternatively, the bargaining round could take place before the budget, thus giving the Chancellor discretion to adapt his tax measures to the bargaining out-turn. Each option has its advantages and disadvantages, but either would lead to a greater degree of co-ordination than has existed in the past.

The T.U.C. has expressed no official views on the C.B.I. proposals, but some union leaders have indicated that they would be reluctant to go so far as the C.B.I. has proposed. Many employers, as was made clear at the first C.B.I. national conference, held in the fall of 1977, also fear that a tripartite policy on pay may too strongly encourage the trend towards corporatism. While not endorsing the C.B.I.'s proposals, the Prime Minister, Mr. Callaghan, stated in December 1977 that "as for full collective bargaining I ceased to worship that ten years ago," and he added that "there must be a continuing discussion about ways and means of improving the system."

Mr. Tom Jackson, general secretary of the Postal Workers' Union, bluntly uttered the same sentiments at the Annual Congress of the T.U.C. More recently, the man who has become one of the most influential and powerful figures on the General Council of the T.U.C., Mr. David Basnett of the General and Municipal Workers' Union, suggested that for the public sector, the T.U.C. should establish a new Public Services Committee. There should also be established permanent review bodies in the public service which would replace one-off emergency inquiries.

Others, such as the Labor M.P. Mr. Douglas Jay, would go further and re-create a national review body or tribunal, which would have no legal powers to enforce a decision, but which would handle pay disputes of major importance to the economy. The trade unions are not prepared to accept an impartial body with statutory powers to enforce its findings, but they may well be prepared to accept a body without enforcement powers.

Mr. Healey, the Chancellor of the Exchequer, has made it clear that the Labor Party would seek to persuade the unions and the leaders of industry that a continuance of pay restraint was necessary after the end of phase three. In spite of a bitter attack by the unions on the continuation of the Labor Government's limitation on pay bargainings it is likely, if the Labor Party remains in office after the next election, that it will support the reform of collective bargaining so as to prevent a recurrence of the runaway inflation of pay increases that have been a feature of the mid-1970s.

Although the leader of the Conservative Party, Mrs. Thatcher, has strongly condemned pay controls and supported a return to free collective bargaining, it is unlikely that she would be opposed to the ideas put forward by the C.B.I., so long as they stopped short of the establishment of a statutory board, or other means of determining and enforcing pay levels by law.

The long-term outlook is then one in which there is likely to be further development of tripartitism, which may go further under Labor than under the Conservatives, but will exist whichever party is in office. Success in coping with the problem of unemployment may be the factor which determines the extent to which free collective bargaining will be tolerated. If unemployment continues to rise and the political pressures on the government to stimulate the economy become irresistible, but the unions are unable or unwilling to limit their power to take advantage of easier monetary and budget policies voluntarily, the imposing of controls will almost certainly be felt by the government to be a political necessity.

Employment and Unemployment

After the Second World War, until the 1970s, unemployment had not been an issue of great social importance since it had usually been below 3 percent, a level which was generally accepted as constituting full employment. With the advent of runaway inflation in 1974 and 1975 there came coincidentally a rapid rise in the level of unemployment. This increase was due in part to the world recession which was brought on by the quadrupling of the price of oil and made worse by the effects of inflation on the price level of British goods.

It is now widely thought that it is unlikely that there will be a quick return to the 3 percent concept of full employment. This problem is not unique to Britain; it is common to most of the advanced industrial countries. Perhaps the most surprising fact is that there has not been a violent political response to unemployment levels of 6 percent. Some years ago it was believed that such a level of unemployment would be intolerable and would be accompanied by serious social unrest. This has not happened. The unions have tried to make unemployment a major issue, but they have not persuaded the government that creating jobs should have a priority over finding a solution to the problem of inflation.

The unions are convinced that the main cause of the persistent high levels of unemployment is the failure of private industry to invest sufficiently to create an adequate number of new jobs. The low level of investment has clearly been an important factor in Britain's poor growth performance. It is equally obvious, however, that it is not the only factor. The steep decline in the output of steel, ships, and many other commodities has not been caused by lack of investment, but by lack of demand. Indeed more investment would have made the unemployment worse in these industries, since fewer workers would have been required if any modern equipment had been installed.

There lies one of the basic problems facing unions and management in the future. If British industry is to compete effectively, plants must be modernized and the massive overmanning which the unions have forced management to accept must be brought to an end. The achievement of greater efficiency and lower costs through more realistic manning has always been difficult, and it has been made more so by the making of lay-offs increasingly socially unacceptable and costly. Nevertheless experience has shown that it is possible to buy out union opposition to the introduction of new machinery and the closure of old and inefficient plants. This policy is being encouraged under the terms of the Labor Government's income policy, but the government, which itself has ultimate responsibility for the employment of one-third of the labor force, has been extremely reluctant for political reasons to tackle seriously the many instances of heavy overmanning in the public sector.

Paradoxically, although there is a relatively high level of unemployment, there are also manpower shortages, notably of highly skilled manual workers and in certain occupations, such as nursing, which have traditionally been low-paid and with relatively onerous conditions of employment. During the past decade, and especially in the past few years, training programs provided by the state have been greatly expanded. A new tripartite Manpower Services Commission, responsible for the employment and training services, has been established, and new programs have been developed.

In addition to long-term manpower policies, short-term job creation programs have been put into effect. The cost effectiveness of these policies is the subject of much debate, and they have also been looked upon with some suspicion by the European Commission as endangering the Community principles of fair competition. Subsidies have also been given on a substantial scale to the shipbuilding industry as a means of keeping men in employment.

It is widely recognized that these measures of job creation are largely palliatives that are no substitute for a genuine economic recovery and expansion of industrial activity. On the achievement of these objectives management, unions, and government are united, but there is less than unity on the strategy which the government, with the support of unions, is bent upon following.

The ultimate impact of higher levels of unemployment on industrial relations cannot be precisely forecast. It is possible that a higher level of unemployment will lead to changes in attitudes. It could lead to even greater resistance to change than in the past, and on the other hand fear of job-loss might lead to more cooperative attitudes and less resistance to change which promised long-run job security.

There is a danger that the effect of prolonged periods of unemployment on young workers and minority groups could produce social behavior that might be extremely disturbing. In an endeavor to mitigate the consequences of high levels of unemployment it is likely that the unions will press for a shorter work-week, longer holidays, and earlier retirement ages. If the net effect of conceding their demands was to raise British labor costs relative to those in other countries, this would lead to a worsening rather than an improvement in the level of unemployment. For this reason there has already been some indication by British unions that they would like to see common policies throughout the European Community on these matters.

Participation in Industrial Planning and Development

The problem of securing a rate of economic growth that will in the years ahead prevent the unemployment rate from soaring to dangerous heights is likely to provide a critical test for the philosophy of tripartism, and the Labor Government's industrial strategy which is strongly supported by the unions. Tripartism has been long established as an instrument of industrial planning. Trade union and employer organization representatives have for many years played a prominent role on the National Economic Development Council and its many offshoots at the industry level. The N.E.D.C. was established to promote closer relations between the government, the leaders of industry, and the unions in the encouragement and planning of industrial growth.

The T.U.C. has not, however, been satisfied with this role; it has been its aim to bring about a more direct influence on the investment decisions of the boards of directors of the major corporations. To that end it has been a strong supporter of the principle of planning agreements. These agreements were advanced by the Labor Government after its return to office in 1974, as a main instrument of its industrial strategy by which it hoped to bring about a substantial increase in investment and a rapid improvement in the growth rate.

Under legislation which established a tripartite National Enterprise Board, funds were made available for assisting private enterprises to reorganize and re-equip. A condition of the receipt of N.E.B. assistance is that companies enter into a planning agreement. A central feature of such an agreement is that the unions concerned must be fully involved. They are entitled to be consulted and to be given all the information the company may be called upon to provide to the National Enterprise Board. The unions, in short, are to become an active partner in the monitoring of the planning agreement. Through this procedure the aim of the T.U.C. and government was to give the unions the opportunity to exercise an influence without them incurring the same degree of responsibility as the management of the company.

The union leaders and the T.U.C. in general have been greatly disappointed by the fact that so far very few planning agreements are in prospect. the only planning agreement that had been entered into two years after their launching was one made by the Chrysler Corporation as a *quid pro quo* for the substantial grant-in-aid provided by the government to enable the corporation to avoid closure of its plants in the United Kingdom. It is difficult to judge what contribution the agreement has made to the recovery of the Chrysler Corporation, but clearly it has not proved a panacea for its production problems, and the future of the company is by no means certain.

Most companies have been hostile to the idea of planning agreements since they fear that to enter into such an agreement would be to give the unions a right of veto over their production plans and a continuing opportunity to interfere without carrying any responsibility for the effects this might have on the success of the company.

The Trend Toward Industrial Democracy

The desire to exercise much greater influence on the investment and manpower decisions of industry was a major element in the significant change in the attitude of the T.U.C. towards the role of the union in the enterprise over the past decade. Traditionally the T.U.C. has been firmly committed to the notion that collective bargaining must be the predominant function of the unions. Although in the 1930s the T.U.C. had flirted with the idea of parity representation on the boards of nationalized industries, at the end of the Second World War it supported the nationalization of the basic public utilities, but went no further than to demand that union leadership should be considered a relevant experience for appointment to board membership, and it approved the principle that on appointment a union officer would have to sever his connection with the union to which he had belonged. There could be no acceptance of the concept of representation, since this would make it difficult for the man appointed to accept the full responsibility of a board member, and it would cloud the bargaining role and obligation of the union to its members.

Signs of an important change in policy came with the evidence submitted by the T.U.C. to the Royal Commission on Trade Unions and Employer Associations, in 1966. The T.U.C. now argued that the distinctions in function had been "unduly sharp." The conflict of interest which might face trade unionists on a board was more a theoretical than a real concern. The T.U.C. also withdrew the distinction it had made between participation in nationalized and private industries. It now saw no reason why trade union representatives should not be represented on the boards of private as well as public industries.

There were a number of reasons for the change. One was that the distinction made in 1944 between bargaining functions and consultative functions no longer existed. These two functions had become integrated and were exercised at different levels by one body, the shop stewards' committee. Personalities had changed, and a new generation of trade union leaders were beginning to look at the role of trade unionism as one that extended far beyond collective bargaining in the traditional sense. They believed that there were many decisions made by boards of directors that had a great impact on the well-being of their members that they were unable to influence.

The T.U.C. enthusiasm for participation in management was not shared by the members of the Royal Commission, who dismissed the proposals in little more than a page of discussion. In the minds of the Commission participation was largely a red herring which distracted attention from the main issue, which they saw as the need to strengthen the process of collective bargaining.

Following the publication of the Royal Commission's report the T.U.C. announced that it would undertake a study of industrial democracy, but this idea was temporarily shelved as a result of conflicts that arose in the wake of the Commission's report. The relevance of industrial democracy was, however, raised again in 1970 by the Department of Employment, which was anticipating the entry of Britain into the European Community. This led to the T.U.C. establishing a working party to review European experience and the implications of adopting a system of industrial democracy in Britain.

Trade unionists had been appointed to the regional boards of the nationalized steel industry from 1967. There were proposals to appoint worker directors under a bill to nationalize the ports in 1970, and it was indicated that the same policy would be followed in the transport industry.

The T.U.C. committee eventually reported in 1973, and member unions were asked to submit their views in time for a final report to Congress in 1974. At the same time a joint committee of the T.U.C. and the Labor Party had come to an agreement that if a Labor Government was elected at the next general election it would, among other things, introduce a company law reform bill that would enable trade union representatives to be appointed to the board of directors.

The final report of the T.U.C. emphasized the continuing importance of collective bargaining and the need to extend its scope, but it also stressed the need to secure trade union representation on the main policy-making boards in industry and for the unions to play a greater role in the process of national economic planning.

Specifically, the T.U.C. called for the introduction of a two-tier board system on the German model, with the unions having the right to elect 50 percent of the members of the supervisory board who would be accountable to the trade unions. The management board, which would be appointed by the supervisory board, would be responsible for the running of the company and would carry out collective bargaining with the unions.

The 1974 Report also called for new arrangements in the nationalized industries and in the public services including health, education and local government.

These proposals for the widespread extension of industrial democracy brought a sudden awareness to the trade unions, which had largely failed to grasp the significance of the change that was being planned in T.U.C. policy. They also aroused a good deal of critical comment from industrialists and politicians.

The 1974 Congress revealed more clearly what had become apparent in the previous year, that there was powerful opposition within the trade union movement against the ideas for the establishment of industrial democracy which were now being vigorously pursued by the dominant group on the

General Council of the T.U.C. At this Congress a resolution was moved and supported by some of the most powerful unions affiliated to the T.U.C. which stated "that the overriding role of the unions is the advancement of the interests of their members. It, therefore, requires that any extension of trade union participation in industrial management shall be, and shall be seen to be, an extension of collective bargaining and shall in no sense compromise the unions' role as here defined."

The resolution rejected the legal imposition of supervisory boards and called for alternative legislation. This resolution was judged by the General Council as not being in conflict with the Council's own resolution and was accepted on this basis. It was not the first time the T.U.C. had passed resolutions that left it facing both ways, and the passing of similar contradictory resolutions in 1976 and 1977 underlined the ambiguity of its position.

The Committee on Industrial Democracy and Proposed Legislation

In 1975 the government announced that it intended to carry out its promise to legislate on industrial democracy before the next election and to this end was setting up a Committee on Industrial Democracy. After running into serious difficulties in finding a chairman the government announced that a distinguished Oxford professor, Lord Bullock, who had written the biography of Ernest Bevin, one of Britain's most famous trade union leaders, had agreed to undertake this task. The Committee consisted of three trade union leaders who were ardent supporters of co-determination, three employers, two academics, a lawyer, and the director of the Consumers Council. The balance of the Committee was clearly tipped towards the T.U.C. policy, since no representative of the opposition trade union view was on the Committee.

When the terms of reference were published, it was made apparent that the government had been persuaded by the T.U.C. that the Committee should confine its report to examining the feasibility of its proposals.

The majority report of the Committee departed from the 1974 T.U.C. report in one important respect, but with the agreement of the General Council. It rejected the concept of the two-tier board, on the grounds that this would exclude the trade union representatives from participating in decisions of key importance to their members. It, therefore, favored representation on the traditional British management board.

The majority report endorsed the principle of employee representation on boards of directors, subject to the limitation that they must be nominated by a joint representative council of the trade unions recognized in the company for collective bargaining, thus maintaining the T.U.C. insistence on single-channel representation. The appointment procedure was to be triggered by an application from the unions for a ballot vote for the employees. Only the unions recognized by the company were to have this right. If a majority vote of the employees (so long as this was not less than one-third of the total employees) was secured, the unions must then establish a Joint Representative Council which would be responsible for electing the employee representatives. These would be equal in number to those elected by the shareholders. The two groups would then jointly appoint a third group that had to be smaller than the trade union and shareholders' representatives and always an odd number. Thus on a board of 15 there would be six shareholders, six unionists, and three jointly appointed members.

The concept of works councils was rejected as contrary to the principle of single-channel representation. The report also rejected the notion that trade union representatives should have a different status and responsibility from the shareholders' representatives. But it was agreed that the trade union representatives should report back to the Joint Representative Council, which would also have the power to remove a representative that it believed was not effectively fulfilling his or her responsibilities.

This concept of parity co-determination based upon union representation alone was severely condemned by the minority report signed by the three employer representatives.

The minority would go no further than agree to support the E.E.C. proposals in the draft European Company statute of one-third shareholder, one-third trade union and one-third neutrals, on a supervisory board. It was also strongly in favor of the establishment of works councils which would be representative of all the employees whether union members or not.

In the event the government's own proposals, published in May 1978, differed in significant respects from the Bullock Committee's proposals. They reflected known divisions in the Cabinet and the fact that the government was faced by the virtually unanimous opposition of employers and managers. They had criticized the Bullock Report on the grounds of its impracticability and that it would lead to an extension of collective bargaining from the shop floor to the board room. The net effect, as they saw it, would be to promote conflict rather than cooperation and to slow down the pace of decision-making at the expense of managerial efficiency.

Even more disturbing from the point of view of the government was the announcement by a number of unions that under no circumstances would they agree to participate in making the Committee's proposals effective.

Faced by this chorus of criticism the government preferred not to push ahead with legislative proposals. It did, however, allow schemes of participation to be introduced in the nationalized industries where these were desired, as in the Post Office, but the parity principle was not conceded in any of these schemes.

The White Paper on Industrial Democracy indicated the lines on which the government will legislate if it wins the election it must face before the end of 1979. In one respect, the government's proposals follow the Bullock Committee fairly closely. The introduction of a system of employee representation on the boards of company's will be by way of an initiative by either the company or recognized unions organized, as the Bullock Committee suggested, in a Joint Representation Council. All employees will be eligible to vote in a ballot which must first be held, and a majority would have to be in favor to activate the scheme. Thereafter, however, it will be for the unions represented on the J.R.C. to decide how the representatives shall be chosen, but the White Paper offers the possibility that if a union or a substantial homogeneous group of employees felt the scheme were unfair they could have the right of appeal either to a new Industrial Democracy Commission, or alternatively, if this was not established, to the Advisory Conciliation and Arbitration Service. The government departs from the Bullock Committee in two major respects. It rejects the Bullock Committee's proposal that the traditional British system of a unitary board of directors be retained and it will legislate so that a "two-tier board with separate policy and management boards is an option for any company." The top board will be a policy board concerned with the formulation of company policy, and it is on this board that employees' representatives will have a statutory right to be appointed. The policy board will not be involved in the day-to-day running of the company, which will be the responsibility of a professional board of management, but it will have a greater degree of control over the activities of the management board than would be the case with the German supervisory board. The model which the White Paper has followed is that which prevails in Denmark, where the "upper board has considerable powers over the determination of policy and the taking of major decisions and within prescribed limits it is possible for individual directors to be members of both boards."

Through this concept of fairly closely linked policy and management boards the government hopes that it will meet the criticisms levelled by the unions against the rigid separation of the two boards and the limited power of regulation and control exercised by the supervisory board. On the other hand, the government recognizes the importance of ensuring that management has a reasonable freedom to make its decisions and equally that the bargaining role of the unions with management is not unnecessarily confused with their role as participants in the determination of company policy. Whether, in practice, the government's solution to the problems which face both management and unions are effective will depend upon the ability of both parties to develop an understanding and respect for each other's essential role.

The government has also rejected the Bullock Committee's parity of representation formula and favors instead limiting the statutory right of employers to appoint only up to one-third of the policy board. This it sees as a first step that may be extended by voluntary agreement or in the light of experience by subsequent legislation.

The limitation of union membership to one-third ensures that the shareholders will remain in control of the company in the last resort. The power of management will continue to depend, however, on the extent to which it is able to win the confidence of the employees. This will be achieved not only by the sharing of power through participation, but through the efficiency with which management carries out its primary functions. It will be necessary for the unions to recognize that unless they play a constructive role, it is likely that industrial efficiency will be impeded and slowed down. If this were to happen, it would be surprising if political support for a further extension of their representation on policy boards would be forthcoming. A major element in the government's strategy is, as far as possible, to encourage the unions and employees to set up their own schemes without resort to the statutory assistance and the statutory model proposed in the White Paper. In this connection, the government fully recognizes that there are strong union objections to representation on boards of directors, as well as management reservations. Neither side is to be forced into participation until at least four years have elapsed from the establishment of the Joint Representative Council.

Although there has been a more favorable response to the government's White Paper than there was to the Bullock Report, there is still strong employer hostility to even the limited degree of compulsory appointment of employee directors now proposed. It is likely that a Conservative Government would wish to seek to associate all employees more closely with the appointment of employee directors than contemplated in the government's White Paper and would wish the Joint Representative Council to be established on a basis that would make this possible.

The general election will decide whether the government will go ahead with legislation on the lines of the White Paper. If the Conservatives win it is unlikely that they will rush into legislation, since employer opposition to a compulsory model of any type is likely to be considerable.

Quality of Working Life

There can be little doubt that British workers are mainly motivated toward work by what they earn. Many studies have shown the extent to which pay dominates their behavior.[3] Although it is often suggested that industrial disputes are caused by a complex of factors, which lie behind the ostensible reason, it is difficult to get away from the fact that the issues on which most strikes are called are ones relating to pay.

British workers are apparently often ready to put up with very bad working conditions so long as they are adequately compensated. There has, however, been a significant growth of concern for improvements in the working environment. The Health and Safety at Work Act provides for the establishment of safety committees and union-nominated safety representa tives in every plant.

It is often claimed that the most significant improvement in the quality of working life is likely to come from the growth of effective schemes of employee participation in the actual carrying out of their normal employment tasks. There have been many experiments in job enlargement and work restructuring so as to provide for a greater degree of selfmanagement. The creation of a work environment in which the worker can enjoy a more satisfying daily working life is strongly urged by many students of industrial relations, but there is relatively little union interest. Although management increasingly recognizes the importance of improving the working environment as a means of winning greater cooperation and reducing absenteeism and labor turnover, experience suggests that these advances will not necessarily bring immediate improvements in industrial relations if the economic and social context is one which creates stress and conflict.

Conclusions

The British system of industrial relations has become much more participative at all levels, at the shop floor, plant, enterprise, and at national levels. This development has taken place both through the evolution of the collective bargaining system and through direct methods of participation. However, the system is far from in a stable equilibrium. Although a recent survey of strikes in manufacturing industries has shown that in the three years 1971–73, which included a number of years that were well above the average of the previous decade, some 95 percent of the enterprises had not experienced a stoppage. The picture was very different, however, when the large enterprises, defined as employing more than 1,000, were examined since the figure fell to 42 percent. These figures suggest that in the larger enterprises, which not only employ a large proportion of the total labor force in manufacturing, but are also responsible for a very high proportion of total output, the problem of industrial conflict is more serious (although it is important to note that a substantial proportion of the large companies had no stoppages of work in the period). The figures confirm what common sense suggests—that the poor performance of British industry has something to do with its industrial relations. Unfortunately there is little evidence that the very large changes that have occurred over the past few decades bringing about a great increase in trade union power, in the power of the shop stewards, and in the development of collective bargaining in the larger enterprises have made a significant contribution to the improvement of industrial relations in either the private or public sectors.

Industrial relations, if measured by the total number of strikes and man-days lost, are clearly much worse than they were in the 1930s and the 1950s. Undoubtedly the lower level of overt industrial conflict in those periods owed a good deal to the relative weakness of the trade unions. They are now much more powerful. What is perhaps most significant is that there has been a greater deterioration in the quality of industrial relations in the public sector than in the private sector. The large increase in strikes and their spread to groups of employees such as civil servants, firemen, airline pilots, doctors, and nurses is indicative of the change in attitudes and values that has taken place since the Second World War.

Relatively high levels of industrial conflict, measured by man-days lost through strikes, may not be a major obstacle to high levels of efficiency as the experience of the U.S.A. indicates. Nevertheless, it is also significant that in Europe it is the countries with relatively bad strike records, such as the U.K. and Italy, that also have poor records of economic performance. The problem is not so much the number of man-days lost, since this figure may be considerable but be less damaging than a relatively large number of short but unpredictable stoppages, which is very much the situation in Britain. Strikes are, of course, only one measure of industrial conflict. Work-to-rule, go slows, refusal to work overtime, and a straightforward refusal to accept a new method of working which might be necessary to obtain the benefit of new machinery are very often resorted to by shop stewards in Britain, but there is no quantitative assessment of the effects of these actions on output. Many managers are convinced that the difficulties they encounter in these aspects have a major impact on the performance of their plants. The most extreme manifestations of local bargaining power have been exposed in the Swan Hunter and British Leyland Triumph conflicts which resulted in large-scale redundancies, but it is believed that there are many other similar situations which have extremely damaging consequences without necessarily resulting in plant closures. What is quite clear is that the power of shop stewards is far greater and the frequency with which they refuse to cooperate with management is far more common than in any other advanced industrial country. The reasons for this are complex, but if they are to be overcome both management and union leadership at national levels will have to take more vigorous and positive steps.

It is evident that the nature of ownership is not in itself a prime cause of the state of industrial relations, since good and bad industrial relations exist in both private and public sectors. What is at issue is at one level a conflict between managers, who draw their authority from those who own the assets of the enterprise, whether it be the state or private shareholders, and the workers who have acquired collective strength through unionization. At another level the conflict is no longer one of social class in the Marxist sense, between those who own the means of production and those who do not, but between occupational groups which wish to improve their status and income, both absolutely and relatively. However, the inheritance of class attitudes is of great social significance. The industrial relations problem is, therefore, one of conflict both between managers and employees and between employees and employees. It is a pattern of conflict which cannot be solved through a system of collective bargaining which is based upon ideologies and structures that are fundamentally inimical to cooperative industrial relations.

It remains to be seen whether it will be possible in Britain to bring a reconciliation of conflicting interests through the development of integrating participative structures and processes at the national and enterprise levels. For such a development to be successful it will be necessary for collective bargaining as it now exists to be greatly changed and ultimately to give way to more effective methods of settling issues relating to pay and the making of decisions essential to good government and the efficient management of enterprises. Although there are many signs that change in this direction must come, it is not likely to arrive quickly, or without great difficulty, since the problem is not only one of overcoming deeply entrenched interests, but also one of bringing about changes in the law, institutions, and behavior throughout society.

The British industrial relations system has moved closer to the systems which exist in Europe. It is more regulated by law, which has followed continental practice in providing a greater degree of legal protection of individual rights of employees. It remains, however, a much more voluntaristic system in terms of collective action. Both employers and unions prefer to limit the role of the law as a matter of general principle, but as a matter of practice they are ready to see an extension of legal regulation which protects their particular interest. Since governments are influenced by the pressures exerted by the unions and industry, the outcome is a legal framework which falls substantially short of either the European or the American model. Although the forces of voluntarism remain strong, the trend is towards a greater degree of legal regulation.

There are those who fear that the restructuring of the industrial relations system will only be achieved at the expense of creating a corporate state. What is certain is that with over 50 percent of the gross national product now being spent by the government, tripartitism is unlikely to diminish. There is a danger when at the same time trade union membership rises above 50 percent, as it has now done, and the law entrenches collective rights above those of individual rights that corporatism will become dominant. Ironically, it may be the conflict between unions, which is manifest in their structure and their schizophrenic attitude towards the role of the law that will prevent Britain from going rapidly down the road to the corporate state, as almost certainly would have happened had British trade unionism developed a more logical structure and British employers' organizations developed the cohesion and strength of the Scandinavian employers' organizations. Paradoxically, this weakness in the British system of industrial relations might turn out to be its principal strength.

Notes

1. Roy Lewis, "Historical Development of Labour Law", *British Journal of Industrial Relations*, Vol. XIV, No. 1, March 1976.
2. *The Future of Pay Determination*, Confederation of British Industry, London, 1977.
3. J. H. Goldthorpe, D. Lockwood, *et al.*, *The Affluent Worker*, Cambridge, Cambridge University Press, 1968.

7
Japan

by H. OKAMOTO

Introduction

This present essay is an attempt to review manifest and latent trends of worker participation in modern Japan, focussing on manufacturing industries in the private sector of the economy and developments in the last two decades in order to explore some long-term possibilities. As such it is an attempt stimulated by the underlying question as to whether similar or dissimilar developments to those within Europe are a likely possibility in view of trends in industrial relations and changes in economic, political, social and cultural forces.

At the outset, a few remarks about the major features of Japanese trade unions may be in order. Under the present legal framework of industrial relations which was introduced in the aftermath of the Second World War and modelled after the American system, decisions on working conditions and other matters related to workers' concerns are left to a large extent to voluntary processes. The opportunity for worker participation is primarily conditioned by the extent, structure, and influence of trade unions. Admittedly, the role of the state has been pervasive in influencing economic, social and other contextual factors, as has been more or less the case in other modern market economies. Nevertheless, also in respect to decisions on economic and social development, it is largely through trade unions that workers as a social category express their interests and opinions in Japan.

Total trade union membership was 12.6 million in June 1976, which is the second largest among market economies. In the last two decades, trade union membership has had a growth rate roughly on a par with the rate of increase of the employed workforce. In the 1960s it grew from 7.7 million to 11.6, an increase of 4.0 million, and in subsequent years by about 1.0 million. Trade unions cover all major firms in both private and public sectors. Although the majority of organized workers is in the private sector (72.9 percent), trade unions in the public sector have been more coherently organized, with a much higher rate of unionization. They have constituted one of the major centers of influence within the Japanese trade union movement. Broadly, trade unions as a whole have achieved such a magnitude, momentum, and strategic power, that they may be said to have become an influential economic and social force in modern Japan. However, the estimated rate of unionization is presently at the low level of 33.4 percent of employed workers. This level has been relatively constant during the last two decades. While the relative constancy may be seen as a remarkable achievement in view of the dramatic changes in employment structure by industry, locality, occupation, etc., it must be also taken as evidence of the difficulty of penetrating the medium and small business sectors. Moreover, since there has been a comparatively larger share of self-employed and family workers in the labor force (of the order of 30 percent), the rate of unionization has remained at 24 percent or one-fourth of those who work, which is roughly on a par with the level in the U.S.A. and much lower than in major European countries.

One very distinctive feature of the Japanese trade union structure is its highly decentralized nature. The major unit of decision-making in trade union organizations is at the plant, or works, or enterprise, level. Each of these units is a self-governing entity having rights for association, bargaining, and striking. Hence they have been called "enterprise unions." This structural characteristic has been a correlate of a distinctive employment system characterized by life-time employment, the seniority principle, and enterprise welfarism. In view of the intrinsic importance of the employment system for the trade union structure and for the dynamics of industrial relations in general terms, a brief account is necessary of its distinctive features. Although labor mobility in most societies tends to be most prevalent among young workers and females, and relatively less so among adult male workers, that of the Japanese adult male from about 25 years of age up to 55–60 appears to be lower. This tendency seems to apply to both large and medium-scale firms, even if, domestically, the difference between the two sectors has been significant. This phenomenon has been due to the reciprocal norms of providing continuous employment (by firms) and not changing the place of work (on the part of workers) to the maximum extent possible. An important correlate of life-time employment is the seniority principle which governs the improvement of individual workers' relative positions in the hierarchies of roles, status and rewards. An important aspect of this principle is a rather distinctive wage-curve pattern.

Whereas in many other societies, the wage curve correlates with age up to about 35–40, that correlation in Japan has extended up to 55–60. Also, while in many other societies the wage-curve pattern has been different between white-collar and blue-collar workers, in Japan's case it has been identical. Although merit has been taken into account, the seniority principle has been the major premise in personnel administration. Another important correlate of life-time employment is enterprise welfarism. Whereas non-wage labor costs relative to the average wage rate have been lower than in most European counterparts, it is due mainly to the method of contributing to a collective welfare fund for employees at the enterprise, rather than fringe benefits for individuals. The welfare cost of 10 percent or so of the wage bill cumulated annually at the enterprise level tends to generate an enterprise community with its own housing, retirement allowance/pension, hospital, education and training centers, sports and recreation facilities. Under the prevailing pattern of employment with these characteristics, it may be expected that trade unions will have their major bases at the enterprise level, the workers' common interests being strongly conditioned by the economic and social dynamics of individual enterprises. In view of the uniquely decentralized structure and underlying conditional factors, there have been two contrasting views of trade unions in modern Japan. In the most extreme form, one view sees the enterprise union as a "company union," responding readily to the needs of management in return for what the enterprise provides out of enlightened self-interest; the other view is that the enterprise union is super-modern, a decentralized organization capable of ensuring industrial democracy under changing technological and social conditions. While these views have some empirical justification, it must be mentioned that both risk over-emphasizing the "uniqueness" of enterprise unions and so fail to recognize the more intelligible universal elements.

Wage decisions have been based on collective bargaining at the enterprise level, but they have been coordinated industrially for the last twenty years by the formula known as the "Spring Wage Offensive." There are at present 175 industrial federations of enterprise unions or their equivalents and they play coordinating roles in wage decisions. In the immediate postwar years in many branches of the economy, it was the industrial federations which played a leading role in wage decisions, because of significant government subsidies to particular industries. By the early fifties, as government subsidies were suspended, more or less enterprise-based collective bargaining became the predominant pattern. In the meantime, enterprise unions were faced with the problem of bargaining strength, due to smallness of size relative to firms. It was against such a background that the Spring Wage Offensive formula was devised. Since then, the industrial federations have begun to coordinate their demands, with a strategic sequence of negotiations and level of settlement giving a pattern bargaining effect within and among industries. The Spring Wage Offensive had its real start in 1955, involving eight industrial unions and 400,000 members affiliated with Sohyo (General

Congress of Trade Unions in Japan), one of the four national labor centers. Thereafter, it showed rapid and successful development against a background of economic growth and an improvement in labor market conditions. Although industrial federations have been divided in their ideological inclinations and thus are affiliated with different national centers, for example, at present 55 with Sohyo, 28 with Domei (Japanese Confederation of Labor), 4 with Shinsanbetsu (National Federation of Industrial Organizations), and 12 with Churitsuroren (Federation of Independent Unions), the remainder being unaffiliated, most of them *de facto* began to join the wage round. In 1959, Churitsuroren joined with Sohyo and formed the Spring Wage Joint Offensive Committee. After the 1960s Zenro, the predecessor of Domei, began to concentrate wage bargaining of affiliated unions in the spring, as did Shinsanbetsu. By 1961, the offensive involved 4.4 million workers, by 1965, 5.6 million, and by 1971, 9.2 million. Today it involves most of the 175 industrial federations and nearly 10 million union members. By the mid-1960s, a regular sequence of events began to emerge in the wage round. Generally, the decision reached between major steel unions and their firms is followed by other private heavy industries. These in turn are followed by the private railways, resulting in a guiding "wage market price." Usually, at the peak of private railway negotiations, the central labor relations commission is involved through the mediation process. Almost invariably, it confirms the "wage market price." Subsequently the decision in the private railways indirectly influences the decision on pay recommendations of the National Personnel Authority for national government employees and that in turn affects the pay increase of local government employees. Thus a wage-round cycle is completed. Wage decisions at medium and small firms have generally been made after the settlement in the private railway sector, except for a minority of cases where wage decisions are reached before the steel settlement. One economic implication of this development may be shown by a comparison of international wage-cost trends. Japan's annual rate of wage-cost increase in manufacturing industries was in the early half of the fifties one of the lowest among the major industrial market economies. However, in the 1960s it went up to a level roughly on a par with the U.S.A. and France, a level lower than in the U.K. and Italy, but higher than in Germany. Subsequently, in the early 1970s, the rate of increase became one of the highest, second only to the U.K.

Domestically, the development considerably narrowed wage differentials by sectors and many non-unionized firms began to be *de facto* affected by the "wage market price." The Spring Wage Offensive has become, so to speak, the national wage-decision mechanism. A corollary of this was the increase in the bargaining potential of trade unions. After the rise in world oil prices, trade unions began to become oriented towards a social-contract-like strategy.

Major political decisions in Japan have been the function of a political system in which parliamentary processes played the major role, but with the pervasive influence of the government bureaucracy. After passing through a few years of political instability before and after Japan's independence in the mid-1950s, parliamentary processes were anchored firmly in society since extra-parliamentary group activities became less prevalent, although pressure group activities focussing on government bureaucracies remained significant. Trade unions have striven to increase their influence within the political system through support of political parties. Political activity has been an important concern of the Japanese trade union movement, so much so that it has often been characterized as political unionism. The national centers have played a major part in the political and ideological division within the trade union movement. The 4.5 million-strong Sohyo has linked itself almost inseparably with the Japan Socialist Party (JSP), which has in it a variety of Socialists with an ideological leftist majority. The 2.2 million-strong Domei aligns itself with the Democratic Socialist Party (DSP), which has a gradualistic approach toward reforms. The 66,000-strong Shinsanbetsu supports all non-Communist reform parties. The 1.4 million-strong Churitsuroren remains apolitical, although its affiliated unions are inclined to support all non-Communist opposition parties. The remaining independent unions, with 4.7 million members, are generally apolitical. While it is true to say that the policentric split has tended to offset the political influence of any one of the national centers and of the trade union movement as a whole, it is also true that the opposition parties have increased their influence in parliament in the last two decades and therefore the *potential* influence of trade unions on major political decisions. During the 1960s and subsequently, the share of seats by opposition parties in the House of Representatives increased from 35.3 percent, or 175 out of 467, in 1960 to 44.3 percent, or 226 out of 511, in 1976. Their share of seats was almost the same as that of the ruling Liberal Democratic Party, and it induced moves for the unification of the labor front.

The development of the trade unions reflects the increased pressure of demands for an improved quality of life. With this growth has come a greater diversity of political interests among rank-and-file members who generally tend to be less ideologically committed than in the earlier days of trade union development. This evolution has led to the structure of the trade unions at the national level becoming comparatively less stable. Against this background, after the mid-1960s, various moves emerged towards setting up new centers of influence among industrial federations cutting across different national affiliations. One of the earliest examples was the International Metal Federation-Japan Council (IMF-JC) involving Tekkororen (Japanese Federation of Iron and Steel Workers' Unions) of Sohyo, Zosenjukiroren (Federation of Shipbuilding and Heavy Machinery Workers' Unions) and Jidosharoren (Federation of Japan Automobile Workers' Unions) of Domei, Zenkikin (National Machinery and Metal Workers' Union) of Shinsanbetsu and Denkiroren (All Japan Federation of Electric

Machine Workers' Unions) of Churitsuroren. Although the founding of this federation was a reaction to the internationalization of the economy, it was also aimed at closer coordination of the domestic trade union movement, and this was made explicit in the late 1960s by its reorganization into the Japan Federation of Metal Workers' Unions. An implication of this development was an attempt to secure a basis for the pragmatic pursuit of economic and social interests outside the existing policentric structure that has involved political and organizational rivalries. At present the Federation is 1.9 million strong. Subsequently, and following a similar course, the Japan Confederation of Chemical Workers was formed, having a strength of half a million. A similar process is at present going on in food-related industries. In the early 1970s, a much larger confederation was formed—the Confederation for the Joint Action of Private Sector Unions, involving the large-scale industrial federations of Domei, Sohyo-affiliated Tekkororen and Gokkaroren (Japanese Federation of Synthetic Workers' Unions) and independent unions involving Jidoshasoren (Confederation of Japanese Automobile Workers' Unions), etc. At present, it has 5 million members. The purpose of this organization is to increase trade-union influence on national policy decisions on economic and social developments and also to steer the unification of the labor front. Meanwhile, against the background of these developments, established national centers began to develop coalitionist actions. Shinsanbetsu and Churitsuroren played a leading role in this development and are themselves considering the possibility of merging with a large number of independent unions into a new national center. This is the background against which Sohyo and Domei are paying more attention to coalitionist actions. Related to these moves, there has been, since the early 1970s, a conspicuous tendency on the part of each center of influence to formulate economic and social policy demands in such areas as growth targets, employment strategies, price stability, tax reform, social welfare, and public services. There were already embryonic moves of this kind, in the mid-1960s, and they had on occasion been utilized in the wage campaigns. Subsequently, the trade union centers began to negotiate directly with government and, after the oil price rise of 1973, they have done so as part of social contract-like wage offensive strategies. So far, negotiations with government have been conducted separately, the only exception being the 1977 coalition demands for employment stabilization policies. However, since economic and social policy demands have not been dissimilar, various forms of combined action are likely to increase.

There is no prospect, however, of any immediate unification of the labor front or major re-alignment at the national center level, since ideological division is deeply rooted in the respective movements. Also, even more importantly, this ideological division has interlocked with situations conditioned by industrial structure. This fact can be shown by the distinctive membership patterns of the national unions. In Sohyo, there tends to be a significantly larger representation of *traditional heavy industries* with such unions as the 18,652-strong Tanro (Japan Coal Miners' Union), 17,147-strong Zenko (Federation of All-Japan Metal-Mining Labor Unions), 34,719-strong Kamiparoren (National Federation of Paper and Pulp Industry Workers' Unions), 129,291-strong Gokkaroren, and 252,793-strong Tekkororen. With the exception of Gokkaroren and Tekkororen, all these are in industries where employment has been declining for the last two decades. Also in Sohyo, there is stronger representation of unions catering to the *medium-small business sector* and more generally workers who are in relatively weak positions. There are, for example, the 201,587-strong Zenkokukizoku (National Trade Union of Metal and Engineering Workers), 66,667-strong Zenjiko (National Federation of Automobile Transport Workers' Unions), 26,781-strong Zenkokuippan (National Union of General Workers), and the 89,617-strong Zennichijiro (All-Japan Day Workers Union). All these, with the single exception of Zennichijiro, increased their memberships in the last two decades. Where unions of relatively weak workers exist, the public sector unions tend to unite with them. In Sohyo, there is an overwhelmingly large proportion of *public service* workers. There are such unions as the 1,195,795-strong Jichiro (All-Japan Prefectural and Municipal Workers' Union), 642,511-strong Nikkyo-so (Japan Teachers' Union), 332,602-strong Dentsu Kyoto (Joint Council of Tele-Communication Industry Trade Unions), 247,171-strong Kokuro (National Railway Workers' Union), and 202,307-strong Zentei (Japan Postal Workers' Union). Generally, they have increased their membership considerably in the last two decades. An exception to this is Kokuro, which lost members due to the decline of the industry and rationalization. This may have been one of the reasons as to why, together with the 46,959-strong Doryokusha (National Railway Locomotive Engineers' Union), another Sohyo union, it has been one of the most militant. Domei has a different membership pattern. While it has well-established trade unions in traditional industries, like the 56,406-strong Kaiin (All-Japan Seamen's Union) and the 470,476-strong Zensen (Japan Federation of Textile and Allied Workers' Unions), it has significantly stronger representation of the major unions in *modern heavy industries* which have grown rapidly. The 229,334-strong Zosenjukiroren increased its membership during 1961–76 8.5 times, the 192,975-strong Jidosharoren 7.4 times. The 133,619-strong Denroren, operating in power plants, is another union in a growth industry, although its membership increased only moderately, by 8 percent, due to comprehensive automation. The 306,654-strong Zenkin Domei (National Federation of Metal Industry Trade Workers), catering to the growing industrial firms in the *medium-small business* sector, more than doubled its membership. Thus, Domei is the strongest in the private sector of the economy. Shinsanbetsu has a different character. It has strong representation of workers at *medium firms* in western Japan. Churitsuroren has larger representation of unions in *light industries, skilled trades and tertiary industries*. Finally, as may be imagined, unaffiliated unions tend to be those unions catering to *white-collar workers*. Thus, it may be concluded that ideological divisions are related to common interests in the economy. However, along with the narrowing of inter-industry and occupational differentials, political and social inclinations among people who share common economic interests have become increasingly diverse. Related to this, party political support of trade unions at the industrial and regional levels began to develop.

Although the Japanese unions are often seen as very much less strike-prone than in other countries, this picture has been exaggerated. Measured in terms of strike frequency and membership participation rate, Japan has been ranked at the top among major industrialized market economies. In terms of the number of days lost due to strikes per union member, Japan has been roughly on a par with the U.K. and France in normal years during the last two decades. One distinctive aspect of the Japanese situation, however, is that disputes have been more predictable and perhaps more orderly; strikes tended to be concentrated in the Spring Wage Round and in autumn lump-sum bonus negotiations; the crucial issues in the disputes have been mostly related to wages and hours. Broadly stated, while trade unions became socially integrated, their bargaining strength and potential political influence have increased. At the same time, they have expanded the opportunities for worker participation by widening the scope of collective bargaining and also of the more direct methods of participation. Static as it may seem, the changes in the industrial relations system have been profound and pervasive, to the extent of suggesting that a new phase of industrial relations has developed. And it is this aspect that we will be looking at more closely. In 1977, however, the trade unions faced a turning point with the prospect of long-term slower economic growth, unemployment, the threat of inflation, and social change. Although aspects of policy and strategy are likely to change, it appears fairly certain that trade unions will look for occasions for increasing worker participation at various levels.

The Experience of the Joint Management Committee

Although admittedly it was during the unusual and crisis situation of the immediate post-war years, Japan has experienced a period of comprehensive worker participation. The *joint management committee*, then widely in use, clearly had features that were unique to Japan, yet it also included some that were similar to aspects of current models of European worker participation.

Following the end of the Second World War, the growth of unions was striking. Rapid growth continued until 1949 when the number of trade unions reached 34,688, with a total membership of about 6.7 million or 55.8 percent of the employed. It was during this period of initial trade-union growth that the joint management committee became prevalent and played a major role in industrial relations.

For more than one year immediately after the war, management had been in a state of confusion. Being unsure of itself, it had been reluctant to re-open or restore production or services, whose facilities had suffered great damage. About a quarter of the national wealth was lost due to the war. Materials were in short supply, transport was crippled, and inflation was terrifying. Government economic policy was uncertain. International trade was prohibited. Major owner interests, the family combines (*zaibatsu*) were disbanded and influential industrial leaders were purged or voluntarily withdrew from office. Mining and manufacturing production in 1946 remained stagnant at about 30 percent of the pre-war level (1934–36 average). Workshops, works, and firms were in a state of uncertainty and, not infrequently, they were occupied by workers and their unions. It was under such circumstances that the joint management committee was demanded by enterprise unions to secure employment and income and also to extend their rights within the enterprise.

In the early post-war years trade unions were stronger than management. Typically, collective agreements included such provisions as: (1) wages shall guarantee a minimum living standard and shall rise with consumer prices; (2) prior negotiations with the union shall be mandatory for such matters as recruitment, discharge, promotion, wage changes and transfer; (3) welfare facilities shall be administered by the union; (4) *business and managerial decisions shall be referred to the joint management committee*; (5) the company shall recognize time off for employees elected to specified union offices; and (6) the foregoing clauses do not preclude the union from making its own decisions.

The joint management committee had almost invariably equal representation for top union officers and top management at works and/or enterprise levels. In reality, there were varying types ranging from purely advisory consultative organs to *de facto* workers' control machinery. Typically, it was an institutional arrangement for worker participation since joint decision was intended to be reached by way of social dialogue between the two parties. Most typically, not only matters relating to working conditions (exclusive of wages and hours that were handled through collective bargaining) but also production problems and business policies were dealt with in this way. Although in most cases managerial initiative and responsibility were respected for production and business policies, preliminary consultation and negotiation were made obligatory to secure joint decision as frequently as possible. Given the climate of industrial relations of the time, it often meant that approval from the union was mandatory for major corporate decisions. In fact, the agreement of the joint management committee frequently stipulated this explicitly. That of the Kanto Kogyo Corporation, for example, specified the following matters as subject to "joint decision," that is, requiring union approval:

1. Increase or decrease of corporate capital
2. Procurement or investment of capital of a sum of more than 100,000 yen

3. Opening or closure of plants
4. Appointment of directors and auditors
5. Recruitment and discharge of employees
6. Payment to directors, auditors and employees
7. Working hours of employees
8. Disposal of corporate physical assets (land, buildings, machinery, tools and appliances
9. Other matters as deemed necessary by the council

It may be of interest to note that the joint management committee, as an institutional arrangement for worker participation, was a spontaneous demand that arose within the trade unions and was subsequently implemented by union and management. Broadly, it aimed to re-organize the productive and social organization of enterprises and to cope with the complex problems of labor relations arising from the chaotic post-war economic and social environment. At many places, through joint decision involving bi-partite consultation or negotiation processes, the committee functioned to control the causes of unnecessary conflict or hardship and to guide the re-organization of workshops, firms and enterprises, to enable them to adjust to the post-war environment. However, equally, at other places it did not fulfill the purpose of worker participation and at times caused additional conflicts. Two of the then national centers, Sanbetsu Kaigi (General Congress of Industrial Organizations) and Sodomei (General Council of Trade Unions) were not in favor of worker participation. Sanbetsu Kaigi, which was strongly influenced by Communist ideology, tended to regard the joint management committee as a device to induce class collaboration between unions and management, although no doubt some of its leaders saw in it another possibility, i.e., its potential evolution into the enterprise "Soviet" or workers' control committee. The Sanbetsu Kaigi, which was very influential at that time, stressed the need to utilize the joint management committee as the ground for day-to-day conflicts and campaigns. Sodomei, which was a moderate socialist force but at the same time business-oriented, saw the joint management committee primarily in a pre-bargaining function. Underlying the attitudes of the national centers might have been the bitter memory of industrial relations in the 1920s and 1930s when the joint consultative committee was used to exclude trade unions from the works and enterprises. In many places, therefore, the joint management committee tended to become the arena for collective bargaining and day-to-day conflicts. At times it became an instrument for trade union control over the enterprise; in 1946 alone, in no less than 170 disputes, management was locked out by the trade unions in what were attempts to impose workers' control of production.

Nevertheless, since it was clear that in many places the joint management committee performed an unmistakably constructive role in generating consensus over the difficult problems of the extremely anomic post-war period, the Central Labor Relations Commission issued "Guidelines for the Joint Management Committee" in 1946. The commission tried to promote an ideal type of joint management committee which was by and large an amalgam of then existing patterns, although there was also an implicit recognition in the guidelines of the need to check trade influence. On the basic character of the joint management committee, the guidelines said:

The joint management committee is a permanent organization established by collective agreement and as such it essentially aims to enable workers to participate in management of enterprise based on the spirit of industrial democracy. However, the establishment of the joint management committee, does not, because of it, in any way bring about changes in the rights and duties of enterprise executives for overall supervision and leadership. But it gives them the duty to refer to the committee matters which had been hithertofore decided and handled at their discretion and as for matters jointly decided, to handle them as decisions as dictated by the committee.[1]

The guidelines stressed that enterprise executives are ultimately responsible for management of an enterprise and therefore it suggested that whenever matters were not jointly resolvable, enterprise executives should have the responsibility of making the final decision. At the same time, they suggested that any managerial concern could be subject to review by the joint management committee. It must be noted in this connection that the guidelines recognized the possibility of comprehensive worker participation. For example:

To refer to the committee such matters as dividends and appointments of directors is not by itself illegal. But in such a case, it is necessary to be duly prepared for it by so stating in the company constitution. Otherwise, if jointly decided by the committee, the decision may not be binding on the stockholders and therefore trouble may later arise. It is then necessary to prevent it from occurring beforehand.[2]

The guidelines of the Central Labor Relations Commission may be said to have succeeded in calling attention to the joint management committee as an institutional arrangement for effective worker participation. The number of trade unions having provision for joint management committees increased from several thousand, or some 30 percent of the total at the end of 1946, to 11,883, or 42.4 percent a year later, and further to 15,005 or 44.3 percent by the end of 1948. Nevertheless, the guidelines did not necessarily succeed in developing a stable pattern of worker participation. In many places the committee played a pre-bargaining role and/or conflict dominated the scene. Frequently the ability of trade unions to participate effectively was questioned. As the economy gradually began to recover from the devastation of war, management began to regain its strength. The shifting power balance accompanied a decline in worker participation. The process was accelerated by a change in the labor policy of the Allied Occupation Forces, towards excluding radical elements from the labor movement, and also by the change in the labor policy of the government, towards introducing the American model of industrial relations, with the notion of management prerogatives. In place of the joint management committee, it was recommended that three separate institutions be organized: negotiation committees, grievance committees, and advisory production committees. Trade unions generally resisted the changes and a period of "no agreement" ensued. By the end of 1950, the number of trade unions having a provision for joint management councils declined to 6,888 or 23.6 percent of the total. At a significant number of places, the reaction to the tendency of trade unions to dominate was sufficiently strong to destroy the joint management council. The decisive reason for the breakdown of joint management councils was the tragic discrepancy between the considerable power of the trade unions to secure comprehensive worker participation and their inability to assume the degree of responsibility involved in membership of the joint management council. Its decline as an institution was due as much to weakened domestic support as to external pressure, but it cannot be denied that it provided an essential medium for generating consensus in the extremely anomic post-war environment and for bringing about a very dramatic democratization of the social structure of enterprises. It must also be mentioned that the joint management council left some important legacies in succeeding systems of worker participation that could not be replaced by American models of advisory production committee.

The Joint Consultative Committee

The most significant institutional arrangement for worker participation at present operating in Japan is a variety of joint consultative committees. Domei's title for this committee, literally translated, is "labor management consultative committee." By contrast Sohyo calls it the "prior-to-decision negotiation committee."

The distinction is subtle but not insignificant. Although it is a matter of degree, the former values joint decisions made through consultative processes and the latter prior-to-decision negotiations. When the consensus is not achieved, Sohyo unions tend to turn more readily to collective bargaining. Nevertheless, since there have been basic similarities in the structure and function of the two arrangements and since both have generally been referred to as joint consultative committees, this more common terminology will be used here. It is, however, important to bear in mind the existence of the two types; the consultation-oriented and the negotiation-oriented.

The joint consultative committee is a pervasive feature at large and medium firms, although not among unionized smaller firms. About 69 percent of all the 61,571 enterprise unions in the private sector have such a committee. The ratios are respectively 70 percent for unions in enterprises with 1,000 or more employees, 65 percent in those with 500-999, 56 percent in those with 100-499, 36 percent in those having 30-99, and 26 percent in those with less than 30 employees. Joint consultative committees are also usual in most public sector establishments. It must also be mentioned that the absence of the joint consultative committee does not mean complete lack of formally prescribed occasions for consultation, or prior-to-decision negotiation with a union representative or, in his absence, a representative of the employees. Under the Labor Standards Act employers are obliged to consult on and negotiate decisions on final drafts of the Rules of Employment, to be submitted to the local Director of the Labor Standards Inspector's Office. Under the Safety and Hygiene Act, employers are required to consult on or negotiate the appointment of worker representatives to the Safety and Hygiene Committee. Under the Wage Security Act, appointment of the majority of members of the wage deposit committee, which is a voluntary system but nonetheless widespread, is subject to consultation or negotiation. These laws are applicable to all establishments with more than ten regularly employed persons. Since the Rules of Employment are legally required to contain provisions for wages, hours of work, retirement and other basic items pertaining to working conditions then, if taken together with the two Acts, formally prescribed opportunities for consultation, or prior-to-decision negotiation, may be said to be substantial. Moreover, at many of the medium and small non-unionized firms, there has been some sort of joint committee for consultative and social purposes, one common type of which is the joint "friendship society."

The joint consultative committee is in some respects rather akin to the works council (*Betriebsrat*) in West Germany, covering a variety of production and working condition issues. In addition, it also has a function of the economic committee (*Wirtschaft Ausschuss*) in that it normally includes economic and business matters for communication and consultation, although the right of prior-to-decision negotiation is usually not formally established. So far, the joint consultative committee tends to be located at the plant or works level in the case of larger firms and at the enterprise level in the case of smaller firms. Almost invariably it involves an equal number of representatives from management and unions. It is a formal institutional body and usually its major joint decisions and points of discussion are recorded and reported back to rank-and-file members. It is usually a management representative who chairs the meeting. But, since issues relating to rationalization are subject to negotiation, not to speak of those broadly relating to working conditions, it is possible to shift the discussion quickly into collective bargaining processes and thus the joint consultative committee necessarily involves accommodation of reciprocal influences, to varying degrees.

The extent of trade union involvement in decisions through the joint consultative committee varies with the items under discussion. The rights involved in the process are normally specified by collective agreement. First, matters of working conditions involving the concrete application of basic agreements on wages, hours, ergonomic conditions, wage structures and fringe benefit items, are subject to joint discussion or prior-to-decision negotiations. If a decision is reached, it becomes part of a formal agreement or *de facto* a binding promise. If agreement is not reached, the union can refer the matter to collective bargaining. Second, matters involving policies and programs on safety and welfare tend to be subject to joint decision-oriented consultation in that the union's right of veto is respected. It is possible for the union to refer the matter to collective bargaining, but the union tends to prefer that it be solved by joint decision-oriented consultation, in part because the nature of the problem is not likely to induce support for a dispute. Third, matters concerning personnel raise different issues. Those involving policies and standards of recruitment, selection, placement, transfer, education and training, job analysis and job evaluation are usually cases for joint understanding-oriented consultation, in that management reports the policies and rules and consults in an attempt to obtain the opinions and understanding, if not support or approval, of the union. It is possible for the union to refer the matters to collective bargaining, but since the enterprise union embraces a membership differing by trade or job, age, sex, etc., there is a general tendency for the union to refrain from the formulation of detailed personnel rules or their application to individual cases. However, it is not unusual for the union to examine the adequacy of the rules being applied. Questions concerning manning rules, ergonomic conditions, mass lay-offs, periodic or large-scale transfer, discipline, and discharge come within the scope of joint decision or prior-to-decision negotiation. Fourth, matters concerning production, including production planning, scheduling of equipment and machinery, measurement of productivity, and rules of the suggestion system, tend to fall into the category of joint understanding-oriented consultation in that management preserves the right to make decisions but again looks for suggestions and understanding from the union, and possibly support and approval. Fifth, matters related to business decisions involving long-range investment, the financial status of the firm, and departmental polices are covered, in that management outlines its policies and plans in an attempt to obtain the union's views and understanding, if not support and approval. In addition, matters related to community relations, environment and the overseas activities of the company fall into this category. However, when any of these matters relates to "rationalization", that affects employment and working conditions, it becomes a subject for joint decision, prior-to-decision negotiation or collective bargaining.

The joint consultative committee is in general approved of by both union and management. Extensive surveys in recent years invariably reported that by far a majority of people on the labor side and in management, and also independents, think that the machinery has worked effectively. The actual process of consultation is seen as being more that of joint decision-making than merely advisory and information-providing. They also feel that rank-and-file workers show a strong interest in the workings of the institution.

To convey the significance of the joint consultative committee in present-day industrial relations, it is necessary to give a brief historical review of its evolution and of the changes in the overall character of industrial relations. Following the decline of the joint management committee after 1949, the Japanese system of industrial relations turned to the collective bargaining model. During the early half of the 1950s, the development of joint consultation proceeded slowly, as Table 7.1 shows.

Table 7.1.   Joint Consultative Committees by Date of Installation

	Number	Percent of Total
Total Covered	1,168	100.0
1945–49	115	13.3
1950–54	104	8.9
1955–59	131	11.2
1960–64	260	22.3
1965–69	297	25.4
1970–72	182	15.6
Unclear	39	3.3

Source: Computed from the figures in *Industrial Relations Survey,*
Ministry of Labor, 1977, p. 266.

This was primarily a consequence of the conflict between management and the unions which characterized industrial relations at the time. The number of days lost due to strikes per union member stood at as high a level as in the immediate post-war years, despite the fact that the economy had been recovering rapidly. Nevertheless, few would deny that the recovery was just as much a cause of conflict as was the fact that management, having recovered its bargaining strength, was frequently aggressive. As unions were no less prone to engage in power contests, major disputes occurred one after another. The disputes at Toshiba (1949), Hitachi (1950), Nissan (1953), Mitsui Miike Min (1953), and the steel companies of Nihonseiko and Amagasaki-Seitetsu (1954) were examples. All of those prolonged disputes invariably involved mass discharges, including union officers, and issues of management prerogative.

Out of these bitter experiences in the mid-1950s there came a major shift in orientation on the part of management and unions. This is clearly seen in the public pronouncement of the Japan Productivity Center (founded in 1955 by the government, industry, and Zenro, a predecessor of Domei). It declared three principles to be essential conditions for an improvement in productivity: full employment, equity in sharing results, and *joint consultation*. Although the manifesto reflected the history of Japanese industrial relations, it must be mentioned that the German Works

Constitution Acts in 1952 influenced the thinking underlying it. Meanwhile, after a series of painful experiences, Sohyo began to demand, in 1957, the prior-to-decision negotiation system in order to cope with problems of technical change.

The joint consultative committee evolved basically into its present form in the latter half of the 1950s and may be aptly seen as a synthesis of the workers'-control type of joint management committee in the immediate post-war years, and as a reassertion of the management prerogative type of collective bargaining. Under the newer arrangement, while management naturally insists on defending its prerogatives, it concedes such matters to joint consultation. And the union, while understandably desiring to extend the scope of collective bargaining, is not hesitant to refer working condition-related issues to joint consultation, but there have been differences of opinion as to when the content of work and working conditions fall within the scope of collective bargaining. Otherwise, the right to make decisions is preserved by management, but subject to review by the joint consultative committee.

During the 1960s, the joint consultative committee became widespread, and in an era of rapid technological change, provided a means for the parties concerned to have comprehensive dialogue on the problems of rationalization. During this period, collective bargaining generally expanded its scope to cover more detailed rules in the areas of working conditions, personnel relations, and matters related to rationalization. On the other hand, trade unions tended to prefer to refer a substantial portion of the bargaining issues to the joint consultative committee, partly because it allowed for informed judgment and flexible decisions. According to the 1972 survey of the Japan Productivity Center of 1,600 major firms, as much as 52 percent of the 713 firms responding answered that their joint consultative committees dealt with bargaining issues. The same 52 percent replied that when a joint decision is not reached on such an issue, that matter is referred to collective bargaining. Both collective bargaining and joint consultative committees expanded their scope in the 1960s to the extent that the joint consultative committee had evolved as a device through which the trade unions could participate in decisions relating to changes in the technical system without endangering the development of collective bargaining.

Trends in Recent Decades

The joint consultative committee in its mature form, when seen as an institutional device enabling workers to reflect their interests, demands and opinions in relation to decisions affecting their working lives, has some inherent limitations, as can readily be seen from its structure and functions. First, it involves primarily the trade unions, so that workers are involved only indirectly. Secondly, it is concerned mainly with problems at the plant or works level and not so much with decisions of broader dimensions, enterprise-wide or at industry or national levels. But it was at those levels that worker participation became highly significant, concomitant with or as the result of, economic and social changes in recent decades, particularly after the mid-1960s.

WORKSHOP LEVEL

In the late 1940s and early 1950s, the government, through administrative guidance, tried to introduce and inculcate grievance-handling procedures along with the American model of collective bargaining, but in effect, grievance procedures were not widely accepted. This was partly due to the then existing complexity of industrial relations at the workshop level and more basically due to certain cultural constraints on the filing of individual claims.

By the early 1960s, along with the growth in the economy, industrial relations at the workshop level became much more stable. In many branches of the private sector, more grass-roots labor leaders began to change from the aging "democratic league" leaders to a newer generation in their thirties and forties. Influence in particular was secured by those within the workshop who were particularly adaptable to technological change, and the "new model" labor leaders who emerged tended to have positive attitudes toward it. In their thinking they shared much with engineers and middle management. On the other hand, they tended to be methodical in pursuing pragmatic goals within the existing system of industrial relations, and cooperative union-management relations soon emerged. After the mid-1960s, workshops in many private sector manufacturing industries experienced major changes. Technological change went into full swing. There was a rapid rate of increase in the recruitment of post-war generation graduates with at least 12 years of school education, and a striking increase of labor mobility. For a while, a host of adjustment problems, strains and tensions arose, but in retrospect, the management and union reacted to the changes with alacrity. In a very short span of years, management introduced a variety of organizational changes. Four were significant: management by objective, small group task forces or subject-related autonomous groups, ability-development plans, and self-appraisal programs. In a few years, all of these became widespread in industrial establishments.

The one most important change was the small group task force. It was somewhat similar to a task force of professionals to solve problems in the area of their specialization. These groups at plant and/or works level, regional and national levels, are linked to an association. The conference of each association is something like a professional conference, the task forces or autonomous groups report the results of their analyses, experiments, surveys, improvements, and inventions. The autonomous group is being institutionalized, according to the survey by the Ministry of Labor quoted above, in 39.7 percent of the total and 63.5 percent of unionized establishments with 100 or more employees. The number of workers participating in all industries would be many millions. Although at times the autonomous group has been criticized as being "managed," and in fact there is much to improve, the potentially valuable qualities of autonomous groups can hardly be gainsaid. As it evolves it may prove to be a significant breakthrough in the history of industrial work.

Although it seems plausible to the present writer, as well as to many others, to say that worker participation at the workshop level in Japan has been at a comparatively high level, it is an undeniable fact of industrial life that formal channels organized by management have inherent limitations. According to a comprehensive survey by the Ministry of Labor, as many as 68 percent of the workers submitted complaints or opinions regarding work methods and/or workshop environment during a one-year period prior to July 1972. However, only one-third of them felt their complaints and opinions were seriously being considered. And herein lies a significant role for the union. Although management initiative has been marked, insofar as worker participation at workshop level is concerned, trade unions have played important roles. Their handling of grievances through day-to-day dealings with management has been vitally significant in enabling workshop conditions to adjust to change. Also, there have been some signs of increasingly formalized involvement of the union in individual personnel decisions. According to the periodic surveys by the Ministry of Labor, during the five-year period 1967 to 1972, trade unions requiring prior consultation or their approval for individual discharge cases increased from 50 percent to 58 percent of the total, and in the instance of disciplinary cases from 45 percent to 54 percent, and of job transfer from 34 percent to 42 percent. Although the formal grievance procedure does not seem to be much utilized by either workers or their union, the role of the union in channeling individual complaints and opinions into decisions at the workshop level will probably increase. However, a sudden drastic change is not foreseen.

ENTERPRISE LEVEL

The *enterprise-wide* joint consultative committee increased markedly after the mid-1960s. This increase generally accompanied the changes in emphasis in the nature of trade union participation in the decisions of the enterprise. In 1964, Professor Ichiro Nakayama, an eminent economist and leading scholar in industrial relations, stated:

Regarding business policies, production plans, corporate achievements and finance-accounting situations, many enterprises are communicating with trade unions and exchanging views ... As a general trend, it may be said management not only reports the results, but is explaining basic policies or plans to trade unions before implementation and asking for union cooperation. More specifically, the policies and plans being referred to are long-range plans, mergers, plant construction and rationalization.[3]

Clearly, trade unions have begun to be involved in decisions one step beyond those immediately related to rationalization plans. One sign of this is the changing name of the enterprise-wide joint consultative committee. Although a large majority of the 401 cases of the enterprise-wide mechanism, identified by a Japan Productivity Center survey at the end of 1975, used the name of the "Central Joint Consultative Committee," as many as one quarter had a "Joint Management Committee." Another sign is the relative frequency of the types of issue referred to enterprise-wide joint consultative committees. Asked to name the issue most frequently brought before the joint consultative committee during the year beginning December 1, 1974, 33.5 percent of the 204 unions responding mentioned "matters related to business and executive policies," 24.5 percent specified "matters related to working conditions," 17.6 percent named "matters related to production," 16.4 said "matters related to welfare and associated issues," and 1.9 percent "other." The answer from the 263 firms responding were virtually the same. In a survey by Shogyororen (Japan Federation of Commercial Workers' Unions), an item-by-item comparison of the extent of trade union involvement in Japan with the co-determination rights in Germany legislated in 1972 and 1976 suggests that the enterprise-wide joint consultative committee in Japan covers almost identical areas. In respect to about half of the decision items specified, the survey shows similar *de facto* involvement at about 30 percent of major firms. The joint consultative committee has evolved halfway toward a co-determinative mechanism for worker participation in major corporate decisions.

An immediate reason for such an evolution is the development of enterprise-wide collective bargaining. This is, in turn, due to many factors, among which are those that persuaded the trade unions to restructure their organization. As is well known, Japanese trade unions are enterprise-based. Typically in the 1950s they were plant- or works-based. There are complex reasons for this involving economic, socio-institutional, and ethno-cultural factors. Economically, the dual structure phenomenon has been important, because it conditions the duality of the labor market. Socio-institutionally, life-time employment, the seniority system and corporate welfarism have been crucial because they together constitute the framework of working conditions common to all members. Ethno-culturally, the collective orientation has been significant because it tends to foster a certain solidarity at the level of the affiliated organization. However, the plant-based trade union structure, as conditioned by such factors, began to face major challenges around the mid-1960s. First, enterprises grew larger, diversified their products, and began to embrace larger numbers of related firms and subsidiaries. In short, they strengthened their organizational bases and became overwhelmingly powerful. Meanwhile, the dual structure has shown some important changes. The relative weight of medium-sized firms has grown, and with labor in short supply, wage differentials between larger firms and medium-small firms have dramatically narrowed, at least for younger workers. Together with changes in the social values of the younger generation, this stimulated the mobility of younger workers and markedly reduced loyalty to the firm and to the union. Technological changes threatened the seniority system and tended to disrupt the expectations of middle-aged and older workers. These changes, too, tended to weaken loyalty to the firm and to the union. Although the scale and intensity of such developments should not be exaggerated, there were in the latter half of the 1960s unmistakably clear signs of these changes in many branches of the economy. At many of the large firms in a number of industries (including steel, shipbuilding, electrical, automobile, and chemical industries) trade unions began to form a single enterprise union or reorganized the enterprise federation to form a more effective organization. Such developments prompted workers at related firms and subsidiaries to form their own unions and they then began to organize enterprise-group-wide trade union federations. Subsequently, they began to formulate so-called life-cycle demands, to accommodate the claims and aspirations of both young and middle-aged and older workers. These demands involved issues of collective bargaining as well as economic and social questions such as housing, education, taxes, pensions, the environment, and so on. Also, as mentioned earlier, the trade unions tried to strengthen their organizations at the workshop level by restoring closer relationships with rank-and-file members and sought to meet their demands and aspirations through the decisions of the joint consultative committees.

Management, which had come to value stable industrial relations achieved jointly with the "new model" union leaders, was generally receptive to this development. With increased capital investment and the technical integration of production, management began to look for active cooperation from trade unions. The enterprise-wide joint consultative system was the outcome of this interaction of forces. Underlying these, it must be stressed that there was uneasiness or latent criticism among rank-and-file members against the cooperative attitudes of established joint consultative committees. And behind this, there was a deep change in the attitude of rank-and-file members toward worker participation. An extensive survey by the Ministry of Labor on industrial relations conducted in 1972 showed that nearly 80 percent of the approximately 50,000 workers sampled wanted to know more about the economic state of their firms and corporate business policies. Further, 80 percent replied that there was more need to reflect workers' opinions in business decisions. However, 48 percent of the total felt that workers' opinions were not being reflected, and 37 percent of the total mentioned either that there was no mechanism at present for that purpose or that joint consultative committees were not working properly. Taking into account the inherent limitations of such a survey, and also of the general antagonism to business in a year marked by speculation, the results nevertheless appear to reflect certain long-term undercurrents that have been influencing the dynamics of contemporary worker participation.

INDUSTRY LEVEL

In the mid 1960s, there were conspicuous moves to found industry-wide joint consultative committees. At present, there are 25 such bodies in 25 industries by minor classification, or 14 industries by medium classification, covering almost all major areas of manufacturing industry. Four major types stand out.

The first is formed of unions under pressure from major changes in the industrial structure. Examples are the Japan Textile Industry Joint Committee, involving Domei-affiliated Zensendomei (Japan Federation of Textile Workers' Unions) and founded in 1956, Coal Mines Voluntary Stabilization National Joint Committee, involving the Domei-affiliated Zentanko (National Union of Coal Mine Workers) and set up in 1958, and the Metal Mining Joint Conference involving Sohyo-affiliated Zenko (Federation of All-Japan Metal Mine Labor Unions) and started in 1971. Their functions may be illustrated by the first of these. It meets every three months and confers on industrial re-structuring policies. It has also promulgated a joint policy on the voluntary restriction of exports to the U.S.A., and has developed standards for environmental control. In 1952, Zensendomei experienced major lay-offs. It subsequently prepared an industrial strategy and pressed the government to organize a tripartite industrial deliberative council to draw up a comprehensive plan for restructuring the industry, based on a long-term demand-supply forecast. This council's plan had considerable impact on the situation. Ever since, the union and management have jointly engaged in preparation and guidance of restructuring strategies.

The second type includes those unions that had to cope with problems arising from technological change and international competition. Falling into this category are the Automobile Industry Joint Committee involving the independent Jidosharoren (All Japan Federation of Automobile Workers' Unions), the Shipbuilding Industry Joint Council involving Domei-affiliated Zosenjukiroren (Federation of Shipbuilding and Heavy Industries Union), and the Electrical Industries Joint Council involving Churitsuroren-affiliated Denkisoren (All Japan Federation of Electric Machine Workers' Unions). The Automobile Industry Joint Committee meets every six months. It deals with such problems as safety and pollution, automobile taxation, and international relations. It may be noted in this connection that the Jidosharoren organized the Nissan and Toyota Automobile Workers World Conference in September of 1973, at the request of the International Metal Workers Federation. In 1974, it reached an agreement with the United Auto Workers, which was demanding an import restrictions bill from the U.S. Congress, that, in exchange for voluntary restrictions on exports, this request would be dropped.

The third type involves those enterprise unions confronted by environmental and resource problems. The Steel Industry Joint Committee of Five Major Firms involving Sohyo-affiliated Tekkororen (Japanese Federation of Iron and Steel Worker's Unions), and the Electrical Power Joint Council involving Domei-affiliated Denroren (Federation of Electric Workers' Union of Japan) are examples. The Steel Industry Joint Committee meets every six months. It makes a review of the industry and deals with industrial strategy, safety, environmental policies, manpower, and energy problems.

The fourth type includes unions which have great influence on the labor market. The Maritime Joint Committee involving the Domei-affiliated Kaiin (All Japan Seamen's Union), and four industry-wide consultative committees in metal and engineering industries involving Domei-affiliated Zenkindomei (National Federation of Metal Industry Trade Unions), fall into this category. The Maritime Joint Committee meets every six months. It deals with industrial strategy, employment policies, safety and hygiene problems. It must be noted in this connection that Kaiin took the initiative in the early 1960s in generating policies for restructuring the maritime industry, which resulted in two legislative acts on amalgamation within the industry.

As is indicated above, there are many factors which account for the development of the joint consultative committee: the necessity for industrial reorganization, internationalization of the economy, environmental and energy problems, labor market adjustment and so forth. There are, however, at least two major factors operating within the system of industrial relations that are important. One of these is the increasing bargaining potential of trade unions through unified industry-wide actions. The other is industrial strategy demands by industry-wide trade union organizations.

TRADE UNION WAGE-BARGAINING STRATEGIES

Under the spring wage cycle formula, unions have increased their bargaining potential. This may be shown by subsequent wage movements in relation to productivity trends and the implication for prices (see Table 7.2). The annual rate of increase in wage costs (defined as 100 + wage increase rate/100 + productivity – 100) was 3.2 percent. Other things being equal, this would affect consumer prices, since the productivity increases diffe. inevitably between sectors and tend to be generally lower in the consumer-related production sectors. Thus consumer prices increased annually at a rate of 6.3 percent, while wholesale prices rose by 3.1 percent.

The increase in wage costs of 3.2 percent a year during the two decades is not by any means below average for the major industrialized economies. But what is more important is the trend. It was -2.0 percent per annum for the half-dozen years in the latter half of the 1950s. But subsequently it rose to 2.6 percent in the early half of the 1960s. And although it declined to 1.4 percent in the latter half of that decade, it went up to 11.7 percent in the early 1970s.

Table 7.2.   Trends in Wages, Productivity and Prices, 1955–75
(percentage increase over previous year or period)

Period, Year	Wages (manufac- turing)	Wage Round	Produc- tivity	Wage Costs (manufac- turing)	Consumer Prices	Wholesale Prices	Real Wage (manufac- turing)
1955–75	12.2	12.7	8.7	3.2	6.3	3.1	5.6
1955–60	6.0	6.7	8.2	-2.0	1.8	0.5	4.1
1960–65	10.2	10.8	7.4	2.6	6.3	0.5	3.7
1965–70	15.0	13.6	13.4	1.4	5.5	2.1	9.1
1970–75	17.9	19.5	6.2	11.0	11.7	9.6	5.5
1970	17.8	18.5	8.5	8.5	7.2	2.3	10.0
1971	13.4	16.9	4.7	8.3	6.8	-0.8	7.2
1972	16.2	15.3	14.6	1.4	5.3	3.2	10.3
1973	23.2	20.1	17.8	4.8	16.0	22.6	6.3
1974	27.4	32.9	-5.2	34.3	21.7	23.4	4.6
1975	9.9	13.1	0.7	9.4	10.5	2.1	-0.6

Source: Japan Institute of Labor, *Japan Labor Statistics,* relevant years.

Related to this was the increase in the strength of the leadership and in coordination among the industrial unions. With some notable exceptions, although industrial unions were not directly involved in the collective bargaining processes, they by now generally exerted a strong influence in the formulation of targets or demands, by conducting related surveys, guiding strategies and settlements and, in some cases, pooling strike funds. By the end of the 1960s, having established their impact on wage decisions, the industrial unions had begun to exert influence over negotiations on other matters including bonuses, lump-sum retirement allowances, retirement-age provisions, and reductions in working hours. Also, there was a marked increase in coordination between industrial unions. This was a factor in the development of the Japan Federation of Metal Workers Union and the Japan Confederation of Chemical Workers Unions. Though not as coherent as these developments, there emerged after the mid-1960s a trend to organize councils or conferences of the industrial unions, for closer liaison on wages and other concerns. There are at present about a dozen such organizations which have helped to make the very great increase in the impact of the industrial union on wage decisions.

In 1970, average wages in manufacturing industry increased by 17.8 percent as a result of the 18.5 percent rise in the leading wage "market price." This meant wage costs increased 8.5 percent. In the following year, the wage increase was 13.4 percent, and in the wage "market price" 16.9 percent, which meant a wage cost increase of 8.5 percent. There was strong reaction to this development. Employers re-emphasized "the productivity principle" for wage decisions. The government, as well as the monetarist Bank of Japan, pronounced "the need to deliberate on introducing an income policy." Subsequently, in 1972, a research committee was organized. The committee focussed its attention on the twelve-year wage trend from 1960 to 1971. It thus excluded both the late 1950s when the spring wage offensive was as yet in the early stages of development and also the years after 1973, which have in many ways been unusual. It may be argued that the committee focussed on trends under normal conditions. During the twelve years after 1960, wages increased by 12.7 percent a year and productivity by 9.8 percent. Clearly the long-term gap between the two rates was not large. During the same period, although consumer prices rose 5.9 percent a year, wholesale prices were stable with a small annual increase of 1.1 percent. In addition, the proportion of income of employees in total national income (labor share) remained relatively constant: 50–55 percent in the early half of the 1960s, 53–56 percent in the second half, and 54–57 percent in 1970–72. Because of these long-term trends, the committee concluded in 1972 that there had not as yet been clear signs of wage-push as a major cause of inflation, and that there was no clear evidence of labor market control strong enough to generate wage-push inflation. It was stated that, as of 1972, the time was not yet ripe for introducing an incomes policy and that the inflation of the early 1970s was mainly due to factors other than wage increases, such as administered prices, excessive liquidity, commodity flow mechanisms, overseas inflation, and inadequate industrial, financial and monetary policies. The committee's findings were widely supported. As was rightly pointed out, enterprise unions, by their very structure, tended to lack the capacity for exercising strong control over the labor market. Nevertheless, the committee was fully aware that enterprise unions, by having industry-wide coordination, were increasing their bargaining strength. In the report, it was implied that under normal conditions, wage decisions were *de facto* being made so that the increase in wages did not much exceed that of productivity. It was also implied that the strong wage push arose in years when firms and the government behaved abnormally or did not fulfill their responsibilities: the report, it must be remembered, was prepared in years of strong anti-business and anti-government sentiment. Probably it was because of such underlying feeling that this pro-union report was so widely supported.

In the Spring Wage Offensive of 1974, immediately following the rise in oil prices, the leading wage "market price" increased 32.9 percent, and this raised the manufacturing wage level by 27.4 percent. Although this was largely due to reaction against the unusually high price rises of the previous year (consumer prices rose 16.0 percent and wholesale prices 22.6 percent), it was obvious that it would worsen the stagflation trend. Since, as was more or less expected, productivity declined markedly (by 5 percent) that year, wage costs increased by 34.3 percent. Consumer prices increased by 21.7 percent and wholesale prices by 23.4 percent. Had this continued, it is obvious that the economy would have collapsed. The experience was a painful lesson for those involved in industrial relations. Employers were shocked at the bargaining strength of their unions, but the unions were disappointed with a real wage rise of only 4.6 percent.

The government was convinced of the need for price stabilization. In subsequent years, the wage increase in the leading wage "market price" decelerated: to 13.1 percent in 1975, 9.0 percent in 1976, and 8.8 percent in 1977. The annual rate of increase in consumer prices also fell: 15 percent by early 1975, 8 percent by early 1976, and 7 percent by early 1977. Serious and immediate stagflation was thereby avoided. The de-escalation of the rates of increase was due largely to the "social contract-like" self-restraint of wage demands by the trade unions. But this went hand-in-hand with efforts by other parties. Government strengthened its price stabilization measures and employers risked their profits to maintain employment security. These two were important parts of the "social contract-like" self-restraint on wage demands.

There were naturally strong differences of opinion within the trade union movement as to the extent to which wage demands should be restrained. Nevertheless, all of the national trade union organizations or their equivalents reduced their wage demands. Whatever differences there might have been among the leaders, wage decisions through the Spring Wage Offensive were not something that could have been readily determined by a minority of leaders. They involved decisions by at least 140,000 negotiators. There were, in other words, certain underlying common assumptions influencing union-management interactions over wage decisions that were latent in the structure of trade unions and more generally in the nature of Japanese industrial relations.

Strange as it may seem, the "social contract-like" self-restraint on wage demands and the subsequent reduction in the rate of wage increase did not, in fact, mean a drastic break from the past in so far as the logic of wage decisions was concerned. In 1976, the Ministry of Labor undertook a comprehensive regression analysis of the wage movement in the period 1960 to 1974. It concluded that the wage movement had been closely associated with changes in the ratio of job offers over job seekers, the rate of increase in consumer prices, and the general level of corporate income (defined as the share of corporate income in the total national income). It was pointed out that this formula largely explained the 1975 leading wage market price of the Spring Wage Offensive. As for the subsequent settlement, the predictive capability of the formula was not insignificant, although obviously consumer prices had begun to play a much greater role than in preceding years. It may be said that the logic of the wage decision was meaningfully related to the "unique" aspects of Japanese trade union structure and union-management relationships. While the enterprise union must more or less live with the demand-supply situation of the labor-market, owing to its limited control of that market, the union is under pressure to take consumer price changes into account when making wage decisions, as price changes are of concern to all members in the varied occupations and trades represented. While the enterprise union structure is a determinant in the corporate income situation, more or less influencing wage trends, it enables individual unions to enter into bargains on a wide range of issues apart from wages, such as fringe benefits, personnel policies, and so forth. Unions may extend their influence to issues not part of the usual bargaining through the joint consultative committee. Cumulative experiences such as these appear, in turn, to have developed a propensity for informed pragmatic decisions. Not a small number of trade unions make their own analysis of corporate accounts.

Quite apart from these factors related to collective bargaining, there was another and more immediate major influence. That was the general trend among industrial unions to formulate a trade union "industrial strategy." The aim of the strategy is to identify the locus and structural characteristics of a given industry in the economy and in the international setting, identify the manifest and latent problems as seen from the workers' and civic points of view, and call for action from enterprises, employees' associations, and government, and if necessary the public, to bring about change. The strategy was designed for use in various negotiations and campaigns. The development of a trade union industrial strategy is still in an embryonic stage but, nevertheless, it has emerged out of cumulative experience in coping with problems of rationalization. One of the earliest examples appeared in the midst of the long and bitter industrial strife in the coal industry in the late 1950s and early 1960s. Tenro (Japan Coal Miners' Union) demanded changes in national coal policy and in government policies relevant to the industry's problems. This had a significant impact although one of the major demands, the nationalization of the industry, was not realized. Thereafter, the demands for policy changes became a conspicuous feature of the counter-rationalization struggle of Sohyo unions. Even earlier, Zensendomei formulated an industrial strategy calling for the restructuring of the textile industry which had considerable effect.

This example was an important precedent within the labor movement for not only Domei but others as well. The years immediately following 1965 saw a wave of moves to set up industrial strategies. Underlying causes for this were employment insecurity and the prospect of slim wage increases. The first half of the 1960s was a period of "volume boom" in that production quotas increased, but corporate income remained stagnant as the result of excessive investment and therefore of intense competition. As a result, demands came from abroad for the internationalization of the economy with immediate trade liberalization to be followed by capital liberalization by the end of the decade. The outcome, however, was a vigorous nationally coordinated and systematic reorganization of industries in order to strengthen international competitiveness. These rationalization plans implied threats to employment, mass transfers and other problems for labor.

In addition, 1965 was a year of major recession. Major industrial unions in the private sector began one after the other to formulate industrial strategies, in short, counter-rationalization plans. Basically, these demanded policies of full employment and higher wages and stressed the beneficial effects of their implementation. Symbolic of such moves were attempts by the national federations to formulate a comprehensive economic development plan—a master plan for industrial strategies. In 1967 Domei set up specialized committees on industrial strategy and in the following year published its own economic development plan. In 1967, Sohyo followed suit and set up a supervisory committee made up of 19 industrial unions and subcommittees for metal and engineering, transport, local government, and underground industries. In 1968, Shinsanbetsu decided to pursue its own "industrial policy" to counter "capitalistic rationalization." In Sohyo, however, there was considerable difficulty in reaching agreement among the affiliated bodies over the propriety of formulating an economic strategy while demanding major changes in the economic and political system. Consequently, Sohyo's attempt has remained at the halfway mark. But meanwhile many of its affiliated bodies pursued industrial strategies to oppose rationalization. Among them Zendentsu (All Japan Telecommunication Workers' Union) formulated a sophisticated industrial strategy and ever since has been exerting substantial influence over the major decisions of the Japan Telecommunication Authority, both through political pressure group activities and through the joint prior-to-decision negotiation committee. The union formulated its counter-plans to match both corporate long-range and short-term plans. Compared with Zendentsu the industrial strategy of many unions is as yet underdeveloped, although since the mid-1960s attempts to generate counter-plans have become widespread. Broadly speaking, the latter half of the 1960s turned out to be a period of unprecedented growth and prosperity, so major rationalization went relatively smoothly. A few years after the mid-1960s, giant oligopolies of international standing gained prominence in many major industries. These large firms began to restructure the economic order in their respective industries to allow "cooperative" competition and started to coordinate plans for investment, production, and major projects for rationalization. By then the Spring Wage Offensive was well institutionalized. The industrial unions had become sufficiently strong to have substantial influence over the decisions of their affiliated enterprise unions. In the latter half of the 1960s, employment security was more or less stable and wages continued to rise rapidly. For a time, the enthusiasm of trade unions for industrial strategies waned. But they quickly became very significant in the early 1970s, when industries had to face the problems of the environment, energy, inflation and stagflation, international adjustment, and the economic slump. However, this time, it was possible for the trade unions to exert their influence to some extent through industry-wide joint consultative committees.

NATIONAL LEVEL

As of January 1975, there were in all 246 legally established standing mechanisms, including deliberation councils, research boards, and examining committees, involved in various legislative and administrative decisions. Although the material significance of such mechanisms is arguable, apart from support for political parties, pressure group activities and letters to editors, they are the major institutional channels through which the trade unions and, indirectly, workers can influence decisions of national significance. Although trade union leaders are today involved in 51 important deliberative councils, a few qualifying remarks must be made as to the significance of their representation. First, many are appointed members not as representatives of trade unions but as experts in their respective areas. There are exceptions in cases where tripartite representation is mandated by law, as in the deliberative councils related to the Ministry of Labor. Secondly, the total number of trade union leaders among the expert members is not large—169 among a total of 1,436, or 11.8 percent. It must be concluded that the degree of trade union involvement in the processes dealing with national policy formation has been as yet limited. Nevertheless, it must be mentioned that it is clearly increasing, as was particularly evident in the early 1970s. As late as the end of the 1960s, the number of deliberative councils involving trade union leaders was 28: today it is 51. Until only recently, the involvement of trade union leaders was limited to those councils related to the Ministries of Labor and Welfare. However, they are now involved in procedures for deliberation at the Ministries of Finance, International Trade and Industry, Agriculture, Transport, Construction, and Local Government. In retrospect, this is an impressive development. In the early 1960s, when the National Income Doubling Plan (1961–70) was drafted, there was not a single trade unionist among the 30 official members of the National Economic Deliberation Council. The number of members personally appointed increased subsequently to one for the mid-term Economic Plan (1965–75) and to three for the plan for the second half of the 1970s. In addition trade unionists began to be appointed in consultation with at least two of the major national federations, Sohyo and Domei. It may be concluded that the involvement of trade unionists in national policy formation has been increasing rapidly in recent years. Two questions follow. One concerns the reasons why the degree of such involvement has so far been very limited; the other with the causes for the recent increase.

In respect to the potential influence which trade unions might exert on national policy formation within the existing economic-political system, it can hardly be denied that the policentric structure of the trade union movement undermined the significance of its total numerical strength. Also, political unionism tended to inhibit trade union involvement in national policy formation. Although this was particularly true of Sohyo, it was by-and-large true of the others as well until about the mid-1960s. Also the government and employers were, to a considerable degree, inclined to avoid trade union involvement in policy decisions of national significance. However, there have been some changes in this picture.

In so far as the philosophies of national federations are concerned, their attachment to political ideologies may be said to have remained unchanged. However, in the last two decades, the basic orientation of the more immediate policies and programs has changed toward more economic and pragmatic reform. The trend has been most conspicuous in the case of Sohyo, which has been the most politically oriented. Sohyo was formed in the 1950s on the initiative of "democratic league" leaders soon after the collapse of Sanbetsu, Kaigi which was strongly Communist-influenced. Against a background of "Cold War" relations, diplomatic complexities and domestic uncertainty with respect to plans for the future social order in the soon-to-be independent Japan, "peace and democracy" became the major goals and ethic for Sohyo. In the field of international policy Sohyo stressed positive neutrality as its principle, but partly as a reaction to the strong links of the Japanese establishment with U.S. elites, and also as a result of the rapid dominance of its leadership by the socialist-left, Sohyo had a distinct propensity to regard the USSR, China, and the unions of the World Federation of Trade Unions as allied forces of "peace and democracy." It opposed Japan's peace treaty of 1952, which did not involve the Eastern Bloc, and after the mid-1950s was against the U.S.-Japan Security Treaty. In internal affairs, it organized protest campaigns against civil order legislation and policies designed to strengthen the role of the state. It may be said that such campaigns have had a political and social impact on modern Japan. There was, however, a major change in the basic tenor of the movement in the 1960s due to developments in both international and domestic relations. The Cold War was replaced by detente and peace, and policentralization became pronounced within the Eastern Bloc and among the unions of the World Federation of Trade Unions. Domestically, the economy began to grow at an unprecedented rate. In 1960, the leadership of Sohyo changed from popular front organizers who stressed united protest with every militant left-wing pressure group to leaders who valued economic strategies more and emphasized the relative importance of wage-earners in the reformist movement. As the Spring Wage Offensive gained momentum under this leadership, the strategic significance of wage-earners' solidarity was more formally pronounced in Sohyo's declaration of the "Japanese model of trade unionism." In the meantime, against a background of continuous economic growth and related social changes, popular demands for an improvement in living conditions became important to the movement. While essentially following the Japanese model of trade unionism the leadership which came to power in 1970 began to place increasing stress on "people's demands" for social welfare and public services involving such issues as social security, taxation, transport, prices, and the environment. The latest leadership (installed in 1975) essentially follows these lines and, in addition, has become more attentive to the possibility of allied action with other federations, due partly to the need to exert effective pressures in national politics and partly to the need to meet demands for unification of the labor front, which has become of importance outside Sohyo's influence.

There is another factor of considerable significance and that is developments in political power relations. During the past decade and a half, the ruling Liberal Democratic Party (LDP) has suffered a continual decrease of its seats in the House of Representatives as well as in the House of Councillors. After the November 1960 election, it had over 60 percent of all the seats in the House of Representatives. By 1976 this number had declined to 50 percent.

It became more important therefore for the government party to secure the understanding and cooperation of the opposition parties and social groups behind them, of which trade unions are a major part. Developments in the political power structure, however, have been no less favorable to the major national labor federations. During the same period, both the Japan Socialist Party (JSP), supported by Sohyo, and the Democratic Socialist Party (DSP), backed by Domei, did not, on the whole, add to their relative influence in the House of Representatives and the House of Councillors. In contrast, the Komeito (Clean Government Party) and the Japan Communist Party, both of which have stronger bases among the unorganized economic sector, markedly increased their share. The changes in the share of seats in the legislature do not exactly reflect the extent of the decline or stagnation of the established political parties because of the disproportionate ratio of seats to votes. The changes in popular voting for the House of Councillors highlight the trend. During 1962–74, the Japan Socialist Party's share of the total number of seats continued to decline, as did that of the Democratic Socialist Party. While trends in voting for local candidates are likely to indicate political currents within local communities, the changes in votes for national candidates may reflect the response of the rank-and-file membership to candidates supported by national trade union federations. The two trends suggest that political pluralism has become widespread both inside and outside labor organizations. Although there is no reason to believe that the same trend will continue in the future, it is unlikely that union-supported parties will suddenly multiply their influence. With increased political pluralism among the membership, extra-parliamentary political campaigns became more difficult to organize. It may be concluded that with this political change the relative significance to the trade unions of the deliberative councils increased as one channel through which they could influence decisions of national significance.

COMMUNITY LEVEL

Trends essentially similar to those on the national level may be discerned, with respect to trade union involvement, in policy formation at the community level, at times to a much lesser degree and at other times more dramatically. Enterprise unions are linked together territorially and form regional and district organizations. The regional organizations are utilized for mutual exchange to promote trade union activities in localities and to coordinate activities on common concerns. However, there is a *de facto* tendency for there to be more than one center of political power. Sohyo has close relationships with its related regional councils located in each of the fifty-two prefectures and with related district councils in 12,000 municipalities or equivalent areas. Although such territorial organizations are not constitutionally branch bodies, or affiliated units, the "related" regional and district organizations are generally strongly influenced by the former. Regional councils are well organized, have full-time officers, although few in number, and have a part of their expenses covered by Sohyo. Although they engage in a variety of activities, including unionization of non-union shops, the main emphasis is on organizing campaigns during elections and, more generally, in dealing with local authorities through negotiation, participation and protest actions. The 12,000 district councils frequently have as members unions which are not affiliated with Sohyo. Many of them tend to be Churitsuroren unions, although in a few instances, Shinsanbetsu and Domei unions are also members. In a majority of Sohyo's related district organizations, public sector unions tend to account for the largest proportion of membership. However, district organizations are still relatively underdeveloped with only about 20 percent of them having one or more full-time officers. Domei has a similar set-up at the prefectural level. Domei's regional confederation includes all Domei unions, affiliation being obligatory, and for other unions on a basis of voluntary affiliation. Domei has about 170 district confederations in major industrial centers. Shinsanbetsu has two regional organizations, one in the Kansai region and another in Yamagata Prefecture. Churitsuroren has seven regional organizations, which are voluntary associations formed on the initiative of its affiliates in their localities. The relatively weaker development of the district-level organizations, and the strong links of regional offices to their national centers are common features except in the case of Churitsuroren. These structures, due to their inherently weaker day-to-day relationships with enterprise unions and their limited influence in community policy formation, have become rather unstable as the demands for improving the environment, social welfare and public services at the community level increased among rank-and-file members. Against this background, the unions of large firms at many of the major industrial centers in the late 1960s began to set up new community organizations for private sector unions. At present, there are 22 such organizations along the Pacific industrial belt. Three of these are "block" organizations covering two or more prefectures and the others are prefecture-based. Regional councils of private sector unions, as they are called, are at present essentially associations of unions at large firms, related firms and subsidiaries. In the early 1970s these regional bodies formed a nationwide association, the National Liaison Conference of Regional Councils of Private Sector Unions. This development represents an attempt to unite labor at the community level. Meanwhile established national trade union federation-linked community organizations began to put forward local demands for a better quality of life than in the past. Since then, changes in the political power structure at the community level have been even more dramatic than at the national level, with trade union participation in deliberative councils at the community level increasing markedly. Although the scale and intensity of this development should not be exaggerated, it is potentially very significant in view of the fact that there have been comparatively few institutionalized opportunities for civic worker participation owing to the minimal development of political, social and cultural associations within the community. Nevertheless, it must be added that the significance of this development is still very limited because of weak organization at the district level and the still strong traces of having acted as campaign agencies for national organizations.

Reactions to European Developments

WORKER DIRECTOR

In the early 1970s European developments in worker participation almost immediately caused great concern in Japanese industry and labor. In October 1973, Domei, which since the end of the 1960s had been stressing increased worker participation as a goal, formally proposed periodic discussions on the subject with Nikkeiren (Japan Federation of Employers' Associations). Subsequently, Domei organized at its head office the Committee on Worker Participation, and Nikkeiren, the Committee on All Employee and Worker Participation, to study the problems and possibilities. In July 1974, the first meeting was called. Thereafter, meetings were held at about six-month intervals. In June 1974, a civic tripartite body, the Shakai-Keizai Kokumin Kyokai (National Conference on Economic and Social Problems), which has employers and independent experts among its leaders, set up a Special Committee on Worker Participation. In the following year, the Ministry of Labor created a reasearch and study group on worker participation at its head office. Meanwhile, the Japan Productivity Center, a tripartite agency involving government, employers and Domei, engaged in a series of surveys on the domestic situation and overseas developments. In 1977, it published its recommendations and advocated the need for a "Japanese type of worker participation." To present a balanced picture of Japanese reactions to European developments, it is perhaps necessary to describe the views of these bodies and locate them in the framework of debate in the centers of opinion in Japan.

In December 1974, Domei issued an interim report by its committee on worker participation. This stressed the need for strengthening worker participation by all means and at all levels, through collective bargaining, joint consultative committees and trade union involvement in the government decision process. Regarding the worker-director scheme, it stated:

By recent revision of the Commerce Law, auditors' roles have been strengthened in Japan. They are now given the right to audit the way in which decisions are executed by members of the board of directors and also to attend meetings of the board [in addition to the customary role of auditing finance and accounting—author's note] — We, the Domei, look for labor representation in the board of auditors. It should be initiated wherever readily practical.[4]

Domei's standpoint was subsequently rephrased more moderately. It would study the matter and examine the long-term possibility of worker participation on the board of auditors by securing the right of trade unions to nominate a number of the auditors, not as members of a particular union, but as general representatives to review and check executive decisions, bearing in mind the broad interests of the workers and of the unions. As for the immediate situation, it re-emphasized the importance of strengthening the joint consultative committee.

Sohyo, Shinsanbetsu, and Churitsuroren so far have remained silent on the subject. However, Sohyo-affiliated industrial unions have generally been against the idea of introducing the worker-director scheme in view of its potential restrictions on the rights to bargain collectively and to strike, and the possible loss of trade union identity by assuming some managerial responsibilities. However, a number of the major unions appreciate the need for strengthening trade union influence in managerial decisions and the role of self-governing elements in the running of workshops. In 1977, Zendentsu, one of the major public sector unions, used its political influence to make the Japan Telecommunication Authority set up an advisory management policy committee, independent of both the board of directors and the auditors. It is made up of management representatives and a substantial number of individuals nominated by the union. It is designed to discuss major policy decisions as an advisory organ to the president of the corporation. For some time the union has been exerting influence on major decisions through the joint prior-to-decision negotiation committee under whose jurisdiction long-range plans on facilities and equipment are made by agreement. As was stated earlier, through these devices and through pressure group activities directed at the Diet and Ministries, Zendentsu has been successful in achieving decisions based on its counter-policies and plans. As far as the union is concerned, the management policy advisory committee has permitted greater access to information, auditing, and prior-to-decision negotiation while not being bound to whatever consensus is reached in the committee. Another case is that of Zenkowan which has been advocating worker self-government since the mid-1970s. Its aim is to strengthen the prior-to-decision negotiation position as directed, toward worker control at the workshop level. Admittedly, these are two rather extreme cases. They nevertheless reflect the general trend among the Sohyo unions to reemphasize the importance of prior-to-decision negotiation (a minority remains opposed to any arrangement other than collective bargaining). The general climate within Shinsanbetsu is supportive, favoring strengthening the joint consultative committees, while tending to be negative toward the worker-director scheme. Within Churitsuroren, there are diverse trends. One of the major unions, Denkiroren (All Japan Federation of Electrical Machine Workers' Unions), decided in 1977 to demand worker participation. Although it is still unclear as to the concrete structure of the scheme, judging from the demand of some of its affiliated unions some sort of management (policy) committee of a joint consultation nature is likely to be involved. Among the unaffiliated federations of enterprise unions, Shogyororen (Japan Federation of Commercial Workers Unions) decided to examine the possibility of setting up a management policy committee of a joint consultative type involving top management and top union officers to discuss topics equivalent to the agenda of the board of directors. The union intends to demand the right to make a joint decision or to impose a veto on the appointment of the board members in charge of personnel relations.

EMPLOYERS

Three of the four major national federations of employers' associations made their stance on participation public in 1976. Nikkeiren (Federation of Employers' Associations) representing employers in labor relations, and made up of about 100 regional and industrial employers associations covering large and major medium-sized firms, stated in January 1976 that "the conditions and timing for a worker-director scheme have generally not yet been ready except at enterprises having special [i.e. harmonious—author's note] labor relations." Nissho (The Japan Chamber of Commerce and Industry), comprising more than 400 chambers of commerce and industry covering a considerable number of medium-small businesses, issued a statement in October 1976 that concluded by saying, "leaving the question of future possibilities aside, at present, there is no necessity nor urgency to diffuse European-style worker schemes." Keizai Doyukai (Committee for Economic Development), an organization of about 1,000 top management people who are members in an individual capacity, mentioned also that "as it now stands, it is difficult to find the necessity for introducing such an institution." But since a minority of its members insisted on deliberating this question positively, it qualified the remark by saying that "for the medium or long-term view, taking into consideration various situations as they develop, in order to secure a higher degree of efficiency and social justice, it may be necessary to look for, among other things, the possibility of having representatives of the trade union participate as directorial members, providing that responsibility and loyalty are clearly defined and that legal preparations are duly made." The Keidanren (Federation of Economic Organizations) made up of 102 financial, industrial and trading associations and nearly 800 major firms, has for the moment remained silent on this question.

Although employers' associations are against the introduction of a worker-director scheme, this does not mean that they are against the notion of worker participation in major corporate decisions. All three employers' associations stressed the significance of a joint consultative committee, in that joint decisions have been made through this arrangement. It is important to note that two of them, Nikkeiren and Nissho, specifically note the possibility of creating management policy consultative committees as one way to speed the evolution of joint consultation as an institutional arrangement for worker participation. More specifically, Nikkeiren stated:

In this case, one improvement would be to set up a management committee or a management deliberation council separately from the customary joint consultative committee providing that its character is as an advisory organ.[5]

Nissho stated:

It is worth considering as one method for worker participation in top management decisions such mechanisms as are already operative through which officers of trade unions and employers periodically consult on major managerial matters.[6]

Although Doyukai's statement did not mention this possibility specifically, judging from the context of the statement and the character of its organization, it is possible to say that it is also positive toward such a possibility, perhaps even more so.[7]

INDEPENDENTS

Of the organizations involving independents, the Japan Productivity Center, backed by government, industry and Domei, has been one of the most vocal on this question. Its latest recommendation was made in March of 1977. Essentially it advocated strengthening the joint consultative committee. More specifically, it stressed inclusion in the consideration of the committee such items as the following:

1. Basic business policy and long-range plans
2. Promotion of worker welfare and ability development
3. Relationships between enterprises and communities

The major reason for the advocacy was phrased as follows:

[The recommendation] does not deny, in so far as the type of agenda for joint consultation or discourse goes, the importance of productivity-increasing measures or matters related to rationalization. Rather it recommends the shift in the main concern of the enterprise joint consultative committee from matters related to daily problems or immediate short-term issues, to matters on a higher plane, involving such matters as basic business policies, major management programs or enterprise conduct in the community. These are matters requiring long-term vision which would form the framework of the enterprise, congruent with the requirements of the coming decades. The main purpose is to form those frameworks through joint consultation. Due to the nature of such a subject, setting up a *management policy committee separately from the customary joint consultative committee may well be a way.* It goes without saying that this will not infringe upon the rights of decision-making of the enterprise as prescribed by the present law. The subject of promotion of worker welfare and ability development was specifically mentioned along with others to enable workers to create a viable self-identity and autonomous individuality, instead of being de-individualized masses within the enterprise and thus to maintain the vitality of the industrial society.[8]

Shakai-Keizai Kokumin Kaigi, which has an extensive influence on those involved in industrial relations, made the following statement in February 1975:

1. Worker participation through joint consultation has been, in the cases of other societies whose worker participation was institutionalized, by way of legislation. In view of the fact that Japanese industrial relations have different historical legacies and customs, the use of legislation requires careful deliberation. Although it may be anticipated that in future years the time may come which would require legislation, at present, the most realistic approach is, by way of voluntary agreement between labor and management, to advance the joint consultative committee at the levels of industry and enterprise.
2. For the longer term, one form of participation would be the involvement of worker representatives, recommended by the union, in the auditor's board.[9]

Gendai Soken (Study Group on Modern Society), made up of representatives of independent organizations and some union leaders of a variety of non-extremist views, published a pamphlet prepared by six scholars in September 1976 which stated:

Worker participation related to top management is a method of overcoming the evils of industrial bureaucracy by introducing the principle of democracy into enterprises under conditions wherein the danger of managerial arbitrariness has become greater as stockholders' influence degenerated, and as trustees lost effective control. Worker participation could be drawn from representatives of employees, local inhabitants and consumers. But as for now it would be practical for them to nominate representatives of employees, trade unions outside the firms or independents. As to the structure, participation in the stockholders- assembly (use of ownership rights by way of participation in ownership), participation in the board of directors, as auditors on one of the two tiers are possible or some newer management committee can be thought of. But for the moment, the norm for co-determinative participation is *the parity formula whereby important matters are jointly decided.*[10]

The official position of the government on this question is still not clear. However, the Ministry of Labor is inclined to think that improving the capacity of joint councils to meet changing functional requirements is a realistic approach. But since there are divergent opinions among various sectors of society, the Ministry has withheld from active involvement until a wider consensus can be obtained.

THE POSSIBILITY OF A "JAPANESE MODEL"

Despite divergent reactions from various groups it seems that there are four areas of agreement:

1. To improve the joint consultative committee, including its sub-type, the joint prior-to-decision negotiation scheme, in order to increase the significance of worker participation or worker influence on major corporate decisions
2. To develop a management (policy) committee separate from the joint consultative committee, but basically as a sort of extension of the latter
3. To promote the above processes not by legislation but by voluntary agreement collective bargaining
4. To meet future needs that may arise from introducing worker participation in the board of auditors

As was described earlier, the joint consultative committee has been on the verge of evolving into a co-determinative mechanism for worker participation. In effect, European developments in the early seventies accelerated the trend. According to a Japan Productivity Center survey administered in 1976 to 500 firms and unions, in which 263 firms and 204 unions provided detailed information on the actual workings of the joint consultative committee and in which the firms and unions assessed its adequacy as a device for trade union involvement in business and managerial decisions, 75.7 percent of the firms and 74.5 percent of the unions responded that it was satisfactory and other means were not required. Nevertheless, 27.4 percent of the firms and 48 percent of the unions responded that much improvement is needed if the committee is to serve that purpose (see Table 7.3). Current major problems raised by the unions are that not enough materials and information are being provided by the firms (50.1 percent) and that not enough professional or technical knowledge is possessed by the unions (76.9 percent). As to concrete improvements in the present arrangement, many unions stressed the need to increase the number of items subject to joint decision, the number of meetings, and joint study by specialized sub-committees. In view of the fact that the joint consultative committee is being reviewed and modified to

Table 7.3. Evaluation of Joint Councils as a Device for Trade Union Involvement in Business and Management

	Firms					Unions				
Size	Respondents (number)	Sufficient (percent)	Much Need for Improvement (percent)	Other Means Required (percent)	Unclear (percent)	Respondents (number)	Sufficient (percent)	Much Need for Improvement (percent)	Other Means Required (percent)	Unclear (percent)
Very large	54	63.0	14.8	7.4	14.8	S 20	30.0	50.0	--	20.0
Large	136	43.4	30.9	8.8	16.9	D 71	31.0	50.7	14.1	4.2
Large-medium	42	50.0	26.2	--	23.8	S[a] 3	66.7	--	--	33.1
Medium	17	35.0	35.3	5.9	23.5	C 25	32.0	40.0	4.0	24.0
Small	14	50.0	35.7	14.3	--	U 85	18.8	49.4	16.5	15.3
Total	263	48.3	27.4	7.2	17.1	204	26.5	48.0	12.2	13.3

Source: Japan Productivity Center, *Roshi Kyogisei Sono Jittai to Unei* (Joint Consultation, the present status and its operations), March 1976.

Note: S = Sohyo, D = Domei, S[a] = Shinsanbetsu, C = Churitsuroren, and U = Unaffiliated.

promote worker participation, it may be safely concluded that it is advancing toward the envisaged management policy consultative committee.

A few management policy committees existed before European developments in the early 1970s had stimulated wider interest in worker participation, but they have increased markedly since then. Three major types are discernable—co-determinative consultation, prior-to-decision negotiaton, and co-deliberative consultation. An example of the first is found in the Hitachi Shipbuilding Company, where the agreement on a management policy committee specifically stated that the management shall voluntarily refrain, in principle, from finalizing decisions if its union has strong objections. Joint prior-to-decision negotiations at the Japan Telecommunications Authority are more of a mechanism for inter-party discourse and, if agreement is not reached, the parties are not bound to make decisions. Although secrecy is kept by gentleman's agreement, major disagreement over basic policies is to be made known to the rank-and-file and to the public. Co-deliberative consultation can be found in the Shin-Nihon Steel Company. The firm provides information and discusses matters of major importance with the union, and tries to reach a consensus. It is explicitly stated that union representatives, in their capacity as committee members, do not exercise the right of collective bargaining. At present, co-deliberative consultation is probably the most common form. But since the existence of sub-types permits a certain flexibility, it is possible that management policy committees may eventually become widespread and become the Japanese model of worker participation in major corporate decisions.

Compared with this, worker participation on the board of auditors as it now stands remains only as a long-term possibility. It does not exist at the present time since the current legal framework does not allow for such arrangements, but as a long-term possibility, the chances are by no means nil. There are a few cases in which, because of legal difficulties, some alternative arrangements similar to auditor participation have been devised. One of these is the appointment of part of the auditors from independent organizations, based on trade union recommendations. This scheme has been introduced at the Hitachi Shipbuilding Company, a giant firm, and at Yanase Batteries, a medium-sized firm. It is not impossible to find other such cases among medium- and small-sized firms. Another possibility is to have union representatives participate as observers at meetings of the board of directors. There are at least two such cases. One is Sankei Newspaper Company, a major firm, and the other is at the France Bed Company, a medium-sized firm. The scheme at Kanebo Textile Company, a major firm, may be a kindred case, because it has union representatives participating as observers at the management committee or, more exactly, the standing directors' meeting which is the *de facto* center of top management decisions. Again it is possible to find similar cases in the medium- and small-sized sectors. The instances cited above admittedly are few in number but, nevertheless, they tend to imply that they occur in response to the need for rationalization, due either to intense competition or to stagnation in the industry, provided that union-management relationships have been stable. It is possible, if legal barriers are eliminated, there will be more cases. On the other hand, since a large majority of employers and trade unions alike are cautious of, or antipathetic to, worker-director schemes, and likely to remain so unless they are forced to change, this type of worker participation is only a long-range possibility. Meanwhile, it is likely that management policy committees will continue to increase.

With worker participation increasing at various levels, there have, of course, been large-scale and profound social changes in recent decades. First of all, there was the conspicuous increase in employed workers in the total working population. In the mid-1950s, it was 44 percent, and two decades later 70 percent. Meanwhile, changes in the needs and values of individuals and in their economic and social situation have been considerable. These have been accompanied by both integrating and disintegrating social tendencies. In terms of standard of living, there has been a marked increase in the tendency to identify one's position as within the middle class. Those viewing themselves as middle class and above were 45 percent of the population in 1960 and a decade and a half later, 68 percent.

To explain this simply as false self-perception is difficult, since there have been economic and social changes clearly related to the trend. During the past decade and a half, the real wage went up by 6.4 percent a year, or 2.4 times. Differentials in household income narrowed to a point that was one of the lowest among the major industrial societies. Differentials in capital holdings also became smaller. Occupationally, white-collar workers, including professional, technical, managerial, clerical, and sales staff, increased from 28.8 percent in 1960 to 41 percent in 1975. Meanwhile, as a result of mechanization and automation, there was a marked decrease in heavy manual work and an increase in "grey-collar" workers. The general rise in educational levels in the labor force was considerable. The proportion of senior secondary school graduates and above was already 30 percent by 1960, but went up subsequently by nearly 10 percent. Urbanization was rapid. In 1960 the metropolitan share of the population was 63.5 percent; in 1975 about 80 percent. Family size fell. Average mambers per household were 4.6 in 1960 but declined to 3.4, with the decline in the birth rate, the increase in prolonged and higher education of children, and the gainful employment of housewives. The life cycle changed considerably. Working hours decreased, leisure time increased, and the average life expectancy rose from 65 to 72 years for males and from 70 to 77 for females.

Nevertheless, it is important to note that growing middle-class identification does not in itself imply a positive evaluation of living conditions by the population. Much of the research on general satisfaction with living conditions tends to show either that there has been no significant change, or even that it is declining. A comprehensive opinion survey conducted by the Ministry of Labor in September 1974, for example, showed that workers in the private sector who were generally dissatisfied with their present living conditions outnumbered those who were satisfied; and that those who were dissatisfied with their present work situation and leisure opportunities outnumbered those dissatisfied with their own income and property conditions. There has been a growing demand for improved leisure facilities among the young, for housing among the middle-aged, and for social welfare among the aged. Admittedly, there have clearly been changes in the levels of aspiration, needs, and values, but while the economic growth in the 1960s was spectacular (at a real rate of 10 percent per annum), it was accompanied by a set of economic-social imbalances. There were problems of environment, inflation, public service, quality of work, social welfare, and stagflation. In the 1950s, there arose a desire to improve the material standard of living, in reaction to the prolonged poverty of war and the immediate post-war years, reinforced by knowledge of the American life-style. By the early 1960s, a national attitude emerged that economic growth was the panacea for poor living conditions and the solution of many impending social problems. But within the present decade, the demand for an improvement in the quality of life has become strong, and growth-worship has begun to show signs of decline. These were important factors in the increasing demand for worker participation.

Around 1970, the basic emphasis of government, social, and economic development policies shifted from production to welfare. The government upgraded pension and other social security provisions to a level equal to other advanced industrial societies. Also, the law for the Promotion of Workers' Property Accumulation was promulgated. (This law was subsequently modified, in 1975.) Although the Japanese system is still comparatively underdeveloped compared to the current German model, the property accumulation law functioned as part of an important and active social policy. Briefly, the law has two major purposes, the promotion of saving for property formation and of housing construction. The scheme for the former includes, first of all, favorable tax treatment for workers who save to add to their property holdings. Interest on capital holdings up to 5 million yen is tax-exempt. As of March 1975, about 4 million workers with qualified savings totalling about 430 billion yen were participating in this scheme. Secondly, the scheme provides incentives to firms to contribute to the worker's efforts to achieve capital accumulation. This is again through special tax treatment, for property accumulations plans meeting specified conditions. An important part of the program is the provision of subsidies to medium and small firms to encourage them also to have such plans. The scheme for housing construction includes low-interest loans to employers, employers' associations, and labor banks, sponsored by trade unions, which construct houses for workers to rent or purchase. Secondly, it provides low-interest loans to individual workers. Workers' property formation plans in Japan, then, so far are based either on special tax treatment or on loans, and not on premiums or stock ownership. There are reasons for this. The propensity of Japanese workers to save has been outstandingly high. Particularly in the large firms there have been various schemes to promote worker property formation, involving such things as corporate savings plans, loans, share-holding, life insurance, lump sum retirement allowances, and pensions. Also, management within the firms has usually had a major influence on these decisions, and not the stockholders. Moreover, it has been the banks that have supplied capital to the firms, the stock market usually being only secondary. For these reasons, the formula of worker participation in capital formation, as conceived by some European unions, is not unlikely to develop in Japan. However, worker property formation plans are likely to be continued and strengthened, as this is the objective of all the parties involved in industrial relations, although they differ in their concepts of these plans.

Future Prospects for Japanese Development

Recently, faced with the possibility of a deep recession and the prospect of slower economic growth in the long term, the National Conference on Economic and Social Problems (Shakai Keizai Kokumin Kaigi) conducted a prognosticative survey on the future of Japanese industrial relations. Labor leaders, opinion makers from independent organizations, and presidents or directors of major firms were consulted on likely developments in the final quarter of this century. The survey was conducted in 1976–77, with responses from 625 persons. In what follows, their prophecies of the likely development of worker participation will be introduced to show likely similarities and differences relative to European trends, followed by a scenario to account for perceived convergences and divergences.

A large majority of those surveyed foresee that the dominant pattern of Japanese industrial relations will converge with German and Swedish patterns, defined as outstandingly participative and pragmatically reformative. This view implies that Japanese industrial relations will move toward a stable equilibrium, since this has been the Japanese image of German and Swedish patterns (see Table 7.4). On the other hand, a minority of respondents foresee that significant development of Japanese worker participation in major decisions at the enterprise level will be through further evolution of the joint consultative committee, and not through the worker-director system as in Germany and Sweden, nor through collective bargaining as in the United States. Also, they do not see the likelihood of a workers' capital ownership system developing as in Germany and Sweden, implying that the present Japanese arrangement of workers' property formation will be further improved. Thus, those polled foresee a major convergence to a distinctively participative type of industrial relations, and at the same time predict diverging institutional arrangements (see Table 7.5). Why? The answer to the question is implicit in the discussion which follows.

Table 7.4. Future Pattern of Industrial Relations in Japan, 1976–2000

	(percent of respondents)			
	Total	Labor	Management	Independents
Class conflict type (as in Italy and France)	0.7	1.2	0.5	0.5
Participative revisionistic types (as in Germany and Sweden)	64.4	72.0	61.4	61.2
Collective bargaining centered-type (as in U.S.A.)	21.5	22.4	21.0	21.3
Workers' self-management type (as in Yugoslavia)	1.4	0.6	1.9	1.6
Communist-type (as in Soviet Union and China)	0.0	0.0	0.0	0.0
Others	11.4	3.7	15.2	13.7
No response (percent of total)	0.5	0.0	0.0	1.6
Number of respondents	620	190	234	196

Source: Shakai Keizai Kokumin Kaigi, *Henbosuru Roshikankei* (Changing pattern of industrial relations), Tokyo, 1977, p. 265.

Table 7.5. Most Significant Prospective Arrangements for Worker Participation, 1976–2000

	(percent of respondents)			
	Total	Labor	Management	Independents
No change	4.5	3.7	5.7	4.5
Out of the question	1.3	1.2	1.0	1.3
Worker-director	5.8	11.8	2.9	5.8
Collective bargaining	11.7	11.2	11.9	11.7
Consultative committees	64.6	69.5	68.1	64.6
Workshop participation	8.7	1.9	7.1	8.7
Worker stock ownership	1.4	0.0	0.5	1.4
Workers' self-management	0.5	0.0	0.0	0.5
Other	0.2	0.0	0.0	0.2
No response (percent of total)	1.3	0.6	2.9	1.3
Number of respondents	620	190	234	196

Source: Shakai Keizai Kokumin Kaigi, *Henbosuru Roshikankei* (Changing pattern of industrial relations), Tokyo, 1977, p. 266.

REASONS FOR CONVERGENCE

(a) Maturity of economic development, slower growth and major shift in industrial structure toward post-industrial pattern. The general level of economic development will show a convergence, if measured by *per capita* national income, in one decade or so. The age level of the population is also converging with other countries. Social security and welfare expenditures relative to GNP will converge in one or two decades. By the year 1990, the general level of welfare and public service provisions will be at comparable levels, except for such matters as housing, commuting facilities and parks, where there are geographical constraints. Economic and social adjustment to levels such as these, however, will be difficult since they will be in conditions of slower economic growth. It is not unlikely that the growth rate will decline from 9 percent per annum for the twenty years ending in 1975 to 6 percent in the next decade (1976–85) and to 5 percent (1986–95) and eventually 4 percent or so at around the turn of the century (1996–2005), in view of the increasing gravity of energy problems and international economic adjustments. One thing is clear. The industrial structure must be changed to a post-industrial pattern that is less energy-consumptive and more knowledge-intensive. Tertiary and quarternary sectors in the total working population will increase from 52 percent as of the mid-1970s to 57 percent by 1990 and 60–64 percent by the year 2000. Major rationalization will be inevitable. However, there is a likelihood of long-term unemployment. Even assuming substantial employment policies, the ratio of job vacancies over job seekers at public employment exchanges will be somewhere between 1.0 and 0.5 throughout the decades preceding the year 2000, a long-term situation hitherto not experienced by Japan.

(b) Inflationary potential, macro-economic wage adjustment, and changes in crucial issues in industrial relations. There will be inflationary pressure due to energy and resource problems. Macro-economic wage adjustment will be inevitable. As a result, long-term wage decisions are likely to be based on something like the following logic. Given a 5 percent per annum GNP growth rate in real terms for the decade 1986–95 and 4 percent or so in the following decade, and given labor-input growth rates after taking into account the annual reduction of working hours of 1 percent in each decade, the productivity increase will be 4 percent and 3 percent respectively. Given this, if the rate of inflation is to be controlled within the 2–6 percent level for 1986–95 and 3–7 percent for 1996–2005, and if the increase in real wages is proportionate to the increase in productivity, the wage increase in nominal terms will be 6–10 percent a year for the two decades. This, however, may be too optimistic. Depending on the rate of increase in productivity and inflation, the annual increase in real wages may well be much lower at 2–4 percent for 1986–95 and 1–3 percent for 1996–2005, which could well generate something like a social contract between parties in industry and

government. Connected with this, the relative significance of national and industrial federations in wage decisions will increase. Nor is it unlikely that the wage negotiation cycle may shift from an annual to a biennial or triennial basis, with sliding clauses to cover the in-between years.

(c) Social change, social responsibility of enterprises, and the changing role of trade unions at the enterprise level. Employed workers will increase their share of the total working population in coming decades, and achieve greater economic and social significance. Their needs, aspirations, and social values will continue to change as material standards of living reach a level of affluence and continue to improve, even though at a slower rate. The "social malaise" common to industrially advanced societies will become pronounced; there will be more turnover as allegiance to the enterprise community declines, more refusal to transfer as rights-consciousness becomes stronger, and more problems with industrial morale as social discipline degenerates. However, if needs, aspirations, and social values are properly appreciated, and the population values social consensus, social obligations, quality of life, equitable distribution of income and wealth, participation in decisions and organic solidarity in social relations, such problems will be socially controlled and major conflict in industry and society as a whole may be avoided. Thus, there will be increased pressure for social responsibility on the part of the enterprise. Around the turn of the century, three of the major expressions of social responsibility by the enterprise will be to provide conditions for life fulfillment of workers, to secure mutual trust of consumers and the general population, and to expand employment opportunities. Concerns such as stockholders' interests or pursuit of profit for its own sake will rate minimal interest. Related to these changes, the role of trade unions at the enterprise level will also change. In addition to the traditional role of improving working conditions, three other items will become prominent, business policies and long-range plans, retirement systems, and humanization of working conditions (see Table 7.6).

(d) Major change of the economic-political system toward a functional social democracy. Economic and social pressures will demand more plan-oriented development strategies and involve larger roles for mass-based organizations in the process. There will be a major shift of economic and political systems from the present liberal democracy to a social democratic system. Since building a welfare society is implied as the major goal, and changes in the political power structure are not necessarily implied, the envisaged new system is a welfare democracy involving a plan-oriented economy and implyng a decentralized political system.

BACKGROUND REASONS FOR DIVERGENCE

(a) Historical legacies of worker participation. The respondents to the survey implied that the divergence of institutional arrangements for worker

Table 7.6.   Significant Items Most Likely to Increase in Importance in
Negotiations and Consultation, 1976–2000

	(percent of respondents)			
	Total	Labor	Management	Independents
Business policies and long-range plans	41.0	56.6	38.6	30.0
Retirement systems, lump sum allowance, pension	38.6	27.4	45.8	40.4
Humanization of work and working conditions	23.8	29.2	21.4	21.8
Wages, bonus and other monetary rewards	23.4	21.2	22.8	26.2
Working hours, holidays, vacation	17.8	16.8	17.6	19.2
Social responsibility of enterprise	15.0	19.2	11.4	15.4
Employment security and opportunity	12.0	7.2	14.2	13.6
Education and ability development	11.4	6.2	12.4	14.8
Housing, welfare, quality of life	8.2	8.0	7.6	8.8
Promotion, upgrading personnel rules	6.6	5.6	5.8	8.8
Number of respondents	620	190	234	196

Source: Shakai Keizai Kokumin Kaigi, *Henbosuru Roshikankei* (Changing pattern of industrial relations), Tokyo, 1977, p. 263.

participation is due to the essential continuity of the major characteristics of Japanese industrial relations in the coming decades and perhaps beyond the year 2000. This point will be amplified in what follows. First of all, there are significant historical legacies of worker participation which will continue to influence the parties in industrial relations. The joint consultative committee since the mid-1950s has provided certain practical benefits to both parties in that it has enabled management to maintain its prerogatives within the enterprise, and the union to increase its influence, if, in addition to its bargaining strength, it exercises sufficient moral authority and expertise to appeal to rank-and-file members and the general public.

(b) Dual allegiance and the employment system. The co-institutionalization of bargaining and consultative arrangements at the enterprise level may be seen as a reflection of the psychological tendency towards dual allegiance among Japanese workers. Generally, trade unions are transactive or confrontative in collective bargaining, and advisory or discursive in joint

consultation or prior-to-decision negotiation. Given that the enterprise community has been conditioned by life-time employment, the seniority principle and enterprise welfarism, dual allegiance tends to become pervasive and produces both bargaining and consultative systems. However, at the same time, the joint consultative committee must be seen equally as a reaction to strain within the enterprise community. There have been strains within the employment system, and the social meaning of lifetime employment, the seniority principle, and enterprise welfarism have changed significantly during the last two decades, as labor mobility has become more practical, working conditions more standardized, and social welfare improved. It was in part to deal with the adjustment required by such changes that the joint consultative committees became widespread.

(c) Meritocratic tendencies and egalitarian demands. The dynamic of adjustments in the employment system either through collective bargaining or through joint consultation may be illustrated by looking at three aspects. With the prospect of slower economic growth and all that implies, even our economic Delphians are split on the future of lifetime employment. More than half of the management consulted wish to abandon the *status quo*, while labor is overwhelmingly against the idea. Regarding the seniority wage system, both foresee significant changes. Yet management insists on differentials by merit, and the union sees changes that would narrow the age differentials to avoid individual differentials by merit as inevitable. In respect to welfare, management may favor selective application of benefits, while the union insists on universal application. Generally the former asserts meritocratic principles, the latter egalitarian demands. Since there can be no complete meritocracy or egalitarianism in a human organization, the results tend to be a compromise to avoid a major breakdown of the community. Lifetime employment is being modified by using more temporary or outside workers, narrowing retirement allowance differentials by length of service, providing education and training for generalized skills, and introducing incentives for voluntary separation. The seniority-based system is being modified by allowing a degree of meritocratic criteria and narrowing age differentials. It is possible that the wage curve itself will be changed to shift the peak from 55 to 50 or 45 years in the near future. Even so, however, Japan remains distinctively seniority and wage-oriented, if compared with those other Western societies which have a wage-peak at ages 35–40. Enterprise welfarism is being modified by increasing the share of contributory social insurance schemes and shifting the emphasis from livelihood supplements to retirement allowances and the quality of working life. In short, they are undergoing modifications, and not major changes. Due to the pressure of unemployment, there will be difficulties and conflict as in the early 1930s and late 1940s. However, it must be remembered, it was exactly in such turbulent years that the Japanese-type employment system was further refined and developed.

(d) Managerial authority and trade union leadership. The formal organization of Japanese top management is akin to the American model, having a board of trustees and management committee (committee of standing directors in Japan's case). *De facto*, however, it is a single board system, the two tiers being filled by an identical team. The team has usually been made up of employee-directors of the enterprise since the early years of industrialization. Typically, the team is a combination of experts in various fields—production, marketing and sales, finance and accounting, engineering, R&D, planning, and industrial relations. Most of the boards have features of a meritocratic elite, each member having a diploma from a well-known higher educational institution, and promoted from within after long years of service. Major decisions are usually made by the committee of standing directors, based on consensus. Normally, they are free from shareholder control as the stock market plays an insignificant role in supplying capital. Banks are significant, but enterprises usually diversify their banks so as to maintain autonomy. Their authority, then, is based on the social dynamics within the enterprise, within the team itself, with middle management, and with other members of the enterprise community. Important correlatives to this are the extensive participation of middle management in top decisions and the closer involvement of top management in industrial relations. It is typically a senior member of the team who represents management in collective bargaining and joint consultation. Almost invariably, there is at least one member specializing in industrial relations. Not infrequently, there is at least one person in the top team who has held one of the three top positions in the enterprise trade union at one time in his career, as president or vice president or general secretary. Such, according to a recent survey, was the case at 59.5 percent of enterprises with 5,000 or more regular employees. In the Japanese setting, this phenomenon is usually not seen by workers as abnormal or to be opposed. It has prevailed not only in industry, but also in hospitals, schools and in government. Co-determination in such a structure may mean either a sort of complete fusion of relationships, which would result in "undesirable" collaboration, or a complete breakdown of social relations in the enterprise community.

In turn, there are certain problems inherent in the positions of trade union leaders which inhibit co-determination. Trade unions have rather strong organizational bases in the enterprise. They have, on average, one full-time officer per 300 members, one elected executive committee member per 20-30 members, and one shop steward per 10-15 members, which is a high ratio of officers unparalleled in other market economies. Most unions have union shop, check-off provisions, and time-off rights for officers and even members. They have rights to use enterprise facilities such as office space, conference rooms, and bulletin boards. They have a financially stable base: the dues of 1-3 percent of basic wages come in every month almost 100 percent. Major periodic meetings are attended by a large majority, and these meetings are frequent. Decision-making rules give the impression of what Sydney and Beatrice Webb called primitive democracy, in which everybody in the unit gets together and makes decisions each time issues of common concern arise. This has been all the more important to adjusting the different interests of members and in securing bargaining strength *vis-à-vis* management, owing to the heterogeneous composition of members by occupation, education, length of service, age and sex. However, this situation at the same time discouraged the development of representative democracy and the accumulation of expertise and leadership, or conversely encouraged the dominance of clique- or sect-based leadership and technocrats in decision processes. Either state is remote from that in which union leaders can claim full-scale co-determination. Although committed leaders, technocratic staff and representative democracy patterns of decision making have tended to increase, it will be a long time before a system of co-determination becomes a realistic possibility.

(e) *Harmony in balance and ideological division.* Some years ago Professor P. Hessling, of Erasmus University, Rotterdam, conducted an experimental study on decision-making patterns among middle management of various countries and concluded that the Japanese pattern showed a striking degree of dissemination of information within the team and among related teams, and distinctively frequent consultations. Although tendencies in a simulated situation should not be confused with patterns in reality, it seems empirically tenable to say that there are certain cultural propensities favoring joint consultations or prior-to-decision negotiations within a group or among groups, if they see themselves as insiders within a social system. Both patterns are in fact institutionalized in Japan in the formalized decision making arrangement known as *ringi seido* (circuit decision system) in which junior staff prepare drafts for decision by seniors, through consultative processes with other related units, sections, or departments. It would seem plausible to say there is a cultural tendency to solidify relationships among insiders of a collective entity in response to a major stimulus, be it at the level of family, community, industry, or nation.

Relatively cohesive social relations within a group or a social system, however, tend to be accompanied by at least two major disequilibriating tendencies. One of these is its strongly alienating effect on people within the same collectivity who identify themselves as insiders. An important cause of such a situation in Japanese enterprises has been the cleavage in career streams owing to educational background or meritocratic differentiation of categories. The differentiation of career possibilities has been related to the diversity of factions within the trade union movement and the latter tended to coincide with ideological divisions. Another tendency is the distinct division between insiders and outsiders in the enterprise community. Thus outside workers, temporary workers, and more generally workers at medium and small businesses have tended to be alienated. This also coincided with ideological divisions, as has been illustrated in some detail. Most forecasters foresee that the ideological divisions within the trade union movement will continue. It is then also implied that sharp differences in trade union attitudes toward co-determination are unlikely to disappear, at least before the year 2000.

Notes

1. Central Labor Relations Commission, *Keieikyogikai no Shishin*, 1946, p. 5.
2. *Ibid.*, p. 6.
3. Ichiro Nakayama, *Roshi Kyogisei*, Japan Institute of Labor, 1964, p. 93.
4. Zen Nihon Rodo Sodomei, *Sankakeizaitaisei no Kakuritsunotameni*, Sodomei Series, No. 26, 1974.
5. Nikkeiren, *Zeninsankaku Keiei*, 1974.
6. Nihon Shokokaigisho, *Keieisanka ni Tsuite no Kenkai*, 1975.
7. Keizai Doyukai, *Keieisanka Shoiinkai, Hokokusho*, 1974.
8. Nihonseisansei Honbu, *Nihongata Keieisanka no Teishō*, 1977.
9. Shakai-Keizai Kokumin Kaigi, *Keieisanka Mondai Tokubetsu Iinkai Hokokusho*, 1975.
10. Gendai Sogo Kenkyushudan, *Rodosha Sanka no Jitsugen no Tameni*, 1976.

8

United States of America

by G. LODGE and KAREN HENDERSON

The American economy in the 1970s faces a number of problems which have serious implications for the future interrelationships between business, the labor force, and the government. Rising energy costs imperil profits and expansion. Productivity in the United States has grown more slowly than in other industrialized nations, giving some companies in those areas a competitive advantage over U.S. firms, particularly in labor-intensive manufacturing industries. Inflation has slashed the purchasing power of the U.S. consumer, with the result that an increasing amount of every family's income must be allocated to high-cost essentials such as health care and housing. Working Americans are concerned over the fact that wages and salaries are not keeping pace with rising costs and taxes; their worries are exacerbated since rapid progress in education has raised their expectations.

In Europe, post-war economic troubles and worker unrest have fostered the growth of co-determination, work participation on boards of directors, and various means of increasing the union role in corporate policy-making. In most or all cases, the governments have been centrally involved in changes in industrial relations; European governments have sometimes initiated radical changes by way of new laws. However, it does not seem likely that these European patterns of action will be duplicated in the United States. It is certainly possible to discern innovation in U.S. industrial relations today, some of which is consciously influenced by European models, but it seems clear that the United States, as in the past, will develop its own models. Although some patterns are emerging, the variety and heterogeneity of the

American experience keep them as yet obscure and uncertain. American employer-employee relations have historically been decentralized affairs even in unionized industries, with settlement left up to the private parties and government intervention avoided. These circumstances inhibit uniformity of action on a national level.

This paper will examine American industrial actions of business, labor, and government which may prove most significant. It will also suggest some trends which are likely to mark the future.

U.S. Labor: Statistical Background

CHARACTERISTICS OF U.S. LABOR FORCE

In America it is inaccurate to speak synonymously of the workforce as a whole and of organized labor, since less than 30 percent of non-agricultural employment is organized. This figure includes some 22 million persons who belong to labor unions, and another group of less than 3 million who belong to associations such as those for police and employees in education. While American unions are large and affluent compared to many elsewhere, labor unions overseas have the advantage of representing about 35 percent of non-agricultural employees in Japan and Germany, more than 50 percent in Great Britain, and 60 to 80 percent in the Scandinavian countries. The absolute number of American labor union members has continued to grow with the population, but the percentage of non-agricultural employees who are members has declined from a peak of about 36 percent in 1945.[1]

In 1975, the total U.S. civilian labor force consisted of 92.6 million persons, of whom 84.8 million were employed and 7.8 million or 8.4 percent were unemployed. The unemployment rate was 5.5 percent in 1960, dropped to 4.5 percent in 1965, and since then rose steadily to its 1975 figure. It is significant that in the 1970s high inflation has existed at the same time as high unemployment, a finding which complicates the formation of national economic policy. From the Second World War through the early 1970s, if unemployment in the U.S. was relatively high, inflation was relatively low, and *vice versa*. Full employment goals now threaten to yield more inflationary impact than formerly. Within the subgroup of unemployed persons, the unemployment rate in 1975 for white males was 7.2 percent, for white females 8.6 percent, for black and other males 13.7 percent, for black and other females 14.0 percent, and for persons 16 to 24 years old 16.1 percent.

Non-farm employment occupied 96 percent of the civilian labor force in 1975, up from 92 percent of civilian workers in 1960, and 85 percent in 1946. The most important trends in the composition of the non-agricultural workforce are apparent from Table 8.1. The most dramatic shifts are the decline in manufacturing's share of employment and the rise of services, and state and local government employment.

Table 8.1. U.S. Nonfarm Employment Patterns, 1960–75

Economic Sector	Percent of Total Wage and Salary Workers		
	1946	1960	1975
Manufacturing	35	31	24
Mining	2	1	1
Contract construction	4	5	4
Transportation and public utilities	10	7	6
Wholesale and retail trade	20	21	22
Finance, insurance, and real estate	4	5	5
Services	11	14	18
Federal government	5	4	4
State and local government	8	11	16

Source: *1977 Economic Report of the President,* p. 224.

Note: Totals may not add to 100 due to rounding.

CHARACTERISTICS OF U.S. LABOR UNIONS

The special character of American labor unions and collective bargaining practices has been delineated by Derek Bok and John Dunlop in their book, *Labor and the American Community,* and the following discussion owes a considerable debt to their work. Certainly it is hard to argue with their premise that decentralization is one of the most significant aspects of American industrial relations. There are about 150,000 separate union-management contracts now in force in this country. Participating in these contractual relationships are more than 175 national unions with 71,000 locals, and 35 national associations with 14,000 local chapters. Although there are a number of important multi-company, national labor-management agreements in the United States, such as in railroads and basic steel, and although some companies negotiate nationally or regionally, most contracts are negotiated with a single employer for a single plant. In contrast, most union members in Europe and Australia are represented by general agreements negotiated for large groups of employees on a multi-employer basis.[2]

The ten largest unions in the U.S., as of 1974, were the Teamsters; United Auto Workers; Steelworkers; Electricians; Machinists; Carpenters; Retail Clerks; Laborers; State, County and Municipal Employees; and Service Employees, each with more than 500,000 members. If employee associations were included, the National Education Association would rank third on the list. The majority of national and local unions are affiliated with the AFL-CIO. Transportation, construction, and manufacturing industries tend to be highly organized; more than half of all government employees are also members of unions or associations. In contrast, trade and service industries tend to be less organized, and since the growth of employment in this sector has been more rapid than in the economy as a whole, it has been difficult for union representation to gain ground among the total workforce. The large employment of women in clerical and sales occupations and in service industries helps explain the lack of union organization, since women have tended not to join unions even in highly organized industries.

Union membership in the U.S. is concentrated geographically. The most highly organized state is New York, with 45.4 percent of non-farm workers in unions or associations, followed by Michigan, West Virginia, Pennsylvania, and Washington. Southern states, on the other hand, have relatively few union members, and the 20 states which retain "right-to-work" laws are mostly in the South. North Carolina, whose textile companies are notorious for their resistance to union organizers, has only 6.9 percent organized non-farm workers; South Carolina, Mississippi, Florida and Texas all stand at 13 percent or less. Since the long-term shift of the nation's manufacturing base is to the South and Southwest (because of factors including superior transportation, cheaper energy, lower taxes and living costs, and incentives to attract business), it is clear that labor unions face a difficult task in keeping their membership from eroding further. The South historically has a strong anti-union bias, and even highly organized industries such as automobile manufacturing are resisting organization of new southern plants.

Union membership is concentrated in relatively few unions. In 1972, fifteen unions, less than 10 percent of the total number, accounted for 56 percent of union membership.

American labor laws are designed chiefly to promote collective bargaining and to ensure the fairness of union representation; but the Congress and the courts have generally acted to legitimize labor's gains only after they have been won. Clearly, this governmental stance is much different from that of European governments which take a leading role in labor-management affairs. For the comparative purposes of this study, it seems appropriate here to list other significant ways in which American industrial relations appear unique:

1. One union serves as the sole representative for all the employees in a plant or other appropriate bargaining unit.

2. Collective agreements literally specify wages and terms of employment, and individual workers may not negotiate different terms on their own behalf; nor are minority unions allowed to negotiate.

3. Because most contracts involve only one employer or even one plant, collective agreements tend to be very specific about wages, working conditions, fringe benefits, discipline, procedures for grievance, promotion criteria, transfers and layoffs, schedules, and a wide varity of other work rules. Unilateral action by the employer is thus very restricted.

4. There is no political party based solely on working-class support; American union members tend to vote the Democratic ticket but do not consider themselves bound to do so.* Upward mobility and a lack of class barriers are part of American tradition. Indeed, in the U.S. there is no working class in the European sense of the term.

5. Local unions maintain considerable power, in part because many contracts cover only one plant. Even where the national union is large and influential, as with the Auto Workers and Steelworkers, local unions generally retain the right to strike over local issues.

6. The central federation of American unions, the AFL-CIO, has few formal powers. In keeping with the decentralization of the system as a whole, the federation has little influence over the bargaining policies or other activities of its members. It may investigate and suspend members for corruption, and it maintains a research department and lobbying operations, but member unions retain their autonomy.[3]

The Winds of Change: Tensions Within the System

Through decades of industrial conflict and bargaining experience, American unions have become an institution. Some unions have the reputation of being corrupt, of mismanaging their finances, or of excessive political wheeling and dealing. It must be acknowledged at the same time, however, that American unions deserve substantial credit for the relatively high standard of living of most American workers, and for the protections they have in the workplace. These benefits accrue to non-unionized as well as unionized workers. If union lobbying helps raise the minimum wage, unorganized workers also gain; similarly, union agitation has helped focus attention on unsafe working conditions even in industries without unions.

Like many large organizations, however, unions have acquired their share of institutional inertia. The labor crusades of the 1930s are long past, and it is no longer as easy for unions to attract dedicated young members. Attendance at many local union meetings is small. The unions are beginning to face a serious problem of having an insufficient number of trained younger leaders coming up through the ranks. It is noteworthy that George Meany, head of the AFL-CIO, is 82 years old, and there is still no clear indication as to who will succeed him. Douglas Fraser, the new president of the Auto Workers, is 60 years old and was in fact Leonard Woodcock's principal opponent for the job in 1970. Lloyd McBride, the newly elected president of the Steelworkers, is 61, and William Winpisinger, the new head of the Machinists, is 52. In general, the elective political process of selecting national union leaders tends to make change less likely and slower than in corporations.

Naturally, unions are not alone in facing unprecedented problems in the

---

*This is by no means always the case. Labor voted heavily for Eisenhower in 1952 and 1956 and for Nixon in 1972.

1970s. Among the most pressing issues confronting American business is that of productivity. Measured simply in terms of manufacturing output per hour, U.S. productivity has risen less than that of other industrial nations since 1966 (see Table 8.2). The strength of foreign competition, particularly in labor-intensive industries, and the high cost of manufacturing operations in the U.S. is causing many companies to locate new plants overseas and even to close down existing plants here.*

Table 8.2.   Average Annual Increase in Output per Man-hour, 1966–75 and 1970–75

Country	1966–75 (percent)	1970–75 (percent)
U.S.A.	2.0	1.8
Canada	3.9	3.0
Japan	9.0	5.4
France	4.9	3.4
West Germany	5.3	5.4
Italy	5.8	6.0
Sweden	5.8	4.4
United Kingdom	3.3	3.0

Source: *International Economic Report of the President,* 1977.

Certain intangible factors also seem to be hurting U.S. productivity. Higher absenteeism in certain industries, problems of employee loyalty, labor turnover, and even sabotage of products are symptoms of malaise which have received a great deal of attention in recent years. How to interpret these problems, however, is the subject of much disagreement among observers. William Winpisinger of the Machinists' union champions the view that "blue-collar blues" is a media myth perpetuated by academicians. He believes that only better wages and working conditions, the kinds of goals that unions have traditionally fought for, can satisfy workers. At least part of American workers' current disaffection may be traced to the fact that their spendable earnings are not keeping pace with inflation. The average weekly disposable income of an American employee, measured in 1975 dollars, was $147 in 1960, rose to $162 in 1965 and has hovered near that level ever since, reaching $166 in 1970, but slipping back to $164 in 1975.

Other observers, however, argue that "employee alienation" is not so much an economic as a social phenomenon. In the view of Professor Richard

*There are, of course, other reasons for locating plants abroad, including access to new markets and raw material suppliers.

Walton, for instance, the underlying cause is that employee expectations have risen in the last decades. Levels of income and security have climbed, so that a regular paycheck is taken more for granted. Some workers have come to resent the monotony of fragmented jobs and lack of opportunity to exercise their own judgment. At the same time, in society as a whole, many traditional values such as ambition, duty, and obedience to authority seem to have lost force.[4] Irving Bluestone, vice president of the UAW, who is responsible for working with General Motors Corporation, believes there is great potential for stress in the disparity between a worker's role on the job and in the rest of his daily life. At home and in his community, he has the chance to make decisions concerning his and his family's life, to control his time, and to take part in the political process if he so desires. On the job he is expected to labor quiescently in an authoritarian, hierarchical system that is directed by others.

No matter on which side of this argument one's opinions happen to fall, the fact remains that labor productivity must climb if the U.S. is to compete successfully in world markets. High absenteeism and high employee turnover work to the advantage of no one—management, union, or employee—and therefore these problems are receiving considerable attention. A variety of techniques are being tested and evaluated. According to Professor Walton:

Companies in a variety of industries in many countries have found that they can create a more satisfied, committed, and capable work force and can obtain equal or better quality and quantity of output by restructuring work along different lines: by combining jobs to create whole tasks; by assigning these tasks to teams with responsibilities for inspection, maintenance, planning, scheduling, and work assignment; by cross-training workers for broader flexibility; by adopting more participative management patterns; and by designing pay schemes to reward individual learning and group productivity.[5]

It is easy to see that radical work restructuring is difficult to accomplish in an existing workplace or where a union contract with a tight network of work rules is in force. Thus, in the United States, experiments in the total restructuring of work have generally taken place in new plants: either non-union, as in the case of the General Foods pet food plant in Topeka, Kansas, and the TRW ball-bearing plant in Gainesville, Georgia; or unionized, such as Rockwell International's Off-Highway Products Division in Battle Creek, Michigan.

In existing plants, particularly in heavy industry, it is much more difficult and often completely impractical to attempt immediate redesign of work processes. For this reason, the UAW has focused its attention recently on improving democratic processes in the workplace. The steelworkers' union, on the other hand, considers "quality of working life" a chimera when the jobs in question involve tending a blast furnace. Their goals are to avoid union-management conflict and to increase productivity in order to salvage the steel industry's ability to compete with foreign steelmakers.

Still other companies approach the twin goals of high productivity and employee satisfaction from the point of view that these are the aims of any competent management, and that it is not necessary to subscribe to any one school of thought in order to pursue them. Many large American corporations seem to operate this way; IBM and Texas Instruments are examples of non-unionized companies with excellent reputations for efficiency and thoughtful personnel management. Some other corporations are quietly conducting their own experiments with different models of job redesign or participative management, but, like Procter & Gamble, they shun publicity and prefer not to allow outside observers.

At this point it is appropriate to examine some of the visible innovations in U.S. industrial relations in detail, and to try to assess their future significance.

Some Attempts to Improve Employer-Employee Relations

EMPLOYEE PARTICIPATION ON BOARDS OF DIRECTORS

Since employee participation in corporate decision-making at the board level is an important feature of the development in industrial relations in a number of European countries, it is important to indicate at the start that this practice is non-existent today in the U.S.A. There is virtually no interest at all in seating workers on boards of directors, on the part of either workers and unions, or, predictably, of corporations. Phillip I. Blumberg commented recently in the *Harvard Business Review* that "discussion of the concept must be regarded as merely interesting, and perhaps even useful, speculation, completely separated from political realities."[6]

It is widely reported in this country that what makes employee representation at the board level feasible abroad is the existence of the two-tier board system in Germany and some other European countries. Under this system, employee representation is restricted to the upper or supervisory board which is concerned with policy-making rather than with management. This situation might be compared in American terms to seating a worker on the board of directors when, in fact, all the important decisions had been made ahead of time in the executive committee meeting. Since American unions and corporations do tend to view the idea this way, it is not hard to understand the lack of interest. The dissenting votes of a few worker-directors would have little symbolic or practical value to an American union, assuming that they would be unlikely to muster other directors' support.

Another way of examining this issue is in terms of the separation of powers, which is central to the American political system. American unions traditionally have cherished their adversarial posture because it has enabled them to act as watchdogs over management on the workers' behalf. There is no easier way for an American union to lose its members' support than to be seriously suspected of collaboration with management, as could well occur were a union member to be seated on the board of directors. Naturally, there is no theoretical reason why a non-unionized corporation might not also have employee representation on its board, but it is hard thus far to imagine a set of circumstances under which it might feel compelled to do so.

About a year ago, Douglas Fraser of the UAW made a joking reference in public about wanting to put a worker or two on the board of directors at Chrysler Corporation. His remark was picked up by reporters present and received wide press as a serious proposition. The union demanded employee representation during the 1976 contract negotiations; but as Professor Herbert R. Northrup suggested, "if the UAW officials had exchanged some cents per hour for a place on Chrysler's Board, I suspect they would soon be among the unemployed."[7]

The official position of the AFL-CIO was summed up in some widely quoted remarks by George Meany's executive assistant, Thomas R. Donohue. "We do not want to blur in any way the distinctions between the respective roles of management and labor in the plant," he said. Any union which attempted to become a partner in management would find itself "most likely, the junior partner in success and the senior partner in failure." Perhaps more important, Mr. Donohue said, American unions already "bargain on more issues than the number we might have any impact on as members of a board of directors."[8]

STEEL: THE EXPERIMENTAL NEGOTIATION AGREEMENT

By all accounts, one of the most interesting recent developments in American industrial relations involves the United Steelworkers Union and the ten basic steel companies. This latest chapter in their history began in 1971, at a time when the U.S. steel industry was no longer comfortably dominating the world market. Fierce foreign competition particularly from Japanese producers, had left the American steel industry with slow growth, stagnating profits, and chronic overcapacity, all of which was complicated by its high labor costs.

In the 1971 basic steel negotiations, the steel industry broached its serious problem of productivity with the union, and they negotiated a new contract provision which established joint advisory committees on productivity in each plant of the industry, about 250 committees in all. The stated purpose of the committees was to work with management on ways and means to:

1. Improve productivity
2. Promote orderly and peaceful relations with employees and achieve uninterrupted operations in the plants
3. Promote the use of domestic steel
4. Achieve the desired prosperity and progress of the company and its employees
5. Review matters of special concern consistent with the purpose of the committee and provisions of the collective bargaining agreement

The agreement emphasized that the job security of employees was not to be threatened by any increases in productivity, and that the functioning of the committees could not be used to circumvent or abrogate any terms of the Basic Labor Agreement.

The progress of these joint labor-management committees has varied from plant to plant. According to the union, best results have been obtained when the plant-wide committee acts as a steering committee and organizes subcommittees in all plant departments including both workers and managers. Problems of poor workmanship, absenteeism, or waste of materials or time may thus be addressed by those most familiar with them, and some locations have reported significant improvement.[9]

No matter how successful the committees have been, however, they could not solve one long-standing problem in the industry: the customers' traditional practice of stockpiling steel in anticipation of a work stoppage before the negotiations for a new contract. This created an artificial demand as buyers bought up foreign steel to hedge against a halt in their normal supply. The aftermath in the U.S.A., whether or not there was a strike, was large-scale unemployment and permanent loss of jobs. To overcome this problem, I. W. Abel, as president of the Steelworkers International, in 1973 negotiated an experimental agreement in which the union gave up the right to strike the steel companies on an industry-wide basis, and both parties agreed to resolve disputed issues by arbitration. The agreement continued the practice of allowing local unions to strike individual plants over local, non-economic issues and to ratify basic steel contracts.

Many observers at once praised the Experimental Negotiation Agreement as a breakthrough from the industry's habitual, destructive conflicts. It was not clear for some time, however, whether the 1.4 million members of the Steelworkers saw it this way, or believed that their union was selling them out. The issue was complicated by the fact that only about a third of the members were actually subject to the Basic Steel Agreement, while the others worked in such diverse industries as mining, chemicals, heavy construction, and even cemeteries. The test of the membership's views came early in 1977 at the election for the USW presidency between candidates Lloyd McBride and Edward Sadlowski.[10]

Mr. McBride was the chosen successor of retiring President I. W. Abel; he was a man of moderate views who enjoyed the backing of the USW bureaucracy and was expected to carry on Mr. Abel's policies (probably including the Experimental Negotiation Agreement) if elected. Mr. Sadlowski, 38 years old, was an outspoken dissident candidate who sharply attacked the Experimental Negotiation Agreement, and promised a return to more militant unionism. Mr. Sadlowski's candidacy had the support of many basic steelworkers in large locals, of the large ethnic group of Polish workers, and even of some well-known outside supporters including economist John Kenneth Galbraith, lawyer Joseph L. Rauh Jr., and former

UAW official Victor Reuther. These outside supporters helped raise funds for Mr. Sadlowski; Mr. Galbraith and Lewis D. Sargentick urged financial support in a letter which included the following quotation: "Sadlowski is in the forefront of a movement that is sweeping the steelworkers and many other unions—a movement to turn the American labor movement around and make it into the democratic, progressive political and economic force its founders intended it to be."[11] Sadlowski's support from outside intellectuals drew a broadside attack from George Meany, who ordinarily refrains from all comment on the internal politics of AFL-CIO member unions.

When the election was concluded, however, it was clear that Mr. Abel's policies had won over the USW membership, because Mr. McBride was the victor by about 80,000 votes. Said Mr. Abel: "The vote says to Sadlowski that he hasn't known what it's been about up to this time, that he hasn't kept up with what this union has been doing or the feelings of the membership, and that he has been used by some . . ."[12]

Later in the spring, union leaders negotiated a new contract with the steel industry which they intend to be a new start towards lifetime job security for all steelworkers. In addition to a total wage increase, including cost-of-living adjustments, of about 30 percent over three years, the new agreement provides much higher supplemental unemployment benefits for all laid-off workers. Workers who are laid off or disabled may now retire after 20 years if their age and length of service total 65 years, and their pensions will be supplemented by $300 a month until they are eligible for Social Security.

The negotiation of the new contract does not by any means seem to indicate that all troubles are past for steel. The 800 union local presidents failed to ratify the new contract by a vote of 148 to 143 the first time it was presented to them. The threat that the entire contract would go to government arbitration unless they approved it was a major reason for their eventual ratification, 193 to 99. Similarly, it was reported that the steel companies chose not to contest the size of the wage increase because they also wanted to avoid arbitration. The two sides agreed only narrowly to use the Experimental Negotiating Agreement in 1980. By itself, the money settlement continues the trend of pay increases rising faster than productivity in steel, and steel imports continue to fall not very far short of 1971's worrisome peak of 18.3 million tons.

THE UNITED AUTO WORKERS

(a) *General Motors.* The automobile companies, like other American industries, have been plagued by foreign import competition and serious worker absenteeism and lack of motivation. After several years of experimentation, General Motors in 1971 began a serious effort to combat these problems. It split the personnel function in the corporation into two with a vice-president in charge of industrial relations and another in charge of personnel administration and development. GM hired Stephen Fuller, who had been associate dean at the Harvard Business School, as Vice President of Personnel and Development in charge of the new programs of Organizational Development, leaving George Morris to continue as Vice President of Industrial Relations. The chairman of the board at GM, Richard Gerstenberg, explained the corporation's attitude: "Productivity is not a matter of making employees work longer or harder. . . . We must improve working conditions and take out the boredom from routine jobs. . . . We must increase an employee's satisfaction with his job, heighten pride of workmanship, and as far as is feasible, involve the employee personally in decisions that relate directly to his job."[13]

At first the activities of the Organizational Development (OD) staff were directly solely toward management personnel. Shortly, experiments were undertaken involving some hourly employees as well, including a very successful program at the Lakewood, Georgia, plant of the General Motors Assembly Division. There each employee was for the first time given access to all information about the plant's functioning, and was encouraged to take part in making decisions and solving problems regarding his or her own job. Labor grievances dropped 50 percent in two years, and the manager of the Lakewood plant was named director of personnel development for GM, reporting to Fuller.

The UAW became concerned over the unilateral activities of the OD department, and began to hold talks with General Motors regarding the union's participation in future experiments at both the union international and local levels. During the 1973 auto-industry contract negotiations the UAW submitted proposals to Chrysler, Ford and General Motors to establish union-management committees for improving the quality of work life. Although each company confirmed an agreement creating a union-management committee, only the GM committee has taken noticeable action.

The GM-UAW National Committee to Improve the Quality of Work Life constitutes a formal system for management and the union to cooperate on mutual concerns and objectives relating to the quality of work life of bargaining-unit employees, apart from the traditional collective bargaining process. The union is represented on the committee by two high-level officials of the International Union, while two officers of the corporation responsible for personnel and industrial relations matters represent management. The committee meets periodically to review quality-of-work-life projects in the corporation and to encourage further management-union cooperation in this area.

During a panel discussion on quality of work life at the annual meeting of the Society of Automotive Engineers in March, 1977, George B. Morris Jr., GM's vice president in charge of the industrial relations staff, discussed GM's relationship with the union on quality of work life. "Today, in General Motors, we are giving major attention to improving the quality of work·life of all GM employees. We have formed a close partnership with the

UAW to better achieve quality of work life objectives where bargaining unit personnel are concerned. It's an exciting and challenging area of cooperation and holds the promise of substantial benefits for GM employees." With respect to the National Committee's part in improving the work climate, Morris stated, "The role of the National Committee is to encourage and stimulate local joint efforts, to serve as a resource, and to be a key agent in diffusing throughout the organization the basic principles that are involved. This means helping the local organization understand and apply these principles."

At the plant and divisional level, General Motors reports that cooperative efforts on quality of work life are increasing:

At one GM car division, a series of meetings have been held involving executives of the division and the union leadership. Additional seminars then were held within each of the division's plants, bringing together plant management and plant union representatives to explore cooperative action on quality of work life.

The top management of another multi-plant division has made a concerted effort to improve the relationship between management and employees and between management and the union. One result has been a marked reduction in the number of unresolved grievances. Compared to the same period three years ago, the number of unresolved grievances has been reduced by about 75 percent.

Management and the union at an assembly plant are actively cooperating on a project designed to increase employee participation in decision making through team problem solving. Training in team problem solving was conducted jointly by union and management representatives. Following a successful pilot on one area of the plant, the concept and related training are being extended throughout the plant.

Another GM facility is organized into five separate operating units, or business teams. Each business team is comprised of members from production and related support activities and functions as a separate business. During the local contract negotiations in 1976, each business team became directly involved in the negotiations. Subcommittees made up of business team members and union personnel met with hourly and salaried employees who would have firsthand information and opinions about the demands on the table. In this way, those who raised the issues had an opportunity to be heard and the people who had to live with the settlement were, in effect, charged with the responsibility of making that settlement. This approach taken during the last negotiations illustrates the growing spirit of cooperation between management and the union in this particular plant. The plant continues to be a leader in measures of business effectiveness and through the cooperative efforts of management and the union and concerns and needs of employees are being dealt with promptly and effectively.

It should be noted that in addition to quality-of-work-life improvement, GM and the UAW are actively cooperating in many areas: alcoholism and drug abuse, orientation of new employees, selection and training of apprentices, equal opportunity in employment, administration of employee benefits, health and safety, and various activities such as the United Way campaign and the Payroll Savings Plan drive.

General Motors supports and encourages a total effort to improve the quality of work life in a number of ways: an annual executive conference that focuses entirely on the quality of work life, measurement of the quality of work life of GM employees (some 50,000 salaried employees have participated in the survey made available to GM units in late 1976), and a corporate activity that is responsible for conducting employee research and for providing quality-of-work-life information, training, and consulting services within the corporation.

Since GM and the Auto Workers have agreed not to publicize the precise nature of the projects undertaken pending further time to experiment and evaluate, it is difficult to supply further details at this time, though some comments may still be made. The first is to point out that the projects are directly undertaken by the local management and the local union. The corporation and the national union make no attempt to urge a project on a particular plant if the local parties are unwilling, and after a project is under way the national representative will act only in a consultative capacity. Second, the adversarial positions of company and union are still sensitive enough so that productivity boosts are not a stated purpose of the joint programs. Anything that resembles a speed-up or threatens to reduce the total number of jobs is avoided entirely; what productivity gains may result from cooperation are in the form of reduced waste or better quality, for instance. Third, it is noteworthy that the two parties are making joint efforts to help employees who suffer from alcoholism, drug addiction, or emotional ailments.

A final comment from Irving Bluestone, vice president of the UAW and director of its GM Department, may serve to sum up the state of the union-management relationship:

Wages, fringe benefits, job security, etc., remain in the collective bargaining arena and I see no contradiction between enlarging the scope of cooperative effort where mutual interest and concern dictate this to be the best course of action while, at the same time, the parties remain adversaries with regard to subjects which lend themselves more naturally to the hard business of confrontation collective bargaining.[15]

(b) *Harman International Industries, Bolivar, Tennessee.* Since few precise data are available about the quality-of-work-life experiments at GM, it may be useful to examine another project with which the UAW has been involved.[16] One such is an attempt to improve working conditions and employee-management relations at an automobile-mirror manufacturing plant in Bolivar, Tennessee. This factory, with about 900 employees, is a unit of Harman International Industries, Inc., a Long Island-based corporation which is principally engaged in the manufacture of high fidelity sound equipment.

During the 1960's the factory turned in an adequate profit and received little attention from the company's headquarters. Physical working conditions were very poor and human relations in the plant seemed to be steadily deteriorating. In 1972 the company's president, Sidney Harman, who had recently acquired a Ph.D. in organizational psychology, took a fresh look at the plant and decided that the quality of life there needed substantial improvement. He discussed the situation with Irving Bluestone, vice president of the UAW, and the company and the UAW signed a shelter agreement setting up a joint program to improve work in the plant for all personnel while maintaining the necessary productivity for job security. Dr. Michael Maccoby, a psychologist, and the director of the Harvard Project on Work, Technology, and Character, became the program's director.

One unusual aspect of the Bolivar program was that it did not begin with a predesigned plan of action, but instead asked workers what changes they wanted most. Beginning at first with experiments in two departments, the employees were interested in finding ways to solve bottlenecks in the production process and make performing their own jobs more convenient. Once they had achieved their production goals for the day, they wanted to go home; many of the employees farmed their own land after working hours, and others were women with children, so that they valued extra time very highly. Neither company managers nor union officials were enthusiastic about the "earned idle time" idea but, since there was great demand by the employees, each department was allowed to develop its own plan to help workers earn more free time.

Some changes in management were undertaken as well. The plant manager at the time the program began was an industrial engineer whom Mr. Harman perceived to be out of tune with the new developments in the plant. He was given a new position, solely with engineering responsibilities, and a man who was a native of the Bolivar area and had worked his way up through the ranks was named plant manager. Seminars were held to educate supervisors about pollution control and job safety, in the hope that they would spend less time watch-dogging individual workers and more time working on larger problems within their areas. Workers were given more access to financial and other data about the plant's operation, and in 1976 one group of workers took equal part with the bargaining committee in setting standards for their department. While decisions about pricing, production scheduling, capital expenditures, finance, and control were still held to be "management prerogatives," the union actually helped the company to estimate costs for a recent General Motors mirror contract. (The company won the contract.)

As of 1977, the Bolivar program has been in operation for four years, and has generally been considered a success. It must be remembered, however, that the program has received considerable infusions of funds from foundations and government and is still relatively dependent upon the help of outside academicians. The factory and employees received much publicity in 1975 and 1976, which cannot help but affect the participants' attitudes. Further, it cannot yet be determined what long-term effect the concept of earned idle time will have on the plant's productivity and profits; the company states that productivity has improved but does not disclose detailed financial data. Finally, not enough time has elapsed for anyone to gauge the effect on the company of the departure of Mr. Harman to assume the post of Under-Secretary of Commerce in the Carter administration. Since Mr. Harman must divest himself of his holdings, an agreement has been signed for the company to be acquired by Beatrice Foods pending approval of the Harman shareholders.

EMPLOYEE SHARING IN CORPORATE GAINS

The chapters on Sweden and Germany have discussed the possible trends toward employee participation in the distribution of capital in those countries. There is nothing in the U.S.A. comparable with either the proposed scheme in Sweden or the actual scheme in Germany or France's scheme of obligatory capital distribution to employees. However, there are in this country many cases in which employees do own stock in corporations or otherwise profit directly from a company's financial gain, and it seems appropriate to discuss these here.

(a) *Employee stock ownership plans.* Under the Employee Retirement Income Security Act of 1974 (ERISA), Congress is encouraging workers in the private sector to share in the ownership of corporate capital, and is giving special benefits to companies which establish employee stock ownership plans (ESOP's). Congress believes that ESOP's will ease capital shortages in this country because they allow corporations to borrow large amounts of money quickly and easily. In addition, the Tax Reduction Act of 1975 gives an additional 1 percent investment tax credit to the corporation adopting an ESOP, and legislation is pending which would tie further tax benefits for business to the establishment of such plans.

In brief, the mechanism of a tax-qualified ESOP, as designed by Louis Kelso, works as follows. The sponsoring company sets up an Employee Stock Ownership Trust (ESOT), which borrows money from a bank with a guarantee of repayment by the company. With the cash it has borrowed from the bank, the ESOT purchases stock from the company or from other shareholders. The sale of stock by the company results in an increase in working capital and net worth. Each year the company contributes up to 15 percent of its payroll cost to the ESOT, and these payments are fully tax-deductible. The ESOT then uses these yearly pretax contributions by the company to repay the bank loan.[17]

Employee participants or their beneficiaries become direct shareholders on retirement, death, or separation from the company as specified by the terms of the plan. During their terms of employment, their accounts in the ESOP are credited with contributions, within specified limits, made to the plan by the company in proportion to their levels of compensation; contributions by participating employees are usually not required or permitted. The Tax Reduction Act of 1975 provides the 1 percent investment tax credit to companies only as long as the credit flows to the trust, vests immediately, and gives voting rights to participants on the stock purchased.

The *World of Work Report* estimates that at least 200 qualifying ESOP's have now been established.[18] In rare instances, ESOP's have enabled employees to buy up the stock and assume ownership of companies in grave financial straits. The 500 employees of South Bend Lathe, Inc., recently purchased this subsidiary from Amsted Industries for $10 million in cash by borrowing the full purchase price; half the loan came from the Federal Economic Development Administration at low interest. The employees will become full owners of the corporation as they become vested through the years in the stock held in the ESOT. One or two other companies are known to be involved in similar arrangements.

Since the formal ESOP concept is relatively new, there are few data to indicate whether or not any significant improvement in productivity or worker satisfaction may result from ESOP's. American unions, however, tend to be very suspicious of the plans since they may be used as last-ditch borrowing efforts by failing companies, or used to displace existing pension plans. Frank L. Fernbach of the Steelworkers has written:

With regard to profit-sharing schemes via worker ownership of stock—currently, the fashionable Kelso plan—the AFL-CIO is officially neutral. I am decidedly negative.

Bitter experience with employee stock-ownership plans, dating back to the 1920s, teaches us that there is no magic in these undertakings. In my judgment, workers' savings should seek liquidity and safety, perhaps via credit unions rather than enticement into more speculative ventures. Besides, the Kelso plan has been launched and subsidized by another new and questionable Federal tax loophole, the type we have long sought to close.[19]

(b) *Scanlon plans.* The "Scanlon Plan" was invented by a steelworker named Joe Scanlon in the 1930's and seems to be enjoying an increasing vogue in recent years. Now in operation at about 100 factories in the U.S.A., the plan entails direct employee participation in company efforts to boost output and cut costs, and offers hefty bonuses to all employees when their efforts are successful.[20] The earlier firms who adopted Scanlon plans were relatively small and family-owned, such as non-unionized Donnelly Mirrors, but in the past few years larger corporations, including Midland-Ross Corp. and Dana Corp., have successfully introduced Scanlon plans to some unionized workplaces.

A formula which establishes the baseline of productivity and labor costs over a fixed time-period such as the quarter-year is a primary ingredient of the plan. Then the plant's actual payroll cost as a percentage of production is calculated each month. If baseline payroll averages 27 percent of the worth of goods produced, but actual payroll ends up costing only 22 percent due to increased efficiency, the 5 percent difference is added to a bonus pool. Then, 25 percent of this difference is set aside to smooth out the pattern for poor performance months, 25 percent is returned to the company, and the remaining 50 percent is paid out in bonuses to employees proportional to their earnings. Midland-Ross Corporation reports that in 27 months of Scanlon plan operation at its electrical products plant in Athens, Tennessee, productivity was up 15 percent. Hourly employees received an average $1,500 each in bonuses in 1976, and the plant's managers received an average $2,500 each.[21]

Where true Scanlon plans are in operation, cost savings are achieved because employees scrutinize their own jobs and make many suggestions about ways to improve processes, tools, and work patterns. For these efforts to succeed, the managers must encourage suggestions and be willing to accept open criticism gracefully. These prerequisites are often greeted skeptically by workers and managers alike, but where Scanlon plans take hold they seem to function well. In general, the plan is first tried in a plant for one year and employees must then decide by vote whether or not to adopt it permanently. Unions that are represented in plants with Scanlon plans include UAW, the United Rubber Workers, and the International Brotherhood of Electrical Workers.

WORK REDESIGN IN NON-UNION SETTINGS

Realistically, any attempt to assess American developments in employer-employee relations must include some discussion of work restructuring in non-union settings. This is true, first, because the great majority of American workers do not belong to unions or associations. Second, many of the best-known and most radical experiments in work redesign have taken place in non-union workplaces, where changes are manifestly easier to implement. This is true even of large corporations which may have some unionized sites but tend to select non-unionized ones at which to test new approaches.

Available information on work redesign or participative management in non-union workplaces indicates that the cases in question separate naturally into two groups: companies which are conducting small, sometimes radical, experiments such as General Foods' pet food plant in Topeka, Kansas, and TRW's ball-bearing plant in Gainesville, Georgia; and companies which integrate progressive personnel management throughout their organization, such as IBM and Texas Instruments. Examining in more detail the experiences of General Foods and Texas Instruments will clarify the differences in their styles.

(a) *General Foods: The Gaines Pet Food Plant.* The 70-man pet food plant which began operation in 1971 has become probably the most widely publicized American example of a team production process in action. With the consultation of Professor Richard E. Walton and research funds from The Ford Foundation, the plant was organized around self-managing teams of 7 to 14 members. Professor Walton has summarized the basic elements of its design:

> Activities typically performed by separate units—maintenance, quality control, custodianship, industrial engineering, and personnel—were built into the operating team's responsibilities. For example, team members screen job applicants for replacements on their own team.
>
> An attempt was made to design every set of tasks to include functions requiring mental abilities such as planning, diagnosing mechanical problems, and liaison work. The aim was to make all sets of tasks equally challenging, although each set would comprise unique skill demands. Consistent with this aim was a single job classification for all operators, with pay increases geared to the mastery of an increasing number of jobs. Employees were encouraged to teach each other; there were no limits on how many team members could qualify for higher pay brackets.
>
> In lieu of the "foreman," a "team leader" position was created with the responsibiliy for facilitating team development and decision making. Operators were provided data and decision guidelines that enabled them to make production decisions ordinarily made by higher levels of supervision.[22]

Unlike many other publicized examples of work redesign, the Topeka plant has now been in operation long enough for some evaluation over time. The first two years were a period of adjustment: the teams coalesced, start-up production problems were solved, and events including a rail strike tested the plant's functioning. Morale during this time was high, and almost all the plant's workers and managers seemed committed to its system.

From 1973 to 1976, however, the atmosphere in the plant became less enthusiastic. Professor Walton's 1976 evaluation explains the problem areas. Once start-up was accomplished, the company began to emphasize production volume, and it became more difficult to find time for team meetings. Recently hired employees were not developing as great a commitment to the system as the original workers. Three of the four managers most responsible for the Topeka system had left General Foods, and it was widely held that "as a result of their pioneering work they had lost rather than gained in career progression within GF."[23] However, frank acknowledgment of troublespots does not imply that the plant is suffering from insurmountable difficulties; instead, it seems more reasonable to assume that the plant is simply in the midst of a new phase of its evolution. It remains to be seen whether General Foods will expand upon the experiment, transferring its principles to other worksites, or will confine it to Topeka.

(b) *Texas Instruments.* Headquartered in Dallas, Texas, Texas Instruments employs about 66,000 persons, producing semiconductor components, electronic equipment, and metallurgical and chemical materials in 44 plants in 18 countries. The company attributes its success in large part to its program of "People and Asset Effectiveness," which focuses on productivity improvement, cost reduction, and employee motivation. As of 1976, the company calculated its return on assets to be near 10 percent, with a profit after tax per employee of about $1,500 and assets per employee of about $16,000.[24]

Texas Instruments puts a high premium on profitable growth and productivity, as is to be expected given its considerable success within a high-technology and highly competitive industry. The company's processes in solid state electronics depend on high volumes to bring unit costs down, and it creates market growth by making its products affordable to great numbers of users. To accomplish this, the company's people must be creative enough to decide what a new product's selling price and performance must be, years in the future, and then design the product and the equipment for producing it to meet the required cost and performance goals. Each employee has a part to play in this process; TI maintains that its personnel are involved "to the greatest extent practical in the planning and controlling, and not just the doing, of their own work." However, the company's chairman, Mark Shepherd, Jr., injects a note of caution:

Motivation is a vital element, but it must be achieved in a way that is compatible with the required distribution of planning and control. The lathe operator should have maximum control over how he plans his work, does his work, and controls his work, but he should not decide what part to make.[25]

The exact implementation of Texas Instruments' management philosophy differs among its plants, and often is determined by regional or national custom. In general, however, the company relies upon teams of natural work groups, frequent attitude surveys, and an "open door" policy at all management levels to keep employee involvement high. In the United States, the company also provides a combination of financial benefits to employees which includes company pension, profit sharing, and a stock option purchase plan. Texas Instruments intends its employees to own about 25 percent of the company by the 1990's.

GOVERNMENT'S ROLE IN LABOR-MANAGEMENT RELATIONS

The role of government in American labor-management relations has been left out of this discussion thus far for clarity's sake in order to limit the number of variables. Yet it must be understood that government influence over business and labor is all-pervasive. To quote Professor Robert A. Leone: "If the pervasivenss of government regulation were to determine which industries were in the 'regulated' sector, today, the unregulated sector would be an empty set."[26]

The groundwork of current U.S. industrial relations is the body of labor laws, including the National Labor Relations, Taft-Hartley, and Landrum-Griffin acts, which spell out in considerable detail regulations for union representation and collective bargaining. The minimum wage law, Social Security legislation, and the Employee Retirement Income Security Act (ERISA) also have substantial impact on businesses and employees. In general, it is assumed that Democratic administrations are more apt to pass pro-labor legislation, and that Republican administrations will look more favorably upon the legislative wishes of business. The Carter administration seems to be indicating thus far that its main concern with regard to business and labor is the creation of jobs rather than the paying off of political debts that may have accrued to organized labor. Of the five legislative goals that the AFL-CIO announced in 1977, Congress has already voted down the common sites picketing bill, which would have allowed a single union with a grievance to shut down a whole construction site, and the administration refused to endorse a proposed increase in the minimum wage to $3 per hour as labor wanted. A third aim, the repeal of Section 14B of the Taft-Hartley Act which allows individual states to pass right-to-work laws, seem unlikely to succeed. The administration has failed to win sufficient support to persuade the Congress to pass perhaps the most important element of the legislative package, at least symbolically—the reform of the National Labor Relations Act to protect workers further against unfair management practices. Winning for public employees the same collective bargaining rights as workers in private industry, also still awaits Congressional action.

Outside of specific labor-related legislation, a plethora of government agencies and activities affect the environment in which business and their workers must function. Primary examples are the government's efforts to monitor and promote wage and price stability, its controls over imports and exports, and its ability to alter take-home pay and profits through taxation. The Department of Labor, Department of Health, Education, and Welfare, and the Environmental Protection Agency, and subunits such as the Occupational Safety and Health Administration (OSHA) and the Office of Federal Contract Compliance for Equal Employment Opportunity, perform a bewildering variety of functions and seem to be increasing in impact over time. Companies complain that the cost of compliance with governmental regulations and requests for information amounts to billions of dollars annually for U.S. companies, but others say benefits outweigh costs.

All these government departments and agencies are not centrally coordinated. It is not unusual to find government operations (with regard to industrial relations or any other subject) overlapping or, on occasion, even conflicting. This is because a principle of decentralization has generally applied in American government just as it has for American labor and management, with an underlying object of obstructing the growth of absolute power. If there has been a problem to be solved, the classic U.S. approach has been to create a new agency to address it rather than to give new powers to an existing agency; once in existence, such agencies are very difficult to disband. In the United States, government agencies quickly develop political constituencies such as management, labor or groups devoted to particular issues. In their support for the programs and goals of particular agencies, those constituencies give the agency a political life as real, although not as well-defined, as that of an elected official. And while it is a subject seldom mentioned in public policy debate in the U.S., state and local government employment has been growing much faster than new federal hiring. From 1960 to 1975, employment by state and local governments increased three times as fast as federal employment.

It is not easy to assess the overall impact on U.S. labor-management relations of government activities. Relations between labor unions and companies are altered sometimes in unpredictable ways by government action. Many government regulations such as those handed down by the OSHA, ERISA, and EEO, impinge directly on questions of health and safety, retirement security, and seniority, which were previously decided through the collective bargaining contract. Some businessmen feel government safeguards are so broad now that they have weakened unions by obviating the need for protection of workers' rights beyond that provided by the government. Naturally union leaders and members tend to disagree. In any case, both management and labor acknowledge that the effects of government policy are a major element in the environment in which collective bargaining operates.

In specific instances of government action, union and management may react by uniting in common cause against what they perceive to be unwarranted government interference. At the opposite extreme, government action may provoke or exacerbate union-management conflict. In specific cases where government has threatened to close down plants due to environmental pollution, the prospect of economic hardship to the company, its workers, and sometimes entire communities has worked to spur the formation of a united labor-management front. But American Telephone and Telegraph Company's settlement with the government's affirmative action staff, which had claimed that AT&T's hiring and promotion policies discriminated against women and minority group members, led the union to an unsuccessful suit, charging that the compensation and promotions given to women and minorities violated the contractual seniority rights of many union members.

As a general rule in the U.S.A., direct government intervention with regard to labor relations is undertaken only when the government perceives a compelling reason to do so. Where the relationship between business, the work force and the community is perceived to be satisfactory or at least unobjectionable, as in the majority of instances, direct government intervention is avoided. Because this is true, efforts on the part of U.S. government agencies to promote better cooperation between unions and management have been reasonably limited and more passive than active in their approach. For instance, the Federal Mediation and Conciliation Service's role is to assist in situations where union and management have reached an impasse in strike or contract negotiations. The Service will not, however, take an active part in negotiations unless both the union and management request it to do so.

In spite of government's reluctance to interfere in labor relations, there are some exceptions: various government agencies have provided "seed money" to help finance demonstration projects in union-management cooperation such as the Harman International project in Bolivar, Tennessee, described above. The Economic Development Administration of the Department of Commerce and the Health Resources Administration of HEW have been active in supporting a number of "quality-of-work-life" improvement programs with the cooperation of the unions and managements involved. There is also a bill called the Human Resources Development Act currently in committee in the House of Representatives which would make additional government funds available under contract with the Labor Department to projects involving employers and employees in efforts to increase productivity, enhance job satisfaction, and create new jobs. The bill, sponsored by Rep. Stanley N. Lundine (D., N.Y.), would also provide incentives for employers to keep workers on the job during periods of economic downturn.

Another instrument of government's policy encouraging change is the National Center for Productivity and Quality of Working Life in Washington. The Center is an independent government agency. Its Board of Directors includes prominent leaders of business, labor, and government, and the Center considers itself accountable to all three groups. Its primary concern is monitoring and increasing productivity both in industry and the federal government. For this purpose it also promotes and catalogues information about cooperative activities between unions and management outside of the collective contract. However, the staff of this agency is small and its budget only $2 million a year, which limits the scope of its activities. In addition to the National Center, there are a handful of state and local government efforts to encourage union-management cooperation, such as those in the Commonwealth of Massachusetts and Jamestown, New York.

Future Trends

There are two perfectly valid ways of interpreting the phenomena described above. One can stress the continuity of American labor relations and argue that there are no clearly discernible changes of any significance or that what changes there are form part of a continuum of change. This approach leads to the prediction that leaders of business, labor and government will continue as they always have in an experimental way, responding pragmatically to a myriad of crises and pressures without any clear pattern or trend emerging. Such a formulation makes it difficult and, in fact, unnecessary to compare U.S. practice with that of Europe and Japan; it emphasizes the heterogeneity, variety, and uniqueness of the American experience. It seems to be the preferred approach of traditional specialists in the area.

On the other hand, one can look at the new developments, at the continuum of change from which they have sprung, and at the evolution of the political, social, cultural and ecological context in which they occur, and argue that there is not only a clear pattern of development but that it seems likely that this pattern will continue and become more widespread between the U.S.A. and Europe and Japan.

We shall set forth both approaches.

Experimental Continuity

Unquestionably, enormous gains have been made in establishing orderly industrial relations in the U.S.A. over the past forty years, and there is some evidence that formal cooperative efforts between unions and managements, away from the adversarial atmosphere of contract negotiation, are on the rise. The National Center for Productivity and Quality of Working Life published in 1976 a directory listing 180 labor-management committees in the U.S.A. Some of these committees, such as those of the retail food and railroad industry, consist solely of union chiefs and corporate executives, and cannot be said to include worker participation in their discussions. The National Center estimates that labor-management committees at the company and plant levels "are in a position to affect the working lives of over 554,000 workers in 33 states," or about 0.6 percent of the civilian workforce.[27]

Interpreting the significance of these recent cooperative efforts is difficult; the opinions of industrial relations experts vary widely. Some authorities maintain that labor-management committees are nothing new in the United States; they existed in many U.S. companies during the Second World War and are practicable only when they fit the needs of a specific union and management. For other experts, the more recently established labor-management committees are seen as the agencies of a new era of goodwill and reduced industrial strife.

One possibly helpful way of examining industrial relations in this country is to examine data on work stoppages over time (see Table 8.3 and

Table 8.3. Work Stoppages in the United States, 1946–76

Year	Number of Stoppages	Workers Involved (thousands)	Number of Idle (thousands)
1946	4,985	4,600	116,000
1950	4,843	2,410	38,800
1955	4,320	2,650	28,200
1960	3,333	1,320	19,100
1965	3,963	1,550	23,300
1970	5,716	3,305	66,414
1971	5,138	3,280	47,589
1972	5,010	1,714	27,066
1973	5,353	2,251	27,948
1974	6,074	2,778	47,991
1975	5,031	1,746	31,237
1976	5,600	2,500	38,000

Source: U.S. Bureau of Labor Statistics, *Monthly Labor Review,* April 1977, p. 127.

Figure 8.1). Certain peak years of strikes stand out dramatically, including 1946, when the United Mine Workers kept 400,000 bituminous coal miners out for months, and 1959, the year of a lengthy steelworkers' strike. Outside of these peak years, however, no confirmed trend toward an increasing or decreasing number of work stoppages is visible. Using as an index the percentage of total estimated working time lost in a given year, the figure for 1976 was 0.19 percent, close to the median for the years 1946 to 1976.

Figure 8.1 Incidence of Strike Activity in the United States 1946–76.

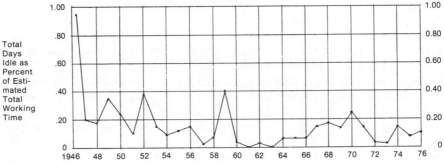

Source: U.S. Bureau of Labor Statistics, *Monthly Labor Review*, April 1977, p. 127.

The fact that strikes do not seem to be disappearing in the U.S.A. should not be read as a failure of the American collective bargaining system, because strikes may well be counted as an integral part of the bargaining relationship. Strikes are not entered upon in haste and are used as a tool for specific purposes. For example, the UAW no longer leads workers on long, costly strikes which GM is financially able to weather; instead, when the union wishes to make a point it directs workers at strategic parts plants to take a three- or four-day weekend, thus disrupting GM's immensely complicated logistics and proving that the union is serious about the issue(s) under dispute. In contrast, the most controversial strikes and slowdowns of recent years have been those of public employees—such as teachers, police, and sanitation workers—who are newly organized and who lack the same collective bargaining rights and formal channels for protest as private sector employees.

There is, in fact, no guarantee that a strike-free workplace is a healthy one, although it may be. Peaceful labor relations can result if either management or union is weak; in the first case, efficiency will be threatened, and in the second, the rights of workers suffer and grievance rates tend to be high. The bare fact that a labor-management committee exists at a company cannot be used as proof of anything except that the specific union and company have seen fit to sit down together and discuss issues which are not covered by the contract. The presence of such a committee may or may not reduce strikes; it does not necessarily indicate that union-management relations are in a good balance, or that union influence over management decision-making is any more than in the average company. Labor-management committees in the U.S.A. are still too rare to be statistically significant, and they are not analogous in structure or function to works councils in Europe.

The relative rarity of labor-management committees, quality-of-work-life projects, and similar innovations draws an observer to the conclusion that for the vast majority of American businesses, whether their employees are organized or unorganized, the relationship between worker and management has not appreciably changed in recent years. Where change has taken place, it frequently has been in a troubled industry such as domestic steel, or in efficient, prosperous companies, such as Texas Instruments or General Foods, which have the money and staff to devote to improving employee satisfaction and motivation.

Trade unionists and other observers from overseas often express surprise at the lack of interest of American workers in any kind of joint consultation or co-determination with management. It is not accurate to say that American workers are totally uninterested in the decision-making process, because in reference to decisions that specifically affect their own jobs and work areas most employees are gratified to be consulted and eager to share the benefits of their own work experience. Increasingly, managers are sharing information with employees and asking for their help in making decisions that affect them, because their approach makes good sense in human terms and managerial terms. Few American companies would be so rash as to try to introduce a new technology without ample consultation with the employees involved. Some suggest that it is easier to bring technological change to a unionized workplace than to a non-unionized one because American unions have learned through experience to reach a compromise, to accept change, but fight to safeguard the job security of those already on the payroll.

Thus, it often seems to Americans as though other countries underrate the influence of American labor over management, simply because there are no workers on boards of directors. The decentralized nature of U.S. industrial relations has tended to make each plant a unit into itself, with the local union holding enough power to make it a significant counterbalance to management. Writing in 1960, Professors Sumner H. Slichter, James J. Healy, and E. Robert Livernash provided an analysis of union influence on decision-making which is still apropos today:

Management may, as a matter of practice, submit proposed decisions to the union for review and comment since the union officers may see aspects of the problem that escaped the attention of management. All of this means that the decision-making process has been broadened in many cases to include consultation. Consultation occurs in some instances simply as a matter of practice: management does not agree to consult, but in practice does consult. In other instances management may *agree* to consult before taking action, while retaining the right to make decisions subject to challenge as to their reasonableness or conformity with the agreement.

. . . It is true that few workers participate directly in determining their working conditions and rate of pay, but they belong to organizations that do participate. Hence, the ordinary worker does not feel left out. He knows that important changes cannot occur in markets and technology without their effect on him being considered.[28]

The degree of influence that American unions fought for over the years has also extended in practice to workers in non-unionized workplaces. Many newer companies have successfully avoided unionization by adopting similar or better personnel policies (including high wages, good working conditions, and other benefits) as their unionized competitors.

What the future may hold in store for collective bargaining and worker-management relations in the U.S.A. is not at all clear from data presently available. There are many strains on the system, as have been discussed previously in this paper. But these strains do not seem to be pushing the system toward any clearly visible outcomes as yet. Any drastic change—as in the United States' supply of energy or rate of inflation, a dramatic shift in government policy, or America's entry into armed conflict—would doubtless precipitate significant change in the relationship among labor, management, and government. But such occurrences are impossible for anyone to predict. One may cite as an example of such an unpredictable event the financial calamity of New York City. The City's inability to pay its bills has transformed its public employee unions, forcing them to give up any thought of strikes or wage hikes. Today they behave instead like banks, lending their pension funds to help the City stay afloat. The unions intensely dislike their new role and their new decision-making authority.

Ten years ago no one would have believed that New York City could ever come to such a pass. Similarly, American businesses and workers tend to regard any major realignment of their traditional roles as unlikely at best, given the strengths of the system. There is a strong commitment in this country to improving productivity and job satisfaction on an individual basis, as a company and its employees see fit to do. The experiments and innovations that have been discussed in this paper seem indeed to be still in an experimental state, and it will take years to see which trends, if any, endure. Any thoroughgoing shake-up in the industrial relations system of the U.S. will follow—not precede—changes in the economic, political, and social realities of America.

IDEOLOGICAL TRANSFORMATION AND STRUCTURAL CHANGE

Here is a different way to view the same data.

Varied and uncoordinated as is the American experience, there is a clear pattern of change if we think in ideological terms.

Such thought is peculiarly difficult for Americans because the very notion of ideology is foreign to us. We have tended to think of ourselves as a pragmatic people who do what needs to be done to meet the requirements of the time. We have supposed that ideology was something which we happily left behind in Europe with our ancestors—a theoretical bag of confusion that has trammelled up socialism and Communism and the other "isms," from which hardheaded Americans are fortunately free.

This, of course, is nonsense. We are just as deeply imbued with ideology as any other community—maybe more so. It is the basis of our motivation; it is the collection of ideas we use to make our great institutions legitimate and to give their leaders authority; it is our national "collective unconscious." To assert that we are free of it is as absurd as to assert that a person exists who does not have a subconscious mind. Ideology is the framework of ideas which a community uses to define, apply, and institutionalize timeless values such as survival, justice, economy, self-fulfillment, and self-respect. It is the bridgework, as it were, by which these ideas are given life in the real world. And as the real world changes, the ideas naturally change.

If one looks, for example, at the real world of Japan—many people crowded onto several hundred small islands dependent upon outsiders who have traditionally appeared hostile—we can readily understand why Japanese ideology has necessarily differed from that of the United States. Historically, we had a relatively small population widely dispersed in what amounted to a wilderness in which the major task was to exploit our abundant resources and to grow. It is obvious that these two communities have used quite different ideas to describe and to justify the role of the individual in society; the functions of business and unions, of managers and employees; the role of government, and the means and ends of government-business relations.

Similarly, differences between U.S. and European institutional development and practice can be clearly seen in ideological terms. The United States is alone in the Western World in the extremity of its individualism (a term which we shall shortly explain). We are the only nation not to have known medieval communitarianism (another term we shall explain); a Briton or Frenchman, for example, has in his heritage the organic, hierarchical traditions of feudalism. When the ideology of individualism came to Great Britain in 1688 and to France about 100 years later, it was tempered by the existing communitarianism. European society today is deeply affected by centuries of tradition—the notion of class, for instance, and its counterpart, socialist egalitarianism. The differences between U.S. and European labor relations can only be understood against this background.

THE TRADITIONAL IDEOLOGY OF THE U.S.A.

Our traditional ideology is not at all hard to identify. It is composed of five great ideas that first came to America in the eighteenth century, having been set down in seventeenth-century England as "natural" laws by John Locke, among others. These ideas found fertile soil in the vast, underpopulated wilderness of America and served us well for a hundred years or so. They are now in an advanced state of erosion.

The Lockean Five are:

Individualism. This is the atomistic notion that the community is no more than the sum of the individuals in it. It is the idea that fulfillment lies in an essentially lonely struggle in what amounts to a wilderness where the fit survive—and where, if you do not survive, you are somehow unfit. Closely tied to individualism is the idea of *equality,* in the sense implied in the phrase "equal opportunity," and the idea of *contract,* the inviolate device by which individuals are tied together as buyers and sellers, employers and employees. In the political order in this country, individualism evolved into *interest group pluralism,* which became the preferred means of directing government and society.

Property rights. Traditionally, the best guarantee of individual rights was held to be the sanctity of property rights. By virtue of this concept, the individual was assured freedom from the predatory powers of the sovereign. These rights also provided the cornerstone of managerial legitimacy, the source of management authority.

Competition—consumer desire. Adam Smith most eloquently articulated the idea that the uses of property are best controlled by each individual proprietor competing in an open market to satisfy individual consumer desires. It is explicit in U.S. antitrust law and practice.

Limited state. In reaction to the powerful hierarchies of medievalism, the conviction grew that the least government is the best government. We do not mind how big government may get, but we are reluctant to allow it authority or focus. And whatever happens the cry is, "Don't let it plan—particularly down there in Washington. Let it be responsive to crises and to interest groups. Whoever pays the price can call the tune."

Scientific specialization and fragmentation. This is the corruption of Newtonian mechanics which says that, if we attend to the parts, as experts and specialists, the whole will take care of itself.

There are a number of powerful American myths associated with these ideas: John Wayne as the frontiersman; rags to riches with Horatio Alger; and, most fundamentally, *the myth of material growth and progress.*

Implicit in individualism is the notion that man has the will to acquire power, that is, to control external events, property, nature, the economy, politics, or whatever. Under the concept of the limited state, the presence of this will in the human psyche meant the guarantee of progress through competition, notably when combined with the Darwinian notion that the inexorable processes of evolution are constantly working to improve on nature.

If we consider the past 5,000 years of human history, we are struck by the extent to which this atomistic, individualistic ideology constitutes a fundamental aberration from the historically typical communitarian norm. It stands as a radical experiment that achieved its most extreme manifestation in America in the nineteenth century. Since that time it has been steadily deteriorating in the face of various challenges—wars, depressions, new economic and political systems, the concentration and growth of populations, institutional as well as environmental degeneration, and a realization of scarcity.

Even though deteriorating, the five components of the old ideology retain great resilience. They are in a sense the hymns we sing: the assumed source of legitimacy and authority for our great institutions. The difficulty is twofold.

The old ideas perform less and less well as a definer of values in the real world of today, and many of our most important institutions—notably, but by no means exclusively, the large, publicly held corporations and their unions—have either radically departed from the old ideology or are in the process of doing so in the name of obedience to the law, efficiency, economies of scale, social justice, consumer desire, productivity, crisis, and necessity.

Although many small enterprises remain comfortably and acceptably consistent with the Lockean Five and, it is hoped, can remain so, the managers of large institutions in both the so-called private and public sectors are forced not to practice what they preach. It is this gap between the behavior of institutions and what they sometimes thoughtlessly claim as a source of authority that causes trauma. If we were to ask, what then is the ideology which would legitimize the behavior of these institutions, we would come up with five counterparts to the Lockean Five. (See Figure 8.2 for a summary of the two ideologies as bridges between the values and the real world.)

THE NEW IDEOLOGY

They are:

Communitarianism. The community—New York City, for example—is more than the sum of the individuals in it. It has special and urgent needs as a community, and the survival and the self-respect of the individuals in it depend on the recognition of those needs. There are few who can get their kicks à la John Wayne, although many try. Individual fulfillment for most depends on a place in a community, an identity with a whole, a participation in an organic social process. And further: if the community, the factory, or the neighborhood is well designed, its members will have a sense of identity with it. They will be able to make maximum use of their capacities. If it is poorly designed, people will be correspondingly alienated and frustrated. In the complex and highly organized America of today, few can live as Locke had in mind.

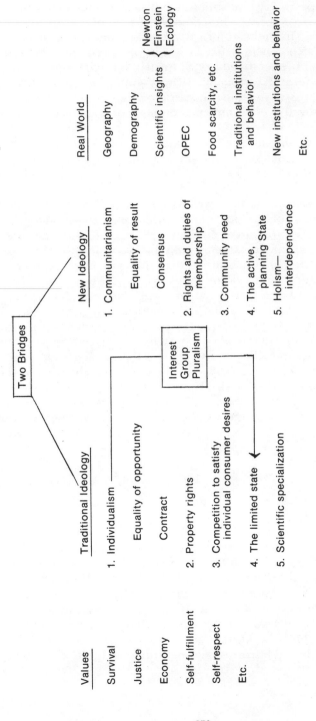

Figure 8.2. Ideologies: Bridges Connecting Values to the Real World

Unions, corporations, and government have played leading roles in the creation of the circumstances which eroded the old idea of individualism and created the new. But, invariably, they have been ideologically unmindful of what they have done. Therefore, they have tended to linger with the old forms and assumptions even after those have been critically altered.

The bank employee, or the assembly-line worker, for example, has been led to believe by unions, management, parents, and TV that the old idea of individual fulfillment is valid. But he finds himself constrained by an inescapable work setting dramatically unlike anything that he has been led to expect. He is liable to strike out, perhaps violently. Or he may join the absentee lists, taking Fridays and Mondays off to eke out some spurious individualism via drugs, drink, old movies, or—if he is lucky—a walk in the hills.

Paradoxically, such behavior puzzles both management and unions. They linger with the traditional individualistic ideas of the contract long after the contract has ceased being individualistic and has become "collective," unmindful of the inevitable dissonance between the idea of contract and the new forms of *consensus* toward which communitarianism is tending.

Our former social policy attempted to guarantee that each worker have equal opportunity. This was an individualistic, indeed an atomistic, idea. The lawyers enforcing equal employment legislation, however, have taken quite a different tack. In the case of AT&T, for example, they argued that discrimination had become institutionalized; it had become endemic to the AT&T community, and women, for example, had been slotted into certain tasks. When this kind of argument is being accepted, it is no longer necessary to prove individual discrimination in order to get redress. The government then moved to change the makeup of the whole of AT&T so as to provide, in effect, for *equality of representation* at all levels. Without any specific charge having been brought, the company in turn agreed to upgrade 50,000 women and 6,000 minority-group workers and—perhaps most significant—to hire 4,000 men to fill traditionally female jobs such as operator and clerk. The company also agreed to pay some $15 million in compensation. Thus the issue became one of *equality of result*, not of opportunity; a communitarian idea had superseded an individualistic one.

Given this definition of the issue, the company's task was to redesign itself according to certain overall criteria, in recognition (a) of the fact that individuals are unequal in many important respects and (b) of the dictum that the good organization is one which adapts itself to those inequalities to assure equality of result.

As we have mentioned, the union at AT&T protested bitterly, since the government's action was a direct threat to the contract which previously had been the device used to resolve inequities in seniority and promotion policies. The company itself has had commensurate difficulty in meshing its old thinking with the specific steps demanded by the representatives of the new ideology. Yet the changes are being forced forward, in one fashion or another, nonetheless. The trend is clear.

One recalls a story by Kurt Vonnegut Jr., in which he described a distopian community of the future in which everyone who ran fast had to wear a lead belt. That, of course, is one form which equality of result could take. There are, however, other more efficient and fulfilling possibilities which AT&T is diligently pursuing. One of the uses of ideological analysis is that it dramatizes our choices.

Rights and duties of membership. Today there is a new right which clearly supersedes property rights in political and social importance. It is the right to survive—to enjoy income, health, and other rights associated with membership in the American community or in some component of that community, including a corporation.

These rights derive not from any individualistic action or need; they do not emanate from a contract. They are rather communitarian rights that public opinion holds to be consistent with a good community. This is a revolutionary departure from the old Lockean conception under which only the fit survive. President Nixon, apparently unaware of what was happening, said once: "If you underwrite everybody's income, you undermine everybody's character." Well, of course, that depends on the definition of self-respect.

Escalating rights of membership have strained the ability of governments to pay the bill. New York City hovers on bankruptcy. Inevitably, therefore, comes the necessity of *duties* of membership. The question comes: Who decides the duties? The banks and the union pension funds? The individual or the state? If government is to be employer of last resort, does that impose an ultimate obligation to work at a job prescribed by government? Some today answer yes. The new ideology presents us with clearly ominous choices.

The utility of property as a *legitimizing* idea has eroded as well. It is now quite obvious that our large public corporations are not private property at all. The 1.5 million shareholders of General Motors do not and cannot control, direct, or in any real sense be responsible for "their" company. Furthermore, the vast majority of them have not the slightest desire for such responsibility. They are investors pure and simple, and if they do not get a good return on their investment, they will put their money elsewhere.

Campaign GM and other similar attempts at stockholder agitation represent perhaps heroic but naively conservative strategies to force shareholders to behave like owners and thus to legitimize corporations as property. But such action is clearly a losing game. And it is a peculiar irony that James Roche, as GM chairman, branded such agitation as radical, as the machinations of "adversary culture . . . antagonistic to our American ideas of private property and individual responsibility." In truth, of course, *GM is the radical*; Nader *et alia* were acting as conservatives, trying to bring the corporation back into ideological line.

But, the reader may ask, if GM and the hundreds of other large corporations like it are not property, then what are they? The best we can say is that they are some sort of collective, floating in philosophic limbo, dangerously vulnerable to the charge of illegitimacy and to the charge that they are not amenable to community control. Consider how the management of this non-proprietary institution is selected. The myth is that the stockholders select the board of directors which in turn selects the management. This is not true, however. Management selects the board, and the board, generally speaking, blesses management.

Managers thus get to be managers according to some mystical, circular process of questionable legitimacy. Under such circumstances it is not surprising that "management's rights" are fragile and its authority is waning. Alfred Sloan warned us of this trend in 1927:

There is a point beyond which diffusion of stock ownership must enfeeble the corporation by depriving it of virile interest in management upon the part of some one man or group of men to whom its success is a matter of personal and vital interest. And conversely at the same point the public interest becomes involved when the public can no longer locate some tangible personality within the ownership which it may hold responsible for the corporation's conduct.[29]

We have avoided this profound problem because of the unquestioned effectiveness of the corporate form *per se*. In the past, when economic growth and progress were synonymous, we preferred that managers be as free as possible from stockholder interference, in the name of efficiency. But today the definition of efficiency, the criteria for the limitations of growth, and the general context of the corporation are all much less sure. So the myth of corporate property is becoming a point of vulnerability.

We are now in the process of finding new means to legitimize the large corporation and to make it responsive to community demands. Several options seem possible:

Effective shareholder democracy might work in small companies.

More comprehensive and intelligent regulation by the state might be a possibility.

Involvement of workers in what had been managerial decisions is another possibility. In such cases management derives its authority from the managed.

Federal corporate charters that define corporate purpose, management rights, and community authority might be successful "legitimizers."

Finally, there is nationalization, perhaps the most brutish and inefficient way to legitimization. And, oddly enough, experience seems to show that government ownership may actually decrease the capacity of government to control. The socialists did not adequately assess the politics of bureaucracy.

Community need. It is apparent that a variety of community needs are upon us which have little to do with consumer desire. Reliance on the old idea of competition to satisfy those desires as a means of controlling corporations consequently becomes less effective or acceptable. Consumers desire large cars, the community needs small ones. Breaking up the auto companies in the name of competition will not necessarily secure the new need. The state is defining community needs and will continue to do so, and the new definitions will touch on a number of areas of direct significance to labor relations: the place of American business in the world economy, return to the U.S. balance of payments, economies of scale, ecological balance, employment, and inflation.

As has already been suggested, increasing constraints imposed upon business by community needs may well bring management and labor closer together, contributing to *consensualism* (to be taken here as distinct from *contractualism*). One result of the increased consensus in the steel industry, for example, could quite possibly be higher wages and prices, with both management and labor asking government to protect them from foreign competition. Any sort of rational response from government would necessitate some sort of coherent thought—a plan—about the strategic place of American business in the world economy.

In the face of the serious pressures from Japanese and European business organizations, which emanate from ideological settings quite different from our own, there will be more and more reason to set aside the old idea of domestic competition in order to organize U.S. business effectively to meet world competition. Management and labor will probably welcome if not urge such a step; they may, however, be less willing to accept the necessary concomitant: if, in the name of efficiency, of economies of scale, and of the demands of world markets, we allow restraints on the free play of domestic market forces, then other forces will have to be used to define and preserve the public interest. These "other forces" will amount to clearer control by the political order, in some form or other.

Active, planning state. It follows that the role of the state is changing radically—it is becoming the setting of our sights and the arbiter of community needs. Inevitably, it will take on unprecedented tasks of coordination, priority-setting, and planning in the largest sense. It will need to become far more efficient and authoritative, capable of making the difficult and subtle trade-offs which now confront us—for example, between environmental purity and energy supply.

Government is already big in the United States, probably bigger in proportion to our population than even in those countries which we call "socialist." Some 20 percent of the labor force now works for one or another governmental agency, and by 1980 it will be more. Increasingly, U.S. institutions live on government largesse—subsidies, allowances, and contracts to farmers, corporations, and universities—and individuals benefit from social insurance, medical care, and housing allowances. The pretense of the limited state, however, means that these huge allocations are relatively haphazard, reflecting the crisis of the moment and the power of interest groups rather than any sort of coherent and objective plan.

The web of interrelated factors which together constitute the energy crisis is the direct result of governmental *"ad hoc-*ism" and the lack of an integrated plan.

Significantly, our political leaders from Franklin Roosevelt on have found it necessary to plan. But they cloak their departures from the limited state in the language of the old hymns, attempting to make their interventions appear pragmatic, ignoring the ideological implications. This is worse than merely confusing and hypocritical; it delays the time when we will recognize the planning functions of the state for what they are and must be.

If the role of government were more precisely and consciously defined, the government could be smaller in size. To a great extent, the plethora of bureaucracies today is the result of a lack of focus and comprehension, an ironic bit of fallout from the old notion of the limited state. With more consciousness we could also consider more fruitfully which issues are best left to local or regional planning and which, in fact, transcend the nation-state and require a more global approach.

The emergence of a planning state in America will bring new challenges to business and labor. What will be their connection to the planning process? How will their views be received, organized, and acted upon? Japan has had long experience with such processes and has been relatively successful. European experience has been marred by fragmentation, division, lack of consensus, and ancient class enmities.

America goes to communitarianism never having been there, so that at least it is possible for us to devise entirely new models, different from any the world has ever seen. We hope we can learn and benefit from the experiences of Japan and Europe, aware obviously of the basic differences in our ideological roots.

Holism—interdependence. Finally, and perhaps most fundamentally, the old idea of scientific specialization has given way to a new consciousness of the interrelatedness of all things. Spaceship earth, the limits of growth, the fragility of our life-supporting biosphere have dramatized the ecological and philosophical truth that everything is related to everything else. Harmony between the works of man and the demands of nature is no longer the romantic plea of conservationists. It is an absolute rule of survival, and thus it is of profound ideological significance, subverting in many ways all of the Lockean ideas.

IMPLICATIONS OF THE TRANSITION

Let us look again briefly at some of the examples cited earlier in this report, and consider their significance in terms of this ideological transition. Ideological analysis should make clearer the issues which experience may tend to blur; it helps us to see the forest and not only the trees.

When the pieces of General Motors were born around 1910, they were clearly consistent with the traditional ideology. GM's various components were clearly owned by individualistic entrepreneurs: Louis Chevrolet and his counterparts at Buick, Oldsmobile, Hyatt Roller Bearing, and so on. Their authority and legitimacy were clear. Young men came out of the hills hungry for work in Detroit; thousands massed outside the hiring gates. Survival was at stake. The rights of property were secure, and the contract which followed from them was authoritative. Mr. Chevrolet offered the terms, and workers took them or left them.

Time passed, and workers demanded more power. They submerged their individualism into an interest group, the United Automobile Workers. Management, acting out of a sense of property rights, resisted. Violence ensued. The UAW finally won, and the contract became collectivized— almost a contradiction in terms, if one thinks of the contract in its pure, individualistic form.

Also, property rights were themselves eroded by becoming a subject for bargaining in an adversary procedure. These rights were further diluted by the emergence of an entirely different type of management, one divorced from ownership. Nevertheless, the structure worked efficiently, and the United States accepted it because of its respect for the automobile and for material growth *per se*.

Then in the 1960s, the UAW started to splinter, individual locals, and individual workers within locals, feeling needs which could not be embraced by the already bloated contract. Survival having been assured by the community, the workers began to demand avenues to individual fulfillment in a communitarian setting where it could not be found.

By this time, too, the ownership of GM had become immensely diluted, and the legitimacy of its function was increasingly suspect. In 1964, Sloan wrote of flying over the countryside, delighting in the "splash of jewel-like color presented by every parking lot."[30] Such a lyrical description falls a bit flat today.

So the legitimacy and power of management, on the one hand, and of the labor contract and thus the union, on the other, deteriorated. But the hierarchies on both sides naturally tended to stay with the old ideas, singing the familiar hymns. For a while, management's answer was to pay workers more for their unhappiness, a recourse suitable to the contractual form. The union hierarchy on their side had roughly the same idea—a fatter contract. Absenteeism, sabotage, and lowering productivity continued, however. Meanwhile, at Toyota, when the night shift went off duty it cheered the day shift on to harder and harder work.

In the face of crisis, the company, as has been described, sought ways to meet the workers' needs outside of and beyond the contract, through organizational development (OD) programs. Those in both management and labor, whose legitimacy and authority were tied to the ideas of property rights and contract, were threatened. OD and other such developments in American employer-employee relations are clearly communitarian, seeking to tie management and labor more by consensus than by the adversarial contract. These developments carry with them also the idea of rights of membership, that is, that an employee of the corporation has rights to health, employment, and other benefits which for him are undoubtedly more important than whether or not he owns property, and if there are rights there must be duties, and the definition of those duties becomes less the responsibility of a manager employing the authority of the shareholder/ owners than it does the judgment of the group, the team, or whatever.

If the new way threatens the old hierarchies, it is natural to begin such efforts rather secretly at the bottom of the organization where they will be less noticed, hoping that by the time they hit the top the new models will be strong enough to withstand the attacks of the *status quo*. But this is plainly chancy. At General Motors, apparently, there was a fortunate coincidence: the presence of two leaders in both labor and management, Fuller and Bluestone, who could work for an understanding of consensus at the top, at the same time as efforts were made at the plant level below.

The steel industry is a good example of the introduction of consensus at the top without taking into account the implications for those committed to the contract on the shop floor. Sadlowski, far from being the radical many supposed, was ideologically the conservative seeking to retain the adversarial relationship of the contract, resenting the consensus at the top which had failed to include those down the line and which he thus perceived as being "elitist."

As organizations go to consensus from contract, whether in Europe or the U.S.A., whatever the form may be, it is probably necessary for the process to be carried out simultaneously at the top and the bottom. This means that divisions within labor or management organizations impede consensual arrangements just as much as do divisions between the two.

A variation on the same theme is seen in the case of the Topeka pet food plant. Note the radical implications of this experiment. In a real sense, the legitimacy and thus the authority of the management of the Topeka plant comes from the workers as a whole, not from some outworn conception of property rights. This fact feeds the workers' sense of fulfillment and thus contributes to the high productivity and profits of the operation.

But the top management of the company faces some excruciating questions:

"Do we extend this idea to other plants—maybe to headquarters itself—to increase ROI, even though it will undercut our jobs?"

"If we do it anyway, what happens to the myth that we are answerable to the board of directors, who represent the shareholders?" (The answer to this one is complicated by the fact that shareholders appear to be getting a better return on their investment from Topeka. Perhaps the management hierarchy, or part of it, *should* be dispensed with.)

It is indeed difficult to open one's eyes to the possibility—the mere possibility—of extinction.

Also, note the threat to the idea of equality when an organization moves to consensus from contract. Each team is responsible for hiring replacements; presumably it selects those who will get along well with the group. If the group objects to certain persons, they will not be hired. Race might be involved. Collectivism can be dehumanizing unless it is controlled by a definite social theory—an ideology.

Moving from contract to consensus obviously threatens unions as well. The Topeka plant is small and new, with an innovative management and no union. To apply the same principles in the automobile or steel or utilities industries, however, raises additional structural problems. (See Figure 8.3 for different models of employer-employee relations described here.)

It seems reasonable to predict that the transition from individualism to communitarianism in the United States will continue. Surveys of approximately 2,000 managers made by Lodge and the *Harvard Business Review* during the past seven years show quite clearly that even though managers prefer Lockeanism (about 70 to 30 percent), they are quite convinced that communitarianism is either here or on its way (again by about 70 to 30 percent).[31]

If this is true, then the examples of change cited in this essay are not insignificant fragments, they are the forerunners of what is inevitably coming in one form or another.

The forms which consensualism will take in America will differ from those of Europe. But in both places there will be similarities.

Managers will derive less and less authority from property rights and more from either the managed or the state. Where community needs are paramount, that authority will tend to come from the state, consumer desire continuing to function in the marketplace where it is appropriate. Where the issues concern operations—productivity, motivation, and the rights and duties of membership—authority may most effectively come from the managed.

The contract will diminish in importance as the connecting link between managers and the managed, collective bargaining moving increasingly to establish instead a continuing consensus. Once the new procedures are in place the introduction of changes into the workplace will require more time and care.

Ownership of corporations will become increasingly distinct from control. Shareholders in the equity marketplace will, as they have done, invest their money where they can obtain the greatest promise of return. They will neither want nor expect control. In these circumstances both employees and employers of a particular firm have a common interest in being able to compete effectively with other firms for equity. What is important is that they trust one another. At Bolivar, for instance, there is no reason for the UAW to be any less mindful of the importance of dividends than the managers.

There will be increasing dispute about what the salary differentials between managers and managed should be. These differentials will be

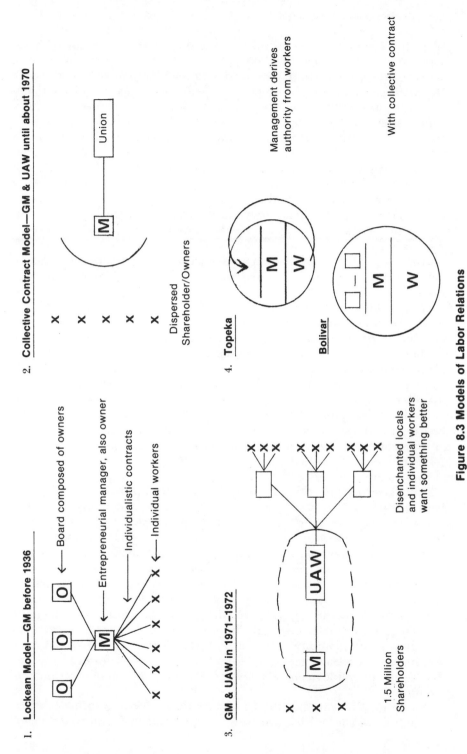

Figure 8.3 Models of Labor Relations

1. Lockean Model—GM before 1936

Board composed of owners
Entrepreneurial manager, also owner
Individualistic contracts
Individual workers

2. Collective Contract Model—GM & UAW until about 1970

Union
Dispersed Shareholder/Owners

3. GM & UAW in 1971–1972

UAW
M
Disenchanted locals and individual workers want something better
1.5 Million Shareholders

4. Topeka

Management derives authority from workers

Bolivar

With collective contract

279

especially important symbolically. Indeed all of the symbolism of management—limousines, yachts, perquisites of all kinds—will cause increasing resentment. One is reminded of the Honda company where we are told there is a machine shop open on weekends to which all company employees are free to come to try out new ideas. It is reported that on a Sunday afternoon one is apt to see the chief executive working elbow to elbow with a young machinist on some new device to make the Honda a better car.

With the passage away from contract, many of the treasured attributes of the contract will be sorely missed. The contract after all was invented to protect individual liberties and rights from the pressures of the group. As with all elements of the old ideology, careful thought will need to be given to how we preserve and protect its most valuable attributes including, indeed, democracy itself.

Consensus will tend to bring management and labor closer together in ways that may adversely affect the community as a whole. This may increase pressures upon government to introduce controls of prices and wages as well as those relating to the environment and the national economy.

The trend toward lifetime employment and security will increase, introducing problems of mobility and flexibility. There will be increasing emphasis on training, especially to prepare workers for many different jobs in the organization.[32]

Finally, successful leaders of business and labor will develop an exceptional degree of objectivity, a willingness to sacrifice their particular power and prestige for the long-run good for their respective institutions. To the extent that they do not do this voluntarily, they face either coercion by government or institutional deterioration and death.

The particular forms of the transition in the United States will be many and varied and will differ from Europe in several ways.

The "class struggle" being non-existent or less significant in the U.S.A., there will be less emphasis—perhaps none—on workers' participation in ownership, the "owning class" as it were. Since boards of directors theoretically represent the owners, Europeans will regard membership on these as significant whereas Americans will not. In both places the issue may become academic if ownership is seen as clearly distinct from control.

Government will play a more central and active role in Europe than in America because of the politicization of European labor and the different notion of the role of the state. But, even in America, new forms of partnership between government, business, and labor seem likely to emerge, as demands for government planning increase. For four years the UAW has been working in Congress to get legislation on plant closings, for example, and other issues of employment security are likely to command governmental attention.

Europe may be ahead of the United States in devising forms of trans-nationalism which will be increasingly significant in Japan, Europe, and the United States face increasing pressures of globalism. There is surely a new reality upon us in which nation-states are becoming antiques, plainly unable to deal with the inexorable pressures of world-wide resource allocation and control. If one looks at the evolution of events around food, oil, and money, for example, one sees an inevitable internationalization taking place. This will have serious implications for relations between business, government, and labor, causing great strains and animosities in particular communities which feel short-changed by the workings of the world.

It is worth noting in conclusion that the three areas examined in this book are all going to communitarianism. Japan has been there for a long time and thus has some interesting advantages. Europe goes to a new communitarianism which is being forged out of a combination of its two traditional ideologies, one medieval communitarianism and the other post-1700 individualism. The United States* is going to communitarianism for the first time, which provides it with some interesting and potentially refreshing possibilities.

*This paper does not deal with Canada but there are signs that there too significant communitarian developments are underway.

Notes

1. Statistics cited in the first section of this paper are from U.S. Department of Labor Statistics, *Directory of National and International Unions*, 1973; U.S. Department of Commerce, Bureau of the Census, *Statistical Abstract of the U.S., 1976;* United States Government, *Economic Report of the President*, January, 1977.
2. Derek C. Bok and John T. Dunlop, *Labor and the American Community*, New York: Simon and Schuster, 1970, pp. 42–53.
3. Bok and Dunlop, *ibid.*, pp. 208–14.
4. Richard E. Walton, "Innovative Restructuring of Work", in Jerome M. Rosow, ed. *The Worker and the Job*, Englewood Cliffs, N.J., Prentice Hall, Inc., 1974, pp. 145–48.
5. Richard E. Walton, "The Quality of Working Life", in *Encyclopedia Britannica Yearbook 1975*, p. 402.
6. Phillip I. Blumberg, "Implications of Representation Trend for U.S. Corporations", *Harvard Business Review*, January–February 1977, p. 50.
7. Herbert R. Northrup, "Employee Participation, Union Power, and the American Scene", presented to *International Conference on Employee Participation in Management Decision Making*, Personnel Association of Toronto, Toronto, Ontario, December 6, 1976.
8. Thomas R. Donohue, "The Future of Collective Bargaining", International Conference on Trends in Industrial and Labour Relations, Montreal, Canada, May 26, 1976, *AFL-CIO Free Trade Union News*, September, 1976, p. 6.
9. I. W. Abel, "Employment Security and Plant Productivity Committee: Ten Coordinating Steel Companies", presented to *The National Commission on Productivity and Work Quality*, December 12, 1974.
10. Information concerning the Steelworkers' 1977 election and contract negotiations is drawn chiefly from published reports in *The Wall Street Journal, Business Week,* and *The New York Times*.
11. Quoted in John T. Dunlop, "American Labor Organizations", draft paper prepared for *Daedalus*, January 7, 1977, p. 6.

12. Quoted in "McBride Seems Victor in Steel Union Voting", *The New York Times*, February 9, 1977, p. 22.

13. Information about OD at General Motors is drawn from George C. Lodge, "Contract and Consensus at General Motors, 1908–1975", Intercollegiate Case Clearing House, Boston, MA; Irving Bluestone, "A Role for the Psychologist in Employer-Employee Relations", presented to the *American Psychological Association*, Chicago, Illinois, August 31, 1975.

14. George B. Morris, Jr. Paper read at Annual Meeting of the Society of Automotive Engineers, March 1977.

15. Irving Bluestone, A Changing View of the Union-Management Relationship. Paper read at the Waldorf Astoria Hotel, October 20, 1976.

16. For a fuller analysis of the Harman project, see Karen S. Henderson, "Bolivar," Intercollegiate Case Clearing House, Boston, MA.

17. For a full account of the advantages and disadvantages to corporations of ESOPs, see "Employee Stock Ownership Plans: Pluses and Minuses," in the July–August 1976 issue of the *Harvard Business Review*.

18. David Robison, "Employee Stock Option Plans Under New Scrutiny", *World of Work Report*, Vol. 1, No. 7, Sept. 1976, Work in America Institute Inc., p. 4.

19. Frank L. Fernbach, "Challenges Facing Labor", presented to *The Future of the Free Enterprise System*, The Minneapolis Foundation, October 4, 1976, p. 6.

20. Henry Tracy, "Scanlon Plans: Leading Edge in Labor-Management Cooperation", *World of Work Report*, Vol. 2, No. 3, March 1977, Work in America Institute Inc., p. 1.

21. Bernard Wysocki Jr., "A Midland-Ross Plant, Others Raise Output With a 'Scanlon Plan' ", *The Wall Street Journal*, December 9, 1976, p. 1.

22. Richard E. Walton, "Work Innovations at Topeka: After Six Years", draft version, December 8, 1976, pp. 1–2.

23. *Ibid.*, p. 14.

24. Mark Shepherd Jr., "The Competitive Value of a Motivated Work Force", presented to *European Management Forum*, Davos, Switzerland, February 1, 1977, p. 8.

25. *Ibid.*, p. 20.

26. Robert A. Leone, "The Regulatory Boom", draft prepared for *Harvard Business Review*, February, 1977, p. 1.

27. National Center for Productivity and Quality of Working Life, *Directory of Labor-Management Committees*, Washington, D.C., October, 1976.

28. Sumner H. Slichter, James J. Healy, and E. Robert Livernash, *The Impact of Collective Bargaining on Management*, Washington, D.C., The Brookings Institution, 1960, pp. 949, 960.

29. Quoted in Herman E. Droos and Charles Gilbert, *American Business History*, Englewood Cliffs, N.J., Prentice-Hall, 1972, p. 264.

30. Alfred P. Sloan Jr., *My Years With General Motors*, Garden City, Doubleday, 1964.

31. Lodge and William F. Martin, "Our Society in 1985—Business May Not Like It," *Harvard Business Review*, November–December, 1975.

32. See S. Prakash Sethi, "Behind the Facade of Lifetime Job Security", *The New York Times*, June 5, 1977, Business Section, p. 5, and also Sethi, *Japanese Business and Social Conflict: A Comparative Analysis of Response Patterns with American Business*, Cambridge, Mass., Ballinger Publishing Co., 1977.

Index

Abel, I. W., 249–50
Albeda, W., 10
Altmann, N., 31
American Telephone and Telegraph Company (AT&T), 261, 271–72

Basnett, David, 177
Bluestone, Irving, 246, 253, 254
Blumberg, Philip I., 247
Boersma, M., 125
Böhle, F., 31
Bok, Derek, 242
Britain, 13–14, 164–89; A.C.A.S. (Advisory Conciliation and Arbitration Service), 168–69, 185; autonomous work groups, 13–14; Bullock Committee's Report, 14, 183–86; C.A.C. (Central Arbitration Committee), 169; C.B.I. (Confederation of British Industry), 175–77; C.I.R. (Commission for Industrial Relations), 168; collective bargaining, 13, 14, 19, 166, 170–76, 181; Committee on Industrial Democracy, 183; Conservatives (government), 167, 172, 175, 178, 186; Department of Employment, 182; employee participation in management, 13–14, 181–87; employment problems, 178–79; Employment Protection Act, 168, 169; Health and Safety at Work Act, 186; industrial democracy, 181–83; industrial planning and development, 180–81; Industrial Relations Act, 167; inflation, 172–75, 178; labor law reform, 167–70; Labor Party (government), 14, 166, 167, 172, 173,

175, 177, 179, 180, 182; Manpower Services Commission, 179; National Board for Prices and Incomes, 172; N.E.B. (National Enterprise Board), 180; N.E.D.C. (National Economic Development Council, 180; pay bargaining, 175–78; plant bargaining, 171; price control policy, 172–75; quality of working life, 186–87; Royal Commission on Trade Unions and Employers' Associations, 166–67, 170, 181–82; shop stewards, 170–71, 181; strikes, 23, 187–88, Trade Union and Labor Relations Act, 168; T.U.C. (Trades Union Congress), 165, 167, 173, 174, 177, 180–83; unemployment, 178–79; unions, 6, 13–14, 164–73, 176–78, 181–89; wage control policy, 172–75; wages, 172–77; White Paper on Industrial Democracy, 184–86; workplace organization, 170–72
British Leyland Company, 171, 172, 188

Callaghan, James, 177
Chrysler Corporation, 248, 251; British, 180
Communitarianism, 269, 271–72, 278, 281
Community needs, 273–74
Competition, ideology of, 268
Consensualism, 274, 278
Corporations, legitimizing of, 272–73

Denmark, 144, 185
Den Uyl, M., 125
de Pous, J., 120, 129

283

Sweden, 130–63; Center Party, 138, 149, 159, 161; centralized union organizations, 131–40; codetermination, 14, 146–50; Codetermination Act, 139, 148–51; collective bargaining, 14–15, 18, 19, 130–47, 160–61; Collective Bargaining Board for State-owned Enterprises, 131; Commission on Labor Law (Article 32 Commission), 147, 148; Communists, 140, 141, 159; Democracy at Work Act, 14; economic democracy (Socialism), 151, 154; EFO group, 135–36, 138, 139, 142; employee participation (industrial democracy), 145–62; Haga policy, 138, 143, 155; inflation, 138; Japan influenced by, 231; Labor Law Commission, 162; laws on employee participation, 147–50; Liberal Party, 138, 151, 155, 159, 161; LKAB iron mines, strike, 137, 140, 147; LO (Swedish Trade Union Confederation), 130–40, 142–48, 150–62; LO-SAP group, 157–59, 161–62; Meidner report, 7, 152–55; Metal Workers' Union, 138; OECD report on, 144; profit sharing, individual, 151–52, 157–59; Promotion of Employment Act, 148, 150; PTK (Private Salaried Staffs' Cartel), 132, 134, 137–40, 142, 144, 150; SACO (Central Organization of Swedish Professional Workers), 132–33, 135, 137, 138, 145; SACO-SR, 133, 159; SAF (Swedish Employers Association), 130, 133–40, 142, 145–47, 150–51, 157, 159; SALF (supervisors and foremen), 134, 136, 137, 139; Saltsjöbaden Agreement, 130, 146, 148; SAV (National Collective Bargaining Office), 131, 134–35, 137; Security of Employment Act, 148, 150; SF (state employees), 135, 137; shopfloor participation, 150–51; SIF (clerical and technical employees in industry), 134, 136, 137; Social Democratic Party (government), 132, 133, 140, 143, 147, 150, 152–59, 161–62; SR (federation of civil servants), 133, 137; strikes, 137, 139–42, 147, 150, 160, table, 141; Swedish Federation of Industries, 157; taxes, 138, 142–43, 160; TCO (Central Organization of Salaried Employees), 132–39, 143, 145–48, 154, 159–61; unions, 5–7, 14–15, 131–56, 159–62; wage-earners' front, 160–61; wage-earners' funds, 152–61; wages, 133, 135–39, 142–44; Workers' Protection Act, 148; works councils, 145–46
Switzerland, 11

Texas Instruments, 247, 258–59, 263
Thatcher, Margaret, 177
Treu, T., 12
TRW, 246, 257

United Kingdom (see Britain)
United States of America, 240–82; AFL-CIO, 242, 244, 248, 260; class mobility, 244; collective bargaining, 2–5, 19, 243, 244, 264, 278; Department of Health, Education, and Welfare, 260, 261; Department of Labor, 260, 262; Economic Development Administration, 261; employee participation on boards of directors, possibility of, 247–48; Employee Retirement Income Security Act, 255; employee sharing in corporate gains, 255–57; employee stock ownership plans, 255–56; Employee Stock Ownership Trust, 255–56; Environmental Protection Agency, 260; equality of opportunity, 271; European influence in industrial relations, 240; Federation Economic Development Administration, 256; Federal Mediation and Conciliation Service, 261; government, role of, 268, 274–75, 280; government in labor-management relations, 243, 259–62; Human Resources Development Act, 262; ideological change, 2–4, 266–81; inflation, 11, 240, 241, 245; International Brotherhood of Electrical Workers, 242, 257; Japanese automobiles imported, 210; Japanese treaties with, 218; labor force, statistics on, 241–42, table, 242; labor laws, 259–60; labor-management committees, 263–65; Landrum-Griffin Act, 259; management, rights and power of, 272–73, 276–78; minorities in industry, 261, 281; National Center for Productivity and Quality of Working Life, 262, 263; National Labor Relations Act, 259, 260; non-unionized companies, work restructuring, 246, 247, 257–59; Occupational Safety and Health Administration, 260, 261; Office of Federal Contract Compliance for Equal Employment Opportunity, 260, 261; political parties, 244; productivity, 245–47; quality of work life, 245–46, 252–54, 262; Scanlon plans, 256–57; service industries, 241, 242; state and local government employment, 241, 260; steel industry negotiation agreement, 248–50; strikes, 3, 244, 263–64, table, 263; Taft-Hartley Act, 259, 260; Tax Reduction Act, 255–56; unemployment, 241; union participation in management, 248–55; unions, 3–5, 19, 20, 242–44, 247–48, 261, 264–66, 271; United Automobile Workers, 242, 246, 250–55, 257, 264, 276, 278, 280; United Mine Workers, 264; United Rubber Workers, 257; United Steelworkers, 242, 244, 246, 248–50; wages, 245; women in industry, 243, 261, 271; workers' dissatisfaction (alienation), 245–46

Van Zuthem, Professor, 122

Walton, Richard E., 245–46, 257–58
Webb, Sydney and Beatrice, 238
Winpisinger, William, 244, 245
World Federation of Trade Unions, 218

Yanase Batteries, 228